# Israelpolitik

MANCHESTER
1824

Manchester University Press

**Key Studies in Diplomacy**

Series Editors: J. Simon Rofe and Giles Scott-Smith

Emeritus Editor: Lorna Lloyd

The volumes in this series seek to advance the study and understanding of diplomacy in its many forms. Diplomacy remains a vital component of global affairs, and it influences and is influenced by its environment and the context in which it is conducted. It is an activity of great relevance for International Studies, International History, and of course Diplomatic Studies. The series covers historical, conceptual, and practical studies of diplomacy.

**Previously published by Bloomsbury:**

*21st Century Diplomacy: A Practitioner's Guide* by Kishan S. Rana
*A Cornerstone of Modern Diplomacy: Britain and the Negotiation of the 1961 Vienna Convention on Diplomatic Relations* by Kai Bruns
*David Bruce and Diplomatic Practice: An American Ambassador in London, 1961–9* by John W. Young
*Embassies in Armed Conflict* by G.R. Berridge

**Published by Manchester University Press:**

*Reasserting America in the 1970s* edited by Hallvard Notaker, Giles Scott-Smith and David J. Snyder
*Human rights and humanitarian diplomacy: Negotiating for human rights protection and humanitarian access* by Kelly-Kate Pease
*The diplomacy of decolonisation: America, Britain and the United Nations during the Congo crisis 1960–64* by Alanna O'Malley
*Sport and diplomacy: Games within games* edited by J. Simon Rofe
*The TransAtlantic reconsidered* edited by Charlotte A. Lerg, Susanne Lachenicht and Michael Kimmage
*Academic ambassadors, Pacific allies: Australia, America and the Fulbright Program* by Alice Garner and Diane Kirkby
*A precarious equilibrium: Human rights and détente in Jimmy Carter's Soviet policy* by Umberto Tulli
*US public diplomacy in socialist Yugoslavia, 1950–70: Soft culture, cold partners* by Carla Konta

# Praise for Israelpolitik

'In their policy towards Israel, the two German states carried out their ideological conflict during the Cold War on the political stage of international relations. This has always been about coming to terms with the National Socialist past. Lorena de Vita shows in an impressive way how the fronts in the German-German conflict shaped this field.'

Sybille Steinbacher, Director of the Fritz Bauer Institute and Professor of the History and Impact of the Holocaust, Goethe University Frankfurt am Main

'This book is an incredibly nuanced investigation of the inter-German rivalry in the Middle East that serves to illustrate the multifaceted complexity of the global Cold War. It is an important, timely contribution to the growing literature on regional and local cold wars that highlights the agency of middle powers, in this case East and West Germany. A must-read for anyone interested in the history of the German Cold War, German-Israeli ties, and the politics of memory.'

Sergey Radchenko, Professor of International Relations, Cardiff University

'At long last – a book about German-Israeli relations that reaches beyond the conventional story. The reader is exposed to the complex interplay between the cold war, the rivalry between the two Germanies, the conflict in the Middle-East, the tensions within the West-German-East-German-Israeli triangle and the role collective memory plays in politics.'

Moshe Zimmermann, Professor Emeritus, The Hebrew University of Jerusalem

'By recasting West German-Israeli relations against the backdrop of relentlessly opportunistic East German pressures, de Vita brings fresh and significant insights to such milestones as the Luxembourg Agreements, the Suez Crisis, Adenauer's meeting with Ben Gurion, and the Eichmann trial. This is finely textured international history at its best.'

William Glenn Gray, author of *Germany's Cold War*

'A fresh, exceptionally well-researched perspective on Cold War diplomacy [. . .] *Israelpolitik* is a remarkably nuanced work that will shape future scholarship not only on German-Israeli relations, but also on the history of modern Germany itself.'

*Kirkus Reviews*

'[A] deft and original study [. . .] *Israelpolitik* provides much new information on the two Germanys' diplomatic tactics and strategies towards Israel and the Arab world. De Vita's scrupulous analysis of the strains of German-Israeli reconciliation represents a model treatment of a complex Cold War subject.'

Carole Fink, Humanities Distinguished Professor, University of Ohio

'An impressive portrait of the triangular constellation between the Federal Republic, the GDR and Israel.'

*H-Soz-Kult*

'De Vita bases her monograph on a wide array of primary sources[.] [. . .] One would be hard-pressed to find another study of the German-Israeli question in the English language that is supported by such a vast array of primary materials.'

Jacob Tovy, Researcher, Herzl Institute, University of Haifa

'[*Israelpolitik*] is simply good history that politely transcends self-serving mythologies.'

Daniel Marwecki, author of *Germany and Israel: Whitewashing and Statebuilding*

'In their policy towards Israel, the two German states carried out their ideological conflict [. . .] on the political stage of international relations. This has always been about coming to terms with the National Socialist past. Lorena De Vita shows [this] in an impressive way.'

Sybille Steinbacher, Director of the Fritz Bauer Institute, Professor of the History and Impact of the Holocaust, Goethe University Frankfurt am Main

# Israelpolitik
## German–Israeli relations, 1949–69

Lorena De Vita

Manchester University Press

Published by Manchester University Press
Oxford Road, Manchester M13 9PL
www.manchesteruniversitypress.co.uk

British Library Cataloguing-in-Publication Data
A catalogue record for this book is available from the British Library

ISBN 978 1 5261 4781 3 hardback
ISBN 978 1 5261 6254 0 paperback

First published 2020

Typeset by Newgen Publishing UK

*To all those who can see the limits of any process of reconciliation
and yet work relentlessly towards it*

# Contents

# Figures

# Maps

# Acknowledgements

It is with great joy and deep gratitude that I acknowledge the individuals and institutions whose support has been crucial to the publication of this book. For financial support, I thank the Aberystwyth University Postgraduate Research Fund; the German Academic Exchange Service (Deutscher Akademischer Austauschdienst); the German History Society; the Partners in Confronting Collective Atrocities Group; the Society for Historians of American Foreign Relations; the Postdoctoral Fellowship Fund of the Foreign Ministry of the State of Israel; the Memorial House of the Wannsee Conference Joseph Wulf Fellowship Fund; and the Research Institute at the Department of History and Art History at Utrecht University. All of these provided fundamental resources that allowed me to conduct the research for this book across Europe, the United States and the Middle East.

I thank the University of Roma Tre for having granted me, in the very distant past, a scholarship to conduct research abroad to write my undergraduate dissertation on German foreign policy – that experience had a profound impact on me, and the double effect of both rewarding and further unleashing my intellectual curiosity. I would have never embarked upon this journey without Leopoldo Nuti's lectures, which introduced me to a wonderful and complex subject, *la storia delle relazioni internazionali*, which I now teach at Utrecht University and where I am proud to be a member of a wonderful group of historians who made me feel welcome in the Netherlands from my very first day. In particular, I am grateful to the members of the History of International Relations section, and especially to Beatrice de Graaf, Laurien Crump, Jacco Pekelder, Liesbeth van de Grift and Jolle Demmers; to research director Oscar Gelderblom and research coordinator Tom Gerritsen; and to the successive directors of the Department of History and Art History, Leen Dorsman, Josine Blok and Maarten Prak, for having supported me in countless ways.

Pursuing my studies at the London School of Economics and at Aberystwyth University taught me more than I could have hoped for. I am especially grateful to Campbell Craig and R. Gerald Hughes, for their unwavering confidence in this project and in my abilities to pursue it successfully. Jenny Edkins, Kamila Stullerova, Jan Ruzicka, Peter Lambert, Claudia Hildebrand and Sergey Radchenko all provided helpful guidance. At the LSE International Relations Department, I was greatly inspired by conversations with Fawaz Gerges, Kristina Dalacoura, Christopher Coker, George Lawson and Ulrich Sedelmeier, and I would have not embarked upon my research without Kimberly Hutchings' gentle encouragement.

Visiting research fellowships in Germany and Israel were, in innumerable ways, crucial in allowing me to develop the argument of this book. At the Jena Center for 20th Century History I was immersed in a lively research environment which profoundly shaped my thinking on German contemporary history. I was greatly inspired by my conversations with Norbert Frei, Kristina Meyer, Dominik Rigoll, Tobias Freimüller, Jacob Eder, Janine Gaumer and Annette Weinke, and it is with pleasure that I note that many of these conversations are still ongoing. At the Joseph Wulf Library of the Memorial House of the Wannsee Conference, I have greatly benefited from conversations and exchanges with Hans-Christian Jasch, Christoph Kreuzmüller and Monika Sommerer. During my time in Israel, I have learnt a great deal from Moshe Zimmermann, Yehuda Bauer, Manuela Consonni, Juliane Brauer, David Witzthum, Guy Laron, Tibor Shalev-Schlosser, Shlomo Shpiro, Hilla Lavieh and Irit Chen. I am in great debt to all the members of the Richard Koebner Minerva Center for German History at the Hebrew University in Jerusalem, but in particular to Ofer Ashkenazi, who provided me with moral, logistical and intellectual support as well as a desk with the most beautiful view of Jerusalem I ever could have imagined, which turned out to be a perfect location for me to finish writing this book.

I am very grateful to all the archivists in Germany, Israel, the UK, the Netherlands, Italy, Austria and the United States who have helped me with my research.

The conversations with eyewitnesses and archivists, as well as with colleagues, friends and mentors, have been a constant source of inspiration. I owe special thanks to Andrew Monaghan, Fawaz Gerges, Oliver Rathkolb, Mark Kramer, Holger Nehring, Stephan Malinowski, Jeffrey Herf, Sybille Steinbacher, Emile Chabal, Roham Alvandi, Piers Ludlow, Jonathan A. Bush, Giles Scott-Smith, Donald Abenheim, Judith Keilbach, Galia Golan, Cian O'Driscoll, Sielke B. Kelner, Turlach O Broin, Ivor Bolton, James Hershberg, Markus Görannson, Aidan Condron, Corina Mavrodin and Ned Richardson-Little. Throughout the years, I have had the privilege of sharing my ideas *in fieri* at international conferences and workshops with talented scholars, whose questions and comments have helped greatly in refining my thinking on the issues I write about in this monograph. I am grateful to those who contributed during discussions at the International Politics Research Seminar at Aberystwyth University; the London School of Economics' International History Seminar; the Cold Warriors discussion at Sciences Po Paris; the Centre for the Study of Modern and Contemporary History at the University of Edinburgh; the German Historical Institute (London); the British Academy; the Partners in Confronting Collective Atrocities experiential conference (2012); the *Doktorandenschule* seminars of the Jena Center for 20th Century History; Charles University in Prague; the *Forschungskolloquium* of the Fritz Bauer Institut at the Goethe University Frankfurt; the Hebrew University in Jerusalem; and the conferences of the Society for Historians of American Foreign Relations, the Political Studies Association, the Practice of International History in the 21st Century Network, and the New Diplomatic History Network. I am indebted to Jacob Eder and Hubert Leber, who organised the 2014 conference on German–Jewish–Israeli relations at the University of Haifa with the support of the ZEIT Stiftung Ebelin und Gerd Bucerius, providing me with the opportunity to share panels and ideas with some of my academic heroes; and I owe special thanks also to the organisers of the European Summer School on Cold War History and the German Academic Exchange Service

Summer School in German Studies for having provided me with an opportunity to present some of my preliminary findings. I am also profoundly grateful to the Institute for German Studies at Birmingham University, and especially its director Nick Martin, for having agreed to support my organisation of a Symposium on '50 Years of German-Israeli Relations: Reflections on History, Memory and International Politics'. I am especially grateful to Amb. Harald Kindermann and Amb. Shimon Shtein for having agreed to share crucial insights based on their ambassadorial experience in Israel and Germany, respectively, and to Ruth Wittlinger for her insightful comments. Ruth's premature passing away has come as a shock to me. I hope that this book will serve as a testimony to just how inspiring she has been for many young scholars.

It is a privilege to work with bright, engaged and inquisitive students. I was humbled by the invitation from Sjoerd van Hoenselaar on behalf of the members of the *Utrechtse Historische Studentenkring* (UHSK study association) to accompany and guide a group of undergraduate and postgraduate students in their visit to Munich and to the Dachau concentration camp. That was an experience that I, as an educator, will never forget. I should also like to thank Celine Mureau, Martijn Kool, Belinda Borck, Yiftach Shavit, Mikulas Pesta and Marcus Chavasse for helping me check some of the references in Dutch, German, Russian, Czech, Hebrew and Arabic and for acting as my sounding boards as I developed the core ideas of the book. And I will never forget the day Frau Donini walked up to me, introducing herself nonchalantly in German. I thank her for having helped me to understand, that morning of many years ago, that *die Grenzen meiner Sprache bedeuten die Grenzen meiner Welt*, and that it was possible – even fun – to keep pushing those *Grenzen* further and further. I am also deeply grateful for having encountered exceptionally wonderful friends during my extensive travelling. They all taught me much, warmly welcoming me into their worlds and making me a much richer person for it. *E naturalmente non sarei riuscita a fare nemmeno un passo in terra straniera se non avessi saputo che dietro di me c'era e c'è un appoggio incrollabile, formato da coloro che in Italia mi sostengono e stravedono per me. Grazie di cuore a tutti voi.*

## Note on translations and transliterations

In the transliteration of names of persons and locations from Arabic, Hebrew, German, Czech and Russian I have chosen to use the transliterations prevalent in common English usage for the sake of clarity. I have received the support of Hagit Kleve and Yiftach Shavit for translations from Hebrew and Arabic; from Marcus Chavasse for translations from Russian; and from Mikulas Pesta for translations from Czech. All translations from German, Dutch, French, Spanish and Italian are my own, unless otherwise stated.

# Abbreviations

| | |
|---|---|
| ADN | Allgemeiner Deutscher Nachrichtendienst |
| AU | Arab Union |
| BND | Bundesnachrichtendienst |
| BRD | Bundesrepublik Deutschland |
| CDU | Christian Democratic Union (Christlich Demokratische Union Deutschlands) |
| CIA | Central Intelligence Agency |
| COMECON | Council for Mutual Economic Assistance |
| CSU | Christian Social Union (Christlich-Soziale Union in Bayern) |
| DAG | Deutsch-Arabische Gesellschaft |
| DDR | Deutsche Demokratische Republik (see also GDR) |
| DP | Displaced Persons |
| FDGB | Freier Deutscher Gewerkschaftsbund |
| FRG | Federal Republic of Germany (BRD) |
| GDR | German Democratic Republic (see also DDR) |
| HVA | Main Directory for Reconnaissance (of the Stasi) (Hauptverwaltung Aufklärung) |
| IDF | Israel Defense Forces |
| JCC | Conference on Jewish Material Claims Against Germany |
| KPD | Communist Party of Germany (Kommunistische Partei Deutschlands) |
| MAI | Ministry for Foreign and Inter-German Trade (Ministerium für Außenhandel und Innerdeutschen Handel) |
| MAKI | Israeli Communist Party (HaMiflega HaKomunistit HaYisraelit) |
| NATO | North Atlantic Treaty Organization |
| NSC | National Security Council |
| SED | Socialist Unity Party of Germany (Sozialistische Einheitspartei Deutschlands) |
| SPD | Social Democratic Party of Germany (Sozialdemokratische Partei Deutschlands) |
| UAR | United Arab Republic |
| UN | United Nations |
| UNEF | United Nations Emergency Force |
| UNGA | General Assembly of the United Nations |
| UNRWA | United Nations Relief and Works Agency |
| WMDs | weapons of mass destruction |

# Introduction: Contextualising reconciliation

The conventional wisdom, and much of the conventional scholarship, presents a powerful narrative. The reconciliation between Germany and Israel in the aftermath of the Holocaust stemmed from German moral atonement. According to this account, the determination of post-war Germany to make amends for the genocidal policies pursued under the Nazi regime represents a vivid example of how moral considerations can explain key developments in international politics. This popular understanding of the moral foundations of the relations between Germany and Israel is based upon important facts. The FRG agreed to pay reparations to Israel seven years after the liberation of the last concentration camp. The agreement that the two countries signed in 1952 was unprecedented and revolutionary in the history of post-genocidal reconciliation. At that time, Benjamin Ferencz, former Chief Prosecutor for the US Army at the *Einsatzgruppen* trial at the Nuremberg war trials, stressed that with the agreement Germany had 'established a milestone in international morality'.[1] Up to that moment, only victors in a war could demand reparations from the vanquished, while the State of Israel did not even exist when Hitler's Germany attempted to exterminate the Jews. The uniqueness and significance of the gesture made by the FRG in the early 1950s and the ever-growing cooperation between the two countries virtually in all fields – commerce, security, research, education – fostered the common perception that German–Israeli relations have historically been based on 'strong moral foundations', as Shimon Peres put it.[2] Academics, public intellectuals and politicians have often invoked the image of the 'moral rearmament' underwent by the FRG upon embarking on the long road towards reconciliation with the Jewish state.[3]

But the history of German–Israeli relations in the aftermath of the Holocaust is much more complex than that. Such an unprecedented process of reconciliation took place in the midst of a geopolitical scenario that encompassed significant tensions stemming from both the Cold War and the intensifying Middle East conflict in the decades following the establishment of Israel and the division of Germany into two separate states, the FRG in the West and the GDR in the East.

Artificially created in the wake of the Second World War, two German states found themselves pitted against one another in a competition that was neither of their own choosing nor of their own making. Yet once placed within it, each German state attempted to exploit the situation to the maximum to defeat the other one politically and emerge as a legitimate and prestigious actor in international affairs. Their competition soon became imperative, all-encompassing, global. The first contacts between Germans and Israelis in the aftermath of the Holocaust took place within this specific historical and geopolitical context.[4] And soon, policy makers in either German state understood that the attitude that their representatives displayed towards Israel – subsumed under the umbrella term *Israelpolitik*, literally 'Israel-policy' – could advance or hinder their respective interests in the competition against the other Germany.

This book argues that the historical context of the global Cold War crucially shaped the making of German–Israeli relations in the aftermath of the Holocaust. This does not imply that each Germany's move in its relations with Israel was dictated exclusively by Cold War considerations. Yet the dynamics of 'mutual antagonism and self-definition' that, in Mary Fulbrook's expression, characterised the competition between the two German states, deeply informed each Germany's behaviour in international affairs at the time of the bipolar rivalry.[5] Indeed, the German Cold War competition for legitimacy, political prestige and new markets, had a global reach and global effects.[6] This struggle to win markets and influence presented much of the same challenges in the Middle East, Africa, Asia and beyond, but the Middle East was a uniquely challenging setting for the two Germanys. The presence of Israel in the region implicitly meant that in the Middle East – like nowhere else in the world – representatives of both Germanys were confronted with issues that uniquely pertained not only to their contemporary rivalry, but also to their past.

Reading a book about the two Germanys and Israel may be surprising for some. After all, East Germany did not even recognise Israel until a few months before its own dissolution, in 1990 – too late for this recognition to have any remarkable effect. The propaganda of the Socialist Unity Party of Germany (Sozialistische Einheitspartei Deutschlands, SED), the GDR ruling party, generally cast the East German citizens as former victims that the heroic Soviet Union liberated from the yoke of the Nazi regime. In foreign policy terms, this implied that the East German regime felt no special obligations towards Israel. There, the central anti-Semitic character of the Nazi dictatorship was reduced to a marginal detail, the focus of the East German regime's faulty memory being on the Nazi persecution of German Communists instead. The fact that internal resistance to Hitler had been virtually non-existent was overlooked, as was the fact that many of the now East German citizens had been socialised in, and had believed in, Nazi Germany.[7] Instead, SED propaganda claimed the moral high ground by portraying West Germany as a hotbed of still fervent Nazis, now loyal citizens and servants of the Federal regime, colluding with Israeli monopolists to subjugate the Arab peoples in a quiet, but powerful, attempt to dominate the Middle East. The West German government officially attempted to take responsibility for the crimes committed by Nazi Germany, by agreeing to pay indemnifications, reparations and compensations to Israel. The fact that the political, judicial and administrative elite of the FRG brimmed with former members of the Nazi bureaucracy complicated the matter further – it was way more convenient for West Germany to strike a deal with Israel and the Jewish organisations rather than go through a thorough process of denazification of its own elites.[8] The history of German–Israeli relations is also the history of two Germanys and of the relationship that each of them chose to have, or not to have, with Israel in the aftermath of the Holocaust – at a time in which each of them attempted to gain legitimacy in the international arena, winning friends and markets, while dealing with the legacy of an 'unmasterable past'.[9]

Yet Israel, and the relationship that West Germany was forging with it, in fact was important to the regime of Communist East Germany and this had regional and even global repercussions. At a time in which the East German state was desperately seeking to win friends in the Third World, GDR representatives deemed that bashing Israel could be a handy tool to woo the political leaders of the non-aligned countries, and come across as the German state that really had their interests at heart, unlike the West Germans who were supporting the 'outpost of Western imperialism and colonialism' in the Middle East, by paying reparations to Israel. To complicate the picture, despite the East German official antagonistic stance towards the Jewish state, contacts between East German and Israeli diplomats and citizens continued to take place in third countries throughout the 1950s and 1960s. Also, the GDR did not refrain from reaching out to the Israeli public opinion at crucial junctures, such as the Eichmann trial, to dig the dirt of the Nazi past on the West German state – in the attempt to look good in the eyes of the world while criticising the FRG.

Studies on German–Israeli relations in the aftermath of the Holocaust generally focus on the relations that *one* German state established (or, in the East German case, failed to establish) with the Jewish state with the assent and support of their respective superpower.[10] This is not surprising, given that the two Germanys developed very different relations to the State of Israel. On the one hand, West Germany agreed to pay restitutions for Nazi crimes to the State of Israel in 1952, and soon the bilateral relationship blossomed into what academic, journalistic and governmental sources generally refer to as the 'special relationship', attracting a rich and diverse body of scholarship.[11] On the other hand, East Germany did not pay any reparations to Israel, and soon adopted an officially hostile attitude towards the Jewish state, as explored in the existing historiography.[12] But while the early history of German relations with Israel might appear to be, essentially, a divided one, this book argues that the history of both Germanys' policies towards Israel is also, crucially, a history of German–German relations and of their peculiar Cold War rivalry.

This study takes a novel approach to the study of relations between Germany and Israel, by tracing the developments in the policies that *both* German states implemented vis-à-vis Israel during the 1950s and 1960s, and by drawing on sources from both sides of the Iron Curtain. Even the most recent works on German–Israeli relations tend to focus on one German state, and especially the Federal Republic of Germany, dismissing the actions of the East German 'petty dictatorship'.[13] Yet, the opening of the Eastern European archives since the end of the Cold War, and the vast amount of recently declassified sources from European, American and Israeli archives, has facilitated research into the making and framing of German–Israeli relations in the aftermath of the Holocaust. The picture that emerges from a multi-archival analysis of the early history of German–Israeli relations reveals the shortcomings of its one-sided treatment in much of the available literature. This book therefore examines the policies that both the FRG and the GDR implemented vis-à-vis Israel (their *Israelpolitik*). By doing so, it also measures to what extent German preoccupations with *Israelpolitik* overlapped with German–German strivings for attaining power and legitimacy in the international domain, at a time in which both Germanys were having to negotiate the legacy of a difficult past, within the context of the(ir) stiffening Cold War rivalry. Writing in the early 1990s, German historian Jürgen Kocka exhorted his colleagues 'to question relations and interactions, interconnections and dissociations among the two German developments [and to] look at the history of the GDR and the FRG in close connection, without reducing them to two separate and independent topics'.[14] This book aims to respond to Kocka's exhortation by examining to what extent an analysis of either Germany's relations with Israel in the aftermath of the Holocaust[15] can reveal a history of German interconnectedness, as well as a more evident one of separation and antithesis.

What follows, then, is a history of the two Germanys' formative years, of their contradictory policies in international affairs. Conceptually, the book pays attention not just to the highest echelons of political power, but also to mid- and low-level diplomatic personnel, located at the heart of these relations, and it engages with the policies and decisions of actors from the propaganda, intelligence and trade sectors, as well as private individuals. The inclusion of propagandists, NGO members and lawyers alongside traditional political and diplomatic officials aims to contribute to pushing the boundaries of the growing field of new diplomatic history, showing that these actors, too, participated in the making, and framing, of German–Israeli relations at home and abroad.[16]

By focusing on German–German perceptions and *Weltanschauungen*, the aim of this work is to contribute to what Tony Smith termed a 'pericentric' study of the Cold War,[17] highlighting the crucial role played by European actors – in this case, the two German states – in projecting the Cold War onto the Middle East. This book contributes to this debate by focusing on actors other than the two superpowers. As Hope Harrison and Jeffrey Herf among others have emphasised, German Cold War history brilliantly illustrates the impact that minor players exerted on the course of the global Cold War.[18] Looking at two decades of German–German rivalry in the Middle East shows that European actors, sometimes willingly, mostly inadvertently, played a crucial role in polarising the Arab–Israeli conflict along East–West lines, and vice versa that Middle Eastern actors, too, fueled the bipolar rivalry.

This book takes the early 1950s as a starting point to analyse the overlap between Cold War dynamics and Arab–Israeli conflict, and it argues that the overlap between Cold War tensions and Arab–Israeli hatreds started earlier than has thus far been understood. It points to the relevance of mutual interconnections and entanglements of political dynamics in diverse regional theatres – in this case, the Middle East and Europe.[19] By examining the debates sparked by the Israeli compensation request, formalised in 1951, and the ensuing talks that representatives from both Germanys had with actors on either side of the Arab–Israeli conflict, the book illustrates how crucial the German–German rivalry was to the projecting of the Cold War onto the region – years before the arms agreement between Czechoslovakia and Egypt, or the onset of the Eisenhower Doctrine.[20]

Covering the critical choices made by the Israeli, and the East and West German establishments in the early 1950s, up to the consolidation of the relations between each German state and the respective Middle Eastern partners in the 1960s, the two decades from 1949 to 1969 were unique in the history of German–Israeli relations, and will be central to this book. Yet this time period also merits particular consideration, as it covers the evolution of each Germany's *Israelpolitik* under a particularly fraught international constellation, marked not only by successive wars in the region, but also by the emergence of the Non-Aligned Movement and the unfolding of the Second Berlin Crisis, which shaped both the dynamics of the global Cold War as well as each German state's margins for manoeuvre within it.

A host of different elements influenced the course of the two Germanys' relations with Israel in the aftermath of the Holocaust. The contradictory attitudes that the political elites in East and West Germany developed vis-à-vis the Nazi past and the continuities in personnel in both German states; the German–German rivalry; the Cold War; Arab–Israeli animosity, inter-Arab competition over the Palestinian question and intra-Israeli debates. All these aspects shaped the political context in which German–Israeli relations developed over the 1950s and 1960s. The interplay between these political forces is woven through the three-phase periodisation which characterises this study. First, by zooming in on the discussions (chapter 1), negotiations (chapter 2) and confrontations (chapter 3) that prompted West Germany to compensate Israel, and East Germany not to, Part I analyses of the emergence of two radically different attitudes vis-à-vis Israel within the West and East German political circles. It also investigates the shades of grey that existed behind these apparently fixed positions. Part II, looking at the years from 1956 to 1961, examines how these attitudes translated into policy at key junctures within the German–Israeli relationship, such as the Suez War (chapter 4), the 1958 Middle Eastern crises (chapter 5) and the Eichmann trial (chapter 6). As domestic and international crises and trials developed in the second half of the 1950s, each Germany found itself increasingly at odds with its respective superpower. This deeply influenced German policy makers and their perceptions of each Germany's international role and was reflected in the East and West German approaches to the region. Part III, covering the years from 1962 to 1969, pays attention to several actors that, willingly or not, impacted upon the making of East and West German–Israeli relations in the 1960s. These include German scientists working in Egypt, accused by the Israeli foreign intelligence services of supporting Cairo's preparation for a pre-emptive war against Israel (chapter 7). They also feature the diplomatic personnel to be first posted to Israel from (West) Germany, and their Israeli counterparts in the FRG (chapter 8). The commencement of diplomatic relations between the FRG and Israel in 1965 was complicated by what many in Israel considered to be the tainted past of several key members of the German diplomatic delegation in Israel. GDR attempts to exploit the situation to make strategic forays in the Middle East at

Bonn's expense, the Arab reactions to Bonn's Middle East crisis, and the Six Day War complicated things further.

To be sure, things had been difficult from the start. By the time of the signing of the reparations agreement, in 1952, Israel was, and had been for years, at an impasse in the armistice – not peace – agreements with its neighbouring Arab states. And West Germany's claims of being the sole representative for the whole of Germany were coming under increasing attack from the countries of the Soviet bloc. Thus, it was perhaps inevitable that the West German decision to transfer contingent reparations to Israel over the next years would draw Bonn, and with it, by degrees, the whole German–German Cold War complex, to clash with the Arab–Israeli conflict. This book provides an account of the origins, and of the unexpected consequences, of such a clash.

# Notes

1  B. J. Ferencz, 'Conscience as an Instrument of National Policy', *Human Rights* 8:42 (1979–80), p. 44.
2  'Address by the President of the State of Israel H.E. Shimon Peres at the German Bundestag delivered on 27 January 2010': www.bundestag.de/parlament/geschichte/gastredner/peres/speech-248112 [Accessed November 2019].
3  N. Balabkins, *West German Reparations to Israel* (New Brunswick: Rutgers University Press, 1971), p. 140.
4  C. Tilly and R. E. Goodin, 'It Depends' in R. E. Goodin and C. Tilly (eds), *The Oxford Handbook of Contextual Political Analysis* (Oxford: Oxford University Press, 2006), pp. 5–32.
5  M. Fulbrook, *German National Identity after the Holocaust* (Oxford: Polity Press, 1999), p. 2.
6  W. G. Gray, *Germany's Cold War: The Global Campaign to Isolate East Germany* (Chapel Hill: University of North Carolina Press, 2003); Y. Hong, *Cold War Germany, the Third World and the Global Humanitarian Regime* (Cambridge: Cambridge University Press, 2015); W. Kilian, *Die Hallstein-Doktrin. Der diplomatische Krieg zwischen der BRD und der DDR 1955–1973* (Berlin: Duncker & Humblot, 2001).
7  M. Fulbrook, *Dissonant Lives: Generations and Violence through the German Dictatorships* (Oxford: Oxford University Press, 2011).
8  J. Herf, *Divided Memory: The Nazi Past in the Two Germanys* (Cambridge, MA: Harvard University Press, 1997).
9  C. S. Maier, *The Unmasterable Past: History, Holocaust and German National Identity* (Cambridge: Cambridge University Press, 1988).
10 Partial exceptions to this include F. Gerlach, *The Tragic Triangle: Israel, Divided Germany and the Arabs 1956–1965* (Doctoral Thesis, Columbia University, 1968) and W. G. Schwanitz, *Deutsche im Nahost 1946–1965: Sozialgeschichte nach Akten und Interviews* (Habilitation Thesis, Freie Universität Berlin, 1998). However, Gerlach's work presents the two German states as acting as one pole of a pre-constituted system (by 1956, when the analysis begins, the system was already in place and by 1965, when the analysis ends, the system had collapsed). The focus of Schwanitz's *Habilitation* thesis, too, differs from the one covered in the present work, because Schwanitz focuses on the social history of German representatives stationed in the Middle East.

11 N. Sagi, *German Reparations: A History of the Negotiations* (Jerusalem: The Magnes Press, The Hebrew University, 1980); I. Deutschkron, *Israel und die Deutschen: Das schwierige Verhältnis* (Cologne: Verlag Wissenschaft und Politik, 1983); L. G. Feldman, *The Special Relationship between West Germany and Israel* (Boston, MD: Allen & Ulwin, 1984); R. Giordano (ed.), *Deutschland und Israel: Solidarität in der Bewährung: Bilanz und Perspektive der deutsch-israelischen Beziehungen* (Gerlingen: Bleicher, 1992); G. Lavy, *Germany and Israel: Moral Debt and National Interest* (London: Frank Cass, 1996); N. Hansen, *Aus dem Schatten der Katastrophe. Die deutsch-israelischen Beziehungen in der Ära Adenauer und David Ben Gurion* (Düsseldorf: Droste, 2002); Y. A. Jelinek, *Deutschland und Israel, 1945–1965. Ein neurotisches Verhältnis* (Munich: Oldenbourg, 2004); D. Trimbur, *De la Shoah à la Réconciliation? La Question des Relations RFA-Israël (1949–1956)* (Paris: CNRS Editions, 2000); M. A. Weingardt, *Deutsche Israel- und Nahostpolitik: Die Geschichte einer Gratwanderung seit 1949* (Frankfurt: Campus, 2002); H. von Hindenburg, *Demonstrating Reconciliation: State and Society in West German Foreign Policy towards Israel, 1952–1965* (New York: Berghahn Books, 2007); D. Witzthum, *Teḥilatah shel yedidiut mufla'ah? Ha-piyus ben Yisra'el le-Germanyah, 1948–1960* (Tel Aviv: Schocken, 2018); M. Borchard, *Eine unmögliche Freundschaft: David Ben-Gurion und Konrad Adenauer* (Freiburg: Herder, 2019); C. Fink, *West Germany and Israel: Foreign Relations, Domestic Politics, and the Cold War, 1965–1974* (Cambridge: Cambrige University Press, 2019); D. Marwecki, *Germany and Israel: Whitewashing and Statebuilding* (London: Hurst, 2020). Specific attention must be paid to the works published by former Israeli ambassadors to the FRG. These include: A. Ben-Natan, *Brücke bauen – aber nicht vergessen: Als erster Botschafter Israels in der Bundesrepublik* (Düsseldorf: Droste, 2005); Y. Meroz, *In schwieriger Mission: Als Botschafter Israels in Bonn* (Berlin: Ullstein, 1986); A. Primor, *"... mit Ausnahme Deutschlands": Als Botschafter Israels in Deutschland* (Berlin: Ullstein, 1997); S. Shtein, *Israel, Deutschland und der Nahe Osten: Beziehungen zwischen Einzigartigkeit und Normalität* (Göttingen: Wallstein, 2011). See also the co-authored volume by two ambassadors, A. Ben-Natan and N. Hansen (eds) *Israel und Deutschland: Dorniger Weg zur Partnerschaft: die Botschafter berichten über vier Jahrzente diplomatische Beziehungen (1965–2005)* (Cologne: Böhlau, 2005). German ambassadors to Israel have been comparatively less prolific in their writing – the biggest exception to this being Hansen, *Aus dem Schatten der Katastrophe*.

12 A. Timm, *Hammer, Zirkel, Davidstern. Das gestörte Verhältnis der DDR zu Zionismus und Staat Israel* (Bonn: Bouvier Verlag, 1997); M. Wolffsohn, *Die Deutschland Akte. Tatsachen und Legenden* (Munich: Ed. Ferenczy bei Bruckmann, 1996 [1995]); S. Meining, *Kommunistische Judenpolitik: die DDR, die Juden und Israel* (Münster: LIT, 2002); K. Kulow, 'Israel, SED und DDR. Zur Geschichte eines tragischen Beziehungskonflikt' in R. Renger (ed.), *Die deutsche 'Linke' und der Staat Israel* (Leipzig: Forum Verlag, 1994), pp. 183–96; S. Lorenzini, *Il Rifiuto di Un'Eredità Difficile: La Repubblica Democratic Tedesca, gli Ebrei e lo Stato di Israele* (Florence: Giuntina, 1998); J. Herf, *Undeclared Wars with Israel: East Germany and the West German Far Left, 1967–1989* (New York: Cambridge University Press, 2016).

13 See, e.g., Marwecki, *Germany and Israel*.

14 J. Kocka, 'Die Geschichte der DDR als Forschungsproblem' in J. Kocka (ed.), *Historische DDR-Forschung: Aufsätze und Studien* (Berlin: Akademie Verlag, 1993), p. 15.

15 I use the phrase 'aftermath of the Holocaust' to refer to the 1950s and 1960s, wary of the fact that in public discourse the term 'Holocaust' only surfaced in the 1970s.

16  K. Weisbrode, *Old Diplomacy Revisited: A Study in the Modern History of Diplomatic Transformations* (London: Palgrave, 2014).

17  T. Smith, 'New Bottles for New Wine: A Pericentric Framework for the Study of the Cold War', *Diplomatic History* 24:4 (2000), pp. 567–91.

18  H. Harrison, *Driving the Soviets Up the Wall: Soviet-East German Relations, 1953–1961* (Princeton: Princeton University Press, 2003); J. Herf, *Undeclared Wars with Israel: East Germany and the West German Far Left, 1967–1989* (New York: Cambridge University Press, 2016).

19  L. M. Lüthi (ed.), *The Regional Cold Wars in Europe, East Asia, and the Middle East: Crucial Periods and Turning Points* (Stanford: Stanford University Press, 2015).

20  F. Gerges, *The Superpowers and the Middle East: Regional and International Politics, 1955–1967* (Boulder: Westview Press, 1994); A. Shlaim and Y. Sayigh (eds), *The Cold War and the Middle East* (Oxford: Clarendon Press, 1997); N. J. Ashton, *The Cold War in the Middle East* (London: Routledge, 2007); D. Little, 'The Cold War in the Middle East: Suez Crisis to Camp David Accords' in M. P. Leffler and O. A. Westad (eds), *The Cambridge History of the Cold War*, Vol. II, *Crises and Détente* (Cambridge: Cambridge University Press, 2010), pp. 305–26.

Part I

# Critical choices, 1949–55

# 1

# Discussions

In April 1950, Kurt Mendelsohn travelled back from his adoptive country, Israel, to his native country, Germany. By that point, he had long ceased to define himself as German, although he still had some difficulties with his Hebrew.[1] He was born into a middle-class Jewish family, in Breslau, in 1902 – a city that by the time of Mendelsohn's journey did not regard itself as German anymore, either, as it was by then known as Wrocław, having been ceded to Poland at the end of the Second World War. As an economist coming of age in a Weimar Republic devoured by a severe financial crisis, Mendelsohn had been an active member of the Republic's leftist union, the Zentralverband der Angestellten, and published his own economic manifesto in 1932, titled: *Capitalist Economic Chaos or Socialist Planning?*[2] He also worked with his wife to translate into German a book, originally subtitled *A Marxist in Palestine*, in which the Belgian former Foreign Minister Émile Vandervelde expounded the potential that that piece of land offered to the Jewish people.[3] Mendelsohn, a socialist economist with fervent Zionist convictions and a doctorate from Heidelberg University, managed to escape Nazi Germany shortly after Hitler's ascent to power. In 1933, he relocated with his wife and son to the Netherlands, where he co-founded Het Werkdrop, a centre organising training courses for Jewish refugees.[4] He kept being involved in the Zionist cause, most notably drafting a fieldwork-based study for the League of Nations on the possible land transfer and population resettlement measures that could be implemented in the near future in British Palestine, to which he emigrated, with his wife, son and adoptive daughter, in 1938.[5] There, Mendelsohn worked for the economic department of the Jewish Agency for ten years, moving to the Ministry of Finance soon after the foundation of the State of Israel in 1948. Of his family members who remained in Europe, none survived the Holocaust.

By 1950, Mendelsohn had become the Director of the Customs and VAT Division at the Ministry of Finance, and he was on his way to Germany because Israeli Foreign Minister Moshe Sharett and Finance Minister Eliezer Kaplan had picked him for a delicate and complex mission: that of exploring the possibility of starting a direct dialogue between the Israeli and the German governments on the question of Holocaust reparations.[6] At the time of Mendelsohn's travels, many in Israel opposed the idea of having economic, political or social contacts with Germany – let alone of accepting any kind of material restitution or compensation for the horrors committed by the Nazis against the Jews. While his mission was not secret (indeed, several newspapers found out about his activities and reported them), it was not to be widely advertised, either, and Mendelsohn tried to keep a low profile throughout his time in Germany.

At that time, Israel's official policy towards Germany was one of economic and political boycott. Formally, Israel declared that it was in a state of war against it on the very same day of its foundation, on 14 May 1948. And yet, in its day-to-day life the Israeli Foreign Ministry was pushed to grant one exception after the other, as commercial exchanges between the two countries, covertly, multiplied. The trade included goods as diverse as citrus fruits (from Israel to Germany) and MAN trucks (from Germany to Israel), and it was driven mainly by the German-Jewish population of Israel (the 'Yekkes') that still had personal and professional contacts with people in Germany, in spite of the official anti-German stance declared by the Israeli authorities. The Israeli consulate in Munich was among the first to have been established abroad, on the insistence of the Jewish Agency's Chaim Hoffmann (later Yaḥil), to assist Jewish displaced persons and facilitate their emigration from Germany.[7] Accredited to the American, British and French authorities, the Munich Consulate received precise indications from Jerusalem to avoid any sort of contact or interaction with the German authorities. But the opposition to dealing with Germany was not shared by everyone in the Israeli establishment, nor in Israeli society.

In fact, some believed that it was necessary, and indeed right, that Germany transfer heirless Jewish property to Jewish institutions; that it give back the goods confiscated from those German Jewish citizens who had managed to relocate to other countries, including Israel; and that it was simply not right that Israel – such a young state, and one that had just emerged victorious from a protracted and very damaging war against all of its neighbours – would also need to sustain, on its own, the costly expenses needed for resettling and integrating Holocaust survivors, many of whom were in need of serious medical assistance and would never be able to work again. Some, in other words, were of the opinion that Germany should pay reparations to Israel.

The idea that Germany should pay some kind of compensation to the Jewish state had been formulated at a time in which Israel had not even been founded. The question dated back to when the Second World War and the attempted extermination of the Jewish people were still underway and it was impossible to assess the exact amount of reparations that Germany would be required to pay – though it was clear that some form of compensation would be demanded, and that it was important not to lose sight of the matter.[8] In 1944, jurists Siegfried Moses and Bernard Joseph (later Dov Yosef) suggested that (what was then) Palestine should be the recipient of compensation from Germany. While the ideas put forward by the two jurists diverged on many aspects, the concept that a future Jewish state could be considered a rightful recipient of German reparations was groundbreaking, for it foresaw not only the defeat of Germany and the formation of a Jewish state in Palestine, but also the possibility that reparations could be paid to an entity, a state, which did not yet exist at a time in which the war was waged.[9] Moses and Joseph's idea was carried forward, and Palestine had a central position in the official memorandum that Chaim Weizmann, on behalf of the Jewish Agency for Palestine, presented to the four wartime Allies on 20 September 1945. In it, the future president of the State of Israel asked for reparation, rehabilitation and indemnification following the 'special war' waged by Germany against the Jewish people. He suggested that part of the reparations extracted from Germany by the Allies be allotted to Palestine and the Jewish Agency to support the rehabilitation and resettlement of those survivors who chose Palestine as their new home.[10] But Weizmann's memorandum did not achieve any concrete results, mainly because it reached the Allies at a time in which the divides among them ran deep, as would be reflected, ultimately, in the division of Germany into two states in March and October 1949: the FRG in the West, and the GDR in the East.

The creation of the two German states in Europe, which followed shortly after the Israeli declaration of independence and the Israeli victory in the first Arab–Israeli war, gave new impetus to the Israeli quest for reparations from Germany. Although victorious, Israel had come out of the war greatly debilitated, its economic resources heavily drained. All of Israel's neighbours had declared war against it just a few hours after David Ben-Gurion, head of the Jewish Agency and first Prime Minister of Israel, announced its very foundation on 14 May 1948. The war effort left the Israeli economy in disarray. The situation was further complicated by the huge waves of mass immigration that characterised much of the first years of Israel's existence. While in the run-up to the declaration of independence the immigrants were arriving in large numbers from Europe, either to escape Nazi persecution or after the liberation of the concentration camps, the end of the first Arab–Israeli war was followed by the mass emigration of Jews from Arab countries and their resettlement in Israel. Many of them had been forced to leave all of their possessions behind in order to be allowed to leave their countries of origins, where the Jewish minorities were being subjected to increasing forms of discrimination from the Arab governments. The Israeli authorities, struggling to provide housing and work to the new immigrants, implemented a strict austerity programme that included the rationing of basic goods and services. At the same time, the government's decision to increase the money supply led to severe inflation and to the blossoming of the black-market economy.[11]

By 1950 Israel was undergoing a severe economic crisis. In contrast, by that point West Germany had been receiving Marshall Plan aid funds for two years and, in 1949, the West German authorities had appealed to the Western Allied powers with the request that they formally end the state of war with Germany. Although France, the United Kingdom and the United States all formally rebuffed the West German request, viewed from Israel, Germany's economic and political prospects seemed to be rapidly and steadily improving. With Israel's delicate economic situation at the forefront of his worries, Finance Minister Eliezer Kaplan looked for a solution that would avert a major crisis that threatened the newly founded Jewish state and, in February 1950, he proposed that an Israeli representative be sent to Germany. His task would be to assess whether, and how much, the Germans were able and willing to pay in restitutions to the Jewish state. Foreign Minister Sharett supported the move, stressing the urgency of establishing a direct dialogue with the Germans soon, for political and economic reasons. He tried to reassure his colleagues by explaining that this would neither mean, nor lead to, the establishment of diplomatic relations between Israel and Germany. Yet even so, some of the Cabinet members were extremely hesitant at the thought of a direct exchange between German and Israeli officials. Agriculture Minister Dov Yosef, the unpopular mastermind of the Israeli rationing programme, tried to look for ways to avoid, as much as possible, the prospect of dealing with the Germans. Although he agreed, in principle, to the idea of 'extracting whatever is possible from them', Yosef questioned whether it was really necessary for the Israelis to have direct contact with the Germans in order to get them to commit to paying reparations. A much more palatable option, he suggested, would be if 'Uruguay, or any other friendly state' could step in and negotiate, on behalf of Israel, with the German side, the perpetrators.[12] His idea, however, was dismissed, and on 15 February 1950, the Israeli Cabinet authorised the Foreign Ministry and the Finance Ministry to initiate contact with the German authorities, in coordination with the Prime Minister's office and the Jewish Agency.

The Israeli initiative to formulate reparations claims against Germany was revolutionary in the history of international law and international relations. Up to the 1950s, the question of reparations had always been linked to the traditional dynamics of war: the vanquished country was expected to pay reparations to the victor. The Israeli claim would be substantially new, and different, for several reasons. First, in order to sustain the reparations claim Israel would have to demonstrate that such a transaction could take place between countries that did not formally exist at the time in which the crimes were committed, given that Israel had been founded in 1948 and the German states in 1949. Second, the claim would need to be very specific about the sum requested by Israel. To further complicate the issue, third, it would be necessary to clarify the grounds for which Israel, as the Jewish state, could be the recipient for such reparations, while negotiating with the many other Jewish organisations that by the end of the 1940s were working tirelessly around the globe to help the victims of German persecution.

## The interview

An important prelude to the discussions in the Israeli cabinet had played out on 25 November 1949 when, during an interview with the editor-in-chief of the weekly publication *Allgemeine Wochenschrift der Juden in Deutschland*, West German Chancellor Konrad Adenauer declared that 'as a first, direct sign' of the West German intention to 'make good for the injustice inflicted by the Nazis on the Jews', the FRG would pay reparations of up to 10 million German marks (DM) to the State of Israel.[13] For a country that was not sovereign and that was not allowed to pursue an independent foreign policy, and so was allowed neither a Foreign Office nor a Foreign Minister, Adenauer's declaration was a bold step. It followed one month after the Chancellor's announcement, on the occasion of his governmental statement to the West German Parliament (Bundestag) on 21 October 1949, that the Bonn government reserved the right to speak in the name of all Germans (*Alleinvertretungsanspruch*).[14] West German representatives would continue to reiterate this message for more than two decades to come.

Obtaining greater room for manoeuvre in international affairs, Adenauer believed, was crucial to ostracising the newly founded East German state. Thus, in 1949 and 1950, the Chancellor often used interviews and speeches as a means to overcome constraints set by the Western powers on the development of West German foreign relations.[15] The Chancellor's declaration of Bonn's readiness to pay reparations to Israel, made during the celebrations of the Jewish New Year (*Rosh Ha-shanah*), was a case in point. Yet the willingness to please the United States may also have played a role. John McCloy, the recently appointed US High Commissioner for Germany, in his conversations with the Chancellor and his closest advisers, often highlighted the importance of West Germany taking concrete measures to signal to the world its readiness to confront the Nazi past and leave it behind.[16]

Betraying the traits that were to become typical of his *Kanzlerdemokratie*, Adenauer had not consulted his Economics Minister, Ludwig Erhard, prior to releasing the statement on restitutions to Israel. Erhard seems to not even have noticed the Chancellor's reparations promise until a few months later, at the end of January 1950, when letters from interested applicants for the funds envisioned by Adenauer started inundating the Economics Ministry. At which point, Erhard checked whether the news was correct, inquiring of Adenauer whether what the *Allgemeine* reported corresponded to the truth, and asked for guidance as to how to proceed with the matter.[17]

Adenauer's unannounced declaration about West German reparations to Israel came as a surprise to many because, despite the aid that the Federal Republic was receiving under the Marshall Plan, in the early 1950s, the economic, social and political situation of the country was still precarious. West German cities were still in ruins, and food and accommodation were scarce.[18] Despite the extent of the destruction brought about by the Nazi regime's policies and wars, population density in West Germany had increased, as expellees from the East, former camp inmates and war veterans resettled in West German territory to rebuild their lives. People that had experienced the Nazi years in completely different circumstances were now living alongside one another. The forced cohabitation lead to an obvious degree of tension and discontent within West German society, where housing, work and food were lacking.[19] Moreover, if social and economic conditions in the new Republic were thorny, the political scene did not seem to offer much hope either.

The new Chancellor, former Mayor of Cologne Konrad Adenauer, had been elected with a majority of just one vote – his own, carped his critics.[20] He was seventy-three years old. Just a few years earlier, in October 1945, the British authorities had been so outraged by his alleged ineffectiveness that they had sacked him from his post as the reinstated Mayor of Cologne and discouraged him from pursuing, 'either directly or indirectly, any political activity whatsoever' in the future.[21] After his election as Chancellor he did not seem particularly impressive in the eyes of the West German voters either, with 54 per cent of the electorate having no opinion about him and 15 per cent actively opposing his policies at the end of the first trimester of his chancellorship.[22] At that time, nobody could have anticipated that 'the Old Man', the first Chancellor of the FRG, would remain at the head of four successive West German governments, ruling from 1949 until 1963. During those fourteen years, the Federal Republic transformed completely. Reconciliation with the State of Israel became a crucial component of West Germany's full transformation into an important, reliable actor in international affairs. Adenauer, just like his Israeli counterpart David Ben-Gurion, would play a crucial role in building the foundations of a special relationship between the Federal Republic and the State of Israel, and his unannounced declarations to the *Allgemeine* were a first step in that direction.

## The meetings

Kurt Mendelsohn stayed on German territory on and off for three months, travelling widely around the country to meet with representatives from both German states. He had brought with him a presentation letter drafted by the Israeli Foreign Ministry, stating that his job was 'to ascertain on behalf of the State of Israel the conditions under which property and funds in Germany belonging and accruing to residents in Israel, may be used for the purchase in Germany of goods required by the State of Israel'.[23] However, as his frenetic activities in Germany made clear, he went above and beyond his written job description. First, he sought to understand whether, and to what extent, German representatives in both East and West were open to the idea of indemnifying individual German Jewish citizens who had relocated to Israel. Further, he also tried to assess whether the option of a broader form of compensation, the Jewish state, could be discussed with official interlocutors in either East or West Germany, or both. He was well aware, and would often remind his interlocutors, that forging a programme of reparations could be very beneficial for either Germany, too, as this could lay the ground for economic exchanges with Israel to blossom in the future – indeed the many exceptions that the Israeli government needed to make when enforcing the boycott were testament to this potential. There was also an element of intelligence gathering to Mendelsohn's trip, as the Israeli envoy tried, and managed, to acquire sources that provided him with unique access to information on the actual state of the German economy.

Mendelsohn tackled the most important meetings first, heading straight to the Chancellery, in Bonn. There, he talked with two close collaborators of Adenauer, Ernst Wirmer and Josef Rust, emphasising that the minimum amount that Israel expected to receive from the FRG was much more substantial than that envisioned by the Chancellor in his *Allgemeine* interview.[24] The meeting did not lead to any concrete promise on the part of the West German representatives, but shortly after Mendelsohn's departure Wirmer urged the members of the relevant ministerial divisions to organise a meeting and discuss the issue of reparations to Israel. Mendelsohn also secured a private audience with Ludwig Erhard's second in command at the Ministry of Economics, State Secretary Eduard Schalfejew, and a meeting with West Germany's Finance Minister, Fritz Schäffer. But while the personnel of the Economic and Finance ministries were sceptical of Mendelsohn's mission, he found a more sympathetic listener in the German industrialist Otto Wolff von Amerongen. Having inherited from his father one of the biggest industrial conglomerates in the country – one whose dealings would later partially merge into big German groups such as ThyssenKrupp and foreign ones such as Exxon – Wolff von Amerongen displayed a vivid interest in the future of the commercial relations between Israel and the Federal Republic. As Mendelsohn highlighted, the Israeli economy was especially in need of the manufactured and semi-manufactured goods that Wolff's industry produced.[25] Thus, if the West German government could be persuaded to accept a programme of reparations in kind (non-cash), these would most probably consist of the goods that Wolff's conglomerate produced, and it was likely that the onset of reparation transfers could lead the way to an expansion of Wolff's trade into a new and blossoming Near Eastern market.

The fact that Mendelsohn managed to secure meetings with members of the West German government and industry sparked the jealousies both of others who had been working on the question of compensation, and of those who somehow wanted to be involved in these discussions. Siegfried Seelig, for example, who worked for one of the biggest raw materials trading companies in Germany, the Vereinigte Stahlwerke AG, and who was a prominent figure within the Association of Jewish Communities in the North Rhine region, wrote an indignant letter to the Israeli consul in Germany, Eliahu Livneh. 'If you think that the small doctors and former lawyers are the right people to come to even the smallest achievements with the German authorities', carped Seelig, 'then you and the others especially in the high echelons of the Israeli government are terribly mistaken'.[26] Seelig had begun reaching out to key figures within the German establishment already in January 1950, attempting to present himself as an intermediary between the Israeli and the German governments.[27] He did not take the news of Mendelsohn's mission well. In turn, in a letter dated June 1950, Mendelsohn lamented that 'all sorts of random people' were involved in the question of getting reparations from Germany, and that a rationalisation of the efforts was necessary if the matter was to be solved successfully.[28] His thoughts were echoed by the Israeli consul, who argued that the problems in proceeding swiftly with the matter of reparations could not just be put down to German unwillingness to act, but they were also due to economic and legal issues that the Jewish organisations and the Israeli state needed to solve before serious negotiations could take place.[29]

Yet not all Jewish organisations ostracised Mendelsohn's work. At the end of April 1950 Noah Barou, the head of the European section of the World Jewish Congress, held a meeting with Herbert Blankenhorn, the director of the political division of what would later become the West German Foreign Ministry (Auswärtiges Amt).[30] Blankenhorn had been an active member of the diplomatic service during the years of the Third Reich, and was one of the many bureaucrats subsequently reintegrated among the ranks of the civil service in the Federal Republic, where he was now serving as Adenauer's chief adviser on foreign policy issues. Discussing the matter of German compensation to Israel, Barou pressed him about the need for the FRG to take an open stance on its commitment to paying restitutions to the Jewish state. Meanwhile, Mendelsohn proceeded with his busy meeting schedule, which now led him to East Berlin, to test the waters for a future possible dialogue between Israel and the GDR.

## Mendelsohn travels eastwards

Although the Eastern part of Germany was highly industrialised and had suffered comparatively less damage than the Western zones during the war, by 1950 the East German economy was in shambles. The crippling amount of reparations that the Soviet occupiers exacted from East German territory impoverished the East German population enormously.[31] The situation was furthered damaged by Soviet-led economic reforms aiming to create a planned economic system in the GDR. Despite this, however, Mendelsohn had concrete reasons to hope that his talks with the East German authorities could in fact lead to some positive results. Preliminary contacts between representatives of the future Jewish state with politicians who would later be in charge of the GDR had taken place already in April 1948, when Chaim Yahil, the director of the Jewish Agency delegation in Germany, secured a meeting with Otto Grotewohl, co-chairman of the political party that was to dominate four decades of East German political life, the SED. Yahil, who was born in Moravia in 1905 and had completed his doctorate in political science in Vienna, had changed his name from Hoffmann when migrating to Palestine for good in 1939. There, he worked for the *Histadrut*, the main trades union in the country. After the end of the Second World War, Yahil was sent to Germany to act as Director of the Jewish Agency office in Munich, where his main objective was to facilitate the emigration of as many survivors and Displaced Persons (DP) camp inmates as possible to Palestine. In his talk with Yahil in April 1948, Grotewohl rejected out of hand the possibility of returning property located in East German territory that had been seized from the Jews by the Nazis. Nonetheless, his response had not been completely negative, as he had kept open the option of pursuing a collective payment to the State of Israel after its foundation. Grotewohl also mentioned that the GDR would provide financial help to assist with the transportation of Jewish survivors from a number of DP camps to Palestine.[32]

In May 1950, two years after the meeting between Yahil and Grotewohl, Mendelsohn managed to secure a meeting with two representatives of the political and economic divisions within the East German Foreign Ministry. His talks with the GDR bureaucrats, just like the ones that he was pursuing in parallel with West German representatives, focused heavily on the question of reparations, trying to assess whether, and how much, the East German authorities would be willing to pay in restitutions to the Jewish state. To Linick and Raphael of the East German Foreign Ministry, Mendelsohn proposed that the GDR pay reparations to Israel in kind, suggesting that this could form the basis for establishing economic relations between the two countries in the near future.[33] The East German bureaucrats did not seem enthusiastic at the thought of adding more reparations to the already burdensome amount the GDR was paying to the Soviet Union, asking whether this payment would necessarily have to be the precondition for starting economic relations between the two countries. They admitted that they did not know how the issue of reparations would be regulated in East Germany and mentioned that, in general, the ministry could not have dealings with representatives of countries with which their government did not have diplomatic relations. The meeting ended with a non-committal East German request for a memorandum on the Israeli demands, and with the assent of the Foreign Ministry personnel to putting Mendelsohn in touch with officials of the Ministry of Foreign and Inter-German Trade (Ministerium für Außenhandel und Innerdeutschen Handel, MAI).[34] Mendelsohn altered his travel plans, so as to remain available for another couple of days should the GDR authorities wish to discuss any further details with him – to no avail. He was not contacted by the East German authorities, and eventually made his way back to West Germany.

By the time Mendelsohn met with Linick and Raphael in East Berlin, Grotewohl's earlier show of goodwill on the question of reparations seemed to have left no trace. In fact, much had changed on East German soil, and in international politics, in just two years. At the time of Yaḥil's meeting with Grotewohl in 1948, the Soviets wholeheart-edly supported the formation of a Jewish state in British Palestine. In their eyes, the creation of the State of Israel signalled a shrinking of the British presence in the Near East that could lead to the broadening of the Soviet room for manoeuvre in the region. Soviet support for the creation of a Jewish state proved crucial to guaranteeing Israel's victory in the war of independence, as the Soviet Union persuaded Czechoslovakia to grant Israel a wide range of military equipment, from bullets to rifles and fighter planes, throughout 1948, circumventing the arms embargo that the United States had imposed on the Middle East at that time and ensuring that Israel received much-needed war materials. Furthermore, Grotewohl's pre-war affiliation with the Socialist Democratic Party (SPD) – a party that had vocally denounced the attacks on the German Jewish community during the Nazi years – may also have influenced his post-war response to Yaḥil.[35] By mid-1950, however, Soviet sympathies for Israel had started to wane, the conditions in which Soviet Jewry lived worsened, and the East German–Israeli dia-logue seemed to lead to nowhere.

## Morphing into the GDR

If Linick and Raphael had seemed rather unprepared for dealing with Mendelsohn's requests, this was also because much was changing in the GDR, too. The official dec-laration of the foundation of the GDR, on 7 October 1949, marked the beginning of a German–German competition for the legitimate representation of the German people. Bonn's representatives fought off the idea of even mentioning the name of the German state in the East, and circulated guidance notes to the Western allies about how (not) to refer to the GDR, alluding to it as 'the zone', meaning the Soviet occupation zone and refusing to recognise any traits of East German sovereignty; or 'Pankow', the area of East Berlin where the Soviet administration was based until 1949. In contrast, the East German leadership frequently mentioned the FRG and its policies. Indeed, attacking and discrediting Bonn soon became the typical East German mechanism for illus-trating the superiority of the GDR and its political system. Furthermore, the GDR's *Israelpolitik* was, substantially, the SED's *Israelpolitik*, given the overall lack of power of state institutions, such as the Foreign Ministry, vis-à-vis party institutions, such as the Politbüro.[36]

The SED, which was to rule the GDR from 1949 to 1990, originated from the Soviet-led merger, in 1946, of the Communist and the Socialist Democratic Parties (KPD and SPD, respectively). This was a move that the Soviets had engineered, in the belief that the establishment of a single strong party in their zone of occupation would improve their ability to control the Eastern German territory and, in turn, promote the establishment of Communist dominance throughout Central and Eastern Europe.[37] Wilhelm Pieck and Otto Grotewohl, two prominent members of the former Communist and Socialist parties, thus became Joint Chairmen of the SED, while Grotewohl also served as Chairman of the Council of Ministers (Ministerrat). Under him, serving (until 1950) as Deputy Chairman, was the 'consummate *apparatchik*', Walter Ulbricht.[38] He would not remain in a subordinate political position for much longer.

In 1950, Pieck and Grotewohl's joint Party Chairmanship was abolished and Ulbricht was elected General Secretary of the Central Committee of the SED. The new East German leader had patiently, though relentlessly, been climbing party ranks from before the outbreak of the First World War through to his return to German soil two weeks prior to the unconditional surrender of Hitler's Germany, in May 1945 – and he had managed to forge ever closer ties to Moscow as he went along.[39] Ulbricht joined the Socialist Workers' Youth Organization when he was just fifteen years old and a simple carpenter's apprentice. Just a few years later he was already known within KPD circles as the 'red soul of Thuringia', the region where he had helped in setting up the local KPD district.[40] During the 1920s, his activism proved crucial for disseminating Moscow's directives throughout Germany. Neither the Nazi rise to power in 1933 and his ensuing escape from the country, nor the outbreak of the Second World War, impaired his ability to be in touch with, and well known within, both the German and Soviet political scenes. It was his ability to be well connected, and very well informed about the German and Soviet political dynamics, that rendered him unique within his party.[41] Indeed, his 'dull'[42] and 'dry'[43] personality notwithstanding, and despite the lack of 'rhetorical gifts, originality (and) brilliance'[44] lamented by several of his biographers,[45] his hard detail-work within the party in his role of obedient functionary, and his constant efforts to further Moscow's political interests in the KPD, put him on the right track to assuming a high profile both in Germany and Soviet Russia.[46] During the early 1950s, as Moscow progressively distanced itself from the pro-Israeli stance it had adopted at the time of Israel's declaration of independence, the East German attitude towards the Jewish state, too, gradually grew more hostile. The hesitancy displayed by the two Foreign Ministry officials in their meeting with Mendelsohn in May 1950 despite Grotewohl's earlier declaration of support for the Jewish restitution claims, encapsulated many of the ambiguities that characterised the GDR during a period in which it was attempting to establish its own credibility as an independent socialist country on German soil while facing the constraints arising from its ties to Moscow.

Thus, despite the signals in 1948 that might have suggested otherwise, it quickly became clear that Israel's chances of getting restitutions from East Germany would be rather slim. Apart from an East German checking of the question of *Wiedergutmachung* laws, Mendelsohn's efforts did not bring about the effect that the Israelis were hoping for,[47] and, from Munich, Livneh lamented that Mendelsohn's visit to Germany did not really achieve much at all. But the Consul's assessment may have been too harsh. In fact, Mendelsohn had been the first Israeli representative to be sent to Germany on an official mission to hold talks directly with the German authorities, on both sides of the Iron Curtain, and this was, in itself, an achievement. One that would contribute to paving the way, slowly, to setting up official discussions among German and Israeli representatives in the aftermath of the Holocaust.

## Tweaking the speech

At the end of May 1950, in Bonn the personnel of the West German Finance Ministry began studying the issue of *Wiedergutmachung* more thoroughly.[48] The discussion focused on two main points. First, on the impossibility of paying the reparations in cash and instead examining the option of paying them in kind, i.e. as material goods to be exported to Israel. Second, on the need to coordinate with other ministries, especially the Ministry of Justice, given that no federal law on the issue of reparations yet existed.[49] While it was clear that the Israeli reparations claims constituted a key problem the avoidance of which would 'seriously harm' future relations between the two countries, in June 1950 discussion on the question of restitutions to the Jewish state came to a halt.[50] Finance Minister Schäffer, requested to refer to the Cabinet on the issue, refused to do so. The news came as a relief to some of Bonn's foreign policy experts, who hoped that this might boost the FRG's credentials vis-à-vis the Arab states.[51] Finance Minister Schäffer explained his decision by pointing out that the FRG simply did not have enough resources at the moment to satisfy the Israeli request. In his opinion, it was futile to discuss the topic because, given the grim economic situation in West Germany and the lack of funds, 'negotiations [with Israel] would go nowhere'.[52] He was soon to be proven wrong.

On 25 June 1950, the armed forces of Communist North Korea crossed over the 38th parallel into South Korea, unleashing a war that would last for over three years. At the United Nations (UN), Israel sided with the United States, de facto publicly taking sides with the West.[53] The external demand for West German raw materials, investment goods and industrial products, arising as a result of the war, boosted economic growth in the Federal Republic.[54] And a wealthier FRG would be in a better position to resume talks about *Wiedergutmachung* to Israel – although it soon became evident that the question of reparations was essentially political, rather than purely economic, in nature.[55]

Twice in 1951 (in January and March), the Israeli government addressed a note to the four occupying powers in Germany explaining 'the basis and nature' of their compensation claims and outlining 'proposals for their satisfaction'[56] – without distinguishing, at this stage, between reparations from the FRG or the GDR and still speaking, in general terms, of reparations from 'Germany'. While no written response came from the Soviet bloc, in July the Western powers replied, encouraging Israeli representatives to deal directly with the West German authorities and without relying on Allied mediation.[57]

A few days later, on 13 July 1951, Alexander Böker, of the Chancellery's administrative unit on Foreign Affairs, had a speech drafted for Adenauer on the subject.[58] Both his superior, Herbert Blankenhorn, and the Assistant US High Commissioner for Policy, Benjamin J. Buttenwieser, revised the draft – and the Chancellor added some changes of his own, too. While addressing the Bundestag on 27 September 1951, signalling Bonn's readiness to enter into negotiations with representatives of the Jewish state, Adenauer explained that:

> During the period of National Socialism there were many Germans, acting on the basis of religious belief, the call of conscience, and shame at the disgrace of Germany's name, who at their own risk were willing to assist their Jewish fellow citizens. In the name of the German people, however, unspeakable crimes were committed, which require moral and material restitution.[59]

The draft speech he had received was less sensational, and somewhat more accurate, than that. It stated that during the Nazi years there had been 'some' who had been willing to help their Jewish fellow citizens.[60] By stressing, before the Bundestag, that Bonn's gesture of reparation to Israel needed to be both 'moral' and 'material' – words that were *not* included in the original draft he had received – Adenauer was pointing to the symbolic significance of the negotiations that were about to begin. At the same time, however, he suggested that Nazism, and Nazi policies including the persecution and extermination of the Jews, had received the support of a mere minority of the German population – a grotesque misrepresentation of the historical truth.[61] Given the high number of professionals working in the Federal Republic who had had connections to the Nazi Party, the option of financial restitution to the Jewish state and Jewish organisations was more feasible, and politically more palatable, than purging the compromised elites of the Federal Republic through judicial procedures.[62] Adenauer's stance in the Bundestag, announcing the onset of West German–Israeli negotiations, conformed to the policies of amnesty and integration that had multiplied in Bonn, under his leadership, in the early 1950s.[63]

Adenauer's speech about the West German willingness to pay reparations to Israel was crucially linked to his ambition to restore the sovereignty, and with it the legitimacy, of the Federal Republic. The year 1951 was very important for the Federal Republic in this respect, as West Germany was finally given permission to establish a Foreign Ministry (in March), Bonn became a member of the European Coal and Steel Community (in April), and the Western allies communicated that the state of war with Germany was officially over (in July). But such legitimacy was a prospect that, in Israeli quarters, was not easily accepted, as the impending discussions at the UN would soon demonstrate.

## Clashing at the UN

Gathered in New York on 13 November 1951, the plenary meeting of the General Assembly of the United Nations (UNGA) debated the controversial prospect of holding all-German elections. The matter had been widely debated in East and West Germany from early 1950 onwards. The American and Soviet viewpoints on this issue – and the West and East German ones – diverged. Free elections represented the first step advocated by Washington and Bonn when discussing the path to German reunification, while the Soviets and East Berlin viewed the elections as a last step of such a process. On 15 October 1951, West German representatives had approached the UNGA with the request to have a neutral commission assess whether the conditions for free elections existed on German soil. The discussion at the UN began quietly, and supposedly rather boringly, until the Israeli delegate at the UN took the floor.[64] As he spoke, a sense of 'unpleasant surprise' pervaded the members of the West German delegation.[65] After all, the UN was deemed a crucial forum in which to show the family of nations that West Germany was, again, a reliable member of it, and the FRG had been making steady progress in gaining appeal in international affairs.[66] Yet the Israeli delegate remained undeterred:

> [To us in Israel] anything tantamount to the readmission of Germany into the family of nations and any acceleration of the process of such readmission cannot in these circumstances but appear as a desecration of the memory of our martyrs, and a triumph of evil.[67]

On 12 December 1951, with forty-five votes in favour, six against and eight abstentions, the UNGA finally resolved to appoint an international commission to investigate whether the conditions existed on German territory (Berlin, the FRG and the GDR) that would allow 'genuinely free elections' to take place.[68] This was an important victory for Bonn, as few had expected the UNGA to vote so clearly in favour of the West German proposal.[69] Interestingly, all the negative votes on the proposal originated from Soviet bloc countries – Russia, Belarus, Czechoslovakia, Ukraine and Poland – except for one, Israel. The Israeli delegation to the UNGA voted against the prospect of holding elections on German territory, on the basis that this would entail a first step towards the restoration of German international legitimacy. Israeli Foreign Minister Moshe Sharett explained that:

> Since the dangers inherent in the resurgence of Germany as a Power, to which we [Israel] drew the attention of the Assembly [have not] been in any way reflected in [the] wording [of the Commission's terms of reference included in the resolution] – I mean the danger of the non-liquidation of the past constituting such a grave menace for the future – we found ourselves compelled to maintain our position by voting against the draft resolution.[70]

The Israeli attitude, Böker commented, had been the 'only unpleasant note' throughout the UNGA discussion.[71] According to the West German report of the UN session, only Arab representatives had intervened to protect West Germany, emphasising that 'a young state such as Israel' had 'no right' to judge other countries.[72] The Israelis, though unable to block the resolution, were voicing exactly the kind of criticism that Adenauer's Germany did not wish to receive, and in such a crucial political forum as Bonn deemed the UN to be.[73] And this was not the only incident of this kind. West Germany's attempts to gain membership of several international bodies in the early 1950s sparked continued debates within the Israeli establishment: how should the Israeli government respond to such German moves? How could Israel repeatedly accept seeing Germany gain even moderate amounts of respectability within the international domain if the issue of Holocaust reparations had not been solved? Israeli diplomats stationed abroad were instructed not to accept the invitations of their German colleagues and to not hold discussions directly with them. Internationally, the Israelis decided to seize any possible opportunity to voice their concern about the FRG making such impressive gains on the path to national sovereignty in such a short amount of time. This, from Bonn's perspective, was not good news. West Germany needed to act quickly to stop such criticism from being publicly and forcefully voiced and initiating official talks of reparations and compensation could be a way of making this happen. Top-level talks between West Germans and Israelis resumed shortly thereafter.

## A secret meeting in London and a painful debate in the Knesset

Sneaking through a back door in order not to be seen dealing with the West German Chancellor, Nahum Goldmann met with Adenauer at Claridge's hotel in London on 6 December 1951.[74] The Chancellor had expressed the wish to meet *one* person authorised to represent all of the Jewish interests involved in negotiating with (West) Germany for *Wiedergutmachung*.[75] The newly elected president of the Conference on Jewish Material Claims Against Germany (JCC), Nahum Goldmann, was the person Adenauer was looking for.[76] Founder and President of the World Jewish Congress, Goldmann represented a minority perspective within it, which argued decidedly against any boycott of Germany. He had long advocated the necessity to act on the question of Holocaust compensation and restitution – most vocally during the 1941 World Jewish Congress conference in Baltimore.[77] The Chancellor later remembered the 1951 meeting as 'very serious and impressive'; his aides noted that an 'exceptionally friendly atmosphere' dominated the encounter between the two.[78] Though originally from modern-day Belarus, Goldmann's family had moved to Germany when he was six years old. Having studied law, history and philosophy in Marburg, Heidelberg and Berlin, he was fluent in German and managed to establish a very good connection with the West German Chancellor in London. At the end of the meeting, Adenauer, at Goldmann's request, put in writing three key points. First, that the Federal Republic recognised that the time had come to begin direct negotiations on the basis of the claims contained in the Israeli note of March 1951. This meant that the sum of US$1 billion was accepted as the starting point for the negotiations. Second, that Bonn viewed *Wiedergutmachung* as a 'moral obligation' of the German people.[79] Third, reparations would be made in kind – which would be beneficial for the West German economy, too.[80]

Now that the ground had, at least partially, been cleared by Goldmann and Adenauer in their talks, the issue needed to be discussed publicly in Israel, and members of the

Figure 1.1 Menachem Begin addresses a crowd of demonstrators, 1952.

Israeli parliament, the Knesset, debated the issue in January 1952 in an extremely fraught atmosphere.[81] All Knesset members agreed that no form of atonement for the crimes committed against the Jews under the Nazi regime would ever be enough to compensate for the crimes committed by the Nazis. However, the Knesset was divided among those who, while recognising that no compensation would ever constitute redress for the violence inflicted to European Jewry, were inclined to negotiate with the Germans and obtain reparations, and those who vehemently opposed the idea of receiving material compensation for the Nazi persecution of the Jews. The debate was tense. Menachem Begin, leader of the Herut party, spoke with his 'heart drunk with blood', and warned those who intended to vote for 'eas[ing] the way for a spiritual cleaning' of the (West) German state with a veiled threat to their personal safety.[82] Some 15,000 demonstrators gathered around the parliamentary building in protest, and the demonstrations soon turned violent. The riot, the rocks that smashed the Knesset windows, interrupted the plenum debate that was taking place inside. The police only managed to regain control of the situation after five hours of rioting, arresting hundreds in the process.

The parliamentary debate ended, after days of tension, on 9 January 1952 with the decision to hold direct negotiations, with a slim but significant majority of sixty-one for and fifty against, and it became crucial to ensure that these would run smoothly. When Adenauer and Goldmann met again in London, the Chancellor gave his word that he would personally monitor the progress of the negotiations, and that his closest collaborators would be taking care of all relevant issues. He expressed the hope, in typical Adenauer style, of preventing the negotiations from getting 'into the morass of the Financial or specialized ministries'.[84] In Bonn, however, the 'specialised ministries' had already started to get involved, pointing to the difficult issues that would certainly arise with the beginning of the negotiations.

Finance Minister Schäffer, for example, repeatedly warned of the dangers of negotiating with the Israelis at the same time as the London Conference was taking place.[85] In London, a West German delegation was negotiating not only the total amount of West Germany's external debt arising out of the unfulfilled payment of the reparations imposed on Germany by the Treaty of Versailles after the First World War, and over the repayment of the occupation costs incurred by France, the United States and the United Kingdom.[86] While recognising that the *Wiedergutmachung* project could also bring Bonn concrete economic benefits, the Economic Ministry, too, warned that Bonn's resources were too scarce to put the FRG in the position of negotiating on both payments simultaneously.[87] The memory of the financial, as well as political, collapse of the Weimar Republic alerted Bonn's Cabinet to the need to ensure that the Federal Republic did not commit itself to payments it was not in a position to sustain.[88] But the Chancellor, during his meeting with Goldmann in December 1951, had already agreed to accept the one-billion-dollar claim against the FRG as the starting point for the negotiations with the representatives of the State of Israel and the JCC. Adenauer recognised the direct connection between the negotiations with Germany's creditors and those with the representatives of the Jewish state and of the JCC. He advised the West German delegates to both negotiations to keep in close contact.[89] Writing of the meeting at Palais Schaumburg, where Adenauer briefed the members of the two delegations on 8 March 1952, deputy chief negotiator in Wassenaar Otto Küster noted in his diary that it was apparent that it was Hermann Abs, the West German negotiator in London, who was the central figure within the whole affair.[90] 'We do not mind playing a modest role', noted Küster. 'We just do not want [our efforts] to be frittered away, and we would like the public opinion to know how little power we have [in settling the question of *Wiedergutmachung* with Israel].'[91] The meeting, which took place less than two weeks before the scheduled beginning of the negotiations with Israel and the JCC, concluded that at present the Federal Republic did not have enough resources to satisfy their requests.[92] Adenauer suggested structuring the negotiations with the Israelis around two key moments: at first, the delegation in the Netherlands, headed by Franz Böhm and Otto Küster, would have to play for time, until the London Conference had settled on the total amount of German external debt. Only then, in a second stage, would the team negotiating with the Israeli and JCC representatives finalise the overall sum owed by the Federal Republic.[93]

Although initially the East German authorities had left open the prospect of future GDR–Israeli cooperation, by 1952 only the Federal Republic had publicly taken it upon herself to negotiate with the Israelis. The Chancellor had put down in writing his commitment to the starting sum of US$1 billion, and had accepted the unique, 'moral' character of the upcoming talks. But with the start date of the negotiations drawing near, Adenauer was becoming nervous. He suggested that his negotiators adopt essentially a wait and see approach – something very different from what Adenauer had agreed upon with Goldmann in December. Uncomfortably aware of this, Böhm and Küster set off to the Netherlands.[94]

# Notes

1 This is clear when reading his papers, e.g. when Mendelsohn writes the German word *Probleme* in Hebrew characters or chooses to insert English words to make sure that his message would be clear. Both examples are in: Israel State Archives (ISA), Foreign Ministry (FM), 1782/16.

2 K. Mendelsohn, *Kapitalistisches Wirtschaftschaos oder sozialistische Planwirtschaft?* (Berlin: Dietz, 1932).

3 É. Vandervelde, *Le Pays d'Israël: un Marxiste en Palestine* (Paris: Rieder, 1929), translated by Jenny and Kurt Mendelsohn as *Schaffendes Palästina: Die jüdische Aufbau heute und morgen. Von einem Sozialisten* (Dresden: Reissner, 1930).

4 For photographic and documentary evidence on *Het Werkdorp* consult the archives of Beit Lohamei HaGetaot (BLGA).

5 K. Mendelsohn, *The Balance of Resettlements: A Precedent for Palestine* (Leiden: Sijthoff, 1939).

6 Although aware of the problematic implications of this term, I employ 'reparations', 'compensation' and 'restitutions' interchangeably because doing so conveys the language of contemporaries. These terms, however, are not synonymous. On this see, e.g., P. De Greiff (ed.), *The Handbook of Reparations* (Oxford: Oxford University Press, 2006). *Wiedergutmachung* was the German term employed at the time (and has been since), and *Shilumim* the Hebrew equivalent. These two terms, however, have very different meanings, as explained by A. Frohn, 'Introduction: The Origins of Shilumim' in A. Frohn (ed.), *Holocaust and Shilumim: The Policy of Wiedergutmachung in the Early 1950s* (German Historical Institute Washington, Occasional Paper 2, 1991), p. 2.

7 Yaḥil would become the first Israeli Consul in Germany. Y. Jelinek, 'Like an Oasis in the Desert: The Israel Consulate in Munich, 1948–1953', *Studies in Zionism* 9:1 (1988), pp. 81–98.

8 N. Robinson, *Indemnification and Reparations: Jewish Aspects* (New York: Institute of Jewish Affairs of the American Jewish Congress and World Jewish Congress, 1944); S. Moses, *Die Jüdischen Nachkriegsforderungen* (1944); S. Goldschmidt, *Legal Claims Against Germany: Compensation for Losses Resulting from Anti-Racial Measures* (New York: Dryden Press, 1945).

9 Sagi, *German Reparations*, p. 14ff.

10 FRUS, 1945/III, The President of the Jewish Agency for Palestine (Chaim Weizmann) to the Secretary of State, 20 September 1945.

11 P. Rivlin, *The Israeli Economy from the Foundation of the State through the Twenty-First Century* (Cambridge: Cambridge University Press, 2010), ch. 3.

12 Israeli cabinet meeting, 15.2.1950 in Y. Sharett, *The Reparations Controversy: The Jewish State and German Money in the Shadow of the Holocaust, 1951–1952* (Berlin: De Gruyter, 2011), p. 26.
13 Akten zur Auswärtigen Politik der Bundesrepublik Deutschland (hereafter AAPD) 1949/1950, Doc. 30, Erhard to Adenauer, 27 January 1950, fn. 3.
14 Deutscher Bundestag, 13. Session, 21 October 1949, p. 308.
15 T. W. Maulucci Jr., *Adenauer's Foreign Office: West German Diplomacy in the Shadow of the Third Reich* (DeKalb: Northern Illinois University Press, 2012), pp. 92ff.
16 T. A. Schwartz, *America's Germany: John J. McCloy and the Federal Republic of Germany* (Cambridge, MA: Harvard University Press, 1991).
17 AAPD, 1949–1950, Doc. 30, Erhard to Adenauer, 27 January 1950.
18 A. J. Nicholls, *The Bonn Republic: West German Democracy 1945–1990* (London: Longman, 1997), chs 1–5.
19 H. Berghoff, 'Population Change and its Repercussions on the Social History of the Federal Republic' in K. Larres and P. Panayi (eds), *The Federal Republic Since 1949: Politics, Society and Economics Before and After Unification* (London: Longman, 1996), pp. 35–73.
20 K. Kellen, 'Adenauer at 90', *Foreign Affairs* 44:2 (1966), p. 257.
21 H. P. Schwarz, *Konrad Adenauer: A German Politician and Statesman in a Period of War, Revolution and Reconstruction. From the German Empire to the Federal Republic, 1876–1952* (Oxford: Berghahn Books, 1995), pp. 322–3.
22 Data gathered in relation to the respondents to the question: 'What do you think of Adenauer's policy so far?', E. P. Neumann and E. Noelle, *Statistics on Adenauer* (Allensbach: Demoskopie, 1962), p. 37.
23 ISA, FM 1782/16, Eytan, 27 March 1950.
24 AAPD, 1949–1950, Doc. 64, Departmental Meeting in the Federal Finance Ministry, 26 May 1950.
25 Stiftung Rheinisch-Westfälisches Wirtschaftsarchiv zu Köln (RWWA), Abt. 72, Otto Wolff AG, RWWA 72-425-1, Mendelsohn to Wolff von Amerongen, 19 April 1950.
26 ISA, FM 1782/16, Seeleig to Livneh, 13 May 1950.
27 PA AA, B10 252, Seelig to Blankenhorn, 13 January 1950.
28 ISA, FM 1782/16, Mendelsohn to Meron, 4 June 1950.
29 *Ibid.* Livneh (Israel Consulate, Munich) to the Economic Department of the Foreign Ministry, 14 July 1950.
30 See T. W. Maulucci, 'Herbert Blankenhorn in the Third Reich', *Central European History* 42:2 (2009), pp. 253–78; on the broader issue see N. Frei, *Adenauer's Germany and the Nazi Past: The Politics of Amnesty and Integration* (New York: Columbia University Press, 2002).
31 B. Ciesla, 'Winner Takes It All: The Soviet Union and the Beginning of Central Planning in Eastern Germany, 1945–1949' in Hartmut Berghoff and Uta A. Balbier (eds), *The East German Economy, 1945–2010: Falling Behind or Catching Up?* (Washington, DC: German Historical Institute/Cambridge University Press, 2013), pp. 53–76.
32 A. Timm, *Jewish Claims against Eastern Germany: Moral Obligations and Pragmatic Policy* (Budapest: Central European University Press, 1997), p. 81. See, e.g., F. R. J. Nicosia, 'Weimar Germany and the Palestine Question', *Leo Baeck Institute Yearbook* 24:1 (1979), pp. 321–45.

33  PA AA, MfAA A 12739/191, Note on the consultation with Mendelsohn, the official representative of the Ministry of Economy and Finance of the State of Israel, Linick and Raphael, 5 May 1950.

34  *Ibid.*

35  Herf, *Divided Memory.*

36  P. Grieder, *German Democratic Republic* (Basingstoke: Palgrave Macmillan, 2011), p. 31; D. Spilker, *The East German Leadership and the Division of Germany: Patriotism and Propaganda 1945–1953* (Oxford: Oxford University Press, 1998), p. 195.

37  See, e.g., V. M. Zubok, *A Failed Empire? The Soviet Union and the Cold War from Stalin to Gorbachev* (Chapel Hill: University of North Carolina Press, 2009), pp. 64ff.

38  V. Baras, 'Beria's Fall and Ulbricht's Survival', *Soviet Studies* 27:3 (1975), p. 381. C. Stern, *Ulbricht: A Political Biography* (London: Pall Mall Press, 1965); W. Leonhard, *Child of the Revolution* (London: Ink Links, 1979).

39  N. Podewin, *Walter Ulbricht: Eine neue Biographie* (Berlin: Dietz, 1995), pp. 19–60.

40  E. O. Maetzke, 'Ein Staat läutert seinen Organisator', *Frankfurter Allgemeine Zeitung* (*FAZ*), 2 August 1973.

41  Podewin, *Ulbricht.*

42  Stern, *Ulbricht*, p. v.

43  Maetzke, 'Ein Staat läutert seinen Organisator'.

44  Stern, *Ulbricht*, p. 41.

45  Except, unsurprisingly, those publishing in East Germany, e.g. J. R. Becher, *Walter Ulbricht: Ein deutscher Arbeitersohn* (Berlin: Dietz, 1958).

46  Stern, *Ulbricht*, p. 47.

47  PA AA, MfAA A 13364/66, Note on the consultation with Mendelsohn, the official representative of the Ministry of Economy and Finance of the State of Israel, Linick and Raphael, 5 May 1950.

48  AAPD, 1949–1950, Doc. 64, Departmental Meeting in the Federal Finance Ministry, 26 May 1950.

49  Balabkins, *West German Reparations to Israel*, p. 40.

50  'Kernproblem' in the original. See AAPD, 1951, Doc. 5, Note, Steg, 8 January 1951.

51  *Ibid.*

52  72. Cabinet Meeting, 9 June 1950, *Die Kabinettsprotokolle der Bundesregierung*, edited by Kai von Jena, Hans Booms and Friedrich Kahlenberg (Boppard am Rhein: Boldt, 1989).

53  Y. S. Ma, 'Israel's Role in the UN during the Korean War', *Israel Journal of Foreign Affairs* 4:3 (2010), pp. 81–9.

54  W. Abelshauser, *Deutsche Wirtschaftsgeschichte. Von 1945 bis zur Gegenwart* (Munich: C. H. Beck, 2004), p. 166; M. E. Spicka, *Selling the Economic Miracle: Economic Reconstruction and Politics in Western Germany, 1949–1957* (New York: Berghahn Books, 2007), p. 97.

55  AAPD, 1951, Doc. 11, Note, Becker, 2 July 1951.

56  Israel Legation, *The Israel Claim for Reparations from Germany: Identical Note to Occupying Powers* (London: Press and Information Department, 1951), p. 1.

57  FRUS, 1951/V, Doc. N: The Secretary of State to the Ambassador of Israel, 5 July 1951, p. 748.

58  PA AA, B150 B171, Böker to Blankenhorn, 13 July 1952, see the attachment, 'Erklärung'.

59 German Bundestag, 165. Session, Bonn, 27 September 1951, p. 6698.
60 AAPD, 1951, Doc 145, Governmental Declaration (Draft) 25 August 1951.
61 S. Engert, 'A Case Study in "Atonement": Adenauer's Holocaust Apology', *Israel Journal of Foreign Affairs* 4:3 (2010), p. 116. On the extent of the support for Nazi anti-Semitic policies in Weimar Germany see M. Wildt, *Volksgemeinschaft als Selbstermächtigung: Gewalt gegen Juden in der deutschen Provinz 1919 bis 1939* (Hamburg: Hamburger Ed., 2007).
62 N. Frei and T. Freimüller (eds), *Karrieren im Zwielicht: Hitlers Eliten nach 1945* (Frankfurt am Main: Campus Verlag, 2001); Herf, *Divided Memory*, p. 283.
63 Frei, *Adenauer's Germany and the Nazi Past*.
64 AAPD, 1951, Doc. 186, Blankenhorn to the Foreign Office, 13 November 1951.
65 *Ibid.*
66 H. von Trützschler, 'Deutschland und die Vereinten Nationen', in E. Moelle (ed.), *Gegenwartsprobleme der Vereinten Nationen* (Göttingen: Mutterschmidt Verlag, 1955), pp. 31–2.
67 UNGA, Official Records, Plenary Meetings 1951–1952, p. 87.
68 UNGA, 356th Plenary Meeting, 20 December 1951.
69 von Trützschler, 'Deutschland und die Vereinten Nationen', p. 47.
70 Official Records of the General Assembly, Sixth Session, *Plenary Meetings, Verbatim Records 6 November to 5 February 1952*, 356th Meeting, 20 December 1952, p. 288.
71 AAPD, 1951, Doc. 200, Böker to the Foreign Office, 5 December 1951.
72 *Ibid.*
73 J. Paulmann, 'Deutschland in der Welt: Auswärtige Repräsentationen und reflexive Selbstwahrnehmung nach dem Zweiten Weltkrieg – eine Skizze' in H. G. Hockerts (ed.), *Koordinaten deutscher Geschichte in der Epoche des Ost-West-Konflikts* (Munich: Oldenbourg, 2004), pp. 63–78.
74 N. Goldmann, *Staatsmann ohne Staat* (Cologne: Kiepenheuer & Witsch, 1970).
75 K. Adenauer, *Erinnerungen 1953–1955* (Frankfurt am Main: Fischer Bücherei, 1966), p. 137, italics in the original.
76 On the JCC, see R. W. Zweig, *German Reparations and the Jewish World: A History of the Claims Conference* (London: Frank Cass, 2002 [1987]).
77 See, e.g., S. Shafir, 'Nahum Goldmann and Germany after World War II' in M. A. Raider (ed.), *Nahum Goldmann: Statesman Without a State* (New York: State University of New York Press, 2009), pp. 207–31.
78 Adenauer, *Erinnerungen 1953–1955*, p. 137; AAPD, 1951, Doc. 204, Blankenhorn to Krekeler, 14 December 1951.
79 Adenauer, *Erinnerungen 1953–1955*, p. 136.
80 D. Witzthum, 'Unique Dilemmas of German-Israeli Relations: A Political Avoidance of Tragedy' in S. S. Chubin (ed.), *Germany and the Middle East: Patterns and Prospects* (London: Pinter, 1992), pp. 55–92. F. Shinnar, *Bericht eines Beauftragten: Die deutsch-israelischen Beziehungen, 1951–1966* (Tübingen: Wunderlich, 1967), p. 29. Balabkins, *German Reparations to Israel*.
81 As Elimelech Rimalt of the General Zionists put it. N. Lorch (ed.), *Major Knesset Debates, 1948–1981* (Lanham: University Press of America, 1993), p. 708.
82 *Ibid.*, pp. 729 and 724, respectively.
83 Y. Jelinek, *Deutschland und Israel, 1945–1965. Ein neurotisches Verhältnis* (Munich: Oldenbourg, 2004), pp. 157ff.

84 Quoted in: Documents on the Foreign Policy of Israel (DFPI) 1952, Doc. 52, Barou to Sharett, 19 February 1952.

85 BAK, B126 51544, Schäffer to Adenauer, 22 February 1952.

86 H. P. Schwarz, *Die Wiederherstellung des deutschen Kredits: Das Londoner Schuldenabkommen* (Stuttgart: Belser, 1982); U. Rombeck-Jaschinski, *Das Londoner Schuldabkommen. Die Regelung der deutschen Auslandsschulden nach dem Zweiten Weltkrieg* (Munich: Oldenbourg, 2005).

87 AAPD, 1952, Doc. 40, Note, Böker, 6 February 1952.

88 G. D. Feldman, *The Great Disorder: Politics, Economics and Society in the German Inflation, 1914–1924* (New York: Oxford University Press, 1997); T. Balderston, *Economics and Politics in the Weimar Republic* (Cambridge: Cambridge University Press, 2002).

89 204. Cabinet Meeting, 26 February 1952. *Die Kabinettsprotokolle der Bundesregierung*, p. 133.

90 ACDP, I-084–001, NL Küsters, Diary Entry, 8 March 1952.

91 *Ibid.*

92 AAPD, 1952, Doc. 72, Departmental Meeting, 8 March 1952.

93 PA AA, B10 1676, Adenauer to Abs, 13 March 1952.

94 F. Böhm, 'Das deutsch-israelische Abkommen 1952' in D. Blumenwitz (ed.) *Adenauer und seine Zeit: Politik und Persönlichkeit des ersten Bundeskanzlers, Beiträge von Weg- und Zeitgenossen* (Stuttgart: Deutsche Verlags-Anstalt, 1976), p. 449.

## 2

# Negotiations

When the negotiations between West Germans and Israelis began, on 21 March 1952, the atmosphere was tense. The opening announcement read by the Israeli delegation stated that no amount of reparation would ever be enough to compensate the Jewish victims of the Nazi crimes. The one read by the West German delegation recognised the unprecedented nature of the crimes committed against the Jews – but it also stressed the importance of recognising Bonn's limited ability to pay reparations under the present circumstances.[1] The slow rhythm of the exchange was marked by the continuous pauses that were needed for the conversation to be translated between English and German – even though German was the mother tongue of all the negotiators, on both sides. Yet the atmosphere also became gradually less tense. As the deputy head of the Israeli team, Felix Shinnar, later recalled:

> On the second day Küster [the second in command in the West German delegation] passed me a note that said, essentially, 'I think I detect a Swabian accent in your English. Am I right?' In short, it turned out that Otto Küster was right. I was born in Stuttgart, went to school there ... It also turned out that we had attended the same *Realgymnasium* [high school] and Otto Küster, one year younger than I, attended the same classes, had the same teachers.[2]

The two decided to write a postcard to a teacher they had had in common, and of whom they both had fond memories. The negotiations, which had begun in English, after four days slowly transitioned into German. While the atmosphere among the negotiators progressively loosened up, however, the progress in the negotiations talks themselves rapidly came to a halt, as various actors across the globe, for different reasons, united in their efforts to impede the progress in the West German–Israeli dealings.[3]

## In Wassenaar

Adenauer had at first envisaged that the negotiations with Israel and the representatives of the Jewish world would be conducted 'under the auspices' of the West German

Figure 2.1 A view of the Kasteel Oud-Wassenaar, where the negotiations between West German, Israeli and JCC representatives took place in 1952.

Foreign Ministry.[4] However, it was the novice Abraham Frowein, who had joined the Ministry only a few weeks earlier, who was to be the only Foreign Ministry representative sent to the Netherlands. Frowein's role would be to support the work of the two heads of the delegation, Franz Böhm and Otto Küster. Both had been persecuted during the Nazi era for their critical stance on the Hitler regime, and both had been removed from their jobs for political reasons: Böhm was stripped of his law professorship at the University of Frankfurt in 1938, and Küster was removed from his employment as auxiliary judge in 1933. Sending them to Wassenaar possibly meant to signal to the Israeli side that Germans, too, had suffered under Nazi rule and that in spite of the recent past a common ground could indeed be found.[5]

The absence of experienced West German diplomats in the negotiations with the Israelis and with the representatives of the Jewish world was telling also. Although the Nuremberg trials had clearly determined the Foreign Ministry's complicity in the pursuit of Nazi Germany's criminal acts and aggressive foreign policy, almost all of the Middle East experts that had been working in the Nazi Foreign Ministry were reintegrated shortly after the Federal Republic was granted permission to establish its own Ministry of Foreign Affairs, in 1951.[6] Then, Cold War pressures led the Allies' originally ambitious denazification plans to wane and, in Adenauer's Germany, an astounding number of officials formerly involved in the Hitler regime were reinstated in positions of power across all sectors of the West German state and society – including the judiciary, the bureaucracy and, indeed, also the diplomatic service.[7] Thus, in Bonn, special attention was given to the personal background of the individuals who would be sent to the Netherlands to negotiate with representatives from Israel and the Jewish groups. In contrast to them, a very different kind of profile characterised the members of the West German team that, simultaneously to the Wassenaar talks, would be stationed in London to negotiate the total amount that the West German government would need to pay to the Western allies, arising out of the unfulfilled reparation payments stemming from the Treaty of Versailles, as well as the Allies' occupation costs.[8] Hermann Abs, who headed the team working on a settlement with West Germany's creditors after the two world wars, had joined the managing board of the Deutsche Bank in 1938, and remained on the board until the end of the war. A skilled banker and businessman who had held such an important position during the years of the Nazi regime, his profile could not be in starker contrast to that of Böhm and Küster. Unsurprisingly, the three would often clash in the coming months, pulling the Chancellor in different directions as to the appropriate course of action to take vis-à-vis the Israeli and Jewish negotiators.

On the opening day of the Wassenaar talks, the Israeli delegation – for the first time – officially distinguished between the amount of restitutions it expected to receive from West and East Germany, claiming US$1 billion from the FRG and US$500 million from the GDR, respectively.[9] Of this sum, DM4.2 billion would be destined to the State of Israel to help it provide for the Holocaust survivors and those who had escaped from the Nazi terror by relocating to Israel and the remaining DM500 million to the Claims Conference, which in turn would provide for the victims in the Jewish diaspora.[10]

The measurement and assessment of how many refugees had entered Israel, for what reason, and when, dominated much of the initial discussions.[11] The numbers provided by the Israeli authorities claimed that at least 500,000 refugees had arrived in Israel since 1933 to escape from, or after having endured, Nazi persecution and extermination attempts. The Israelis also calculated that they would require US$3,000 per refugee in order to guarantee the rehabilitation and integration of the victims of Nazi persecution. But the German side contested Israeli numbers on both counts. While Israel claimed that it needed to resettle half a million refugees following Nazi persecution policies, Bonn's representatives questioned the actual motives behind the refugees' migration to Israel, claiming that many of them were in fact escaping from the menace of Communism, not Nazi persecution, and that they were lured into going to Israel because of the work of Zionist organisations throughout Europe. The question of how much money the Israeli government would have to spend per refugee was also contested, as the West German Federal Ministry for Displaced Persons, Refugees and War Victims claimed that US$2,413 per person was the maximum amount needed to guarantee the welfare of the refugees, while the Israeli government calculated that in order to ensure housing, healthcare and education for all the new incomers, the sum could not go below US$3,000. The Israeli delegates, wary of the dire economic situation the State of Israel was in, pressed to have an answer soon, 'and I need to pull together all of my courage … to halve [their] hopes', jotted down Küster in his private diary.[12]

Only three days after the beginning of the negotiations in the supposedly secret Dutch location, Arab League Envoy Mohamed Ali Sadek Bey paid a visit to the West German ambassador at The Hague. Married to a German woman, and a sophisticated connoisseur of German culture and politics, Bey was displeased at the latest West German foreign policy developments. Over the course of the war between Israel and its Arab neighbours, which had raged between May 1948 and March 1949, some 700,000 Arab Palestinians had fled or were expelled from their homes.[13] The Arab League, founded in 1945, had made it its mission to represent the Palestinian cause internationally.[14] Stressing a connection between West German restitutions to the Israeli Holocaust survivors and calls for Israel to compensate Palestinian refugees of the first Arab–Israeli war, Bey informed German Ambassador Karl Du Mont of the official Arab League intention to be partial recipients of any German payments that would be agreed with Israel.[15]

Approaching the German authorities and linking the question of German restitutions to Israel to that of Israeli compensations to the Palestinian refugees became part and parcel of the League's strategy between 1952 and 1953. During his meeting in The Hague, Bey also enquired as to whether the Federal Republic, upon either the Arab League's or United Nations' exhortation, would be willing to halt the reparation payments. Ambassador Du Mont replied that this matter could only be decided upon by the Federal government and promised the envoy that he would pass on his message to Bonn. The hope of the US Secretary of State, Dean Acheson, that the link between the two issues could be 'scotched promptly' was to remain unfulfilled.[16] Throughout 1952, the unresolved conflict between Arabs and Israelis, though fundamentally unrelated to the question of German restitutions to Israel in the aftermath of the Holocaust, would become increasingly difficult to avoid for German officials stationed in various parts of the globe. And this, in turn, would directly impact the West German–Israeli talks that were going on in Wassenaar, where the discussions continued in and outside the negotiating room.

On Sunday, 30 March 1952, Böhm and Küster went for breakfast with the two Israeli head negotiators, Felix Shinnar and Giora Yoseftal, in the nearby town of Oegstgeest. The atmosphere among the four men was amicable: 'The impression of dealing with marvelous people is growing ever more … we laugh a lot', recorded Küster in his diary.[17] Yet the serenity that characterised that crisp Sunday morning soon disappeared, given the apparent irreconcilability of the West German and Israeli positions, widespread Arab attempts to thwart the West German–Israeli reconciliation process, and – soon – also terror attacks against the negotiators.

## Bonn's ambivalence

On 31 March, the day after the breakfast in Oegstgeest, both negotiating teams woke up to a disturbing piece of news.[18] One man had died and five had been injured in the basement of the Munich police headquarters, while trying to defuse the explosive hidden inside a cut-out encyclopedia, in a parcel addressed to Chancellor Adenauer.[19] Now, the police warned members of both delegations about possible assassination attempts against them, too, recommending them to be wary of any parcels that they may receive. 'And just before our [Böhm and Küster's] departure [to go back to Bonn to discuss the state of the negotiations with the Chancellor], here it is … the bomb [in fact, two small parcels], designated as such by the *Fräulein* (secretary) laughing', which, as 'the radio confirm[ed the following day], it was really highly explosive material'.[20] The group claiming the attack called itself the Jewish Partisan Organization, and was then unknown to the authorities. Four days later, the French police raided several houses in downtown Paris, taking into custody five Israeli nationals.[21] Most of them were affiliated with the Herut Party headed by Menachem Begin, who had so vehemently attacked the idea of the German–Israeli negotiations and of West German reparations earlier that year, with his fierce speeches in and outside the Knesset. All five of them had been members of the Irgun – one of the most radical and violent Jewish underground armed groups in British Palestine.[22] Only one of the five, twenty-seven-year-old Eliezer Sudit, was arrested. Though at that time he did not admit to this, it had indeed been him who had crafted the explosive parcels sent to Germany and the Netherlands. 'I had been a bomb-maker … since I was fourteen', Sudit later recalled in his memoirs, and Begin's passionate denunciation of the German–Israeli talks had been the crucial motivation that had pushed him into action.[23] Sudit spent five months in a French prison, before being allowed to go back to Israel.

Meanwhile, the talks in Wassenaar dragged on without much success. In Bonn, the Cabinet was divided as to whether, when and how much the FRG should agree to pay to the Jewish and Israeli delegations. Economic Minister Erhard argued that in this specific negotiation the best outcome was not necessarily to have the other side agree to the lowest possible amount of payment obligation. On the contrary, he suggested that a higher sum would better serve the West German interests, in three main ways. First, by showcasing Bonn's creditworthiness internationally. Second, 'perhaps' this would also contribute to 'reconciling the Jews with the German past'. Third, showing a 'daring' attitude, which Erhard deemed to be more in line with the 'American mentality' than Bonn's current display of 'ifs' and 'buts', might also augment Bonn's standing in Washington's eyes.[24] This view was in line with Böhm and Küster's position. However, as the Israeli delegation rightly assessed, these two were viewed by the majority of officials in Bonn as 'starry-eyed idealist[s] ignorant [of the] economic implications' of the negotiations and thus, in fact, their take on the matter of restitutions would hardly be taken seriously by the highest echelons of Bonn's financial and commercial circles.[25] Their stance was in stark contrast to that of others, especially that of Finance Minister Fritz Schäffer, and of the chief negotiator in London, Hermann Abs, who stubbornly refused to settle for any amount with the Israelis before knowing the total sum of the pre-war debt that the FRG would have to settle with its creditors.[26]

The two main points of the negotiations with the Israelis – the controversy over the actual number of those who had relocated to Israel because of Nazi persecution and how much the Israeli government would have to pay per person for resettling these refugees – divided the members of the West German Cabinet for most of 1952. Finance Minister Schäffer in particular emphasised that at least 337,000 immigrants had reached Israel *after* 15 May 1948 from countries *within* the Soviet sphere of influence.[27]

Migration from these countries at this point in time, the Minister maintained, had nothing to do with Nazi persecution. Instead, these had to be ascribed to the anti-Semitic wave in Eastern Europe, which led increasing numbers of Jews to leave their homes and relocate to Israel. The bitterness between the London negotiator, Abs, and the Wassenaar negotiator, Böhm, would endure long after the end of the negotiation talks. Giving a talk at the University of Konstanz four decades after the events, Abs still complained that during the 1952 negotiations Böhm 'actually did not see his mission as that of acting in the interest of his country'.[28]

The Chancellor himself seemed to be of two minds regarding which policy West Germany should adopt in the reparations talks with Israel. While he had been the one to declare the West German willingness to pay *Wiedergutmachung* in 1949, and again in 1951, he also understood Abs' and Schäffer's concerns. After his initial alacrity vis-à-vis Nahum Goldmann, in a private talk with his negotiators in late March 1952 he wondered whether it would not suffice to offer just a symbolic *Wiedergutmachung* to the Jewish state, for example by building a hospital in Israel. After the beginning of the talks with the Israelis, his tone had become graver, more cynical and suspicious of the goodwill of the Israeli and Jewish groups. After listening to what his negotiating team had to say, the Chancellor emphasised that no one should nurture illusions as to the real Israeli aims regarding the restitutions, given that 'they' mainly wanted to use German resources to industrialise their country and conquer the markets of the Middle East, and that Bonn could either 'like it or lump it'.[29] He warned Böhm and Küster of the need to pay attention that 'they' not 'con us'.[30] For the moment, with Böhm and Küster he reiterated that the role the West German delegation in Wassenaar had to play was, more than anything, 'psychological' – i.e. that of reassuring the Israelis that the deal would, at a certain point, be concluded, though – as he made abundantly clear – it was important not to agree to anything just yet.[31]

## Ten weeks

Caught between the Chancellor's desire to play for time and the Israeli and Jewish pressures for a quick and successful conclusion of the talks, Böhm and Küster's job became increasingly difficult. The two negotiating sides disagreed over many issues. When confronted with the West German caution in dealing with high sums, 'they [the Israelis] referred to the countless exterminated Jewish families, who had no heirs to whom reparations could have been paid. Above all, they claimed that Israel had received numerous Jews from all over the world, whose stay in their previous homelands had become impossible after we [Nazi Germany] had poisoned the situation, or who no longer *wanted* to live in their countries after they had become venues of horror'.[32] Given the West German reluctance to commit to any concrete sum, and their continuous contestation of the Israeli facts and figures, the negotiations halted eighteen days after they had started, and ten weeks of diplomatic crisis followed.[33] The two German head negotiators resigned in protest – Küster for good, while Böhm would later go back to the negotiating table. Nahum Goldmann wrote to Adenauer to condemn what he saw as the sheer absence of 'any trace of the willingness to make any kind of real sacrifice for the sake of *Wiedergutmachung*':[34]

> A problem of such moral significance as that of the *Wiedergutmachung* to the Jews cannot be solved by means of methods usually applied in commercial negotiations. What had so profoundly impressed me in my talks with you, Mr. Chancellor, was your conception of Germany's moral obligation to render a serious measure of *Wiedergutmachung*, at least in the material sphere.[35]

The Israeli Ambassador to the United States, Abba Eban, repeatedly contacted US Secretary of State Dean Acheson, to emphasise that 'an unsatisfactory reply from Bonn would mark one of the darkest events in the moral history of the human race'.[36] Acheson in turn stressed with the West German side that it was of utmost importance to 'avoid giving public impression Lon[don] n[ego]t[iation] in any way holds precedence over Hague [Wassenaar] talks', and he repeatedly alerted the US High Commissioner in Bonn, John J. McCloy, of the need to highlight with the Chancellor that the negotiations with the Israelis could 'not be allowed to fail'.[37] However, for Acheson it was also important that the United States should avoid making any public statement about the West German–Israeli talks, so as to eschew any West German excuse for getting more financial backing from the United States than it was already receiving at that time, and also to avoid alienating the Arab countries, which were already displeased by what they perceived to be the United States' unjustifiably pro-Zionist stance. Indeed, the Secretary of State recommended to President Truman to only 'privately' push Bonn to settle the Israeli and Jewish claims rapidly and successfully.[38]

Thus, McCloy did his best to nudge the Chancellor towards a successful conclusion of the negotiations, underscoring that without it the Israeli government seriously faced the risk of collapsing, both financially and politically, and that this outcome should be avoided at all costs. Yet the Americans were not the only ones pushing West Germany to accommodate the Israeli requests. During Adenauer's visit to London, in June 1952, the British, too, advised him that it would be 'politically smart and morally right' to conclude the deal with Israel swiftly and successfully. From a British perspective, the agreement would not only be beneficial to restoring Germany's image internationally, but it would also serve a concrete interest of the British government. Lord William Henderson, a British politician who had recently been Joint Under-Secretary of State for Foreign Affairs, encouraged the Chancellor to include a clause in the final agreement that would allow Israel to keep buying British oil using pounds sterling coming from Bonn, which for London was especially important given that the Israeli reserves of British currency were running out.[39] While the French authorities were less adamant in their support of the development of West German–Israeli talks they, too, promised their Israeli counterparts that they could count on Paris's support.[40]

At the same time, pressure also mounted within the West German political scene, both for, and against, reaching an agreement with the Israelis. Finance Minister Schäffer kept opposing the talks and any possible deal coming out of it, dreading the consequences it might have on Bonn's economy. His attitude attracted criticism, but also praise and respect, from many West German citizens. Industrialists who had come to face unexpected sharpness from Arab partners due to the West German stance on Israel wrote him numerous letters to voice their approval of his opposition to the agreement.[41] Members of the sizeable expellees' community in West Germany, who had been forced to leave their homes in the territories that were ceded to Poland and Czechoslovakia after Germany's defeat in the Second World War, voiced their criticism of the notion that West Germany should have to pay compensation 'to the Jews', when they themselves were still facing so many difficulties.[42] Of course, there were also members of the public who despised Schäffer's stance on the matter.[43] But he was voicing concerns that many in the FRG felt, and that were all the more serious given that they were also coming from the internal ranks of the Chancellor's party, the Christian Democratic Union (CDU). In stark contrast to Schäffer and to the majority of the coalition members, chairman of the SPD Kurt Schumacher addressed a private letter to the Chancellor stressing how crucial the treaty would be for the 'moral and political rehabilitation of Germany', pressing for a swift and successful conclusion of the negotiation process, and assuring the Chancellor that the agreement would receive the support of his party.[44]

After weeks of crisis, of prodding by his Western allies, of lobbying of the Jewish groups, as well as that of those who, in West Germany, recognised the importance of the agreement such as Schumacher, in June the Chancellor finally agreed to sign a draft text upon which the West German and Israeli teams in Wassenaar would continue to negotiate. Bonn's Cabinet voted, on 17 June 1952, in favour of the sum of DM3 billion that would be given to Israel in kind as part of the restitutions agreement.[45] Having settled the disagreement over the final sum, the decisive phase of the negotiations opened in Wassenaar on 24 June 1952 and lasted until 8 September 1952. Two days after that, Adenauer, in his dual role of Chancellor and Foreign Minister of the Federal Republic, and Israeli Foreign Minister Sharett signed the agreement in Luxembourg.[46]

The agreement foresaw that the FRG would pay DM3 billion to Israel, plus DM450 million to be destined to the Claims Conference. The West German authorities would transfer the funds into the bank account of the Israeli Mission in Germany, which was allowed to use them only to buy products made in Germany and which would belong to one of the following five categories: 'ferrous and non-ferrous metals'; 'products of the steel-manufacturing industry'; 'products of the chemical industry and of other industries'; 'agricultural products'; and 'services'.[47] As London's politicians had warmly encouraged the Chancellor to do, the agreement also included the provision that DM75 million would be used for the purchase of oil from British oil companies. The transfers would take place over the course of the following thirteen years. And although the general outline of the agreement foresaw that Israel would not be able to sell these goods to other countries, certain commodities – such as iron and oil – were exempted from it. For this reason, and because it provided Israel with a significant amount of essential goods and products, the agreement would have a fundamental impact on the development of the Israeli economy. In turn, it also aided the West German economy significantly, boosting Bonn's industrial activity, and contributing to the reduction in West German levels of unemployment.[48]

Figure 2.2 West German Chancellor Konrad Adenauer (seated centre left) and Israeli Foreign Minister Moshe Sharett (seated centre right) signing the Luxembourg Agreement in September 1952.

Beyond its evident economic as well as historic significance, the agreement also had an important political meaning relative to the West German positioning within the Cold War as the sole legitimate German state. The year 1952 had witnessed crucial developments for the FRG, which made big steps forward along its path to sovereignty and independence within the Western bloc. Apart from following the simultaneous – and ultimately successful – negotiations in London and Wassenaar, in May Adenauer had signed the General Treaty (*Deutschlandvertrag*) with the United States, the United Kingdom and France. While the treaty did not come into effect until 1955, its signing marked a crucial moment in the history of the Federal Republic, as it formally recognised West Germany's sovereign status.[49] Coming a few months after the Chancellor's rejection of Stalin's note, in which the Soviet leader offered German reunification in exchange for neutralisation, the signing of the Germany treaty underscored Adenauer's commitment to a policy of orientation towards the West (*Westbindung*).[50]

In the first half of the 1950s, the initial steps in West German–Israeli reconciliation overlapped with Bonn's gradual progression towards sovereignty. Adenauer's choice to negotiate with the Israelis supported his broader aim of gaining the trust of the Western allies. To be sure, West Germany had not simply followed the lead of the American superpower – Adenauer's initiative in 1951 had been crucial to kick-start the process, and the FRG's (especially Schäffer's) relentless determination to lower the amount of payments to the required minimum testifies to the fact that the West Germans had been active participants throughout the negotiating process with the Israelis.[51] However, by finally accepting the Americans' recommendations to conclude the negotiations successfully, Adenauer attempted and managed to turn the legacy of the Nazi past from a political liability to an element that would emphasise how different (t)his Germany was from the one they had defeated in 1945. Signing the agreement with Israel was thus also meant to reinforce the new image of the Federal Republic as the only legitimate representative of the German people.

## Reaching out to the GDR

Upon learning of the Israeli attempts to receive further indemnification payments from the GDR, US State Department officials requested the Israeli Foreign Ministry to avoid any 'steps liable to be interpreted by the world, or by the Russians, as a de facto recognition of East Germany'.[52] The Israelis, however, would not exactly follow this warning *à la lettre*. From Luxembourg, where he had encountered the West German Chancellor for the first time for the signing of the agreement, Foreign Minister Moshe Sharett made his way to Paris. There, during a press conference at the Israeli Legation, he emphasised the 'historical significance' of the agreement, 'adopted in the exercise of free will and in obedience with the call of moral responsibility', one whose 'importance as a precedent in world history cannot be exaggerated'.[53] Sharett further declared that the success in the negotiations with Bonn rendered Israel all the more impatient to conclude a similar agreement with East Germany, too – a chilling prospect for those on the other side of the Iron Curtain.[54] Mikhail Gribanov, the Director of the Third European Department of the Soviet Foreign Ministry in charge of the policy towards Germany, swiftly circulated his desk's advice on the question of possible East German restitutions and the Israeli pressure to negotiate with the East Germans, too, following their success vis-à-vis Bonn. He recommended his colleagues to avoid reacting to Sharett's statement by all means unless directly and officially addressed by the Israeli diplomatic personnel.[55]

Israeli diplomats stationed in Moscow had long been trying to get an answer on the matter from the Soviet authorities, especially given the mildly encouraging signals dating back to 1948. For example, on 23 October 1951, Israeli ambassador to the USSR Shmuel Eliashiv had solicited the Soviet Ministry of Foreign Affairs to reply to the Israeli diplomatic notes concerning the reparations request, which the Israeli government had sent to Moscow and the Western allies earlier that year. Yet he did not receive an appointment with the Soviet authorities until March 1952, when the talks in Wassenaar were already underway. By that point, two important events had taken place. First, in the course of the negotiations in Wassenaar the Israeli and Jewish delegations had – for the first time – officially distinguished between the amount of compensation they expected to receive from West and East Germany.[56] Second, the Western allies had turned down Stalin's tantalising, though vague, proposal on German unification, which emphasised the importance of the Four Powers signing a peace agreement with Germany.[57] In his meeting with Eliashiv, Semen T. Bazarov of the Foreign Ministry's European Division explained to the Israeli ambassador that 'the problem' of East German restitutions to Israel had to be solved by '[East] Germany itself', and that question could not be solved until a peace treaty with Germany was signed.[58] How ironic, Eliashiv commented, the Soviet stance on East German restitutions was.[59] After all, Moscow had certainly not hesitated to gather reparations for itself from the GDR, regardless of the lack of a peace agreement of any sort with Germany. The point that Bazarov had made in Moscow was reiterated in Tel Aviv shortly thereafter, when the Soviet Minister to Israel, Pavel I. Ershov, during a meeting with Sharett also emphasised that the Israelis should deal with the GDR directly on the matter – to which Sharett responded by asking the USSR to exert all its 'influence on its satellite to induce the government of East Germany to adopt in practice and in public a positive attitude on the question of restitution'.[60]

The Israeli attempts to apply pressure on the GDR and the Soviets were not just confined to discussions in East Berlin, Moscow or Tel Aviv. In a similar vein to how they had operated towards the FRG when pushing the Bonn leadership on the question of *Wiedergutmachung*, Israeli diplomats now attempted to use the occasions on which the GDR was applying for membership of international organisations, in front of a large multinational audience, to denounce the East German passivity and lack of interest on matters of restitutions to Israel – for example, when the GDR applied for membership of the UN's Universal Postal Union. As the Union members were assessing the East German application, the Israeli representative took the floor, accusing that: 'the Germany that today is applying … in no way conveys the image of a society that has undergone any essential moral change prior to returning among the civilized nations'.[61] Although the GDR was still granted access to the Universal Postal Union, the Israeli protests did not make for positive publicity for the young, allegedly democratic, East German regime.

In Moscow, Eliashiv did not accept defeat, and reached out to the head of the Soviet diplomatic mission in the GDR, Georgii M. Pushkin, to discuss the matter of East German reparations with him. When the Israeli ambassador mentioned his interest to examine the topic, in early September 1952, Pushkin replied that he would be happy to consider the question, yet he also stressed that he was 'not well briefed on Israel'.[62] A second meeting between Eliashiv and Pushkin took place on 15 September 1952, again without achieving any concrete results. The Israeli diplomat attacked the USSR for taking reparations from the GDR while preventing other countries from doing the same. Eliashiv emphasised that it was the 'lack of any sign of goodwill' from East Berlin that prevented 'any possibility of direct communication' between Israel and the GDR, contrary to what had been possible to achieve with the FRG in the wake of the Chancellor's public stance regarding (West) Germany's moral duty to pay restitutions to Israel.[63]

It is telling of the state of the East German foreign policy establishment at that time that the East German Foreign Ministry learned only from the Western press that, in Moscow, Israeli and Soviet diplomats were discussing questions concerning the GDR. In late September 1952, initial press reports came out stating that Israeli Foreign Minister Sharett had judged as 'unsatisfactory' the Soviet response on the prospect of East German–Israeli talks – and yet the Ministry in East Berlin seemed to know nothing of the matter.[64] Therefore, its clerks kindly requested information from Moscow, so as to be able to align its position on the matter with the Soviet one. 'Knowing the [substance of] the Soviet note would be very valuable for the relevant departments of our Ministry', explained an East German communication to Moscow.[65] A few weeks later, possibly unaware of the almost total East German ignorance regarding Soviet-Israeli exchanges on the issue, Eliashiv approached the GDR's envoy to the Soviet Union, Rudolf Appelt, directly. He seized his chance as soon as he saw his East German colleague at the opening of the Chinese cultural exhibition in Moscow, to ask him whether and when the talks on possible East German reparations to Israel could take place. Appelt promised to get back to the Israelis with his government's official reply in due course. But the response would take two years to arrive – and it would be a negative one.[66] Shortly after the meeting between Appelt and Eliashiv, the rumour spread that the former GDR Minister of Agriculture and Chair of the Democratic Peasants Party of Germany, Ernst Goldenbaum, speaking at a press conference in Bonn, had spoken of an alleged East German willingness to enter into negotiations with the State of Israel on the issue of reparations, although the latter had thus far showed no willingness to engage the GDR directly on the topic. Goldenbaum himself, a couple of months later, declared that actually these words had not been pronounced by him, but by the deputy Prime Minister Otto Nuschke. For the time being, the East German press dismissed the alleged GDR willingness to negotiate with Israel as mere 'agitation rumors'.[67]

Three main issues accounted for East Berlin's reluctance to deal with the Israelis in the early 1950s. First, the volte-face in the Soviet approach to Israel. Moscow had been the first country to grant Israel *de jure* recognition in 1948, welcoming the news of the British withdrawal from Palestine, which at that time seemed to offer promising avenues for Soviet influence in the region. And Israel had been able to prevail in the first war against its Arab neighbours, in 1948–49, especially thanks to a Soviet-sponsored airlift of weapons from Czechoslovakia. By the early 1950s, however, the initial Soviet support for Israel had drastically diminished and Moscow saw no need to support any kind of rapprochement between Israel and the GDR. Second, in turn, what the Israeli diplomats were saying to one another, and increasingly also to the Soviet authorities, was true: Moscow had not hesitated to extract huge amount of reparations from the GDR itself. Thus, the GDR would not have been in the position to pay reparations to Israel and the Jewish representatives at that time even if there had been local support for the initiative, which in fact was only backed by a minority group within the SED – a group which would soon be decimated amid accusations of being 'Zionist spies'.[68] Third, the events of late 1952 would make it especially clear to the East German authorities that, rather than dealing with Israel, a much more encouraging avenue to realising the East German dream of attaining international kudos and recognition was that of pursuing relations with the Arab states instead.

## Meanwhile, in Cairo

Just as Adenauer met with Moshe Sharett to sign the *Wiedergutmachung* treaty, Arab League representatives were convening in Egypt to discuss what countermeasure to put in place to deter the FRG from pursuing dealings that, in their view, would inevitably end up strengthening Israel's military might. The seventeenth session of the League, which opened in Cairo on 14 September, came at a difficult time for the Arab countries. Egyptian diplomat Abdul Rahman Hassan Azzam, the League's first Secretary General, had just announced his intention to withdraw from the position, thus triggering intense intra-Arab competition as to who would be at the top of the organisation's political echelon. Yet the push to intervene together to undermine any of Israel's moves in international politics proved to be a strong enough glue for the Arab countries to stick together and cooperate to undermine the West German–Israeli agreement. Chancellor Adenauer, who from 1951 also acted as West German Foreign Minister, knew that by signing the Luxembourg Agreement he would anger several important Arab leaders, as testified by his urgent request of support on the part of the United States a few days prior to signing the document in the official ceremony with the Israeli authorities.[69] For their part, amid increasing Arab remonstrations, the US authorities were not eager to appear as sponsors of the West German–Israeli agreement as this 'might easily contribute to [a] new wave [of] anti-American feeling in [the] Arab world'.[70]

As the negotiations of the agreement had progressed, Arab pressure on the West Germans intensified. In early 1952, Syrian Foreign Minister Jamal Farra had discussed the matter with the US Ambassador in Syria, expressing the hope of receiving US support for the 'just and humane' plan to direct the reparations for the Jewish victims of Nazi crimes to 'Arab Palestinian refugees whose homes have been demolished and whose property has been confiscated for benefit of Jews'.[71] The Arab League and the Syrian government addressed letters of protest to the Federal Republic, and the Egyptian, Lebanese and Jordanian governments had remonstrated verbally vis-à-vis their West German colleagues, while Saudi Arabia had rushed to cancel a trade agreement it had signed with a West German firm.[72] On 5 September 1952, Jordanian Prime Minister Tawfiq Abu al-Huda repeated to Adenauer that reparations to Israel would be interpreted as 'a sign of inimical attitude against the Arab and Islamic states'.[73] In a conversation with the Chancellor, Syrian diplomat Manoun al-Hamui had warned him against ruining the relationship between the Federal Republic and the forty million inhabitants of the seven major Arab countries. As late as 5 September 1952, long after the DM3 million sum had been agreed upon by the Bonn Cabinet as the basis for the West German–Israeli agreement, Adenauer showed to be willing vis-à-vis his Syrian interlocutor to revise the sum in order not to alienate the Arab leaders. Although the Syrian General Consul dismissed the Chancellor's proposal as mere posturing, the exchange also made clear Adenauer's deep anxiety concerning the possible countermeasures, especially in the economic field, that the Arab countries could put in place to retaliate against the West German–Israeli agreement.[74] The two chief negotiators in Wassenaar, too, had worried about the Arab attempts to halt and discredit the negotiations. Shortly after the beginning of the talks with the Israelis, Böhm and Küster had highlighted to the Chancellor that it would be beneficial to reach an agreement with the Israelis and the JCC quickly, so as not to give those who resisted the *Wiedergutmachung* project any time to 'organize themselves' and 'assert their propaganda'.[75] The initial West German plan was, like the American one, to 'ignore'[76] the Arab protests. This, however, became increasingly difficult, as certain German nationals close to Arab political circles since the years of the Third Reich began colluding with Arab officials in the attempt to thwart the West German–Israeli agreement.

## Networking from Egypt to Indonesia

'I would be glad if you could find out in due course what truth there is in this story', requested an official of the British Foreign Office upon reading a news item, published in November 1952, which pointed to the hand of German military advisers in Egypt as one key explanation of how the Arab protests against the ratification of the reparations agreement had suddenly become so strong and effective.[77] The British were keeping a special eye on the former Nazis who had migrated to the Arab Middle East in the aftermath of the Second World War. In post-revolutionary Egypt, anti-British sentiments were growing and, according to London's foreign intelligence services, these German nationals were sharing crucial lessons with Egyptian military personnel as to how to perform counter-resistance and guerrilla operations. The Americans, meanwhile, closely watched the evolving West German–Syrian relationship, noting that they, together with their British and French allies, would soon have to contend with 'a new … factor in Middle Eastern politics': German influence in Syria was expected to grow in the near future, especially if the Germans decided to put their military know-how at the service of the Syrian authorities.[78] Indeed, a group of German nationals, including former army officers and former members of the SS, had been stationed in Damascus since the late 1940s, the locals referring to them as 'the German military mission'.[79]

The former SS and Wehrmacht members stationed in Syria, and their colleagues hired as military advisers in Egypt, did widely share the antagonism of the Arab representatives against Bonn's reparations to Israel. Within the West German Foreign Ministry, many noted that the Arab states would never have managed to effectively organise their protests against the FRG had a 'whole series of powers' not come together to galvanise such discontent.[80] For example, not until 1955 – apparently too late for any serious disciplinary measure to be taken – did the West German Foreign Ministry become aware of the private meetings that the West German ambassador to Indonesia, Werner Otto von Hentig, had had with several representatives of the Arab League, in 1952 and early 1953, to discuss the question of Bonn's commitment to *Wiedergutmachung*.[81] A 1941 *New York Times* article described Hentig as 'the principal German agitator among Arabs', but his links with the Arab world dated to even earlier than that. Hentig was a veteran of German foreign policy, having begun his diplomatic career in 1911. After job postings in Constantinople, San Francisco and Bogota, in 1937 Hentig had become the head of the Orient Division of the Reich's Foreign Ministry, focusing especially on German–Arab relations. In that capacity, he had often dealt with figures such as the Mufti of Jerusalem, Amin al-Husseini, and imam Alimjan Idris, who both had a long history of cooperation with the German authorities. Mufti-al-Husseini had even met Hitler in person, while Idris had worked in Muslim prison camps for the Prussian War Ministry in the 1920s and then, from 1933 until the end of the Second World War, worked for the Nazi Foreign Office, first as an adviser to the Orient Division of the political department and later in the propaganda section, which was jointly run by the Foreign Ministry and Goebbels' Ministry of Propaganda. Among his various tasks, the Foreign Office commissioned him to write a Persian translation of Hitler's *Mein Kampf*.[82]

Hentig and Idris met again in the wake of the agreement signed between Israel and the Federal Republic.[83] By that point, Idris worked as a representative of the Arab League and Hentig, without informing the Federal Foreign Office, went on a mission to the Middle East to 'complicate the ratification of the agreement', as an internal ministerial investigation would later reveal.[84] It was Hentig's successor as West German ambassador in Indonesia, Helmut Allardt, who by chance found the correspondence with the Egyptian envoy.[85] He was struck by what he described as his colleague's 'poisonous hate towards the Federal Government and "regime"',[86] as expressed, for example, in a communication to the Egyptian envoy in Jakarta in late 1952. In it, Hentig expressed his disdain for the 'fabulous sum' that Adenauer had agreed to devolve to the Israeli claimants, which 'in now [*sic*] way corresponded to the actual expenses Israel could have had for its people' and which, Hentig explained, was agreed upon by West Germany 'notwithstanding the fact that all individual demands [on behalf of Jewish victims of Nazi persecution] had [by now] already been fully compensated'. As Abraham Frowein would later describe it, this was a 'grotesque' misrepresentation of facts.[87]

## The Arab League in Bonn

By October 1952, the Arab League's members unanimously passed a resolution condemning the West German agreement to pay restitutions to the Jewish state. In addition to this, the League voted to send a delegation to Bonn to dissuade the Federal government from going ahead with the transfers – although Jordan, Saudi Arabia and Yemen decided not to send their national representatives to Bonn and, in the end, the delegation would consist only of one Syrian, one Egyptian, one Iraqi and one Lebanese delegate.[88] West German reassurances that their agreement with Israel had nothing to do with the conflict between Israel and the Arab states; that Bonn considered Israel as trustee for Jewish refugees of Nazi persecution; and that the agreement would not imply a direct subsidy of Israel but rather would be structured around the delivery of specific, non-military, goods – none of these points seemed to have any calming effect on the Arab League representatives, as their mission against the restitution agreement continued.[89] West German attempts to prevent the Arab League's visit to Bonn proved to be futile.

State Secretary Walter Hallstein asked, in vain, for American cooperation on thwarting the Arab attempts to visit Bonn in their tour against the Luxembourg Agreement.[90] But the West Germans did not just hope to get the help from their superpower – they also readily engaged with various Arab countries to show that they were indeed ready and eager to solve any issues that might stand in the way of furthering the economic, and also political, links between the Federal Republic and the Arab world. Director of the Political Division of the Foreign Ministry Herbert Blankenhorn sent one of his subordinates, Alexander Böker, on an informal mission to Egypt at the end of September. A few weeks later, further small special delegations were dispatched to Lebanon, Saudi Arabia and Iraq to negotiate economic deals that would calm down the Arab discontent.[91] And the West German permanent observer at the UN, Hans Riesser, received instructions to donate DM100,000 to the United Nations Relief and Works Agency to alleviate the fate of Palestinian refugees of the first Arab–Israeli war.[92]

However, none of the West German efforts to thwart the Arab protests against the agreement with Israel seemed to be successful and, in the end, the Arab League delegates arrived in Bonn on 21 October 1952. Ahmed Daouk Bey headed the delegation. With him were the military attaché of the Egyptian embassy in Rome, Ahmed Hassan, Syrian representative Ramzi Alajati and Iraqi diplomat Ali al-Safi. The four organised a press conference denouncing the agreement and announcing their firm intention to oppose its ratification. Joachim Hertslet, a shady German businessman with a past in the Reich Ministry of Economic Affairs and who now directed a trade agency which was specialised in trade with the Arab world, accompanied and supported the PR efforts of the four Arab representatives. Politically close to the Arab League – he had become so while being engaged in his long-standing commercial dealings with the Levant – the FRG suspected Hertslet of being in the pay of the Soviets and working to undermine its credibility by helping to orchestrate the Arab League's vehement protests against the agreement with Israel.[93] Walter Hallstein asked all the Cabinet members to avoid meeting any of the delegates without previously informing the Foreign Ministry. He, and Bonn's diplomats, would take care of the issue themselves.

Hallstein was determined to take all necessary steps to contain the protest of the Arab representatives, but after an intense week of meetings in Bonn, the four Arab delegates left more furious at the West German authorities than when they had arrived. They had meetings at the Foreign Ministry every other day, the first and last of which were chaired by Hallstein himself. Yet the talented State Secretary did not seem to be able to cope with the four Arab representatives and, against Hallstein's hopes, the situation quickly heated up. On 28 October the State Secretary promised that he would examine the possibility of having the UN supervise the West German transfers to Israel, as the League had earlier suggested, and vigorously reiterated that, in any case, Bonn's material transfers would not enhance Israel's military capability. This, however, did not deter the Arab delegates. The Lebanese representative, Daouk, responded to Hallstein's allegedly reassuring words by announcing the delegates' intention to meet with 'Bundestag members, journalists, economists and so on'. This, for Hallstein, was simply too much. He requested the members of the delegation to stop spreading 'propaganda against the defined policy of the Federal government'. After days of trying to calm them, in vain, at a meeting on 30 October he eventually asked the Arab delegates to leave the Federal Republic.[94]

Hallstein's attitude, and his attempt to limit the delegation's room for manoeuvre in the FRG, sparked outrage in the Arab world, and especially in Cairo, as Ambassador Günther Pawelke was soon to experience first-hand. Egypt had been the first country in the Middle East to establish diplomatic relations with the FRG, with the West German embassy officially opening in Cairo on 16 October. Less than two weeks later, the newly appointed ambassador had not even finished furnishing his own residence when he already had to face one very uncomfortable encounter. Livid at how the Arab delegation had been dismissed by Walter Hallstein in Bonn, Prime Minister Naguib chilled Pawelke by threatening to cut off diplomatic relations with the Federal Republic, given that the 'honour' of his country was at stake in this situation.[95] This was not the first time that Pawelke had had to deal with the Egyptians' annoyance at the FRG. In an earlier meeting, Egyptian Foreign Minister Mahmoud Fawzi had stressed that the restitutions agreement with Israel was, as he saw it, 'a stab in the back of the Arab world'.[96] Yet the fury which Naguib heaped on Pawelke was rather unprecedented. As the British diplomatic mission in Cairo observed, the mission of the newly appointed ambassador had 'had an unfortunate start'.[97]

For better or worse, Pawelke was not alone in representing the FRG in Egypt. Locally known as the 'Alemanni', the group of German advisers to the Egyptian military establishment which arrived in Cairo in 1950 during the time of King Farouk kept their posts even after the ousting of the monarchy and the Free Officers' rise to power, remaining in their roles as advisers to the Ministry of War.[98] The 'Alemanni' were a rather consistent group, actively involved in advising and training the Egyptians in military and security matters. Having kept in contact with key West German ministries, these advisers also often served as intermediaries between local and German firms, and often reached out to various personalities in the Federal Republic's highest echelons to provide their analysis of the situation on the ground – and on how Bonn may make the most of it. The leading figure among them was Wilhelm Voss, a former member of the prestigious 'circle of friends of Heinrich Himmler' during the Nazi era – a membership he had acquired through his work as SS-Standartenführer, and which made him part of an exclusive club of the forty or so most influential SS members in Nazi Germany.[99] His special interest lay at the intersection between the armament industry, economics and business management, having headed and managed big armament conglomerates in Nazi-occupied Czechoslovakia, which at that time relied on the work of almost two million concentration camp inmates, POWs and forced labourers and which cost the lives of tens of thousands in Voss' area alone.[100] After a brief period of imprisonment in the United States, and later in Germany, he had landed in Cairo in 1950, managing to establish close contacts with the Egyptian leadership.

In the aftermath of the Luxembourg Agreement, worried by the souring of the ties between the Federal Republic and Egypt, former SS Wilhelm Voss reached out directly to Walter Hallstein, urging him to send a high-ranking delegation of industrialists and economic experts to appease the Egyptians by signing further trade deals.[101] As Hallstein quickly recognised, Voss had a point. Indeed, representatives of big German firms, such as Siemens and Telefunken, had been trying for months to get reassurances from the government that their trade with the Arab countries would not suffer in the event of a successful conclusion of the West German–Israeli agreement.[102] To the pressure coming from Cairo and the Arab states, and from the West German industrialists worried about losing their commercial partners in the Levant, Egypt added a diplomatic offensive carried out at the United Nations. Twice, in November 1952, the Cairo government emphasised that they were still 'at war' with Israel and thus opposed to the restitutions agreement. In the wake of the debacle in Bonn, the political committee of the Arab League announced that, should the agreement be ratified, the Arab countries would respond with a total boycott of German goods.[103]

Indeed, from Bonn's perspective it was crucial not to let the issue of restitutions to Israel obstruct the strengthening of the West German ties with the Arab world – and especially with Egypt, a country that represented both an economic and foreign political asset for Bonn. Yet not everyone panicked over the Arab League's latest threat against the Federal Republic. The West German observer mission at the UN, for example, underscored that Bonn should not be fooled by the outer façade of unity presented by the Arab League. West German diplomats stationed in New York noted how Iraq had refrained from protesting to the FRG ('the importance of its economic relations with Germany does not allow for such an adventure'); how Libya and Saudi Arabia had shown 'considerable reluctance' to proceed on the matter; how Syria, 'which has played the leading role in this offensive, is now more cautious about the boycott threat' and how Egypt was 'in the midst of carrying out some industrial projects, the continuation of which depends on the supply of German machinery and German expert guidance'.[104]

Despite the calming advice coming from New York, however, the West German government strove to find a reasonable compromise with its precious Arab partners. The economic exchange between the Federal Republic and the Arab countries in 1951 amounted to over DM420 million, and the trade with Egypt alone formed over one quarter thereof.[105] In the wake of the Arab League delegation's early departure from Bonn, State Secretary Hallstein thus encouraged Pawelke to reassure the Egyptians, reminding them that the goods transferred from Bonn could in no way strengthen Israel's military potential. What might be strengthened, Hallstein acknowledged, was the Israeli economy – yet in this respect the Federal Republic was willing to offer Egypt compensation (*Ausgleich*) via a balancing intensification of economic relations between Bonn and Cairo.[106] Despite the fact that internal West German reports stressed that subjecting the implementation of the agreement to UN supervision was 'legally incompatible with the provisions of the agreement' as well as fundamentally 'impracticable', Hallstein stressed that the Federal Government was ready to bring the question to the attention of the UNGA and to carry out all the measures that the UNGA might pass on the matter. He also promised that the FRG would investigate the best ways by which it could support the capital projects of interested Arab countries, mentioning in particular the West German intention to increase the purchase of Egyptian cotton, and to support Egyptian motorisation efforts, as well as examining specific economic requests that might arise from Cairo. The FRG, Hallstein concluded, was ready to send a specialised delegation to Egypt to discuss the matter further, just as Voss had suggested.

After a series of calmer exchanges with the Egyptian authorities, including another meeting with a much more conciliatory Naguib, Ambassador Pawelke confirmed the Egyptian interest in receiving a West German delegation, comprising representatives of the iron and steel industries, as well as of the mechanical engineering, and electrical and construction industries, accompanied by a leading finance expert and an authoritative representative of the Federal government.[107] The US ambassador to Cairo, Jefferson Caffery, noted how the intercession of leading Egyptian industrialists had 'pressed upon Naguib and [the] military committee [the] importance of German-Egyptian trade relations' – an especially relevant point to counterbalance the Arab League's stated intention to boycott German products should the Federal Republic go ahead with the ratification of the Luxembourg Agreement.[108] However, in a letter to a friend, newly appointed ambassador Pawelke anticipated that the coming negotiations would be extremely delicate. As he confided, 'my political work here is not easy, and certainly it is much more difficult than I was able to anticipate when I left Bonn'. What he lamented, in particular, was that through 'our [West German] fallacious preparation of the German-Israeli agreement, we [the FRG] were able to bring about unity among the states of the Arab League'.[109] Indeed, the newly established Egyptian regime was eager to show that it could lead the Arab world, and the question of West German restitutions to Israel provided an excellent opportunity to project the Egyptian leadership onto the rest of the Arab League, as a curious diplomatic incident in Cairo was about to demonstrate.

# Notes

1  Shinnar, *Bericht eines Beauftragten*, p. 36.
2  R. Vogel, *The German Path to Israel: A Documentation* (Chest Springs: Dufour Editions, 1969), p. 42.
3  AAPD, 1952, Doc. 97, Note, Böhm, 7 April 1952.
4  Quoted in Vogel, *The German Path*, p. 38; F. Böhm, *Das deutsch-israelische Abkommen 1952* (Stuttgart: Deutsche Verlags-Anstalt, 1976), p. 449.
5  E. Conze, N. Frei, P. Hayes and M. Zimmermann (eds), *Das Amt und die Vergangenheit. Deutschen Diplomaten im Dritten Reich und in der Bundesrepublik* (Munich: Karl Blessing Verlag, 2010), p. 574.
6  J. Hürter, 'Das Auswärtige Amt, die NS-Diktatur und der Holocaust. Kritische Bemerkungen zu einem Kommissionsbericht', *Vierteljahreshefte für Zeitgeschichte* 59 (2011), p. 167.
7  Frei, *Adenauer's Germany and the Nazi Past*; R. G. Moeller, *War Stories: The Search for a Usable Past in the Federal Republic of Germany* (London: University of California Press, 2003).
8  Schwarz, *Die Wiederherstellung des deutschen Kredits*; Rombeck-Jaschinski, *Das Londoner Schuldabkommen*.

9 DFPI, Comp. Vol. 1952, Doc. 72, Shinnar and Josephtal to the Ministry of Foreign Affairs, 21 March 1952.

10 The exchange rate was US$1 to DM4.2, C. Goschler, *Wiedergutmachung: Westdeutschland und die Verfolgten des Nazionalsozialismus (1945–1954)* (Munich: Oldenbourg, 1992), p. 11.

11 Sagi, German Reparations to Israel, p. 103ff. C. Goschler, Schuld und Schulden: *Die Politik der Wiedergutmachung für NS-Verfolgte seit 1945* (Göttingen: Wallstein, 2005), p. 147ff.

12 ACDP I-084–001, NL Küster, Diary Entry, 30 March 1952.

13 B. Morris, *The Birth of the Palestinian Refugee Problem Revisited* (Cambridge: Cambridge University Press, 2004).

14 Pact of the League of Arab States, 22 March 1945, https://avalon.law.yale.edu/20th_century/arableag.asp [Accessed March 2020]; B. Boutros-Ghali, *The Arab League, 1945–1955* (New York: Carnegie Endowment for International Peace, 1954).

15 AAPD, 1952, Doc. 84, Du Mont (The Hague) to the Foreign Office, 24 March 1952.

16 FRUS. 1952–1954/IX, Doc. 417. The Secretary of State to the Legation in Syria, 12 March 1952.

17 ACDP, I-084–001, NL Küster, Diary Entry, 30 March 1952.

18 ACDP, I-084–001, NL Küster, Diary Entry, 31 March 1952.

19 H. Sietz, *Attentat auf Adenauer: Die geheime Geschichte eines politischen Anschlags* (Berlin: Siedler, 2003).

20 ACDP I-084–001, NL Küster, Diary Entries of 31 March and 1 April 1952, respectively.

21 Jakow Farshtej, Hermann Fekler, Itzchak Preger, Elieser Sudit and Elieser Shostak, respectively.

22 J. Bowyer Bell, *Terror Out of Zion: Fight for Israeli Independence* (London: Transaction, 2017).

23 Published privately, E. Sudit, *Be-shliḥut matzpunit* (Jerusalem, 1994).

24 AAPD, 1952, Doc. 108, Erhard to Adenauer, 16 April 1952.

25 DFPI 1952, Doc. 88, Israeli Delegation to the Reparations Negotiations to the Ministry of Foreign Affairs, 1 April 1952.

26 AAPD 1952, Doc. 111, Abs to Adenauer, 22 April 1952.

27 228. Cabinet meeting, 17 June 1952, *Die Kabinettsprotokolle der Bundesregierung*, https://www.bundesarchiv.de/cocoon/barch/0000/k/k1952k/kap1_2/kap2_46/para3_12.html [Accessed March 2020].

28 H. J. Abs, *Außenpolitik und Auslandsschulden – Erinnerungen an das Jahr 1952* (Konstanz: Universitätsverlag Konstanz, 1990), p. 13. On Abs see L. Gall, 'Hermann Josef Abs and the Third Reich: "A Man for all Seasons"?', *Financial History Review* 6 (1999), pp. 147–202. Erhard's position later became closer to that of Abs.

29 AAPD 1952, Doc. 95: Meeting chaired by Chancellor Adenauer, 5 April 1952.

30 *Ibid.*

31 *Ibid.*

32 Italics in the original. O. Küster, *Ehrfahrungen in der deutschen Wiedergutmachung* (Tübingen: Moh Siebeck, 1967), p. 28.

33 Y. Jelinek, 'Die Krise der Shilumim/Wiedergutmachungs-Verhandlungen im Sommer 1952', *Vierteljahrhefte für Zeitgeschichte* 38:1 (1990), pp. 113–39.

34 DFPI 1952, Doc. 158, Goldmann to Adenauer, 19 May 1952.

35 *Ibid.*

36  DFPI 1952, Doc. 92, Eban to Acheson, 3 April 1952.
37  FRUS, 1952–1954/IX, Doc. 419, The Secretary of State to the Office of the United States High Commissioner for Germany, at Bonn, 4 April 1952, and Doc. 424, The Secretary of State to the Office of the United States High Commissioner for Germany, at Bonn, 22 April 1952, respectively.
38  FRUS, 1952–1954/IX, Part 1, Doc. 423, Memorandum by the Secretary of State to the President, 22 April 1952.
39  AAPD, 1952, Doc. 162, Memorandum of Conversation, Adenauer-Henderson, 24 June 1952.
40  DFPI, Vol. 7, Doc. 181, Report of Conversation between M. Fischer, Sh. Divon and M. Schumann on 30 May 1952, 5 June 1952.
41  BAK B126 51545, Latzin to Schäffer, 8 January 1953.
42  BAK B126 51544, Löw to Schäffer, 23 May 1952. On the problem of the expellees see P. Ahonen, *After the Expulsion: West Germany and Eastern Europe 1945–1990* (Oxford: Oxford University Press, 2003).
43  BAK B126 51544, Wolffs to Schäffer, 23 May 1952.
44  AAPD 1952, Doc. 131, Schumacher to Adenauer, 10 May 1952.
45  228. Cabinet meeting, 17 June 1952, *Die Kabinettsprotokolle der Bundesregierung*; BAK B126 51545: Memorandum of the Delegation of Arab States to the Government of the Federal Republic of Germany, 31 October 1952.
46  A touching description of the event is in D. Diner, *Rituelle Distanz: Israels deutsche Frage* (Munich: Deutsche Verlags-Anstalt, 2015), pp. 11–34.
47  On this and the following point see, respectively, Article 6(d) and Letter 4a point 2, in: https://treaties.un.org/doc/Publication/UNTS/Volume%20162/volume-162-I-2137-English.pdf [Accessed November 2019].
48  Balabkins, *West German Reparations to Israel*, p. 189; A. Tooze, 'Reassessing the Moral Economy of Post-War Reconstruction: The Terms of the West German Settlement in 1952', *Past and Present* 6 (2012), pp. 47–70.
49  H. J. Küsters (ed.), *Der Integrationsfriede: Viermächte-Verhandlungen über die Friedensregelungen mit Deutschland 1945–1990* (Munich: Beck, 2000).
50  H. P. Schwarz, *Die Ära Adenauer: Gründerjahre der Republik, 1949–1957* (Stuttgart: Deutsche Verlags-Anstalt, 1981).
51  Tooze, 'Reassessing the Moral Economy', p. 60.
52  DFPI, Comp. Vol. 7, 1952, Doc. 438, Aroch (Moscow) to the Ministry of Foreign Affairs, 13 November 1952, fn. 2.
53  JTA, 'German Reparations Payments Are Not "Atonement", Sharett Says', 12 September 1952.
54  Quoted in: PA AA, MfAA 13364/ 59, Israel claims for reparations to the GDR, n.d. 1952.
55  Documents on Israeli-Soviet Relations (DISR), Vol. 2, Doc. 385, Gribanov and Bazarov to Vyshinskii, 27 October 1952.
56  DFPI, Comp. Vol. 7, 1952, Doc. 72, Shinnar and Josephtal to the Ministry of Foreign Affairs, 21 March 1952.
57  See V. Mastny, *The Cold War and Soviet Insecurity: The Stalin Years* (Oxford: Oxford University Press, 1996), p. 134.
58  DISR, Vol. 2, Doc. 406, Eliashiv to the Israeli Ministry of Foreign Affairs, 25 March 1952.
59  *Ibid.*, p. 795. By 1953 the amount of reparations that the Soviets extracted from East Germany would amount to over US$4 billion. Zubok, *A Failed Empire?*, p. 84.

60  DISR, Vol. 2, Doc. 410, Levavi to Argaman (Moscow), 27 April 1952.

61  Quoted in: PA AA, MfAA 13364/59, Israeli claims for reparations to the GDR.

62  DISR, Vol. 2, Doc. 426, Meeting: Eliashiv – Pushkin. Moscow, 4 September 1952.

63  DISR, Vol. 2, Doc. 427, Note of the Israeli Legation in the USSR to the USSR Ministry of Foreign Affairs, Moscow, 15 September 1952.

64  PA AA, MfAA 13364/57, Hausmitteilung: News release: Note of the Government of the USSR to the Israeli Government. Kluge, 25 September 1952.

65  PA AA, MfAA 13364/55, Richter to the Diplomatic Mission of the German Democratic Republic, 29 September 1952.

66  See chapter 3.

67  'Öliges Lächeln und leere Hände', *Neues Deutschland* (*ND*) (18 July 1952), p. 6; PA AA, MfAA 13364/58, Florin (Foreign Ministry) to Oelßner (Politbüro), 24 September 1952.

68  Herf, *Divided Memory*, pp. 115ff.

69  See FRUS, 1952–1954/IX, Doc. 479, The Acting United States High Commissioner for Germany (Donnelly) to the Department of State, 6 September 1952.

70  NARA, RG 59 Box 2966, Telegram, Confidential Security Information Donnelly (Bonn) to Secretary of State, 3 September 1952.

71  FRUS, 1952–1954/IX, Doc. 408, The Minister in Syria (Cannon) to the Department of State, 3 March 1952.

72  PA AA, B150/180, Hallstein, 5 September 1952; 'Der Boykott: Die Araber sind wichtig', *Der Spiegel*, 1 October 1952, p. 15.

73  PA AA, B150/180, Etzdorf, 6 September 1952.

74  PA AA, B150/180, Etzdorf, 11 September 1952.

75  AAPD 1952, Doc. 92, Note signed by Böhm and Küster, 1 April 1952.

76  PA AA, B150, Aktenkopien 1952, Record of the Ambassador Counsellor Kordt, 3 July 1952.

77  BNA: PRO, FO 371/103954, JKP, Central Department, 26 November 1952.

78  NARA, RG 59, Box 2966, American Delegation in Damascus (Eagleton) to the Department of State, 18 August 1952.

79  *Ibid.*

80  AAPD 1952, Doc. 74, Note, Allardt, 20 February 1953.

81  See Conze et al., *Das Amt die Vergangenheit*, p. 581.

82  D. Motadel, *Islam and Nazi Germany's War* (Cambridge, MA: The Belknap Press of Harvard University Press, 2014), p. 44.

83  PA AA, Personnel file, Werner Otto von Hentig 49856, Note. Bauer, 24 March 1955.

84  *Ibid.*, Transcript. Frowein, 6 April 1955.

85  *Ibid.*, Allardt to Blankenhorn, 9 March 1955.

86  *Ibid.*

87  *Ibid.*, Hentig, 27 September 1952.

88  See, e.g., FO 371/98262, British Legation (Beirut) to Foreign Office, 4 September 1952 and Cairo to Foreign Office, 11 September 1952, both in A. L. P. Burdett, *The Arab League: British Documentary Sources*, Vol. 7 (London: Archive Editions, 1995).

89  NARA, RG 59, Box 2966, Division of External German Affairs, US High Commission in Bonn (G. W. Renchard) to the Department of State, 10 September 1952.

90  NARA, RG 59, Box 2966, Gifford (London) to Secretary of State, 27 September 1952.

91  253. Cabinet Meeting, 21 October 1952, *Die Kabinettsprotokolle der Bundesregierung*.

92  R. Steininger, *Berichte aus Israel: Aktenedition* (Munich: Olzog Verlag, 2004), Vol. 3, Doc. 54, Telegram Schöner (Bonn) to Gruber (Wien), 25 October 1952.
93  253. Cabinet Meeting, 21 October 1952, *Die Kabinettsprotokolle der Bundesregierung.*
94  AAPD, 1952, Doc. 222, Memorandum of Conversation, Hallstein-Arab Delegation, 28 October 1952.
95  BNA, PRO, FO 371/97860: Stevenson (British Embassy, Cairo) to Kirkpatrick, 1 November 1952.
96  AAPD 1952, Doc. 216, Pawelke to the Foreign Office, 14 October 1952.
97  BNA, PRO, FO 371/97860, Stevenson (British Embassy, Cairo) to Kirkpatrick, 1 November 1952.
98  B. Rubin and W. G. Schwanitz, *Nazis, Islamists and the Making of the Modern Middle East* (New Haven: Yale University Press, 2014), pp. 209ff.
99  U. Becker, 'Post-War Antisemitism: Germany's Foreign Policy Toward Egypt' in C. A. Small (ed.), *Global Antisemitism: A Crisis of Modernity* (Leiden: Martinus Nijhoff, 2013), pp. 283–286.
100  *Ibid.*
101  AAPD 1953, Vol. 1, Doc 12, Note, Allardt, 9 January 1953.
102  BAI, Vol. 3, Doc. 50, Hartl (Tel Aviv) and Gruber (Wien), 7 September 1952.
103  Harry S. Truman Presidential Library (HSTL), Secretary of State File, Acheson Collection, Memorandum of Conversation with Ambassador Abba Eban of Israel; Minister David Goltein of the Embassy of Israel; Colonel Chaim Herzog; Fred E. Waller; and Patrick T. Hart, 5 January 1953.
104  *Ibid.*
105  S. O. Berggötz, *Nahostpolitik in der Ära Adenauer: Möglichkeiten und Grenzen (1949–1963)* (Düsseldorf: Droste, 1998), p. 466.
106  AAPD, 1952, Doc. 248, Note, Hallstein, 12 December 1952.
107  AAPD, 1953, Vol. 1, Doc. 2, Pawelke to the Foreign Office, 4 January 1953; NARA, RG 59 Box 2966, George L. West, Jr. Chief Division of External German Affairs (Bonn) to the Department of State (Washington, DC), 'Easing of Tension in German-Arab League Relations', 7 January 1953.
108  NARA, RG 59 Box 2966, Telegram Caffery (Cairo) to Secretary of State, 1 January 1953.
109  Landesarchiv Nordrhein-Westfalen (LNW), Bernhard Reismann File, 104, Pawelke (Cairo) to Reismann (Bonn), 29 December 1952.

# 3

# Confrontation

State Secretary Ludger Westrick of the Federal Economics Ministry arrived in Egypt on 1 February 1953, accompanied by Hallstein's best wishes for a 'successful outcome of your certainly not easy task'.[1] He headed a team of ten men, drawn from both the policy-making and the industry worlds, comprising the owners and directors of big German industries which included many of the top West German bankers and industrialists from the fields of textiles, electrical and mechanical engineering, and steel construction – just as the Egyptians had asked, and just as Hallstein had promised. In Cairo, they would be dealing mainly with the Egyptians, although representatives from Jordan, Syria, Lebanon, Saudi Arabia, Yemen and Iraq were also present and willing to engage with the West Germans about a settlement of their dispute.[2] During a press conference organised shortly after the delegation's arrival, Westrick said he was 'sincerely pleased with the spirit of friendship' which had welcomed him and his delegation to Cairo. He reported to the press that Prime Minister Naguib had 'pointed to the possibilities for a German-Arab cooperation in the field of economy [and he had] mentioned the very grave concern which the [Palestinian] refugee problem causes to the Arab authorities – a problem with which we Germans are particularly familiar, as we have in our country 12 million refugees from the Eastern territories'.[3] The German mission looked forward to 'the opportunity to discuss all worries in an atmosphere of harmony and perfect frankness' with the Arab countries, he added. And, indeed, the initial cables sent by the Bonn delegation in Cairo were cautiously optimistic.

However, the Egyptian take on the events was rather different. As he made clear during his talks with the German negotiators, Naguib insisted that the FRG ' "owed" [the] Arab States an "indemnity" ' and that the 'long-term credits to [the Arab States], of which Egypt would get [the] lion's share, should "at least" equal [the] amount of reparations paid [to] Israel'.[4] US Ambassador Caffery worked hard to help the West Germans reach out to the local authorities, and explained to the Bonn delegation the main issues that were behind the attitude of the Egyptian counterparts – i.e. their perceived need to appear strong in front of their domestic audience, especially so shortly after the Free Officers' revolution, and their having to face intra-Arab difficulties in coming up with a united negotiating position. In the days after his arrival in Cairo, Westrick would stress, repeatedly, that 'the delegation is not here to discuss the Israel-agreement' and that (West) 'Germany is not a debtor to the Arab states'.[5] Yet the talks quickly came to a halt less than two weeks after they had started, when an East German trade delegation suddenly, and for the West Germans shockingly, landed in Cairo.[6]

The East German press celebrated how East Berlin's foreign trade policy – including its increasing commercial ties with Egypt – served the purpose of world peace.[7] Yet the developments on the ground had been a bit tenser than the regime narrative would reveal. Following the friction that the signing of the Luxembourg Agreement had created in the relations between West Germany and Egypt, in December 1952 the SED had begun receiving direct input from GDR businessman in loco emphasising that 'now would be the very best moment' to push for economic ties between Cairo and East Berlin.[8] And while the West German Chancellor was sure that the sudden appearance of the East German delegation in Cairo was somehow connected to a Soviet manoeuvre, in fact smaller Soviet bloc countries had pushed the East German regime towards Cairo. In December 1952, Deputy Foreign Minister Vlasta Borek, in Prague, noted that the GDR was in a unique position to exploit Nasser's opening towards the 'peace camp' – i.e. the Soviet bloc – given the Bonn-Cairo skirmishes following the signing of the *Wiedergutmachung* agreement.[9] The previous year, the State Secretary of East Berlin's Foreign Ministry, Anton Ackermann, had sent a note to Walter Ulbricht asking for his assent to forge economic ties with Egypt, a matter on which, in turn, his colleagues at the Ministry for Inter-German and Foreign Trade had been rather vocal.[10] Finally, in February 1953 the Foreign Ministry and the Trade Ministry finalised their instructions for an East German delegation to be despatched to Egypt. The situation was particularly precarious because, as the report noted, this was to be the first time that East German delegates had visited a third country which hosted a West German embassy.[11]

In Cairo, both General Muhammad Naguib and Egyptian Foreign Minister Fawzi apologised to Westrick, explaining that the arrival of the East Germans was due to a 'technical mistake' made by their diplomatic mission in Czechoslovakia.[12] However, given the particular topic of the negotiations between Bonn and Cairo, and that rumours about this move had appeared in the press in December 1952, it really seemed that the Egyptians were attempting – and rather openly, too – to play off the two Germanys against one another.[13] Indeed, they seemed to be using the West German feelings towards the idea of Egyptian–East German dealings to mediate their own regarding the prospect of West German *Wiedergutmachung* to Israel. Hallstein cabled from Bonn that the FRG was 'profoundly shocked' at the news of the arrival of the East German commercial mission. The West German delegation decided to leave Egypt sooner than initially planned and Westrick, upon returning to Bonn early, encouraged the Chancellor to ignore the Arab threats and to proceed with the ratification of the reparations agreement with Israel without further ado.[14] The head of the East German mission, Franz Koch, was thus left to negotiate with the Egyptians undisturbed, sitting on the 'still warm' chair vacated by Westrick, as *Der Spiegel* put it.[15]

On 7 March 1953, the GDR and Egypt concluded their first economic agreement, a barter deal based on the exchange of Egyptian cotton and leather goods for East German mechanical and chemical products.[16] The actual economic result of these negotiations was modest, but the deal also represented an astounding success from the East German perspective: this was the very first commercial deal concluded with a non-European non-Communist country – and, what was more, one that had diplomatic relations with West Germany but had not let the matter deter it from concluding the deal with the East Germans.[17] Five days later, in East Berlin, leading members of the East German Foreign and Trade ministries gathered at Berlin's Ostbahnhof to welcome back the delegation headed by Fritz Koch and celebrate their achievements.[18] The following day, the state-owned museums on East Berlin's Museum Island reopened their Egyptian collections – a further testament to the importance of the closer relationship between Egypt and the GDR, and to the East German willingness to display it to the public.[19] In Bonn, the West German Bundestag ratified the agreement with Israel on 18 March in a climate of bitterness and deep resentment. Not even half of the members of the coalition government voted in favour of the ratification, which succeeded only thanks to the votes of the opposition party.[20] The political turmoil of 1952, culminating with the 1953 concurrent German–German presence in Cairo, had shown how easily the FRG could be pressed by emphasising its burgeoning links with Israel – and exploiting this was a tactic that East Berlin would try to emulate, with mixed results, for decades to come.

The simultaneous presence of two German delegations in Egypt in early 1953 marked a turning point in the German–German Cold War confrontation and, in the months that followed, tensions heightened even further. At home, the East Germans launched an extensive propaganda campaign explaining why the GDR would never sit down to negotiate with Israel. This overlapped with a series of political purges that removed from positions of power those who had strived for a closer relationship between East Germany and Israel and went hand in hand with the official narrative of the SED regime about the Nazi past, which discarded the centrality of Jewish persecution under the Nazi regime and focused instead on the suffering of the German Communists.

## Purging ranks

A series of political purges and show trials took place in much of the Soviet bloc in the early 1950s. These started in Budapest in 1949, with the show trial against former Hungarian Minister of the Interior (between 1946 and 1948) and Foreign Minister (between 1948 and 1949), László Rajk, put on trial because Prime Minister Mátyás Rákosi – who described himself as 'Stalin's best pupil' – felt increasingly threatened by his charismatic and competent Minister.[21] In East Germany, the purge began in August 1950, six months after the establishment of the East German Ministry for State Security (Stasi). Hermann Matern, a long-time Ulbricht associate eager to tighten the SED's control over the East German state, directed the trials. At that time, anti-Semitic tropes scarcely featured in the accusations framed against the Communist defendants, all of whom were of Jewish origins. In 1952–53, however, things would be very different.

Intense, vocal anti-Zionist and anti-Semitic themes characterised the second phase of political repression that took place in East Germany from 1952 onwards – one that would have lasting effects on the framing of East German policies vis-à-vis the State of Israel. Many of those targeted in the purges of 1952–53 supported a different East German stance towards Israel – one imbued with awareness of how significant the racial persecution of the Jews had been within the Nazi political project, and one animated by the conviction that the 'new' socialist German state should engage with the Jewish state, and pay restitutions to the Jewish survivors of Nazi persecution, wherever they may live. Instead, the East German official discourse on the past removed any notion of East German historical responsibility towards the Jews, and failed to identify, in the atrocities inflicted on the Jews by the Nazis, the crucial trope of the Hitler dictatorship.[22] It was both ironic and tragic that the allegedly antifascist Germany would foster anti-Semitic tendencies while officially stressing its pride in having discarded any remnants of Nazism. Nevertheless, once state organs began casting Nazism as the final stage of monopoly capitalism, and the establishment of the new socialist politico-economic order in the GDR as the amputation of any continuity with the Nazi past, the question of paying restitutions to the State of Israel could be, and was, easily dismissed.[23]

The SED's anti-Semitic attacks and purges continued in the wake of another show trial – this time one that was taking place in Prague, against the number two of the Czechoslovak Communist party, Rudolf Slánský.[24] Julius Meyer, the leader of the Federation of the East German Jewish communities, who was both a party member and a member of the East German People's Chamber, was taken in by the Stasi for interrogation on 6 January 1953. He had been present at the initial meeting that Grotewohl had had with Israeli representatives in 1948 to discuss the question of restitutions to Israel. Much of his interrogation revolved around this meeting, his contacts with people living in Israel and his efforts on the question of post-Holocaust compensation.[25] Meyer fled the GDR a few days after his hour-long interrogation. Less than a week after his escape, GDR police stormed the houses and offices of several East German Jewish citizens, while in Moscow the official press agency of the Soviet Union announced that the authorities had allegedly discovered and exposed a network of Jewish doctors, accused of being mercenaries and agents of a foreign power, who had plotted to orchestrate the deaths of several party officials.[26] The so-called 'doctor's plot' would represent the peak of Stalin's anti-Semitic paranoia, and it led to the arrests of thirty-seven doctors, most of whom were Jews.[27] As these developments unfolded in the Soviet Union, in the GDR Jewish East German Communists loyal to the regime began fearing the possibility of being stigmatised as Zionists.[28] The Jewish Agency offices in West Berlin pressed Israeli Consul Livneh to facilitate Jewish emigration from East Germany and, in turn, help East German Jews to migrate to Israel.[29] Leading representatives of the East German Jewish communities, together with over one-quarter of the remaining Jewish population in the country, fled to the West in the wake of the souring political climate for Jews in East Germany.[30]

## *Wiedergutmachung* in East German propaganda

In the wake of the purges, East German propaganda turned to the task of explaining to its domestic audience the reasons behind the East German refusal to grant reparations to the State of Israel. By delving into questions that had to do with the country's past and present, East German formulations of its policy vis-à-vis Israel quickly turned into something broader, and more significant, than a mere justification of the GDR's foreign policy towards a third country. From 1949 to 1951 the SED mouthpiece *Neues Deutschland* had been framing a narrative portraying Israel as a 'satellite', or 'colony', of aggressive American capitalists.[31] However, the tone changed after the signing of the Luxembourg Agreement. On 25 November 1952, the editor-in-chief of the SED newspaper, Rudolf Herrnstadt, published an editorial commentary on the West German–Israeli agreement, titled: 'Reparations, for whom?'[32] This was the first time that the SED had put the party line on West German–Israeli relations in black and white and presented it to the public.[33] The article came out more than two months after Adenauer and Sharett had signed the agreement in Luxembourg, and just three days after excerpts from the indictment in the Slánský show trial were translated into German and published in the same newspaper.

In the GDR, therefore, the news of the Luxembourg Agreement came to overlap with the mass-hysteria about secret Zionist agents fostered by the show trial in Prague. This allowed a smooth assimilation of the image of the State of Israel as a base of Zionist agents, supported by the United States, with the aim of overthrowing socialism internationally. 'The Americans use Zionism as a camouflage for their crimes and as a channel through which to infiltrate traitors and spies, hence their agents are mainly Jews', contended East German propaganda.[34]

As Zionism became synonymous with imperialism and racism in East German media, the line between anti-Zionist and anti-Semitic statements in the governmental propaganda on Israel became blurred.[35] Remarks on 'Jewish chauvinism' overlapped with texts and declarations that described the GDR as fundamentally non-anti-Semitic.[36] Among those who also released such statements were some representatives of East German Jewish communities, prodded to do so by the SED authorities. For example, during the ceremony celebrating the reconstruction of the synagogue in Prenzlauer Berg in September 1953, which had been severely damaged during the 1938 *Kristallnacht*, Israel Rothmann, a representative of the East Berlin Jewish community, praised the East German regime for 'fighting anti-Semitism and respecting every religion'.[37] This was evidently untrue, considering the high number of Jews, including Rothmann's own predecessor Julius Meyer, who had fled from the GDR in the months leading up to that statement. In the following years, SED officials would repeatedly approach prominent members of the East German Jewish community requesting them to endorse the party stance on Zionism, relations with Israel, and the questions of restitutions and indemnification of Jewish victims of Nazism,[38] while at the same time blaming the 'Americans' and 'Zionist organisations' for wanting to 'squeeze out some profits from Auschwitz and Majdanek'.[39]

GDR propaganda highlighted the distinction between Bonn and East Berlin by contrasting East German passivity vis-à-vis the Israeli requests for compensation and indemnification and Adenauer's active endeavour, at least in public, to resolve the reparations issue quickly and successfully. Any accusations of fostering anti-Semitism would be vocally rebuffed, while the Luxembourg Agreement, the GDR press charged, was tantamount to a 'robbery' of the West German economy that would inevitably lead to the remilitarisation of the Federal Republic, posing a grave danger to the German population.[40] At that time, many West German citizens agreed that Bonn's financial burden as defined by the Luxembourg Agreement was excessive. According to an opinion poll conducted in August 1952, 44 per cent of the population viewed the agreement as unnecessary, while of the 35 per cent which agreed with paying reparations to Israel, 24 per cent viewed the amount as far too high[41] – while in fact it only constituted a very small part of the amount of the West Germany financial obligations negotiated in 1952.[42] And, in one of the many ironies that characterised the German–German propaganda skirmishes during the Cold War, the East German denunciations of the economic vexation caused to Bonn's population due to the Luxembourg Agreement came at a time in which the economic welfare of the East German population was increasingly imperilled, as the uprisings culminating on 17 June 1953 would soon render manifest.[43]

## Precarious balance

The worsening living conditions of the population in the GDR fuelled a series of workers' protests that took place throughout East German territory in 1953, culminating in a full-fledged political uprising in East Berlin. It was the armed intervention of Soviet troops, on 17 June 1953, and their enforcement of martial law throughout East German territory, which allowed the GDR authorities to regain control of the situation.

The June uprising was the first serious political challenge to rattle the Soviet bloc following Stalin's death in March 1953, and the men left at the helm of Soviet politics – Prime Minister Georgy Malenkov, Foreign Minister Vyacheslav Molotov, Interior Minister Lavrenty Beria, and Central Committee Secretary Nikita S. Khrushchev – observed the East German events with apprehension. Since their rise to power, the members of the Soviet Presidium had been attempting to conduct international affairs in a more conciliatory way, redesigning the Soviet approach to key foreign relations issues. There were 'no international issues which could not be settled by peaceful negotiation', emphasised Malenkov at Stalin's funeral – a claim that other members of the Soviet political elite would later also endorse.[44] Albeit having been interrupted following a terror attack against the Soviet Embassy in Tel Aviv in the wake of Stalin's renewed anti-Semitic campaign, the Soviet Union and Israel re-established diplomatic relations in July 1953 – though with Moscow clarifying that 'friendly relations with the Arab states', too, were at the top of the Kremlin's international agenda.[45] The members of the Presidium also reassessed the Soviet stance on the German question, even considering removing the intransigent and stubborn Ulbricht from power. The prospect would have been welcomed by many, both in East Germany and the Soviet Union. In the wake of the uprising, all but two of the SED Politbüro members agreed that leaving Ulbricht in power could have 'catastrophic' consequences for the GDR.[46] The Soviet High Commissioner in East Germany, Vladimir S. Semyonov, shared these concerns, and so did Foreign Minister Beria, who had long considered Ulbricht to be 'an idiot'.[47] Yet against all odds, the East German leader managed to stay in power even after the 1953 uprising, as upcoming Soviet leader and party secretary Khrushchev resolved not to abandon him. Domestically, Ulbricht managed to outmanoeuvre and isolate his most vocal critics. Among them was Rudolf Herrnstadt, the editor in chief of the party mouthpiece, *Neues Deutschland*, and author of the first strong attack against the Luxemburg Agreement in the East German media. In 1953, Ulbricht ended up in a stronger and more secure position than he had been prior to the uprising.[48]

With things calming down at home, the GDR's initial attempts at a proactive foreign policy could continue abroad, relying particularly on economic diplomacy and hefty propaganda. Building upon the successful agreements signed with Egypt in March 1953, that same year the GDR managed to sign one more trade agreement with an Arab country – Lebanon – and, in 1954, got the Egyptian authorities to agree that the GDR would open a commercial mission in Egypt. Within the realm of propaganda, continuous attacks against the West German–Israeli agreement featured ever more prominently in East German outlets and in the communications between East German and Arab diplomats.

The SED leadership had closely monitored the Arab League's efforts to impede the ratification of the West German–Israeli agreement, especially between November 1952 and March 1953.[49] Otto Grotewohl's copy of the diplomatic memorandum that the Syrian government had delivered to Bonn in November 1952, which had been forwarded to him from Moscow, shows that the East German Prime Minister had grasped the significance of several key passages about the Arab stance on German–Israeli relations.[50] First, for example, that the Arab League countries considered the West German reparations to Israel to be a 'subvention of the Israeli war efforts against the Arab states'. Second, that in their view Zionism's main goal was the subjugation of the Arab peoples. Third, that Bonn's payments could 'affect relations between the German Federal Republic and the Arab states'. GDR agitprop would insist on all or some of these points from the 1950s until the mid-1980s. And, as the inflammation in Arab–Israeli relations was swelling, the early East German foreign political exploits provided an ideal laboratory in which to experiment with such claims and gauge their global potential.

By stressing its sympathy with the feeling of insecurity that the Arab delegation had expressed while in Bonn, and that Arab diplomats had uttered in public and in private at the UN and key Western capitals, East Berlin attempted to craft for itself the image of a responsible actor in world politics, whose main interest lay in the maintenance and safeguarding of peace in the Middle East and the world. And while the Arab audiences were the main targets of the East German propaganda on the restitutions' agreement, the message received some attention within Israeli circles, too. During the SED's fourth party conference, in April 1954, Mordechai Biletzki of the Israeli Communist Party (HaMiflega HaKomunistit HaYisraelit, Maki), used his speech to endorse the East German party line regarding East Berlin's approach to Israel and to bash Bonn's policy of rapprochement with the Jewish state. Biletzki stressed that the GDR, not the FRG, represented a pillar for peace in Europe. He called 'for friendship with the GDR', and warned 'against deals with the FRG':

> The powerful circles in Israel, on the orders of the American warmongers, insti-
> gate hatred against the German Democratic Republic with the argument of the
> demands for 'reparations'. But our people will not forget the historical lessons of
> the tragedy of the extermination [*strong, long, continuous applause*]. They will
> not forget that there is no better reparation or compensation for the Jewish peo-
> ple, and for all the peoples who have suffered under Nazi barbarism, than the
> impediment of a third world war; than the elimination of German Fascism and
> Nazism; than the reunification of the whole of Germany into a democratic and
> peace-loving state; than the battle of the German Democratic Republic under
> the guidance of the Socialist Unity Party of Germany [*lively applause*].[51]

Biletzki's speech was welcomed by a unanimous standing ovation – at least according to the East German accounts of the event. As his contribution showed, the SED party line regarding the East German stance on the legacy of the Nazi past, the question of post-Holocaust restitutions, and the differences between Bonn and East Berlin, had begun to reach Middle Eastern audiences – in this case, the Israeli Communist one, thanks to the ideological links between brother parties.[52] Yet, from an East German perspective, it was even more important to reach out to Arab interlocutors, to clarify where the GDR stood, especially in comparison to the FRG.

## Contacts in Moscow

The mid-1950s were characterised by important geopolitical changes, in both the Eastern and the Western bloc, ushering in a new era of European political stability. The leadership renewal in Moscow was followed by one in the White House, with Dwight D. Eisenhower starting his term in office as US President just a few weeks before Stalin's death. Eisenhower had campaigned on a tough anti-Soviet stance, promising the American voters that he would roll back Communist influence from throughout the world. However, reacting to the conciliatory message coming from the Kremlin, once in power he, too, voiced his commitment to create a 'chance for peace'.[53] A series of international conferences organised in 1954 and 1955 culminated in the July 1955 Geneva summit that, for the first time since Potsdam, reunited the Soviet, American, British and French leaders, raising hopes of a durable thaw in the superpowers' rela-tions.[54] Such hopes, however, were not destined to last. Throughout the first half of the 1950s, despite paying lip service to their commitment to reunite Germany, both super-powers granted their respective German satellite greater sovereign powers. The Soviet Union, on 25 March 1954, declared that 'the German Democratic Republic shall be free to decide on internal and external affairs … at its discretion'.[55] The Soviets would retain the functions relevant to guaranteeing security in the German Democratic

Republic, but the figure of the High Commissioner would be abolished. Meanwhile, after the entering into force of the 1954 Paris Treaties, in May 1955 the FRG became a full member of the North Atlantic Treaty Organization (NATO). Nine days later, the Soviet Union announced the establishment of a multilateral 'friendship, cooperation, and mutual assistance' framework among Soviet bloc countries, which later became known as the Warsaw Pact. The GDR was invited to join the Pact as a founding member, entering the Soviet security architecture en par with other countries of the Eastern bloc – at least on paper.[56]

Given the two Germanys' progress towards national sovereignty and the renewed superpower contacts about the future of the German question, which spread rumours of a possible upcoming German reunification, both Arab and Israeli diplomats reached out to East and West German representatives to discuss what would happen to the German reparations to Israel should the two Germanys cease to exist and be reunited as one country.[57] Thus, during a meeting in Stockholm, GDR deputy Foreign Minister Georg U. Handtke, reassured a Syrian colleague, reminding him that the GDR had been against the question of reparations well before the agreement between Bonn and Israel was even signed – and promised that East Berlin would remain adamant on the matter even in the eventuality of a German reunification.[58] A united Germany on East German terms, Handtke underscored, meant a Germany that would be free from economic obligations towards Israel, and friendly towards the Arab states.

Worried by such rumours, Ambassador Eliashiv booked a table at one of the best restaurants in Moscow, the Prague, specifically for the resumption of talks with the East German authorities about possible reparations negotiations with them. The invitation for lunch landed on the desk of Christoph Seitz, chargé d'affaires of the East German embassy in Moscow who, baffled by the Israeli note, turned to both East Berlin and Moscow for help. Should he agree to meet the Israeli diplomat? What would he want to discuss, he wondered? The reply of Aenne Kundermann, head of the USSR Department in the East German Foreign Ministry, was not very helpful. The reason why the Israeli ambassador would want to talk with East Germany's representative was 'unknown' to the Ministry, Kundermann wrote.[59] She therefore suggested getting in touch with the Soviets for guidance, adding that in any case the East Berlin authorities expected to receive a 'detailed' report of the meeting, to be sent 'immediately' after its conclusion.[60] Seitz did as he had been instructed and soon got in touch with the Soviet Foreign Ministry. There, he received Semyonov's encouragement to meet with the Israeli Ambassador. Semyonov rightly predicted that the Israelis would probably want to discuss, once again, the issue of restitutions, and gave the green light for the Seitz–Eliashiv meeting to go ahead.[61] When the lunch between the East German and the Israeli diplomat finally took place, Seitz did as Kundermann had instructed. He did not comment at all about the question of restitutions other than to say that he would pass on the message to his Ministry. After leaving Eliashiv, he swiftly sent a report of the meeting to East Berlin – detailed to the point of including what, and how much of each, the two diplomats had consumed at the restaurant.[62] Coffee and cigarettes, mainly, while most of the wonderful food that lay on the table of the Prague remained untouched.

## East Berlin's Nasserist dream

By 1955, Nasser had affirmed himself as a leading political figure in Egypt as well as in the Arab and non-aligned world. At home, he had emerged victorious from the internal rivalries among Egypt's Free Officers, becoming the country's uncontested leader. His references to the problems of the Egyptian people as problems of the Arab peoples, and his emphatic support for the Palestinian cause, allowed him to attract the admiration not only of much of the Egyptian population, but of large sections of Arab public opinion, too.[63]

Nasser's increasing popularity in the Arab world went hand in hand with his ambition to project his leadership beyond Egypt's borders, and to counter the Western presence and influence in the area. In early 1955, he rebuked the invitation to join a British-American initiative to build a Western-sponsored military alliance in the region, the Middle East Treaty Organization (also known as the Baghdad Pact), distancing himself from its founding members, Turkey and Iraq. Nasser's rebuttal of the Pact and his refusal to follow the Western countries' initiatives earned him respect and popularity amongst the masses of the postcolonial Arab world – even though conservative Arab regimes, such as those in Iraq and Saudi Arabia, were extremely wary of his political moves and disapproved of his regional leadership ambitions. In the West, the Eisenhower administration and the Eden government looked at Nasser's political dynamism with increasing dislike.[64]

But Nasser's appeal grew ever stronger throughout the non-aligned world. In April 1955, the Egyptian leader had established himself as one of the dominant personalities at the Bandung Conference, a meeting of twenty-nine heads of state and government from Asian and African countries, which took place in Indonesia and aimed to set forth the creation of a non-aligned bloc of Third World states, aiming to transcend the sternness and limitations imposed by the bipolar Cold War system.[65] US Secretary of State John Foster Dulles remarked that, under the current international political climate, claiming neutrality was an 'immoral' policy.[66] Yet Nasser's presence at Bandung, and his contribution to laying the grounds for the eventual creation of the Non-Aligned Movement, allowed him to project his political allure onto the international stage. In the autumn of 1955, the announcement that Egypt had reached an arms procurement agreement with Czechoslovakia only added to Nasser's magnetism. Coming in the wake of Western refusals to sell weapons to Egypt, the Czech–Egyptian deal nullified the efforts of the US–British–French Near East Arms Coordinating Committee that had attempted to control the flow of weapons to the region following the first Arab–Israeli war, and threatened to tilt the military balance in Egypt's favour.[67] The deal further signalled that the Western position in the region was potentially at risk, and that the Soviets and their satellite countries could and would militarily and economically penetrate the Middle East if given the chance to do so. The West German secret services (Bundesnachrichtendienst, BND) suspected that the Czech–Egyptian arms deal contained a secret clause binding Cairo to diplomatically recognise East Berlin.[68] This suspicion was unfounded – the East German leadership was in fact appalled by the Soviets' decision to push Czechoslovakia, rather than the GDR, to provide weapons to Nasser. However, from the West German perspective the fear of an impending Egyptian diplomatic recognition of the GDR was increased by the fact that the East German government had, in the meantime, managed to: conclude trade agreements with Lebanon (1953) and Syria (1955), and a payments agreement with Sudan (1955); and establish a permanent trade mission in Egypt (1954).[69]

East German propaganda emphatically claimed that these developments showed that West German threats to third countries made 'obviously little impression abroad'.[70] It was an overstatement to claim, as East German propaganda did, that by the end of 1956 Nasser would recognise the existence of two German states.[71] Nonetheless, the treaties that East German representatives signed in the Middle East between 1953 and 1955 did represent a remarkable success for the GDR in international affairs.[72] Then, in late October 1955, Cairo welcomed with open arms an East German delegation headed by Trade Minister Heinrich Rau. The two parties agreed to a series of economic deals, as well as to exchange trade missions – to the disdain of the FRG.[73] Weeks of open and covert West German–Egyptian bickering followed, and the mutual recriminations reached a peak as the Bonn government decided to recall its ambassador, Walter Becker. At which point, however, Nasser blinked.[74] He granted an interview to one of the main West German newspapers, the *Frankfurter Allgemeine Zeitung*, in which he stated that Egypt had no intention to recognise the GDR, nor to establish consular relations with East Berlin. The West Germans, relieved, sent Becker back to Cairo while, unsurprisingly, Ulbricht was furious – and he took out his rage on the man who had been so close to scoring a huge tactical victory for the GDR in Egypt, Trade Minister Rau.[75]

Ulbricht's frustration was so great that the Soviet ambassador to the GDR, Georgy Pushkin, tried to mediate between the two – and he took Rau's side. During a meeting in East Berlin, Pushkin confirmed that all that Rau had claimed about the Egyptian readiness to open a trade mission in East Berlin stemmed from Nasser's own words. And although 'of course one cannot call Nasser a liar in public', the East Germans should wait for the opportune moment to remind the Egyptian leader of the promises he had made to the GDR.[76] More broadly, Pushkin exhorted Ulbricht to slow down the East German quest for international recognition – in the Middle East and elsewhere. He emphasised how dangerous the policy of using the springboard of economic relations to jump to diplomatic recognition could be.[77] Instead, Pushkin highlighted, this would only result in ensuing 'Western countermeasures', without bringing any geostrategic advantage to the Soviet bloc. The dispute between Ulbricht and Rau thus ended up as a quarrel between Ulbricht and his Soviet masters who, in 1955, did not approve of his 'overeager' foreign policy ambitions.[78] The message, however, would not echo in Ulbricht's ears for long.

## West German–Israeli relations and the GDR recognition problem

Throughout the first half of the 1950s, Bonn's astounding progress towards full national sovereignty continued and the economic situation kept improving. In 1953, Adenauer was re-elected Chancellor. After the difficult moments that the West Germans and the

Israelis had gone through in the lead up to the ratification of the restitutions agreement, the ties between the FRG and Israel increasingly strengthened. And, while the decision taken by Finance Minister Schäffer in 1954 to reduce the amount of the yearly transfers to Israel to the lowest possible sum was met with widespread criticism in Israel, it soon became clear that the West German economy would indeed have been able to fulfil the terms of the agreement.[79] In 1955, for the third consecutive time, the Israel Mission in Cologne suggested an economic deal to Bonn; one that was based upon pure commercial interests and was not connected to the reparations agreement. Meanwhile, the West German deliveries of goods carried out within the framework of the 1952 agreement proved crucial to Israeli economic stability and, in turn, they also acted as a small-scale public works programme for Bonn, boosting industrial activity, and contributing to the reduction in West German levels of unemployment.[80]

Not all was easy, of course. As the first (West) German goods started to arrive in Israel, French intelligence services warned their German and American counterparts that Jewish terrorist organisations in loco planned to carry out attacks against German ships and crews.[81] However, gradually Israeli public opinion towards the FRG began to change. In February 1954, the British Embassy in Tel Aviv reported that the 'bitterness and the extent of opposition to dealings with Germany' in the country had 'faded'.[82] While the arrival of the cargoes and goods from Germany also evoked painful memories in much of the Israeli population,[83] as a member of the Israeli Communist Party would later put it to an East German comrade railing against 'Bonn's foreign propaganda' and its successes in Israel: 'Financial, material reparations do play a role among the masses whose life standard is not the highest.'[84] Increasingly, German Jews who had migrated to Palestine to escape Nazi persecution began considering going back to Germany and Israeli applications to migrate to West Germany increased significantly in the first half of the 1950s. In Cologne, for example, Israelis were five times more numerous than any other nationality group of foreign applicants. The case of Cologne was exceptional because the Israeli purchasing mission was based there, but still, as the West German Interior Ministry noted, the increment of Israeli immigrants to Germany in general was noteworthy in its pace and volume.[85]

The rapprochement between the Federal Republic and Israel, spurred by the exchanges relating to the implementation of the reparations agreement, was also encouraged by the Israeli political and diplomatic establishments, as a way to push back against the increasing isolation faced by the Jewish state.[86] In the region, although the armistices signed in 1949 between Israel and its Arab neighbours remained in place, political violence continued to be the main feature of the relations between Israel and the Arab countries. Cross-border skirmishes, featuring violent incursions into Israeli territory from Lebanon, Syria, Jordan and Egypt, and severe Israeli military retaliations, fed a spiral of violence that would soon escalate into another full-out war.[87] At the international level, the arrival of President Eisenhower in the White House had translated into a new American approach to the region – one that attempted to rebalance the US policy vis-à-vis the Middle East by distancing itself from Israel.[88] The increasing Israeli isolation in the diplomatic arena stood in stark contrast to the constant improvement of the West German position in international affairs. As the

*Jewish Observer* put it in May 1955, by that point Israel would not be able to ignore the 'German factor' in world politics for much longer.[89]

Yet the push to assess the feasibility of the exchange of diplomatic representations between the two countries did not stem only from Israel's desire to counter its increasing isolation in international politics. Practical concerns related to the diplomatic representations of the Federal Republic abroad played a role, too. In 1955 the General Treaty (*Deutschlandvertrag*) came into force. With it, the Western allies recognised the FRG as a sovereign state – one that could conduct its own foreign policy and open its own embassies abroad. The British Consulate in Haifa, which had been carrying out most of the work related to the West German interests in Israel, began hoping to reduce its workload. In a communication to the newly established German Foreign Office, the London Haifa Consulate let them know that their work on behalf of the Germans kept increasing; 'We wish to be rid of this commitment as soon as it can be arranged', was the unequivocal request coming from Haifa.[90] Bonn's Foreign Ministry circulated a request to its diplomats scattered around the region, asking them to express their views on whether the FRG and Israel should establish diplomatic ties.[91] In a conversation with the head of the Israel Mission in Cologne, Felix Shinnar, Foreign Minister Brentano claimed that establishing diplomatic relations with Israel was a goal that he had had in mind from the beginning of his term in office – he knew that this would be a delicate process, especially given Arab pressure on West Germany, but promised that he would 'lay the groundwork and advance step by step'.[92] Shinnar came away from the meeting with the impression that it would be possible to finalise the relevant details within just a couple of weeks, and that a West German diplomatic delegation would be on its way to Israel in a few months.[93] Shortly thereafter, the Foreign Ministry in Jerusalem decided that newly issued Israeli passports would no longer include the line 'valid for all countries except for Germany'. And, with the preparations for the exchange of official diplomatic relations with Austria and Italy underway, it really seemed like Israel's position in Europe was gaining traction, and that relations with Bonn would soon follow suit.[94]

Yet many of the respondents to the Foreign Ministry query on the question invited Bonn to exercise utmost caution. Among the most vocal proponents of such prudence was a long-standing authority on Middle Eastern matters: Wilhelm Melchers. Entering the diplomatic service in 1925 and becoming the director of its Near East Department in 1939 – a post he retained until the end of the war, in 1945 – Melchers had returned to his diplomatic activities in 1951, this time on behalf of the Federal government. In 1955, he replied to the Foreign Ministry inquiry in his triple capacity as Bonn's ambassador in Iraq, head of the legation in Jordan, and the diplomat responsible for questions concerning Israel. His assessment of the situation included many points of warning and ended by hinting at one particularly thorny issue: that the GDR could make potential advances in the Middle East as a consequence of the strengthening of the West German–Israeli ties. Melchers highlighted that it was 'very likely' that in the eventuality of an exchange of ambassadors between Israel and the FRG the Arab states would no longer feel obligated to respect their promise not to establish diplomatic relations with the GDR.[95] West German representatives had, time and again, stressed to their Arab counterparts that Bonn would tolerate neither the establishment of diplomatic relations nor the exchange of commercial or consular representations between the Arab states and East Berlin, Melchers noted. Therefore, he argued, Bonn had to draw its own conclusions regarding what would happen if the Federal Republic established diplomatic relations with Israel. He stressed that the Arab states were still at war with Israel, and recounted the appeals, from Bonn's Arab partners, asking the FRG to withdraw from the agreement signed with the 'artificial state'[96] of Israel in 1952. The Arab states might decide to recall their representatives from Bonn, and harm West Germany's 'political, economic and cultural interests', to the advantage – Melchers pointed out – also of the British, who would thus be able to regain strategic ground in the region and enjoy the benefits deriving from Bonn's political setbacks in the Arab world. Melchers' successor as the head of the Near East Department within Bonn's Foreign Ministry was Hermann Voigt. He, too, was a veteran diplomat and he, too, advocated caution.[97] In 1955 he endorsed Melchers' view, noting that the existence of, first, the 'so-called GDR', and second, the 'Israel Agreement' were two 'conceptually dissimilar', though in fact 'interdependent', issues which restricted the West German room for manoeuvre in the Middle East.[98]

Both Voigt and Melchers would soon expand on this point, which gained traction after the West German Chancellor's first and only visit to Moscow, in September 1955. In the wake of his rise to the top of the Kremlin, Soviet leader Nikita Khrushchev had invited Adenauer to Moscow to discuss the prospects for the normalisation of relations between the Soviet Union and the Federal Republic.[99] In spite of the advice he had received from some of his closest aides, as well as the guidance coming from the US State Department, during his visit Adenauer proved that he was willing to negotiate with the Soviets. In exchange for the liberation and return to Germany of some 9,000 prisoners of war, Adenauer agreed to establish official diplomatic relations with the Soviet Union. A few days after the Chancellor's departure from Moscow, Otto Grotewohl also arrived in the USSR for an official visit. There, he signed a document declaring that relations between the Soviet Union and the GDR would now be 'based on complete equality of rights, mutual respect of sovereignty, and non-interference in domestic affairs'[100] – a move which evidently undermined Bonn's claim of being the sole representative for the whole of Germany. In order to stress the exceptionality of the case of Moscow, where from 1956 onwards two German embassies would be stationed, and to prevent other countries from establishing relations with the GDR, the West German government released a statement declaring that from then onward Bonn would interpret any recognition of the GDR as an 'unfriendly act',[101] a foreign political stance which later came to be known as the 'Hallstein Doctrine'.[102]

The Middle East had become the prime extra-European theatre for the German–German Cold War competition. In October 1955, the new West German ambassador in Cairo, Walter Becker, weighed up how much, and how rapidly, the situation in the Middle East had changed over the last couple of months. Becker recommended that the Federal Republic do all it could in order to retain its position in such a strategic area, while signalling that the ability of the Western powers to respond to the seeming expansion of Soviet influence in the Middle East was 'extraordinarily constrained especially because of their obligations towards Israel'.[103] His assessment reinforced the conclusions of some of his colleagues, and he would soon be called upon to unpack it in front of his superiors, at the upcoming 'spectacular' conference of West German diplomats in Istanbul, in April 1956.[104]

## Brainstorming in Istanbul

Bonn's very first diplomatic conference abroad was specifically organised to discuss the Middle East. The conference, which took place in Istanbul, lasted from 3 to 7 April. Its participants surveyed both country-specific issues as well as larger questions, such as that of the Soviet bloc's 'commercial offensive' in the area, or Bonn's need to coordinate its policies with those of the Western powers while keeping in mind particular West German interests.[105] The two minds behind the implementation of Bonn's strategy for the isolation of the GDR, Walter Hallstein and Wilhelm Grewe, had flown to Turkey especially for the occasion. When the conference started, the two were extremely sceptical about the arguments put forth by Melchers, Voigt and others about the existence of a correlation between the German–German and Arab–Israeli rivalries. And yet, by the time they left Istanbul, they were adamant that such a connection existed and that it could, and would, be exploited against the FRG. What made them change their mind was the insistence on the matter displayed by the *Arabisten* they met in Istanbul – as well as a perfectly timed intervention on the part of Nasser.

The conference participants agreed that Bonn's position in the Middle East presented both positive and negative elements. On the one hand, the lack of a German colonial legacy in the Middle East, as well as the fruitful contacts established by German diplomats in the Arab Middle East before 1945, constituted a strategic asset for the Federal Republic. On the other hand, they noted with displeasure how the East Germans enjoyed the same, 'German', reputation. Ambassador Becker commented that the relations with Israel constituted 'the only negative mark' (*der einzigen Schatten*) on Bonn's reputation in Egypt, where he was stationed. He highlighted that, while for the moment he foresaw no alteration in the status of East German–Egyptian relations, this could change easily as a consequence of a transformation, or any kind of upgrade, in Bonn's relations with Israel.[106] Voigt, too, spoke of a specifically West German dilemma in the region: having to choose between relations with Israel, on the one hand, and Arab recognition of the GDR on the other.[107] Not all those present agreed. Hallstein, for example, recalled that, back in 1952, 'almost all Middle East experts [had] prophesised catastrophic consequences that, however, did not materialise' and this 'rather weakens the strength of today's arguments'.[108] 'All the reasons that induced us to conclude the Luxemburg Agreement', observed Hallstein in Istanbul, 'today are of no less importance: it's about the liquidation of a difficult past'. The 'last expurgation of our guilt complex?', Becker asked. 'Yes, exactly', Hallstein confirmed.[109]

In Istanbul, the discussion about the strategic value of international reconcilia-tion with Israel versus the economic and political worth of the West German rela-tionship with the Arab states continued. Grewe highlighted that, while one could say that the Arab states were showing a 'blackmailing attitude', it remained to be seen whether they could indeed blackmail the Federal Republic.[110] West Germany's envoy in Riyadh emphasised that key states that did not have relations with the Soviet Union, such as Iraq, Syria and Saudi Arabia, would, for example, not be in a position to threaten the FRG with a recognition of its arch-enemy. Moreover, given the long-standing good relations between Israel and the Ethiopian Empire, the West German envoy in Addis Ababa suggested that establishing relations with Israel might pave the way for a prosperous entente between the FRG and some African countries such as Ethiopia, whose leader, Haile Selassie, had found refuge in Jerusalem during the Second Italo-Abyssinian War.[111] Also, during his presentation on the Soviet eco-nomic offensive in the region, the Legation Councillor of the Ministry's Middle East Department noted that the signing of the Luxembourg Agreement in 1952 did not have a negative impact on commercial relations between Bonn and the Arab coun-tries at all – despite all the threats that had been made to Bonn in the run-up to the Israel negotiations.[112]

Two days after the beginning of the conference, on 5 April 1956, the first secre-tary at the West German Embassy in Cairo cabled a worrying message to Bonn and Istanbul. President Nasser had declared that: 'If West Germany recognizes Israel and establishes diplomatic relations with it Egypt will recognize East Germany and estab-lish diplomatic relations with East Berlin.'[113] He stressed that, while Cairo had thus far refrained from recognising the GDR in the belief that 'reunification [of the] divided German people would greatly contribute to … peace [in the] world', 'recognition [of] Israel would remove our inhibitions [to recognise the GDR] as it would constitute an act unfriendly to [the] Arab nations'. The note also emphasised that 'other well-informed sources' had hinted that Syria, Saudi Arabia, Jordan, Lebanon, and possibly also Iraq, would 'follow Egypt in recognizing [the] East German People['s] Republic'. Disturbing news, which seemed to confirm the analysis that Bonn's new ambassador in Cairo, veteran diplomat Becker, was presenting to his colleagues at the conference.

Many of the diplomats stationed in the Levant firmly opposed taking the risk of establishing a West German diplomatic presence in Israel. The diplomats based in Afghanistan, Pakistan, Lebanon, Turkey, Syria and Egypt agreed that, as far as the countries they were assigned to were concerned, the reactions to the formalisation of ties between Bonn and the Jewish state would, in one form or another, turn against the FRG and in favour of the GDR. Melchers even predicted that the lives of (West) Germans stationed in Jordan would be at risk after an exchange of ambassadors between Bonn and Israel. By the end of the meeting, Hallstein too was convinced that avoiding any further formalisation of West German–Israeli ties would be the least risky course of action for Bonn's foreign policy.

Having reached this conclusion, the question now was how to communicate the FRG's new decision to the Israeli representatives. For even before the conference took place, upon learning from Brentano that Bonn was concerned about the 'massive consequences' that a 'normalisation' of relations between Bonn and Israel would have for the Federal Republic given the Arab states' possible recognition of the GDR, the head of the Israel Mission in Cologne, Felix Shinnar, had dismissed the argument as 'completely illogical'.[114]

| | |
|---|---|
| **Melchers:** | Could we not [simply] clearly explain our situation [to the Israelis]? |
| **von der Esch:** | The argument about [the fear of] endangering our reunification policy? |
| **von Trützschler:** | Or the argument about [the fear of] playing into the hands of the Soviets? |
| **State Secretary:** | [No], we cannot give in to the [Arab] blackmail [of recognising the GDR]. Instead, the argument that the establishment of diplomatic relations with Israel would give a better chance to the Soviet efforts [in the Middle East] deserves attention.[115] |

Thus, when Hallstein met Shinnar just over a month after the end of the conference, on 14 May 1956, he poured cold water on the Israeli hope that the FRG would have a diplomatic presence in the Jewish state any time soon. In accordance with what had been decided in Istanbul, he explained Bonn's stance in terms of the possible benefits that the Soviet Union would reap in the aftermath of a formalisation of the West German–Israeli ties, making no mention of the GDR.[116]

Shinnar, predictably, protested – though to no avail. He stressed that from Israel's perspective this signified the violation of a promise, and that the Germans should take full responsibility for the future of the bilateral relationship. Yet, he also seems to have taken Hallstein's reassurances at face value. In his report to the Israeli Foreign Ministry, he insisted that he had the impression, still, that a West German proposal for diplomatic relations would come within the next six months.[117] Shinnar was dead wrong – and Sharett, either way, was furious. The Foreign Minister's initial openness to having relations with the Federal Republic had been crucial to pave the way to strengthen the bilateral ties, and now he looked like a fool within his own Ministry. Outraged by the sudden West German volte-face, he announced a pervasive, low-key freeze in the relations with the Germans: all Israeli diplomats abroad were instructed not to respond to invitations from representatives of the Federal Republic, nor to strike up, or respond to, conversations with West German diplomats in third countries. If some kind of interaction was unavoidable, then they should just mention that in Israel the overall impression was that the FRG was not interested in having relations with the Jewish state – a message that should be discussed with common partners, too, so that they would, in turn, question German representatives about Bonn's bizarre behaviour.[118] Sharett's frustration notwithstanding, after the meeting of veteran diplomats in Istanbul the relationship between the Federal Republic and Israel had morphed, in the West German imagination, into a Cold War liability – something that could and would be exploited by the Arabs and the East Germans to take away from the FRG the small victories that, up to that point, Bonn had laboriously managed to score in international affairs.

## Dreaming big in East Berlin

Meanwhile, in February 1956, the GDR ambassadors stationed abroad gathered in East Berlin to discuss the future directions of East German foreign policy. This was not the first meeting of its kind. East German representatives stationed in other Socialist countries had already begun sharing their experiences within structured talks in 1950.[119] However, the 1956 gathering was substantially different in at least one respect: the emphasis put by the highest echelons of the East German state on the importance of worldwide recognition of the GDR, with special attention to Third World countries. According to Ulbricht and Grotewohl, and in stark dissonance with what the Soviet authorities were suggesting, the time had come to dream big in East Berlin. Addressing his ambassadors at the beginning of the conference, Ulbricht highlighted the importance of attaining international recognition from as many states as possible. If outright recognition was not feasible, Ulbricht emphasised, the diplomats' task would become to 'at least pave the way' towards the construction of 'normal relations'.[120] Second, and closely related to the first point, Ulbricht stressed the goal of establishing and developing solid economic ties with interested countries – especially those hesitant, for the time being, to exchange diplomatic representatives with East Berlin. The tasks envisioned by Grotewohl were equally ambitious. Boasting about the GDR's allure in international politics, he stressed that East Berlin had a crucial job ahead: within the next five years the East German state needed to achieve such an enviable level of economic and political stability so as to make it clear 'for each worker in the world' that only the Socialist camp presented the working people with a viable, bright future. He ended with an appeal to continue 'keeping the initiative, keeping abreast of the offensive' so as to not give 'the enemy' the opportunity to put East Berlin on the defensive.

Grotewohl's message was met with disillusion by most of the attendees. Sepp (Max Joseph) Schwab, ambassador to Hungary, lamented the 'lack of courage' that, in his view, characterised the GDR's foreign policy, as well as its 'inability to exploit the possibilities at hand'. Werner Eggerath, East German ambassador to Romania, claimed that, when stationed abroad, he knew very little of the SED's 'general political line and its application to certain specific points'. Johannes König, the GDR's ambassador to Moscow, was even more indignant. He lamented the lack of 'authority' of the East German Foreign Ministry in comparison to that of other countries of the Socialist Bloc. He deemed that the other ministries ('and not just the Ministries!') crucially underestimated the importance of the foreign service and of the diplomats stationed abroad. König highlighted that a fundamental lack of information about what went on in East Berlin between the GDR and the countries the East German diplomats were stationed in rendered the job even more complicated. And the lack of information that the diplomats had about the activities of the FRG was, in his view, *eine Schande* – 'a disgrace'. König also shared with his colleagues a depressing experience he had recently gone through. In Moscow, he had had the chance to meet with Cairo's ambassador to the Soviet Union. König had greeted the Egyptian colleague with enthusiasm, anticipating the day when the GDR would eventually substitute completely for the FRG in its economic exchanges with Cairo. Yet his excitement was abruptly interrupted by the question: 'Can you [really] take upon yourselves the obligations that the West Germans have towards us?' It was clear, König concluded, that 'our own economic strength plays a decisive role in our relations with these countries [and in] the question of the recognition of the GDR'. East Germany still had a lot of work to do if it wanted to appear as strong, and credible, in the eyes of its potential Arab partners. Given the East German ambition to forge ever closer ties with the countries of the Arab Middle East, it was perhaps to be expected that the contacts between East German and Israeli diplomats in Moscow, which had resumed after Stalin's death, would remain fruitless.

## Enter Avidar

East German–Israeli exchanges continued throughout the first half of 1956, with the Israelis insisting on the question of restitutions. On 20 April, Ambassador König met his newly appointed Israeli colleague, Yosef Avidar, who had succeeded Eliashiv after a deterioration in the old ambassador's health. A founding member of the paramilitary organisation of the Zionist movement, the *Haganah*, who lost his right hand while handling a grenade in 1931, Colonel-turned-Ambassador Avidar was not one to buy the East German delusions about their alleged extraneousness to the Nazi past without putting up a good fight. With his East German colleague, he brought up again the inconsistency between a West German state engaging in restitutions talks with Israel, and an East German state – allegedly antifascist – that did not want to confront its own past. In the course of the conversation, Avidar repeatedly reminded the East German Ambassador that 'crimes against the Jews took place in all parts of Germany' – something that, notwithstanding what the SED regime insisted he argue in front of his Israeli counterpart, König had reasons to be aware of. His late wife was Jewish. Their house was wrecked and vandalised during the *Kristallnacht*. Long-standing Communists, they both had been arrested several times by the Gestapo, until they managed to flee the country, in 1938, relocating together to China. Yet, when Avidar communicated his government's intention to begin 'direct negotiations' to reach an agreement that 'would earn for the GDR the appreciation of Jews throughout the world', König calmly explained to his Israeli colleague that this would not happen, and that there was simply no need for East German payments to Israel, because: 'There are two German states, whose developments have unfolded in completely different directions ... One could say that West Germany succeeded fascist Germany. People ... who participated in the creation of the Nuremberg laws and in the murder of many thousands of Jews, today occupy key positions in the Adenauer government. In the GDR, on the contrary ... fascism was eradicated.'[121] König's reply was in line with the previous East German responses on the matter, highlighting the differences between East and West Germany and stressing that, while West Germany was the successor state to Nazi Germany, East Germany was not. To his Israeli interlocutor, the East German ambassador emphasised that having rendered a resurgence of the past impossible, and having eradicated from positions of power the people who had supported the Nazi dictatorship, per se represented the best of all possible reparations that the GDR could make to the Jewish state.

Though much of the East German message was spread via propaganda channels, the record of the conversation between König and Avidar shows that diplomatic meetings, too, were crucial forums to push the message forward. GDR representatives could use such occasions to construct and articulate the East German delusion regarding their alleged complete lack of involvement with the criminal policies that had been put in place in the name of Germany during the Hitler era. The repression of the Jewish question in the GDR, and the denunciation of the many legacies of Nazism in the FRG, were not simply the defining features of a national identity engineered to exonerate the domestic public – they also underpinned the image of the GDR that the SED elites aimed to project internationally.

Avidar gave his East German colleague another aide-memoire, and the meeting ended with König's reassurances that he would notify the East German Foreign Ministry about the document, which he also forwarded to Moscow.[122] Two weeks later, *Neues Deutschland* forcefully denied rumours that East Germany might be anywhere near establishing official relations with Israel, and, in July 1956, the East German Foreign Ministry put together an official response to the Israeli aide-memoire, basically reiterating the message contained in earlier notes – no negotiations, no restitutions.[123] The document was delivered to the Israeli diplomatic personnel in Moscow during a short and impersonal meeting on 9 July 1956.[124] The authorities in East Berlin also rejected Israeli requests of material for the Israeli national library and other museums from the GDR about the history of German Jewry, for fear that these might be used 'for nationalistic propaganda purposes' against states of the Arab Middle East, to whom the East German regime was much more interested in getting close.[125]

From 1953 to the summer of 1956, the official East and West German policies towards Israel aimed to delineate each Germany's new political identity, expanding the respective room for manoeuvre in international affairs – while preferably also limiting that of the other German rival. Among East German circles, it was not only the celebration of 'awkward anniversaries', the construction of contested memorials, and the spread of partisan historiographies that displayed and diffused the GDR's new political identity.[126] Diplomatic encounters, too, were crucial to the redefinition, testing, and reiteration of the party line on the difference between the Germany of the past, the Germany in the West, and the German Democratic Republic in the East. The West German *Arabisten*'s ability to persuade German foreign policy framers that a connection between the German–German Cold War and *Israelpolitik* existed, also testifies to just how malleable the concept of a rigid Cold War system was, in either Germany. It emphasises how issues that originally had little to do with the Cold War, such as postwar German–Israeli relations sparked by the Israeli request to receive compensation for Nazi crimes against the Jews, could be cast as crucially interwoven with it.[127] And in the Middle East, the intensifying intra-Arab rivalries and mounting Arab–Israeli enmities foreshadowed further complications along the way. 'Believe me, Mr Steffen', had warned a Lebanese official in an informal talk with a West German colleague, 'If I may say so among friends, here in the Federal Republic you do not have the slightest idea of what a startling reason for hostility against you, you have given the Arab countries with the Israel Agreement.'[128]

# Notes

1 AAPD, 1953, Vol. 1, Doc. 41, Hallstein to Westrick, 29 January 1953. Adenauer, too, very much hoped it would succeed. See: Doc. 307, Adenauer to Brentano, 12 December 23 1952, in: *Briefe 1951–1953* edited by H. P. Mensig (Berlin: Siedler, 1987).

2 AAPD, 1953, Vol. 1, Doc. 50, Allardt to Blankenhorn, 5 February 1953. A full list of the participants is in: PA AA, B150/183.

3 NARA, RG 59, Box 2966, Caffery (Cairo) to the State Department, 9 February 1953.

4 NARA, RG 59, Box 2966, Telegram Conant (Bonn) to Secretary of State, 12 February 1953.

5 AAPD, 1953, Vol. 1, Doc. 57, Westrick to Hallstein, 10 February 1953.

6 See W. G. Gray, *Germany's Cold War: The Global Campaign to Siolate East Germany* (Chapel Hill: University of North Carolina, 2003), p. 20.

7 *ND*, 'Unsere Außenhandelspolitik im Dienste des Friedens', 31 March 1953, p. 2.

8 Quoted in W. G. Schwanitz, *Deutsche im Nahost 1946–1965* (Habilitation Thesis, Freie Universität Berlin, 1998), p. 171, fn. 43.

9 PA AA, MfAA A 9286, Vizeaußenminister Borek zu Agypten-DDR. Bringmann, 18 December 1952.

10 Reprinted in Schwanitz, *Deutsche im Nahost 1946–1965*, p. 117.

11 *Ibid.*

12 Instead, the East German press referred to 'earlier talks' that had taken place in Berlin. Contrast *ND*, 'Handelsdelegation der DDR in Kairo', 11 February 1953, p. 1. with PA AA, B10/1686, Pawelke and Westrick to Hallstein, 11 February 1953.

13 AAPD 1952, Doc. 253, Pawelke to the Foreign Office, 30 December 1952.

14 Gray, *Germany's Cold War*, p. 20.

15 'Kanonen nach Kairo', *Der Spiegel*, 18 February 1953, p. 15.

16 'Zum Handelsabkommen der DDR mit Ägypten', *ND*, 15 March 1953, p. 2.

17 BAL, DL 2, 5717/51, Report on trade relations between the GDR and the Arab states, n.d.

18 'Regierungsdelegation aus Kairo zurückgekehrt', *Berliner Zeitung*, 12 March 1953, p. 1.

19 'Ägyptische Abteling der Staatlichen Museen wiedereröffnet', *ND*, 13 March 1953, p. 4.

20 The Social Democrats voted *en bloc* for the ratification, in contrast to only 104 of the 214 members of the ruling coalition parties.

21 B. Apor, *The Invisible Shining: The Cult of Mátyás Rákosi in Stalinist Hungary* (Budapest: Central European University, 2017).

22 T. C. Fox, *Stated Memory: East Germany and the Holocaust* (Rochester: Camden House, 1999); M. Wolfgram, *Getting History Right: East German Collective Memories of the Holocaust and the War* (Lewisburg: Bucknell University Press, 2011).

23 Herf, *Divided Memory*, pp. 187–9; J. Herf, '"At War with Israel": East Germany's Key Role in Soviet Policy in the Middle East', *Journal of Cold War Studies* 16:3 (2014).

24 M. Kotik, *The Prague Trial: The First Anti-Zionist Show Trial in the Communist Bloc* (New York: Herzl Press/Cornwell Books, 1987).

25 Herf, *Divided Memory*, p. 132ff.

26 J. Brent and V. P. Naumov, *Stalin's Last Crime: The Plot against the Jewish Doctors, 1948–1953* (New York: HarperCollins, 2003).

27 Herf, *Divided Memory*, p. 133.

28 K. Hartewig, 'Die Loyalitätsfälle – jüdische Kommunisten in der DDR' in M. Zuckermann (ed.), *Zwischen Politik und Kultur: Juden in der DDR* (Göttingen: Wallstein Verlag, 2012), p. 58.

29  Timm, *Hammer, Zirkel, Davidstern*, pp. 98ff.
30  See, e.g., A. Weigelt and H. Simon (eds), *Zwischen Bleiben und Gehen: Juden in Ostdeutschland 1945 bis 1956, zehn Biographien* (Berlin: Text, 2008), pp. 111ff.
31  G. Krauss, 'Die zionistische Agentur des USA-Imperialismus', *ND*, 6 December 1952, p. 7.
32  R. Herrnstadt, 'Wiedergutmachung – für wen?', *ND*, 25 November 1952, p. 1.
33  A. Timm, 'The Image of Jews and the State of Israel in Eastern Bloc Media', in Tudor Parfitt and Yulia Egorava (eds), *Jews, Muslims, and the Mass Media: Mediating the Other* (London and New York: Routledge Curzon, 2004), p. 125.
34  'Den Zionismus entschieden bekämpfen!', *ND*, 10 February 1953, p. 5.
35  Timm, 'The Image of the Jews', p. 121; see also J. Herf (ed.), *Anti-Semitism and Anti-Zionism in Historical Perspective: Convergence and Divergence* (London: Routledge, 2007).
36  G. Krauss, 'Die zionistische Agentur des USA-Imperialismus', *ND*, 6 December 1952, p. 7.
37  'Größte Synagoge Deutschlands in Berlin eingeweiht', *ND*, 1 September 1953, p. 6; 'Jetzt alle Jugendlichen für den Frieden gewinnen!', *ND*, 22 August 1951, p. 1.
38  This remained the case well beyond the 1950s, e.g. CJA 5B1/211/1, Rede des Vizepräsidenten des Verbandes der Jüdische Gemeinden in der DDR auf der internationalen Pressekonferenz am 20 February 1967.
39  V. Stern, 'Den Zionismus entschieden bekämpfen!', *ND*, 10 February 1953, p. 5.
40  '8,2 Miliarden D-Mark könnten für die Werktätigen verwendet warden', *ND*, 23 August 1953, p. 2; 'Remilitarisierungsmaschine auf Hochtouren', *ND*, 9 September 1953, p. 2.
41  E. Noelle and E. P. Neumann, *The Germans: Public Opinion Polls 1947–1966* (Allensbach and Bonn: Verlag für Demoskopie, 1967), p. 188.
42  Tooze, 'Reassessing the Moral Economy', p. 54.
43  See, e.g., H. Timmermann (ed.), *Juni 1953 in Deutschland: Der Aufstand im Fadenkreuz von Kalten Krieg, Katastrophe und Katharsis* (Munster: LIT, 2003); C. Ostermann, 'The United States, the East German Uprising of 1953, and the Limits of Rollback', *Cold War International History Project (CWIHP), Working Paper No. 11* (Washington, DC: Woodrow Wilson International Center, 2003).
44  CIA Report: 'Resignation of Malenkov', 12 September 1955, CIA (CREST/FOIA), www.cia.gov/library/readingroom/docs/caesar-12.pdf [Accessed November 2019].
45  Y. Ro'I, *Soviet Decision-Making in Practice: The USSR and Israel, 1947–1954* (New Brunswick: Transaction Books, 1980), p. 470.
46  J. Granville, 'Ulbricht in October 1956: Survival of the *Spitzbart* during Destalinization', *Journal of Contemporary History* 41:3 (2006), p. 481.
47  Quoted in M. Frank, *Walter Ulbricht: Eine deutsche Biographie* (Berlin: Siedler, 2001), p. 241.
48  H. Wentker, *Außenpolitik in engen Grenzen. Die DDR im internationalen System 1949–1989* (Munich: Oldenbourg, 2007), p. 121.
49  BAL- SAPMO, NL Grotewohl NY 4090/ 495: Memorandum submitted by the Government of Syria to the Government of the Federal Republic of Germany on reparations to Israel, 17 November 1952.
50  *Ibid.*
51  Italics in the original. 'Begrüßungen der Bruderparteien an den IV. Parteitag der SED: Genosse Dr Mordkhai Biletzki, Mitglied des ZK der KPI Israels', *ND*, 8 April 1954, p. 6.

52 'Begrüßungen der Bruderparteien an den IV. Parteitag der SED: Genosse Dr Mordkhai Biletzki, Mitglied des ZK der KPI Israels', *ND*, 8 April 1954, p. 6.

53 D. D. Eisenhower, '"Chance for Peace" Address Delivered Before the American Society of Newspaper Editors', 16 April 1953, www.eisenhowerlibrary.gov/sites/default/files/file/chance_for_peace.pdf [Accessed November 2019].

54 G. Bischof and S. Dockrill (eds), *Cold War Respite: The Geneva Summit of 1955* (Baton Rouge: Louisiana University Press, 2000).

55 'Statement by the Government of the German Democratic Republic Concerning Sovereignty', 27 March 1954 in B. Ruhm von Oppen (ed.), *Documents on Germany Under Occupation, 1945–1954* (Oxford: Oxford University Press, 1955), p. 597; 'Statement by the Council of Ministers of the USSR on the Repeal of Soviet Military Administration and Soviet Control Commission Legislation', 6 August 1954, in *ibid.*, p. 600.

56 M. M. V. Byrne and M. Klotzbach, *A Cardboard Castle? An Inside History of the Warsaw Pact, 1955–1991* (Budapest: CEU Press, 2005); L. Crump, *The Warsaw Pact Reconsidered: International Relations in Eastern Europe, 1955–1969* (London: Routledge, 2015).

57 Y. Govrin, *Israel-Soviet Relations 1953–1967: From Confrontation to Disruption* (London: Frank Cass, 1998).

58 PA AA, MfAA A 682/2, Notes on a conversation with the minister plenipotentiary and envoy extraordinary Minister of the Republic of Syria in Sweden, Mr Farra, Handtke, 11 February 1954.

59 PA AA, MfAA A 682/4, Kundermann to Seitz, 25 July 1955.

60 *Ibid.*

61 PA AA, MfAA A 682/3, Memorandum of the conversation in the 3rd European Department of the Ministry of Foreign Affairs of the USSR. Seitz, 27 July 1955. On the same day Seitz wrote to the Foreign Ministry in East Berlin regarding the same issue, PA AA, MfAA 13364/45 Note, Seitz, 27 July 1955.

62 PA AA, MfAA A 682/5, GDR Embassy Moscow. Memorandum of a conversation with the Israeli ambassador S. Eljiashiv, Seitz, 3 August 1955.

63 J. Lacouture, *Nasser: A Biography* (New York: A. A. Knopf, 1973); A. Alexander, *Nasser: His LIfe and Times* (London: Haus, 2004).

64 S. Yaqub, *Containing Arab Nationalism: The Eisenhower Doctrine and the Middle East* (Chapel Hill: University of North Carolina Press, 2004).

65 The Non-Aligned Movement was formally founded in 1961, but the 1955 Bandung Conference represented a major stepping stone in this process. See, for example, N. Mišković, H. Fischer-Tiné and N. Boškovska (eds), *The Non-Aligned Movement and the Cold War: Delhi – Bandung – Belgrade* (London: Routledge, 2014).

66 R. B. Rakove, *Kennedy, Johnson and the Nonaligned World* (New York: Cambridge University Press, 2013), pp. 10–11.

67 G. Laron, 'Cutting the Gordian Knot: The Post-WWII Egyptian Quest for Arms and the 1955 Czechoslovak Arms Deal', *CWIHP Working Paper* No. 55 (2007).

68 Gray, *Germany's Cold War*, p. 257.

69 The Egyptians, however, did not open their GDR consulate until three years later.

70 'Minister Rau im Außenministerium Indiens', *ND*, 5 November 1955, p. 1.

71 'Vom ganzem Herzen Glück … ', *Freies Volk*, 1 August 1956.

72 S. Wippel, *Die Außenwirtschaftsbeziehungen der DDR zum Nahen Osten* (Berlin: das Arabische Buch, 1996), p. 17.

73 PA AA, B11 381, West German Embassy in Cairo to Federal Foreign Ministry in Bonn. 'Establishment of diplomatic relations between Egypt and the Soviet Occupation Zone', Mirbach, 7 January 1955.

74 Gray, *Germany's Cold War*, p. 53.

75 BAK, B 206/614, Intelligence Report: Disagreements between Ulbricht and Rau, 29 December 1955.

76 PA AA, B12 238, Memo: 'Controversies in the so-called GDR about the question of international recognition', Voigt, 7 January 1956.

77 BAK, B 206/614, Intelligence Report: Disagreements between Ulbricht and Rau, 29 December 1955.

78 PA AA, B12 238, Memo: 'Controversies in the so-called GDR about the question of international recognition', Voigt, 7 January 1956.

79 To DM 250 million instead of DM 310 million. Balabkins, *West German Reparations to Israel*, p. 174.

80 *Ibid.*, p. 189.

81 NARA, RG 59 Box 2,966, Foreign Service Dispatch, George L. West Jr. (Bonn), 24 March 1953.

82 BNA, PRO, FO 371/111063, A. R. Moore (Tel Aviv) to A. Eden, 16 February 1954.

83 See, for example, Amos Oz's recollection of his first journey made aboard a German train in Israel, in A. Oz, *Israel und Deutschland. Vierzig Jahre nach Aufnahme diplomatischer Beziehungen* (Bonn: Bundeszentrale für politische Bildung, 2005), p. 13.

84 PA AA, MfAA A 11926, Memorandum of conversation with the foreign policy editor of 'KolHaHaam', Tel Aviv. Heilmann, 4 November 1960.

85 PA AA, B12 1018, Report: Federal Ministry of the Interior on repatriation applications from Israel, 7 December 1956.

86 Jelinek, *Deutschland und Israel*, p. 268ff.

87 B. Morris, *Israel's Border Wars: Arab Infiltration, Israeli Retaliation, and the Countdown to the Suez War* (Oxford: Clarendon Press, 1993).

88 P. Hahn, *Caught in the Middle East: US Policy Towards the Arab-Israeli Conflict, 1945–1961* (Chapel Hill: University of North Carolina Press, 2004), p. 164; Yaqub, *Containing Arab Nationalism.*

89 'The Return of Germany', *Jewish Observer and Middle East Review*, 13 May 1955, p. 8.

90 PRO, FO 371/115819, 16 May 1955.

91 See Hansen, *Aus dem Schatten der Katastrophe*, p. 367; F. E. Shinnar, *Bericht eines Beauftragten: die deutsch-israelischen Beziehungen 1951–1966* (Tübingen: R. Wunderlich, 1967), p. 112; R. Stauber, 'The Israel Ministry of Foreign Affairs and the Debate over the Establishment of Diplomatic Relations with Germany 1953–1955', *Yad Vashem Studies* 37:2 (2009), pp. 153–95.

92 DFPI Vol. 11, Jan–Oct. 1956, CV, Doc. 59, Shinnar (Cologne) to the Ministry of Foreign Affairs, 28 January 1956.

93 *Ibid.*

94 H. M. Sachar, *Israel and Europe: An Appraisal in History* (New York: Knopf, 1998).

95 Jelinek, *Zwischen Moral und Realpolitik*, Doc. 99: Aufzeichnung des bundesdeutschen Gesandten Wilhelm Melchers in Bagdad und Amman, an Abteilung 3. AA, über die Aufnahme diplomatischer Beziehungen zu Israel, 28 July 1955.

96 *Ibid.*, Doc. 98, Aufzeichnung der Gesandtschaft der Bundesrepublik Deutschland in Bagdad über Beziehungen zu Israel, 26 July 1955.

97 Conze et al., *Das Amt und die Vergangenheit*, p. 574.

98  Jelinek, *Zwischen Moral und Realpolitik*, Doc. 111: '*Referat von Generalkonsul I, Voigt, AA, über die politische Lage im Nahen Osten*', 23 January 1956.

99  A. Fursenko and T. Naftali, *Khrushchev's Cold War: The Inside Story of an American Adversary* (New York: Norton, 2006), p. 50.

100  V. Gransow and K. H. Jarausch (eds), *Uniting Germany: Documents and Debates 1944–1993* (Oxford: Berghahn Books, 1994), p. 13.

101  'Jede Anerkennung der "DDR" ein unfreundlicher Akt', *Bullettin der Presse- und Informationsamtes der Bundesregierung*, 13 December 1955, p. 1.

102  The phrase 'Hallstein Doctrine' originated in the pages of the *Frankfurter Allgemeine Zeitung* in 1958, originally as the *Hallstein-Grewe-Doktrin*. W. Kilian, *Die Hallstein-Doktrin. Der diplomatische Krieg zwischen der BRD und der DDR, 1955–1973. Aus den Akten der beiden deutschen Außenministerien* (Berlin: Duncker &Humblot , 2001).

103  My italics, PA AA, B11 381, Diplogerma Kairo. Welck, 15 October 1955.

104  Schweizerische Gesandtschaft bei der Bundesrepublik Deutschland, 5 April 1956, Bauer. http://db.dodis.ch/digitalObject/156693.

105  PA AA, B2 94, Minutes of the Middle East Conference in Istanbul from 3–7 April 1956, n.d.

106  PA AA, B2 94/150, Ambassador Becker: Political report on Egypt, n.d.

107  PA AA, B2 94/208, Consul General Voigt: Political report on the Middle East and the Israel Problem, n.d.

108  PA AA, B2 94/246, Minutes of the Middle East Conference.

109  PA AA, B2 94/247, *ibid.*

110  Gray, *Germany's Cold War*, p. 81.

111  G. Rochat, *Le Guerre Italiane, 1935–1943: Dall'Impero d'Etiopia alla Disfatta* (Turin: Einaudi, 2005).

112  PA AA, B2 94/262, Legation Counsellor Weber, Report: The Soviet trade offensive in the Middle East, n.d.

113  Original text in English, in: PA AA, B12/89, Telegramm: Schirmer (Kairo) to the Foreign Office, 5 April 1956.

114  'Aufzeichnung über den Besuch des israelischen Gesandten F.E. Shinnar im Auswartigen Amt vom 27.1.1956', in Jelinek, *Zwischen Moral und Realpolitik*, p. 359; 'Bericht von Dr. F.E. Shinnar, isr. Gesandter in Köln, an Außenminister Moshe Sharett über die Unterredung mit Außenminister von Brentano in Bonn, 31 January 1956', *ibid.*, p. 375.

115  PA AA, B2 94/244, Debate notes, n.d.

116  DFPI Vol. 11, Jan-Oct. 1956, CV, Doc. 247, Shinnar (Cologne) to Sharett, 14 May 1956.

117  'Telegramm von Dr. F.E. Shinnar, Gesandter Köln, an Moshe Sharett, isr. Außenminister, über ein Besuch im Auswärtigen Amt vom 14. Mai 1956', 14 May 1956, reprinted in Jelinek, *Zwischen Moral und Realpolitik*, pp. 397ff.

118  DFPI Vol. 11, Jan-Oct. 1956, CV, Doc. 264, Sharett (Jerusalem) to the Israel Missions abroad, 27 May 1956.

119  I. Muth, *Die DDR-Aussenpolitik, 1949–1972: Inhalte, Strukturen, Mechanismen* (Berlin: Links Verlag, 2000), p. 103.

120  SAPMO-BArch DY 30/11348, Grotwohl's speech at the Ambassadors' Conference, 1 February 1956. The following quotes from the conference are from this file.

121 For the Israeli communication see PA AA, MfAA A682/27, Government of Israel, Aide Memoire, n.d.; for König's response, see PA AA, MfAA A682/29, Botschaft Moskau. Embassy Moscow. Report about the visit of the Israeli ambassador Joseph Awida to ambassador König, 20 April 1956, Krolikowski.

122 PA AA, MfAA A 13364/3, Krugmann to Grüttner. Telegram from Moscow, 21 April 1956 and PA AA, MfAA A 13364/2, Memorandum of conversation between Ambassador König and the Head of the Third European Department in the Soviet Foreign Ministry, Comrade Lapin on 20.4.1956.

123 'Keine diplomatische Beziehungen zu Israel', *ND*, 19 June 1956; PA AA, MfAA A 682/32, Botschaftr DDR Moskau. Aktenvermerk ueber eine Unterredung mit dem Geschäftsträger a.i. der Botschaft Israel in Moskau, Herrn Schlusch, und dem Unterzeichneten am 9.7.56 um 10.00 Uhr. Roßmeisl, 9 July 1956.

124 Timm, *Hammer, Zirkel, Davidstern*, p. 138.

125 PA AA, MfAA A 17594/2, Handke to Eisermann, 17 January 1956.

126 Fulbrook, *German National Identity after the Holocaust*, p. 79.

127 A. Stephanson, 'Fourteen Notes on the Very Concept of the Cold War', in S. Dalby and G. Ó Tuathail (eds), *Rethinking Geopolitics* (London: Routledge, 1998), pp. 62–85.

128 PA AA, B11 1397, Ref. 308. Vermerk, Steffen, 4 March 1955.

Part II

# Dilemmas and contradictions, 1956–61

# 4

# Crises

In July 1956, Konrad Adenauer was in Bühlerhöhe, his favourite inn in the Black Forest region, enjoying his escape from Bonn's hectic political life in the company of his son, relishing the quiet of the place. But the Chancellor's break was interrupted by worrying news coming from Cairo – Gamal Abdel Nasser, who had recently removed his former ally Naguib from power and assumed the presidency of Egypt, announced in a live broadcast that he would nationalise the Suez Canal Company. The Company was a British–French enterprise which, thanks to the political efforts of French diplomat Ferdinand de Lesseps, by 1956 had been operating the Canal for nearly a century. In July 1956, addressing the crowd from Alexandria's main square, Nasser attacked the imperial powers for exploiting Egypt's resources, taking advantage of its strategic location for hundreds of years, and for humiliating it. 'Today we are going to get rid of what happened in the past', he declared.[1] The Egyptian army had been on standby throughout Nasser's broadcasted speech. Upon hearing the codeword 'Ferdinand de Lesseps', it started the seizure of the Canal, as instructed before Nasser went on stage.[2]

To Adenauer in Bühlerhöhe, and to much of the political establishment in Bonn, the news came as an unpleasant surprise. The Chancellor had long been worried about Nasser's bold leadership style, sometimes referring to him as 'the little Hitler'.[3] The sudden nationalisation only reinforced his concerns about Nasser's expansionist tendencies and about other moves he may have up his sleeve in defiance of West Germany's closest allies. What worried the Chancellor even further, was the extent to which the Soviets had penetrated the Middle East in a short span of time. Just a few months prior, Nasser had announced the signing of an arms deal with Soviet-backed Czechoslovakia – news that was as disturbing for Adenauer as it was terrifying for the Israelis.[4]

Interestingly from East Berlin's perspective – and worryingly from Bonn's – in his nationalisation speech Nasser singled out the West German Holocaust compensation payments to Israel as an example of how the Western powers constantly chose to side with Israel, and against the Arab world. Indeed, the Egyptian leader fiercely denounced the United States' hesitance to financially support Egypt especially because, he claimed, Washington was so openly subsidising Israel – among other ways via Bonn's compensations to the Jewish state. Nasser's seizure of the Suez Canal thus presented the East

German authorities with an excellent opportunity to ride the wave of anti-Western sentiment in Egypt and across the Arab world, by portraying themselves as the champions of the anti-imperialist cause as allegedly demonstrated by the East German unwillingness to engage in reparations negotiations with Israel. The Bonn government had good reasons to worry about the nationalisation of the Suez Canal.

## Preparing for London

In their attempt to devise a diplomatic response to the Egyptian crisis, the Western powers scheduled an international conference to take place in London, on 16 August 1956. Among the various issues discussed while drafting the list of attendees, US, British and French representatives confronted the problem of which German state should be invited to London, and on what grounds. The shared idea was to forward invitations to the conference to the successor states of the signatories of the 1888 Convention of Constantinople, underwritten between the Ottoman and European rulers, and which stated that the Suez Canal 'shall always be free and open in time of war as in time of peace to every vessel'.[5] Among the signatories was the German Emperor and King of Prussia. However, doubts arose as to which of the two German states should be regarded as the legitimate successor. French Foreign Minister Christian Pineau told his British and American colleagues that if the invitation to attend the conference was to be forwarded to the successor countries to the signatories of the 1888 Convention, then 'it would be necessary … to invite both East and West Germany'.[6] Walworth Barbour, then US Deputy Chief of Mission in London, dismissed the idea because, 'of course', the United States did not 'recognize East Germany', although he also conceded that an eventual East German attendance would in no way pose any kind of 'serious danger'. Barbour noted that the Soviets 'might well decide not to attend if East Germany [was] not invited', and this 'would be all to the good'. The Western allies therefore decided to invite only Bonn. However, they justified their decision by classifying the Federal Republic as being one of the nations 'largely concerned in the use of the Canal' – as a 'large user' of the canal and not, as Bonn would have hoped, as one of the successor states to the signatories of the Constantinople Treaty.[7] Many in West Germany considered this a serious problem.

In its note of acceptance to the invitation, Bonn made it clear that it 'would have appreciated' receiving the 'invitation in quality of signatory' to the 1888 Convention, emphasising that the FRG continued to embody the 'legal entity' of the German Reich that had signed it; indeed, Bonn was 'identical' to it.[8] At the outset of the conference, Soviet Foreign Minister Dmitri Shepilov did point out that it could not 'be considered normal that just one German state was invited' to participate.[9] The French Foreign Minister replied by defending the West German participation and by emphasising that the three Western powers recognised the FRG as the only successor state of the German Reich. The discussion then quickly moved on to discuss Suez, to the seeming disappointment of the West German delegates. According to a *Der Spiegel* journalist present at the scene, they seemed to be disconcerted by the ease with which the problem of German participation had faded from the conference table.[10]

The importance that Bonn attached to both deterring East German participation in the London Suez Conference and to highlighting that only West Germany could be considered the representative for the whole of the German people testified to the central place that the German–German Cold War occupied in Bonn's official mind at a time of international crisis.[11] The urgency for doing so was augmented by West German intelligence reports regarding the Soviets' intention to use the Suez Crisis to put pressure on the West; communicating that the GDR was eager to send personnel to Egypt to aid the local authorities in guaranteeing the continued flow of goods via the Canal and train its military forces; and that, by doing so, East Berlin might gain recognition from Egypt in return. Meanwhile, the BND reiterated the view shared by the majority of Bonn's diplomats stationed in the Middle East, relating that, in the event of an establishment of diplomatic relations between the Federal Republic and Israel, then Egypt and Syria – and possibly the other member states of the Arab League, too – would indeed swiftly recognise the GDR.[12]

From East Berlin, things looked remarkably different. For one, because the GDR had indeed been left out of the international diplomatic consultations regarding the future of the Suez Canal. In fact, the East German authorities had not only not been invited to the London Conference, but also been turned away at the UK border after trying to gate-crash the diplomatic summit.[13] Frustrated by this exclusion, the East Germans turned to the one tool they had at their disposal: propaganda. East German state media emphasised that Bonn's seat at the conference table essentially confirmed the East German allegations about the FRG. As Deputy Foreign Minister Schwab put it, Bonn's foreign policy essentially served 'the interests of the big monopolies':

[The FRG] supports the claims of auctioneers of the nationalized Suez Canal Company [... and] this shows Bonn's real attitude, which for years now has expressed itself through the *material support for Israel* in the battle against the freedom of the Arab peoples.[14]

A West German think-tank studying East Berlin's policy in the region noted that the Suez Crisis led to the 'first, big [East German propaganda] campaign' against West Germany in the Middle East – one that had at its core the emphasis on the ties between Bonn and the State of Israel.[15] The fact that West Germany, and the reparations to Israel, featured in Nasser's nationalisation speech gave credence to a series of claims that the East German propaganda had been making since the West German–Israeli deal was signed.[16] It was now time to exploit the situation.

## Reaching out to the Levant

In the summer of 1956, the Soviet Union pushed Poland to increase its exports of glance coal and coke to East Berlin, with the provision that East Germany could later re-export these materials. This was a boon in the form of economic benefits, aimed to ensure that the GDR would be in the position to intensify its economic exchange with the countries of the Levant, while at the same time also attempting to restrain East Germany's political ambitions in the area. These exchanges were to take place under the umbrella of the multilateral organisation coordinating the Soviet bloc economies, the Socialist Council for Mutual Economic Assistance (COMECON), which in July 1956 had approved the motion that the GDR intensify its contacts with the Levant, with the aim of signing economic and cultural – though not diplomatic – agreements.[17] This was not necessarily good news for the East Germans. GDR authorities had long been complaining about the fact that the Polish deliveries fell far short of respecting their economic obligations towards the GDR.[18] Nonetheless, COMECON support was better than nothing and, in an attempt to reassure the East Germans, Moscow vowed to also increase its exports of precious raw materials to the GDR – ore in the Soviets' case – which would then render East Germany more appealing to the markets of the Arab Middle East.[19]

These COMECON measures were intended as the sop that should have kept the East Germans away from throwing tantrums about political recognition from, and diplomatic relations with, Third World countries. When the East Germans again attempted to forge political ties with two more countries in the region – this time Lebanon and Libya – the Kremlin again intervened to cool down the East German enthusiasm.[20] In an allegedly 'very harsh' exchange in Moscow, Ulbricht pointed out that establishing political, not just economic, contacts with the Arab countries was crucial to strengthening the legitimacy of the GDR. He highlighted that this was especially urgent given the worrying developments that were taking place in Poland,[21] where just a few weeks earlier, a protest for fairer work conditions and political freedoms that had started in Poznań on 28 June had turned into a full-fledged uprising. A change of leadership in the local Communist Party had followed and, in the summer of 1956, Ulbricht was panicking. He pointed to the events in Poznań to stress that the GDR seriously needed to augment its international credibility – and that the Middle East offered the GDR an ideal means of doing so.

The sources of Ulbricht's concerns, and of his renewed sense of urgency to reach out to the Arab Middle East, did not just stem from the volatility of the international scene in the mid-1950s. They were also connected to domestic concerns, and most prominently to his own preoccupation with remaining in power. The unrest in neighbouring Poland was just one of the more visible political repercussions of the changes that were going on in and around Moscow. In February 1956, the newly instated Soviet leader Nikita Khrushchev had delivered an allegedly secret speech at the twentieth congress of the Communist Party of the Soviet Union, denouncing Stalin's cult of personality. The content of the speech was intended to remain secret, but the Israeli intelligence services learned of it and passed the text on to the Eisenhower administration, which leaked it to the press. Without wanting or anticipating it, Khrushchev's words thus reignited hopes of liberal reforms in various satellite countries, sending shockwaves throughout the fragile bloc.[22]

As one of his collaborators put it, 'the shock of 17 June [1953]' in 1956 was 'still in [Ulbricht's] bones'.[23] The East German leader seriously worried that the GDR may be the next Soviet satellite to vacillate under the weight of growing popular discontent and internal cracks among its Politbüro members. Just a few weeks earlier State Secretary Erich Mielke – who was soon to be appointed as the head of the East German security service, the Stasi – had reported news about the growing calls for strikes and protests in various East German cities, in defiance of the regime.[24] In Ulbricht's view, the GDR needed to augment its international credibility, and also to reinforce the stability at the domestic political level, and establishing political ties with the countries of the Arab Middle East could be a way to secure this aim, he repeatedly argued with Moscow.[25] His preoccupation was to intensify later in 1956, as Hungary, too, proved susceptible to popular unrest.

For the time being, however, the Soviets were not to be persuaded. The option of consular or diplomatic relations with the countries of the Levant had to be suspended, Ulbricht's frustration notwithstanding. But if political relations were not to be sought after, at least according to Moscow's wishes, then a way for East Berlin to work around the Kremlin's diktat could be that of *kulturpolitsch* relations. In June 1956 a meeting of the GDR Council of Ministers had voted for the onset of a PR offensive, which seemed all the more relevant after Moscow's stern halting of the East German political ambitions in the Middle East. Such an offensive included a series of cultural programmes and educational exchanges that would accompany the GDR's economic outreach to the Middle East.[26] During the visit of an Egyptian official to the GDR in early August 1956, the party press even hinted at the opening of an Egyptian trade mission in East Berlin in the near future.[27] The previous week, East German President Wilhelm Pieck had sent a message to Nasser to congratulate him on the fourth anniversary of Egypt's Revolution Day, celebrating the Free Officers' seizure of power from the monarchy that began on the evening of 22 July 1952, guided by Nasser and others. The West Germans derided Pieck's note, stressing that the Egyptian leader had announced that from 1956 onwards the celebrations of Revolution Day would shift to 18 June, marking the first anniversary of when the last British troops left the Canal Zone.[28] Pieck's telegraph, West German commentators ridiculed, betrayed the East German lack of eye for detail when dealing with their Middle Eastern partners.[29] Yet Nasser did not seem to mind, and swiftly telegraphed his wishes of 'glory and happiness' back to Pieck. Belittled in the *Frankfurter Allgemeine Zeitung* as 'merely an expression of Oriental courtesy', in fact Nasser's move aroused suspicion and discomfort among top West German foreign policy circles.[30]

## East Berlin's Suez War

Meanwhile, in London, West Germany supported the US proposal to resume international control over the Canal. But Nasser did not budge. Having decided not to take part in the London conference, he rejected the summit's conclusions – communicated to him by Australian Prime Minister Robert Menzies – and instead called for another conference, to be held in Egypt, to discuss the matter further.[31] This time East German diplomats made sure that Moscow would guarantee that the GDR, too, was invited to the negotiating table.[32] East German participation at the conference would imply that the GDR, too, and not only the FRG, was being internationally recognised as a legal successor of the German *Reich* that had signed the 1888 Convention of Constantinople, confirming a point upon which East German officials had been insisting for weeks – although, when dealing with Israeli representatives they had also highlighted that only the FRG was to be considered the successor of the Nazi Reich. The Soviets eventually did support the East German request to the Egyptian authorities to ensure that they would, this time, be allowed to take part in the debate on the Suez Canal and its future. On 29 October, however, the unexpected Israeli military attack against Egypt shipwrecked such developments, preventing the East Germans from enjoying the fruits of the diplomatic invitation they had worked hard to secure for themselves.

Despite this setback, on 2 November Otto Grotewohl addressed the East German People's Chamber. His statement about the Suez events, which was later translated into English and circulated among relevant Middle Eastern diplomatic representations, read: 'The aggression against Egypt reveals all the brutality of imperialist colonial policy.' 'It shows that there is no equality of rights between the colonial powers and the countries marching forward on the way to national independence.' In contrast, Grotewohl asserted East Berlin's 'sympathy' for the Egyptian 'struggle for national independence and self-determination', putting specific emphasis on the difference between East and West German policies:

> The Government of the German Federal Republic … approves of and actively supports the British and French colonial policy. It grants the aggressive circles of Israel more than three thousand million German marks of so-called reparation payments which are used by Israel in her fight against the national independence movement of the peoples of the Near East. During the London Suez Conference the Federal Government supported the viewpoint of the colonial powers and turned against the justified demands of Egypt. The colonial attitude of the Federal Government does not contribute to strengthen the international reputation of the German people. Therefor [*sic*] the Government of the GDR calls on the Government of the German Federal Republic to immediately stop assisting Israel.[33]

In his parliamentary address, Grotewohl made two important points. First, he associated Bonn with the aggressors, the former colonial powers. Second, he identified the West German government as the enabler of Israel's military aggression against Egypt, via its restitutions agreement – a point that had worried Arab representatives since before the agreement was even signed. East German journalists reinforced Grotewohl's statements: 'It is without a doubt that these [West German] deliveries substantially contributed to Israel's military potential', emphasised the party press.[34]

Yet it was not through words alone that the GDR hoped to ingratiate itself with the Egyptians. The SED's public stance on the Suez Crisis came together with a spree of solidarity gestures that East German politicians, at national and local levels, directed to their Egyptian counterparts. These included telegrams of solidarity, shipments of medicaments, food, and clothing, as well as more substantial contributions.

The official youth organisation of the East German ruling party, the Freie Deutsche Jugend, received hundreds of spontaneous applications on the part of volunteers eager to depart for Egypt to fight alongside their Arab comrades.[35] Another mass organisation, the East German Peace Council (*Friedensrat*) arranged and hosted about 250 meetings in six weeks throughout East German territory to alert the population to the events that were taking place in the Middle East, inviting speakers from Egypt, Iraq, Syria and beyond.[36]

To their domestic population, to the Egyptian authorities and to their Soviet masters, East German cadres repeatedly showcased their readiness to send pilots to Egypt, in order to guarantee the continued flow of goods via the Canal following its nationalisation, as well as volunteers from the ranks of the National People's Army, the riot police, border police, and military instructors and engineers.[37] In early November 1956, GDR Foreign Minister Lothar Bolz went to Moscow to assess whether 'the support of Egypt via material help and eventually also the dispatch of volunteers on the part of the GDR' could lead to a 'faster diplomatic recognition' on the part of Egypt and whether this would be in line with the policies of the Soviet bloc.[38] Soviet Deputy Foreign Minister Zorin maintained that there was no need to send East German volunteers to fight.[39] Again, the East Germans were relegated to a secondary role on the international stage. Despite this the SED's Central Committee resolved to make the most of the 'British-French aggression', which, 'undoubtedly' still offered advantageous possibilities to intensify economic and political relations between the GDR and the Arab states.[40]

## Adenauer's discontent

While the East German establishment fervently rooted for the Egyptians, when the Suez War broke out Chancellor Adenauer proved to be a supporter of his European allies. Indeed, as Adenauer asked his ministers during a Cabinet consultation, why should the UK and France allow an Egyptian 'Hitler' to be at their throats?[41] And he became increasingly worried by the way in which the Americans were handling the crisis. The Chancellor had viewed with increasing dislike and suspicion the American reticence to participate in, let alone lead, a military intervention in Egypt. Moreover, Nasser's move had followed less than two weeks after the news of the 'Radford Plan' had been leaked to the *New York Times*, which reported that the Chairman of the US Armed Forces, Admiral Arthur W. Radford, had proposed the reduction of the armed forces stationed in Europe (and elsewhere) by up to 800,000 men by 1960.[42] If the Radford Plan were to be adopted and war broke out between the two superpowers on European soil, German civilians would be at tremendous risk. While the prospect of keeping the peace in the Middle East was, of course, valuable from the West German perspective, if the Americans were ready to come to an agreement with the Soviets over Suez in spite of French and British objections, did this not mean that the two superpowers might one day reach an agreement over the German question in spite of possible German objections?[43] American opposition to any form of military intervention in the Middle East, coupled with the (later retracted) news of the intended reduction in US armed forces for the defence of Europe, alarmed the Chancellor. As he wrote in his memoirs: 'In my opinion the United States had not recognized correctly the situation in the Middle East. They did not recognize that the Soviet Union, as every so often, had modified its offence strategy and that after its unsuccessful attempt to advance in Europe it now tried to advance in the Mediterranean region via the Middle East.'[44] 'And Russian control of the Mediterranean', he reasoned, 'would result in Russian control of Europe.'[45] As he wrote to the US President, 'the particularly close interdependence of all European affairs should serve as an explanation for my deep concern, though at a first glance the Federal Republic is not immediately affected by all pending questions.'[46]

But in the face of Nasser's increasing popularity in the region, of the spectre of Soviet penetration of the Middle East, and of a possible imminent reduction in the US armed forces stationed in Europe, it was easy for the Chancellor to understand why David Ben-Gurion would justify the Sinai campaign as a pre-emptively defensive, rather than an offensive, act.[47] This, in turn, came close to putting the FRG onto a road to covert defiance of the United States, while the relationship between Adenauer and Ben-Gurion, and the West German and Israeli security establishments, grew ever closer.

## The first letter

It was during the early stages of the Suez War that the Israeli Prime Minister reached out directly to Adenauer with a letter that the Head of the Israeli Mission in Cologne, Felix Shinnar, delivered by hand to the Chancellor. Four years earlier, the restitutions issue had been negotiated and decided upon without the two state leaders having any direct contact. At that time, even the fact that Sharett would act as a counterpart to the West German Chancellor, who then also served as Bonn's Foreign Minister, had been considered to be 'beneath the dignity of Israel's minister of foreign affairs'.[48] But on the fourth day of the fighting against Egypt, in 1956, Prime Minister Ben-Gurion wrote to the Chancellor directly, sharing his worries about a rumour that had caught his attention. As his Washington-based diplomats had heard, the West Germans were apparently considering halting their restitution payments to Israel in order to protect their neutrality in the Arab–Israeli conflict and, more broadly, to comply with the rule of neutrality, which prohibits providing support to any UN member state engaged in armed hostilities against another member of the UN. In an aide-memoire to the Prime Minister, Israeli legal experts concluded that halting the flow of West German goods to Israel 'would be a serious breach' of the 1952 agreement.[49]

The rumour had various sources. A few days earlier, at a press conference in Bonn, journalists had pressed the Chancellor's chief spokesman, von Eckardt, about the possibility that the West German government might decide to freeze its restitutions to Israel while the country was at war against Egypt. In Jerusalem, Foreign Ministry officials also reported that the Americans – furious at not having been informed about the attack and the French–British–Israeli plans, and wanting to halt the fighting as quickly as possible – were pressuring Bonn to halt its transfers to Israel. Indeed, while Ben-Gurion's letter was en route to Bonn, the Head of the Trade Department in Bonn's Foreign Ministry, van Scherpenberg, conceded to Robert Pferdmenges, an influential banker and CDU Bundestag member, that the Federal government was currently examining the question.[50] Foreign Minister von Brentano gave a similar reply to the representatives of Syria and Lebanon, who had gone to see him on 30 October, and again on 5 November. To them, Brentano said that the FRG was considering the question and that a decision on the fate of the reparations to Israel had not yet been made. In fact, two days earlier, during the meeting with Shinnar, Adenauer had categorically denied that the issue was even up for discussion, stressing that the FRG would not even consider halting the reparations payments to Israel. Adenauer's trusted aides, Blankenhorn and Grewe, who were also present at the meeting, reinforced the message.[51] 'I cannot believe', emphasised Ben-Gurion in his letter to the Chancellor, 'that any such far-reaching proposal, contrary as it would be to the terms of that profoundly significant agreement of which you were a primary architect … can have your approval or consent'.[52]

Meanwhile, the fighting on the ground continued. France and Britain vetoed ceasefire resolutions at the Security Council and soon landed in Egypt, taking an active role in the fighting and infuriating both superpowers. Soviet Premier Nikolai Bulganin, already under pressure given a new violent anti-Soviet uprising that had begun in Hungary on 23 October, threatened to deploy nuclear and thermonuclear bombs against London and Paris should they not halt the fighting and withdraw from their military positions in Egypt. Worried that the situation would lead to an advancement of the Soviets in the Middle East, US President Eisenhower hurried to find a diplomatic solution to the crisis but, for this, he could count on West German support only to a certain extent. On the one hand, the Federal Republic readily made available its airfields, in support of the President's plans to airlift Canadian troops to Egypt with the aim of interposing themselves between the combatants, thus putting an end to the fighting. On the other hand, the Federal Republic proved much more hesitant to follow the superpower's lead in the crisis – as demonstrated by the Chancellor's repeated statements, to the Israeli representatives and to his own Cabinet, that Bonn would not halt its restitutions shipments to Israel. That West German Foreign Ministry personnel would not stress this emphatically in front of their Arab colleagues did not make this less true – their attitude served to keep the Arabs calm and to curb the effects of the mounting East German propaganda attacks against the alleged consequences of the West German reparations.

The UN ceasefire only came into force on 7 November. By that point, the Israeli military was occupying the Gaza Strip and the Sinai, while British and French troops were stationed on corridors along the Canal. Eisenhower used the threat of economic and oil sanctions to force his European allies to withdraw, which they eventually did, in December 1956. The negotiations with Israel proved to be more complicated. Although Ben-Gurion swiftly announced that Israel would withdraw from all territories seized during the war, negotiations about the conditions attached to the withdrawal, and on the involvement of an international peacekeeping force (United Nations Emergency Force, UNEF), lasted until February 1957. The Israelis refused to leave the Gaza Strip, for fear that *fedayeen* incursions into Israeli territory would continue undisturbed under Egypt's supervision of the Strip; and they shunned the idea of leaving Sharm el-Sheikh unless they received assurances about future Israeli access to the strategically located Gulf of Aqaba.

For the East Germans this was, again, a brilliant opportunity to vilify West Germany's links with Israel. East German Foreign Minister Bolz issued another statement requesting that Bonn halt its payments to Israel. He argued that the Suez War would not have been possible without the transfer of goods from the Federal Republic to the Jewish state – exactly what had worried the Arab representatives. Thus, the statement concluded, Bonn should now pay reparations to Cairo:

> The Government of the German Democratic Republic turns to the Government of the Federal Republic of Germany with the request to transfer to the Republic of Egypt the so-called reparations to Israel, which allowed the armament of the Israeli aggressor, in order to compensate for the damages inflicted upon the Republic of Egypt by the Israeli troops.[53]

The attacks against Israel, and against the ties between Bonn and Jerusalem, had become a tactical device of prime importance to advancing East German recognition claims in the Middle East. The personnel of the East German trade mission in Egypt, reporting to the East Berlin authorities in December 1956, articulated a series of policy recommendations for the Foreign Ministry. The top three were: first, to 'support Egypt's neutrality policy'; second, to 'exploit Egypt's neutrality policy in order to attain political recognition of the GDR'; third, to defeat the 'West German strong influence [in Egypt], for example through further political declarations of the GDR about the relationship between West Germany and Israel'.[54] Directives for the establishment of an East German general consulate in Cairo were dispatched on the same day the French and British troops completed their removal from the area.[55]

Rather than strengthening Israel's negotiating position at the UN and forcing the other countries to compromise, as the Israeli cadres had hoped, the Israeli unwillingness to withdraw from the territories seized during the war backfired, as the Eisenhower administration increased its political and economic pressure on Israel. The possibility of halting West German reparations reappeared on the cards. In February 1957, at a meeting with the FRG Ambassador to the United States, Heinz L. Krekeler, Secretary of State Dulles hinted that West Germany should indeed halt its restitution payments to the Israelis, at least to 'make them get nervous'.[56] A few days later, on 22 February, a coalition of six countries headed by Iraq and Lebanon submitted a resolution to the United Nations calling for an extensive international boycott of Israel – the point at which President Eisenhower decided to push forth with his own sanctions threat, imposing them on both US governmental and private aid to Israel. This would have also included the West German restitutions, for a total of roughly one hundred million dollars per year.[57] Before the sanctions came into effect, however, Ben-Gurion gave in. The last Israeli troops remaining on Egyptian territory received the order to withdraw in March 1957. The Eisenhower administration did not, in the end, impose the economic sanctions; and the West German government had very nearly avoided having to choose between its continuing commitment to upholding the restitutions to Israel or following the lead of its superpower. Something, however, had changed in the West German–Israeli relationship.

## Secret liaisons

Viewed by the Chancellor as an operation to contain Soviet expansion in the region, the Suez War in fact led to Moscow's increased presence in the Middle East.[58] Nonetheless, at the time Adenauer believed firmly that the onset of the crisis and later the war had proved him right.[59] The developments of late 1956 reinforced his belief in the necessity of pushing for rearmament; for a *rapprochement* with France; and for framing a strong and coherent European defence strategy, as he explained to the members of his Cabinet on 5 November 1956.[60] Then, shortly after the end of the crisis, Shinnar contacted Bonn with interesting information. Israel had captured large amounts of Soviet weaponry, which West German officials could inspect if they so wished.[61]

The heads of the Mossad and of the BND established direct contact shortly thereafter.[62] The exchange of intelligence about the Soviet bloc and the Arab countries, the two agreed, would be at the heart of the cooperation between the two services. Israel would be furnishing intelligence about the Warsaw Pact, especially about their weapons, such as the ones that the Israeli military had captured from Egypt in the course of the Sinai campaign, and that the Bundeswehr was eager to study in order to better ascertain the capabilities of Eastern bloc countries, and those of the GDR in particular. In return, the BND would be providing information to the Mossad about the Arab countries' armaments and security establishments, as well as assisting secret operations by Israeli agents on Arab territory.[63] This was a rather contradictory promise, given that Gehlen's organisation had done a lot to support the Arab security services in their anti-Israeli efforts up to that moment. Thus, it was not a coincidence that the Israeli liaison officer selected for this difficult role was himself an expert on the Arab Middle East and their security apparatuses.

Born in Hamburg in 1921, Shlomo Cohen-Abarbanel had fled from Nazism with his family, emigrating first to France and later to Israel. He was a gifted artist and he soon found a way to combine his passion for art with his service for the security of the young Israeli state. Having studied art in Paris, once the Mossad stationed him in Cairo to investigate the network of former Nazis working in the Egyptian security services he posed as a promising French modernist artist, and his cover was so successful that he even managed to get a solo exhibition at the Cairo Museum of Modern Art.[64] In the late 1950s, upon having been relocated to Paris as the Mossad's chief of station, he would liaise with West German intelligence officer Wolfgang Langkau – a former SS-officer who, after the end of the war, swiftly joined the Gehlen Organization, the body which served as a predecessor to the West German intelligence services, the BND. Langkau had served in the same regiment as Gehlen during the war. After 1956, he became the Director of the BND's Strategic Service, an office which was in charge of, among others, developing the BND's international network.[65] Langkau's detractors nagged that he was such a secretive guy that he himself probably did not know he existed.[66] In the wake of the Suez War the contacts between Cohen-Abarbanel and Langkau, and the connection between the West German and Israeli services, code-named Operation Blaumeise, would gradually intensify.[67]

Yet the security liaisons between Bonn and Jerusalem encompassed more than the exchange of intelligence. By 1957, Israel's Ministry of Defense had begun planning to reach out to the Germans to inquire about the possibility of exchanging weapons, aiding both the German and the Israeli arms procurement efforts. 'I have reached the conclusion that we need more allies in Europe', Ben-Gurion had announced at a party meeting that summer.[68] Germany seemed a particularly good choice because unlike other countries such as England, which had too many interests in the oil reserves of the Arab Middle East to act as a real partner to Israel, the Federal Republic did not display any 'Arab complex', it was the 'richest in Europe' and had the 'ability' to support the Jewish state, if it so decided. The Federal Republic had been forbidden from building up their armed forces until 1955, and then had to intensify the quest for armaments to rebuild them from scratch. The Israeli Uzi submachine gun was a simple, inexpensive weapon that had served the Israel Defense Forces (IDF) well in the Sinai campaign, and Minister of Defence Strauss was very interested in it.[69] The Uzi was also very convenient for the West Germans because Bonn would be able to offset the cost of adopting it against war reparations, as the weapon was produced in Belgium.[70]

Both the West Germans and the Israelis involved in security arrangements between the two countries were eager to keep their talks secret. From the Israeli perspective, this was paramount in order not to upset a public opinion which just five years earlier had protested like never before while the country was in the process of negotiating reparations from Germany. Against this backdrop, the idea of Israel selling weapons to Germany was something that politicians such as Menachem Begin, and large parts of the population, would not have accepted lightly. From a West German perspective, given Bonn's ties with the Arab world – and East Berlin's attempts to thwart them – it was paramount to protect the secrecy of these exchanges. It therefore came as a shock in both capitals when the Israeli newspaper *LaMerhav*, on 19 December 1957, published the news that Ben-Gurion was planning to send Mapai Secretary General Giora Yoseftal to Germany to negotiate further arms transfers.[71] The newspaper that had published the news was affiliated to the leftist Ahdut HaAvoda-Poale Zion party, the fifth largest party in the Knesset and whose support was crucial to keep the government's coalition afloat. A severe crisis followed. At the Mapai meeting that took place on 30 December, Ben-Gurion lamented the 'mental burden' that having the responsibility to guarantee the security of the people of Israel placed on him and emphasised to his fellow party members that the issue was extremely dangerous because it exposed the purchase 'from this specific country' of 'very essential equipment for our security'.[72] The leak was also alarming because it could signal to other countries that a possible decision to covertly support Israel in matters of security and defence might be made public, thus breaching their trust and scaring them away from future deals. Ben-Gurion was livid about what he saw as a blow to undermine his own leadership. He repeated that it was paramount that 'all security matters must be kept in complete secrecy' and reminded his fellow party members that just a few years prior, when discussing the prospect of German reparations, after an initial period of animosity the Ahdut HaAvoda ended up 'accept[ing] very eagerly the money we got from Germany'.[73] In public, Prime Minister Ben-Gurion kept vehemently denying that such a trip as that revealed in the leak was about to take place.

## The road to Rott am Inn

Shimon Peres, Asher Ben-Natan, and Haim Laskov, three officials at the top of the Israeli arms procurement efforts, arrived at the holiday house of West Germany's Minister of Defence Strauss, in Rott am Inn, on 27 December 1957. The Israelis had travelled in an anonymous rental car, in order to protect the secrecy of their mission.[74] They had opted for a long drive through snowy back roads between France and Germany. The house in Bavaria, which belonged to Minister Strauss' in-laws, was secluded and therefore well placed to protect the identity of the three Israeli visitors, as well as the content of their discussion with the German Defence Minister. The Israelis arrived there with a wish list that included items such as artillery, anti-tank rockets, and helicopters, and discussed the possible Israeli purchase of German submarines also.[75] The following day, the Egyptian Ambassador to the FRG hastily contacted Bonn's Foreign Ministry to ask about an alleged West German–Israeli security arrangement – and was reassured that nothing of the sort existed, nor would any time soon.[76] Yet, just the previous evening the four had struck a deal that would remain secret for years to come.

The talks in Rott am Inn were the latest development in a long series of covert transactions that had been taking place between the West Germans and the Israelis over the previous five years. The Director General of Israel's leading weapons manufacturer TAAS, Zvi Dar, had travelled to the Federal Republic as early as 1952 to try and forge ties with its defence establishment. His efforts would soon yield important results. Zvi Lidor, one of his colleagues at TAAS, recalled that 'the relationship which Dar developed with the heads of the German Defense Ministry, and with the Minister himself … were unusual in scope and character'. He was 'naturally at ease' in the country, and kept an open mind about the idea that the Federal Republic and Israel may become close security partners, trusting, however, that his colleagues would ensure that he would not come into contact with people who had a clear Nazi past. This attitude allowed him to work well and forge precious partnerships. By 1955, he thanked the personnel of the Israeli Mission in Cologne for having granted him permission to use US$2.25 million from the German reparations payments to stock up Israel's 'emergency inventory'.[77] The Luxembourg Agreement explicitly forbade any kind of weapons transfers between the two countries – yet it did not exclude the possibility that Israel might resell domestically some of the goods transferred from the Federal Republic within the confines of the agreement itself and use those funds to equip its military with more, and better quality, weapons.

Figure 4.1 Ḥaim Laskov (second row, centre), Asher Ben-Natan (first row, left) and Shimon Peres (first row, second from right) at a joint photo of senior IDF staff with Prime Minister and Minister of Defense David Ben-Gurion and and Defense Ministry officials, 1961.

In 1956, a Colonel in the IDF, Avigdor Tal had arrived at the Israel Mission in Cologne as permanent representative of the Israeli Ministry of Defence, tasked with establishing contact with the Bundeswehr and the German Ministry of Defence, and with monitoring the orders of raw materials from Germany to tweak them towards a direction that may benefit the Israeli defence establishment. With his arrival in Cologne, the weapons exchanges between the two countries increased substantially. The Israeli navy received its first motor patrol boat that same year.[78] A second one followed in July 1957.[79] The two ships were motor patrol boats manufactured in Bremen, but the German origins of the boats remained secret for decades to come.

Yet the exchange agreed to by Strauss and Peres in Rott am Inn was qualitatively and quantitatively different. The 1957 talks in Bavaria entailed a bilateral arrangement at the highest levels of both states' defence leaderships and marked a watershed moment in the making of the special relationship.[80] By the end of the year, a new agreement was in place that encompassed the West German acquisition not just of the Uzi but also of ammunition. Strauss told his Israeli interlocutors that the German navy was about to start building its own submarines. Their design had already attracted the interest of the Italian navy, and Strauss suggested that the Israelis get on board with the deal. He suggested a price of US$750,000 per boat, which included the possibility of offering instruction to Israeli officers as to how to manoeuvre the submarines and to provide them with a suitable cover during the whole duration of their stay in Germany for training purposes.[81]

Did the West German approach to the secret talks with the Israelis respect constitutional procedures? They did not. And the trade of weapons between West Germany and Israel was also in direct contradiction of the US approach to the region: after the Suez Crisis, the White House's insistence on a total arms embargo towards the countries involved in the Arab–Israeli conflict had only increased. West German diplomats stationed across the globe found it difficult to believe that such covert security cooperation between Israel and the Federal Republic might be taking place. 'Ben-Gurion must know that he cannot get weapons from Germany. He must above all know that the Federal Republic, because of the problem of recognition of the so-called GDR by the Arab states, needs to be much more cautious [on such matters] than any other NATO member state', commented the West German ambassador in Washington, Krekeler, having heard rumours of Ben-Gurion's project to send Chief of General Staff Moshe Dayan to Germany.[82] Yet unbeknown to Krekeler and to most of Bonn's foreign policy establishment, 'within a few months ... very valuable equipment began to reach the Israeli army [from Germany]', as Peres wrote in his memoirs. 'The quality was excellent and the quantities were considerable.'[83]

## Plausible deniability

How many Egyptian women and children weighed on Bonn's conscience after the aggression in Suez, which Israel carried out allegedly thanks to the resources it had received from the Federal Republic? Building upon the rumours that the Holocaust restitutions agreement signed with the Federal Republic in fact was aimed at strengthening Israel's military might, after Suez the East German party press and state representatives asked this question repeatedly.[84] In early 1957, *Neues Deutschland* disclosed details about a West German ordnance company that was allegedly providing Israel with weapons.[85] And a few months later, a spokesperson for the East German Foreign Ministry declared that West Germany supplied Israel with military hardware 'both through direct shipments and by paying for deliveries from third countries'.[86] This was not news, he added, as the Ministry had been aware of this 'for quite some time' thanks to the work of certain 'reliable sources' operating inside West Germany. In their Middle Eastern embassies and consulates, West German diplomats pointed to the fact that the news had been spread by East German media channels to emphasise that the allegation was baseless – and they did so in good faith. Just like the majority of their Israeli colleagues, most of Bonn's diplomats were genuinely not informed about the developing security ties between the Federal Republic and Israel.

The West German embassy in Cairo rebuffed rumours of West German–Israeli security cooperation by labelling them 'ridiculous nonsense' (*törichter Unsinn*), a display of East Germany's efforts to turn the Arab countries against the Federal Republic in the hope of gaining ground in the Middle East.[87] West German diplomats in

Damascus labelled any rumour about arms transfers 'mere East German propaganda'.[88] And judging by the difficulties faced by East German representatives with their Arab counterparts, Bonn indeed seemed to be succeeding at keeping the expansion of covert security ties with Israel a secret.[89] For example, when the East German representative in the Middle East, Ernst Scholz, insisted on railing against West German–Israeli ties with the Syrian Minister of Foreign Affairs, Salah al-Din al-Bitar, his point did not seem to register very strongly. This was surprising, because when Israel refused to withdraw its troops from Gaza and Sharm el-Sheikh in February 1957, Damascus had presented the Arab League with its official complaints, singling out the West German aid to the Jewish state as a crucial factor that the League needed to discuss, and possibly counteract too. Scholz reminded his Syrian counterpart of the 'political and material support' that the GDR had given Egypt at the time of the Suez War, and of the repeated East German appeals to the FRG to stop providing 'material and financial support' to the State of Israel. Yet when Scholz pressed the Syrian Foreign Minister about the need to establish closer relations between East Berlin and Damascus via the opening of an East German General Consulate in the Syrian capital, al-Bitar replied that his government feared doing so would put an end to the relationship with West Germany. And this, in the Minister's words, would create 'difficulties' for the Syrian side – reparations to Israel notwithstanding.[90]

In spite of the limited rhetorical success of the argument about the different relations that the two Germanies had with Israel vis-à-vis the GDR's Arab partners, East German representatives remained insistent. West German rebuttals of the East German accusations regarding West German–Israeli security ties did not dishearten GDR representatives much.[91] The different attitudes of the two German states during the Suez Crisis were included as one of the main arguments suggested by the Foreign Ministry dossier for the visit of Deputy Chairman of the East German Council of Ministers, Paul Scholz, to Egypt in May 1957.[92] And the Deputy Minister for Foreign and Intra-German Trade, Gerhard Weiss, during a press conference held in Baghdad in 1958 again stressed the different attitudes that the two German states had towards Israel, condemning the 'essential contribution to Israel's material and moral strength' of the 'so-called reparation payments' of the Federal Republic to the Jewish state.[93]

The East German contrasting of the East and West German attitudes towards Israel for the benefit of Arab representatives was not only used with the aim of improving the GDR's stance in the Middle East – but within international organisations, too. During a meeting with the Head of the Economics Division of the League of Arab States, Minister Schwab emphasised that the two German states should be treated equally in the international arena – and in particular within the United Nations Economic Commission for Africa, where the GDR was trying to attain the same status as the FRG. Schwab tried to push the Arab League representative on the issue of the West German transfers to Israel. However, the reply he got was that being the Head of the Economics Division was not the same as being 'responsible for the Boycott Department'. The Arab League representative's remarks remained non-committal and vague, commenting only that a delegation was indeed studying the matter of the West German reparations to Israel, but concluding that he knew 'nothing more'.[94] The fact that his own son was currently living and studying in the Federal Republic may have added to his unwillingness to alienate the West German regime, but broader geopolitical considerations, too, may explain his reluctance. When the first country outside the Soviet bloc, Tito's Yugoslavia, gave in to pressures coming from Moscow and decided to establish diplomatic relations with the GDR on 22 October 1957, Bonn for the first time retaliated by unilaterally suspending diplomatic ties, actually using the Hallstein Doctrine and sending an indirect warning to other non-aligned states that might have been tempted to give in to the GDR's overtures.[95] The ongoing East German attacks against the West German reparations to Israel did not exert any major effect in terms of advancing the relations between the GDR and the Arab states. Nor did this point constitute a sufficient reason for the Arab countries to halt commercial relations with Bonn, nor to favour GDR membership in international forums.

Nonetheless, East Berlin's representatives persisted. Renewed confidence in the future of socialism and Soviet sureness of the GDR's economic potential supported the renewed East German determination to insist on its struggle for international recognition, of which anti-Israeli propaganda, at least from an East German perspective, became an ever more important component. Increasingly, GDR cadres also reflected on what kind of messages its propaganda channels should spread in Israel – not just in the Arab world. This was particularly important given that the West German and Israeli press often mentioned the establishing of diplomatic relations between the two countries as being a rather imminent achievement – and this had the potential to be a crucial development. The establishment of official diplomatic relations between Bonn and Tel Aviv, the East German Foreign Ministry calculated, might well favour East Berlin.[96] If the Arab states responded to such a move by cutting off their ties to West Germany and strengthening ties with East Germany instead, then East Berlin had good reasons to cheer for an imminent establishment of diplomatic relations between Bonn and Tel Aviv.

And yet, the head of the Middle East Division within the East German Ministry of Foreign Affairs, Hermann Simons, recommended attacking the idea vis-à-vis Israeli audiences. He insisted on the need for GDR representatives to support those in Israel who were against the establishment of official diplomatic relations with West Germany. For the prospect of the Arab states breaking off relations with Bonn in response to a probable exchange of ambassadors between the FRG and Israel appealed to East Berlin, but the ongoing criticisms of Bonn might still be a useful tool to carry on the campaign of defamation of the FRG's political establishment, highlighting the anti-Semitic (*judenfeindlich*) character of the West German regime. This was especially desirable given that, as the author of the report himself noted, it was highly unlikely that the 'echo' of the East German defamation campaign against the FRG would be 'strong enough to prevent the establishment of these relations'.[97]

## The geostrategic implications

The attitude that the FRG and the GDR adopted towards Israel in the wake of the 1956 crises testified to each Germany's eagerly sought-after independence in international affairs. In utter contrast to Soviet predictions, which in 1956 envisioned that

Adenauer would not remain in power for much longer, the West German leader won an absolute majority in the 1957 elections – in an astounding electoral success.[98] Thus, although the motto of the electoral campaign that had led him to this landslide victory had been *'keine Experimente!'* (no experiments), in fact he now had all the political room for manoeuvre he needed for experimenting in the national and international political domains – including in the realm of Bonn's special relationship with Israel. For the Federal Republic, this was especially evident in the crafting of the security deal between Strauss and Peres in 1957 – at a time in which doing so was in utter contradiction to the United States' approach to the region, which banned any arms transfer to the countries involved in the Arab–Israeli conflict. These exchanges went on undetected, while much of the Federal foreign policy establishment – including the Chancellor – firmly rejected the idea of establishing diplomatic relations. The threat of Arab recognition of the GDR became a leitmotiv in the West German indefinite postponement of full diplomatic relations with Israel, and the existence of the East German state proved to be an asset for Bonn in the Middle East. West German officials could use the Arab threat to recognise the GDR as a way of resisting Israeli pressure to exchange ambassadors – an issue that Bonn had no interest in furthering if it wanted to protect its political and economic stakes in the Arab world. And covert security ties could develop more or less undisturbed, as the rumours about them were dismissed as East German propaganda by West German diplomats in the region. The crises of 1956 would help cement the closeness of West German–Israeli ties, which now extended to the highest echelons of each country's security and defence establishments, while spurring the East German eagerness to galvanise the Arab states against Bonn.

# Notes

1  *Documents on International Affairs* 1956, 'Speech by President Nasser at Alexandria announcing the nationalization of the Suez Canal Company, 26 July 1956' (London: Oxford University Press for the Royal Institute of International Affairs, 1956).
2  K. Kyle, *Suez: Britain's End of Empire in the Middle East* (London: IB Tauris, 2011).
3  Quoted in G. Buchstab, *Adenauer: 'Wir haben wirklich etwas geschaffen': 1953–1957* (Düsseldorf: Droste, 1990), p. 1027.
4  Laron, 'Cutting the Gordian Knot'.
5  'Convention Respecting the Free Navigation of the Suez Maritime Canal', *The American Journal of International Law. Supplement: Official Documents* 3:2 (1909), pp. 123–7.
6  FRUS, 1955–1957/XVI, Doc. 37: Telegram from the Embassy in the United Kingdom to the Department of State, Barbour, 31 July 1956.
7  FRUS, 1955–1957/XVI, Doc. 53: Tripartite Statement Issued at London, 2 August 1956.
8  Deutscher Bundestag: Haltung der Bundesregierung im Suez-Konflikt. Brentano, 26 November 1956, http://dipbt.bundestag.de/doc/btd/02/029/0202915.pdf [Accessed November 2019].

9  'Suez-Delegation. Was ist normal?', *Der Spiegel*, 22 August 1956, p. 9 and 'German
    Reds Barred: Their Decision to Attend Suez talks Rejected by Britain', *New York Times*,
    14 August 1956, p. 3.

10  *Ibid.* and FRUS, 1955–1957/XVI, Doc. 88, Telegram From the Delegation at the Suez
    Conference to the Department of State, 16 August 1956.

11  Literature on the British colonial experience inspired my use of the term 'official mind',
    e.g. T. Otte, *The Foreign Office Mind* (Cambridge: Cambridge University Press, 2011)
    or F. Heinlein, *British Government Policy and Decolonization, 1945–1963: Scrutinizing
    the Official Mind* (London: Frank Cass, 2002).

12  BAK B 206/621, Report: Arab League against Bonn's recognition of Israel, 23 August
    1956.

13  'German Reds Barred: Their Decision to Attend Suez talks Rejected by Britain',
    *New York Times*, 14 August 1956, p. 3.

14  My italics. 'Bonn – Feind der Araber', *ND*, 9 August 1956, p. 2.

15  Deutsches Orient Institut, *Die Angriffe der SBZ gegen die Nahostpolitik der
    Bundesregierung* (Hamburg: Deutsches-Orient-Stiftung, 1964), pp. 7 and 101.

16  See, for example, G. Weinberger, 'Die Politik des westdeutschen Imperialismus
    während des Suezkonflikts' in H. Tillmann (ed.), *Westdeutscher Neokolonialismus*
    (Berlin: Rütten & Loening, 1963), pp. 165–221.

17  BAK B 206/619, BND Intelligence Report. Statements of the new acting Foreign
    Minister of the 'GDR' Sepp Schwab, 7 July 1956.

18  S. R. Anderson, *A Cold War in the Soviet Bloc: Polish-East German Relations,
    1945–1962* (Boulder: Westview Press, 2001), pp. 114–58.

19  BAK B 206/619, Statements by the new Deputy Minister of Foreign Affairs of the
    'GDR', Sepp Schwab, 7 July 1956. See also S. Lorenzini, 'Comecon and the South in
    the Years of Détente: A Study on East-South Economic Relations', *European Review
    of History: Revue Européenne d'Histoire* 21:2 (2014), pp. 184–6.

20  Wentker, *Außenpolitik*, p. 172.

21  BAK B 206 620/184, Intelligence Report. Reason for the visit of the governmental
    delegation of the 'GDR' to Moscow and earlier clashes about the all-Germany policy
    of the SED, n.d.

22  See S. Radchenko, '1956' in S. A. Smith (ed.), *The Oxford Handbook of the History
    of Communism* (Oxford: Oxford University Press, 2014), pp. 140–55; W. Taubman,
    *Khrushchev: The Man and His Era* (London: Free Press, 2005 [2003]), pp. 270–99.

23  The quote is translated and quoted in Granville, 'Ulbricht in October 1956',
    pp. 477–502; T. Kemp-Welch, 'Khrushchev's "Secret Speech" and Polish Politics: The
    Spring of 1956', *Europe-Asia Studies* 48:2 (1996), pp. 181–206. On the East German
    uprising of June 1953 see, e.g., A. Baring, *Uprising in East Germany: June 17, 1953*
    (Ithaca, NY: Cornell University Press, 1972).

24  BStU, MfS, SdM, 2799/2: Comrade Lieutenant General Mielke reports on the enemy
    activity at the Leipzig Trade Fair, n.d.

25  *Ibid.*

26  BAK B 206/618, BND Intelligence Report. News from the Foreign Ministry of the
    'GDR', 29 June 1956.

27  'Freude über Solidarität der DDR', *ND*, 2 August 1956, p. 1.

28  'Nasser-Telegramm ohne Bedeutung', *Der Tag*, 1 August 1956.

29  *Ibid.*

30  'Telegrammwechsel zwischen Nasser und Pieck', *Neuer Zürcher Zeitung*, 2 August 1956; 'Das Telegramm Nassers and Pieck', *FAZ*, 2 August 1956.

31  R. Louis, *Suez 1956: The Crisis and Its Consequences* (Oxford: Clarendon Press, 1989); D. Tal, *The 1956: Collusion and Rivalry in the Middle East* (London: Cass, 2001).

32  PA AA, MfAA A 9351/25, Memorandum of a conversation General Roßmeisl in the 3rd European Department of the Soviet Ministry of Foreign Affairs on 21.9.1956.

33  My italics. PA AA, MfAA A 9351/16, The Ministry of Foreign Affairs to the Kingdom of Saudi Arabia. For party press reports of the news about the fact that the Foreign Ministry had sent out the note see 'DDR verurteilt Aggression in Nahost', *ND*, 7 November 1956, p. 1.

34  'West Deutschland und der Nahe Osten', *Die Wirtschaft*, 20 December 1956, p. 9.

35  BAK B 206/628, Report: Volunteers for Egypt, 3 December 1956.

36  BAL-SAPMO, DY 30/J 2/2J/311, Stasi report: 'The events in the Middle East and the population of the GDR', Willman, 13 December 1956.

37  E.g. *Information* (ADN), 'nasser dankte patrioten von zella-mehlis fuer sympathie-erklaerung', 25 October 1956; BAK B 206/626, Geldsammlung zugunsten Ägypten soll angeblich Entsendung von Freiwilligen aus NVA, Volkspolizei und Kampfgruppen finanzieren, 13 November 1956; BAK B 206/1960, Information, 'Fachkräfte für Ägypten', No. 16, September 1956; BAK B 206/1960 *Information* No. 18, 'Ausbilder für Ägypten', October 1956.

38  BAK B 206/626, Pushkin stopped 'GDR' aid to Hungary, 16 November 1956.

39  BAK B 206/627, Dr. Bolz reports on meetings with the Soviet Deputy Foreign Minister Zorin in Moscow, n.d.

40  BAK B 206/627, 29. Plenum of the ZK of the SED, 28 November 1956.

41  Schwarz, *Konrad Adenauer*, p. 242; N. J. Ashton, 'Hitler on the Nile? British and American Perceptions of the Nasser Regime, 1952–1970' in L. Freedman and J. H. Michaels (eds), *Scripting Middle Eastern Leaders: The Impact of Leadership Perceptions on US and UK Foreign Policy* (London: Bloomsbury, 2013), pp. 47–62.

42  A. Leviero, 'Radford Seeking 800,000-Man Cut; 3 Services Resist', *New York Times*, 13 July 1956, p. 1. On this see, e.g., C. Craig and F. Logevall, *America's Cold War: The Politics of Insecurity* (Cambridge, MA and London: Belknap Press of Harvard University Press, 2009, 2012), p. 170.

43  J. J. Malone, 'Germany and the Suez Crisis', *Middle East Journal* 20:1 (1966), p. 24.

44  K. Adenauer, *Erinnerungen*, Vol. 3, 1955–1957 (Stuttgart: Deutsche Verlags-Anstalt, 1967), p. 216.

45  *Ibid.* At p. 215, Adenauer wrote that he saw the Suez conflict essentially as a 'conflict between East and West'.

46  Dwight D. Eisenhower Presidential Library (DDEL), Dwight D. Eisenhower Papers (Ann Whitman Files), International Series, Box 15, Adenauer to Eisenhower, 4 December 1956.

47  R. Stauber, 'The Impact of the Sinai Campaign on Relations between Israel and West Germany', *Modern Judaism* 33 (2013), pp. 235–59.

48  Sharett, *The Reparations Controversy*, Rosenne to the Minister of Foreign Affairs, 1 September 1952, p. 343.

49  David Ben-Gurion Archives (DBGA), *Aide memoire*, 1 November 1956, obtained and translated by Yiftach Shavit.

50  Jelinek, *Zwischen Moral und Realpolitik*, Doc. 416: Aufzeichnung, van Scharpenberg, 2 November 1956.

51 Special Session, 5 November 1956, *Kabinettsprotokolle der Bundesregierung*; DFPI, Vol. 11, 1956–1957, Doc. 42: Shinnar (Cologne) to the Ministry of Foreign Affairs, 3 November 1956.

52 DFPI, Vol. 11, 1956–1957, Doc. 29, Ben Gurion to Adenauer, 1 November 1956; see also Documents Diplomatiques Français, 1956, Vol. 3, Doc. 138, Procès-verbal de l'entretien du 6 november 1956 entre le président Guy Mollet en le chancelier Adenauer.

53 PA AA, MfAA A 9286/12, Statement of the Minister of Foreign Affairs on the withdrawal of British and French troops from Egypt, n.d.

54 PA AA, MfAA A 9286/3, GDR Trade mission, Egypt. Preliminary study for a foreign policy line towards Egypt, Stude, 17 December 1956.

55 PA AA, MfAA A 9826/61, Schwab to Scholz. Directive on a proposal to the Egyptian Government for the establishment of a Consulate General of the German Democratic Republic in Cairo, 23 November 1956.

56 FRUS, 1955–1957/XVII, Doc. 110, Memorandum of a Telephone Conversation Between the Secretary of State in Washington and the Representative at the United Nations (Lodge) in New York, 18 February 1957; D. Trimbur, 'American Influence on Germany's Israel Policy 1951–1956' in G. Haim (ed.), *Germany and the Middle East: Past, Present, and Future* (Jerusalem: The Hebrew University Press, 2003), pp. 281–2.

57 Hahn, *Caught in the Middle East*, p. 213.

58 J. L. Gaddis, *We Now Know: Rethinking Cold War History* (Oxford: Clarendon, 1998), p. 173.

59 Special Session, 5 November 1956, *Kabinettsprotokolle der Bundesregierung*.

60 *Ibid.*

61 S. Shpiro, 'Know Your Enemy: West German-Israeli Intelligence Evaluation of Soviet Weapon Systems', *The Journal of Intelligence History* 4 (2004), pp. 58–9.

62 Reinhard Gehlen and Isser Harel first met in person in 1958. S. Shpiro, 'Für Israels Sicherheit paktieren wir sogar mid dem Teufel', *Das Parlament*, 11 April 2005.

63 De S. Gramont, 'Recollections of a Superspy', *Washington Post*, 2 July 1972.

64 S. Setter, 'In the Footsteps of the Mossad Chief Who Went Undercover as a French Artist in Egypt', *Haaretz*, 15 November 2017; S. Shpiro, 'Shadowy Interests. West German-Israeli Intelligence and Military Cooperation, 1957–1982' in C. Jones and Tore (eds), *Israel's Clandestine Diplomacies* (London: Hirst, 2013), pp. 171–89.

65 T. Wolf, *Die Entstehung des BND: Aufbau, Finanzierung, Kontrolle* (Berlin: Links, 2018), pp. 422ff.; K. D. Henke, *Geheime Dienste: Die politische Inlandsspionage der Organisation Gehlen, 1946–1953* (Berlin: Links, 2018), p. 304; J. Adams, *Historical Dictionary of German Intelligence* (Lanham: The Scarecrow Press, 2009), pp. 41, 259–60.

66 H. Zölling and H. Höhne, *Pullach Intern: General Gehlen und die Geschichte des Bundesnachrichtendienstes* (Hamburg: Hoffmann und Campe, 1971), p. 270.

67 J. Adams, *Historical Dictionary of German Intelligence* (Lanham: Scarecrow Press, 2009), p. 41.

68 This and the following quotes are from The Moshe Sharett Israel Labor Party Archive – Berl Katznelson Foundation, File n. 2-7-1957-66, Mapai Party Meeting Protocol, 27 June 1957, p. 62, obtained and translated by Yiftach Shavit.

69 C. McNaub, *The Uzi Submachine Gun* (Oxford: Osprey Publishing, 2011), p. 31.

70 J. Edmiston, *The Sterling Years: Small Arms and the Men* (London: Leo Cooper, 1992), p. 22.

71 'Ha-shliḥut she-butla', 18 December 1957 (*LaMerhav*), p. 2.
72 The Moshe Sharett Israel Labor Party Archive – Berl Katznelson Foundation, File n. 2-23-1957-72, Mapai Party Meeting Protocol, 30 December 1957, obtained and translated by Yiftach Shavit.
73 *Ibid.*
74 S. Peres, *David's Sling* (New York: Random House, 1971), p. 73; F. J. Strauß, *Die Erinnerungen* (Berlin: Siedler, 1989), p. 345; A. Ben-Natan, *The Audacity to Live: The Autobiography of Asher Ben-Natan* (Jerusalem: Mazo Publishers, 2007), p. 120.
75 Strauß, *Erinnerungen*, p. 381; G. Rosenberg, *Franz Josef Strauß und sein Jude* (Munich: Allitera, 2015), pp. 7–9.
76 N. Hansen, 'Geheimvorhaben "Frank/Kol". Zur deutsch-israelischen Rüstungszusammenarbeit 1957 bis 1965', *Historisch-Politische Mitteilungen, Archiv für Christlich-Demokratische Politik* 6 (1999), p. 231.
77 Jelinek, *Zwischen Moral und Realpolitik*, Doc. 106: Zvi Dar (TAAS) to Dr. A. Bergmann, 12 December 1955.
78 Hansen, 'Geheimvorhaben Frank./Col.', p. 234; Peres, *David's Sling*, pp. 73ff.; Strauß, *Erinnerungen*, p. 346.
79 S. Shpiro, 'Intelligence Services and Foreign Policy', *German Politics* 11:1 (2002), p. 31; M. Serr, 'Bilateral Arms Cooperation: The Roots of German-Israeli Relations', *Israeli Journal of Foreign Affairs* 2 (2015).
80 In 1952 the Israeli authorities had already compiled a list of raw materials that might be useful for the IDF. See I. Tal, 'The Evolution of the German-Israeli Security Relations: A Personal Perspective' in M. Uhlmann (ed.), *Die deutsch-israelischen Sicherheitsbeziehungen. Vergangenheit, Gegenwart, Zukunft* (Berlin: Berliner Wissenschaftsverlag, 2008), pp. 16–17; M. Mohr, *Waffen für Israel: Westdeutsche Rüstungshilfe vor dem Sechstagekrieg* (Berlin: Köster, 2003), p. 51.
81 DBGA, Diary entry, 29 December 1957, obtained and translated by Yiftach Shavit.
82 Although in fact Dayan was not present at the meeting. PA AA, B12 1045, Kessel (Washington) to the Foreign Office, 27 December 1957.
83 Peres, *David's Sling*, p. 72.
84 'Todesfabrik am Eichborndamm', *ND*, 23 February 1957, p. 6.
85 For a comprehensive review of East German articles and statements on the topic, see Deutsches Orient Institut, *Die Angriffe der SBZ*.
86 'Bonn der Lüge überführt', *ND*, 29 December 1957, p. 7.
87 PA AA, B12 1045, Telegram, Welck, 31 December 1957.
88 PA AA, B12 1045, Knoke (Damascus), 4 January 1958.
89 H. P. Schwarz, 'Die deutschlandpolitischen Vorstellungen Konrad Adenauers, 1955–1958', in H. P. Schwarz (ed.), *Entspannung und Wiedervereinigung: Deutschlandpolitische Vorstellungen Konrad Adenauers* (Stuttgart: Belser, 1979), pp. 7–40.
90 BAL-SAPMO, NY 4090/495, Notes. Simons, 16 February 1957.
91 PA AA, B12 1045, Telegram (encrypted), Welck, 31 December 1957.
92 Relevant documents can be found in PA AA, MfAA A/9318, Journey of the deputy prime minister Paul Scholz in the UAR.
93 'Erklärung des Leiters der Handelsdelegation der Regierung der Deutschen Demokratischen Republik, Gerhard Weiß, vor der Presse in Bagdad am 27. Oktober 1958', *Dokumente zur Außenpolitik der Regierung der Deutschen Demokratischen Republik*, Band VI, Vom 1. Januar bis zum 31. Dezember 1958 (Berlin: Rütten & Loening, 1959), p. 317.

94 BAL-SAPMO, DY 30 IV 2 / 20 / 373 22, Simons, July 1960.

95 Gray, *Germany's Cold War*, p. 58; M. Anic de Osona, *Die erste Anerkennung der DDR. Der Bruch der deutsch-jugoslawischen Beziehungen 1957* (Baden-Baden: Nomos, 1990); M. C. Theurer, *Bonn – Belgrad- Ost-Berlin: die Beziehungen der beiden deutschen Staaten zu Jugoslawien im Vergleich: 1957–1968* (Berlin: Logos, 2008), p. 112; S. Rajak, *Yugoslavia and the Soviet Union in the Early Cold War: Reconciliation, Comradeship, Confrontation, 1953–57* (London: Routledge, 2011), p. 202.

96 PA AA, MfAA A 12739/35, Memo. Simons an Schwab, 17 July 1957.

97 *Ibid.*

98 BAK, B 206/68, Soviet agitation concerning the German question, 10 September 1956.

# 5

# Adjustments

Originally established in 1953 as a humble operation concerned solely with reparations, under the leadership of Felix Shinnar the Israeli mission in Cologne gradually took on a much more significant role. Slowly but surely, Shinnar laboured to get direct and privileged access to the highest echelons of West Germany's foreign policy, with the ultimate goal of establishing full diplomatic relations between Israel and the FRG. By 1958, Chancellor Adenauer, Foreign Minister von Brentano, and many other leading FRG representatives from across the political spectrum received him on a regular basis to discuss global geopolitical trends and the evolving bilateral relationship.

In his memoirs, Shinnar portrayed the core duty of his mission as promoting cohesion among his subordinates, fostering real team spirit. This was so important to him that, in his memoirs, Shinnar remembered, he had banned the use of the pronoun 'I' at weekly mission meetings – everyone was invited to reflect on the objectives accomplished and the work done, but only in terms of a collective endeavour, using exclusively plural, rather than singular, pronouns.[1] Many in Jerusalem disparaged 'his domineering nature', however, and criticised Shinnar's fixation with high politics. Shinnar's detractors urged the mission to start promoting a real rapprochement between the two peoples, promoting links at social and cultural, as well as policy-making, levels. Initiatives such as organising exchanges between lecturers, journalists, politicians and students, they argued, offered a better way to win West German sympathy for Israel.[2]

Relations between West German and Israeli civil societies had been gradually drawing closer. In March 1957, for example, SPD chairman and Bundestag member Erich Ollenhauer visited Israel in an official capacity and, for the first time in Israeli history, had delivered a public speech in German – a language whose use in public, at that time, was still subject to approval on a case-by-case basis.[3] Later that year, in September 1957, the President of the West German Sports Federation (Deutscher Sportbund), Willi Daume, also made an official visit to Israel, using the occasion to make a financial donation of DM42,000 to the Israeli Maccabi Sports Organization.[4] From that year onwards, West German and Israeli football teams began exchanging expertise, with Israeli coaches travelling frequently to Cologne for training purposes.[5] The links between the German Trade Union Confederation (Deutscher Gewerkschaftsbund) and its Israeli counterpart, the Histradut, also grew closer.[6] But Shinnar maintained his focus on high politics for the time being, fixated on his goal of establishing diplomatic relations. The desire for a closer cooperation with the Federal Republic was something that David Ben-Gurion seemed to be 'possessed by',[7] and Shinnar believed an exchange of ambassadors to be close at hand. In fact, this objective would become ever harder to attain, as the upheavals in the Middle East region, and the East German attempts to capitalise on them, multiplied throughout 1958.

The year started with Nasser's announcement, on 1 February, that Egypt and Syria would unite to form a political union, the United Arab Republic (UAR) – to the dismay and alarm of many of their regional neighbours. On 14 February, in an effort to counter the broad appeal and popularity of the Egyptian-Syrian move, Iraq and Jordan announced their own plans for the 'Arab Union' (AU), a political federation that also aimed to incorporate Saudi Arabia in due course. The news failed to generate anything comparable to the widespread excitement that the formation of the UAR had inspired throughout the region. Worse still, shortly after the AU announcement flopped, news circulated that King Saud, together with the United States, had been plotting a coup in Syria and an assassination attempt against Nasser. These rumours were unfounded, but they still severely damaged the image of the Eisenhower presidency in the region, and the standing of the conservative monarchies in the area, Saudi Arabia in primis. The crisis gradually dissipated with the ascent to power of Crown Prince Faisal, who sought to steer a more neutral course in the UAR–AU rivalry and to lower the Saudi profile in regional power struggles.[8]

But the relative political calm was not to last. By the summer, Lebanese leader Camille Chamoun requested Anglo-French-American support to thwart what he perceived to be lethal attacks against his grip on power. This was soon followed by a similar Jordanian appeal. At first, US and British authorities had been hesitant about how to respond to Chamoun's appeals for political and military support. But, in July, Iraq was shaken by a military-led revolution, which resulted in the execution of ruling King Faisal II and Prime Minister Nuri al-Said and in the rise of Iraq's new, revolutionary political leader Abd al-Karim Qasim. On 15 July 1958, the day after the Iraqi revolution, some 2,000 US Marines were dispatched to Beirut. They were soon joined by another 14,000 military personnel, while the US Seventh Fleet – generally stationed just off the shore of Okinawa in Japan – was relocated to the Strait of Hormuz to safeguard the situation in the Persian Gulf. The British agreed to supply Amman with food and fuel while the US intervention was ongoing in Lebanon.[9] Chamoun and King Hussein had ostensibly asked the Western powers for help for fear of a Communist infiltration of their political systems. In fact, what worried them was the increasing volatility of the Arab political scene and the fear that revolutionary forces might overthrow several other regimes among the conservative Arab republics allied with the West – especially their own. With the Western intervention supporting the conservative Arab states in the region, and the Soviets backing the revolutionary republics, the global Cold War now came to overlap with the Arab Cold War.[10]

## The German dimension

With the formation of the UAR, East German hopes to be finally recognised by Nasser, who now was the leader of a much bigger Arab political entity, ran high. Egypt–GDR trade had grown steadily over the years, and several leading personalities had visited the country in an official capacity – a remarkable achievement from an East German perspective. Hoping to open new avenues for economic and political cooperation with the UAR, the GDR, like its Soviet patron, had readily overlooked Nasser's fierce repression against Egyptian, and, after 1958, also Syrian, Communists.[11]

Formalising diplomatic relations remained difficult, however, for reasons that sounded remarkably similar to those that the West Germans had been presenting to Israeli diplomats of late. As the FRG Foreign Ministry summarised, UAR 'recognition of the GDR could provoke a West German recognition of Israel'. This would, in turn, reflect negatively on the UAR and endanger its relations with other countries in the Arab world.[12] This was one of the most common refrains from the UAR authorities in talks with East German diplomats, although the possibility of a West German economic backlash may have been a more compelling actual reason for the UAR's reluctance to move towards establishing diplomatic relations with the GDR.

Regardless, the situation illustrated the unique deadlock that the two German states, Israel, and the Arab states inhabited by the end of the 1950s. The FRG authorities avoiding establishing diplomatic relations with Israel while alluding to the danger that the Arab countries would retort by recognising the GDR, while UAR representatives refrained from encouraging East German ambitions to establish diplomatic relations because of possible FRG recognition of Israel. Earlier that year, the US National Security Council (NSC) had observed that by 1958 the West Germans were 'without a doubt the most popular of any of the Westerners with the Arabs'.[13] According to the NSC assessment, this was due to the high volume and quality of the goods that the FRG was selling to the countries of the region and Bonn's foreign trade with the Middle East had indeed increased significantly throughout the 1950s.[14]

But the NSC participants also agreed that there was another important factor sustaining Bonn's popularity with the Arab countries – the West German ability to convince their Arab counterparts that Bonn was not an enthusiastic supporter of Israel, 'by hinting in appropriate places that agreement [regarding the reparations to Israel] came about as a result of US pressure'.[15] Over the coming months, the West German foreign policy establishment faced the arduous task of treading the fine line between appealing to an increasingly fragmented – yet politically and economically important – Arab world while maintaining its delicate ties to Israel, adjusting them to make sure they would not be an obstacle to the Federal Republic's rise in popularity and economic leadership in the Arab Middle East.

With the revolution in Iraq, Bonn – and the West as a whole – suddenly and unexpectedly risked losing a reliable ally in the region and, the West Germans knew, the GDR would soon try and make the most of the new regional geopolitical scenario. As was to be expected, in the hot summer of 1958 East German media again portrayed the FRG as a crucial party to an aggressive Western policy to subjugate the peoples of the Middle East.[16] Insistence that, by providing logistical support, 'West Germany plays a special role in the imperialist aggression' became a GDR propaganda leitmotiv for the summer of 1958, accompanied by remarks about Bonn's material support for Israel with 'so-called reparations which [Israel] uses [as] a means to finance attacks against Egypt' and the Arab world as a whole.[17]

In fact, allegations of Bonn's complicity with, and military support of, the British–American interventions were unfounded. Adenauer, to his dismay, had been unaware of the impending Western intervention in Lebanon and Jordan. The same went for Foreign Minister Brentano, who, as the first US Marines landed in Lebanon, was on holiday enjoying the natural beauties of the Odenwald region. The West German press attacked the US intervention, and the Chancellor, while avoiding voicing public criticism of his own, in fact agreed with most of the negative press coverage.[18] Far from the compliant sidekick of GDR propaganda, for Chancellor Adenauer, the regional upheavals of 1958 brought with them a renewed dose of insecurity regarding Bonn's international standing. The fact that neither the British nor the Americans had informed the West German authorities of their impending interventions in the Middle East caused particular disappointment and discontent among Bonn's foreign policy establishment and among the West German public opinion at large. Given that many of the US forces that reached Lebanon did so from US bases located in West German and that the FRG had no constitutional right to impede the US military manoeuvres on its territory, the matter was regarded as especially serious.[19]

## Meeting the comrades

By the time the US troops reached the shores of Beirut, a huge political event was drawing to a close in East Berlin – the Fifth Party Congress of the SED. Communists from forty-five countries had arrived to take part in the gathering. Among them was Esther Vilenska, a founder and legendary member of Maki.[20] SED Central Committee Secretary Kurt Hager had personally fetched her from the airport upon her arrival in the builders' and workers' state. On the fifth day of the Congress, Vilenska took the floor to address the audience with a strong endorsement of the GDR and its policies. 'We, sons and daughters of the Jewish people, feel especially close to you, who fight tirelessly and relentlessly against the re-establishment of National Socialism in West Germany', she stated.[21] She praised the East German regime as 'one of the most important bulwarks ... against fascism and war' while condemning 'the political collaboration between the Ben-Gurion government and the Adenauer government, which is re-establishing Nazism and militarism in West Germany'.[22]

Vilenska's words in East Berlin were important – they signalled that common interests could exist between East German and Israeli Communists, at a time in which the Israeli Communists felt increasingly alienated by the Ben-Gurion government – as demonstrated, for example, by the Prime Minister's decision to exclude all Maki members from the Histradut and by the mass arrests that had taken place in Israel in the wake of the Labour Day demonstrations.[23] The Maki leadership had then contacted the SED organs, among other Communist parties, asking them for support in denouncing Ben-Gurion's iron-fisted measures.[24]

But if the Israeli Communists thought that ideological alignment would motivate the SED cadres to lend them their support, they were sorely mistaken. In the international affairs of the GDR, politics trumped ideology, and pleasing a small group of Israeli Communists was not a priority. On the contrary, it became paramount for the East German leadership to reassure the Arab audiences that the GDR was essentially interested in dealing with them – regardless of the mass incarcerations of Egyptian and Syrian Communists in Nasser's UAR. East Germany's main concern was to break the isolation campaign imposed on it by the West. Any East German initiative that may signal support for Israel was halted – even the smallest ones. When the praeses of the general synod of the Evangelical Church of the old-Prussian Union, Lothar Kreyssig, proposed a societal initiative aimed at fostering reconciliation between Germans, Poles and Israelis, the East German regime firmly forbade any such exchange. The only activities worth pursuing, Kreyssig would learn, were those aimed at improving living conditions in the GDR.[25] His idea instead became a success in West Germany, where hundreds of thousands of young people signed up for his Action Reconciliation (*Aktion Sühnezeichen*) programme.[26] At that point in the GDR the political situation was simply too hostile to Israel for any such initiative. The regime's priorities were different. The Fifth Party Congress had displayed 'a cohesiveness and morale higher than of any previous' meeting, showing that the East German ruling party had 'emerged from the serious ideological and other failings of 1956–57 with remarkable vigor', as the US State Department's Bureau of Intelligence and Research assessed.[27] Khrushchev's renewed support soon translated into further economic credits and assistance. Ulbricht, who seemed in firm control of his party, strived eagerly for his key goal: international recognition of the GDR. The Middle Eastern upheavals would provide interesting opportunities to fulfil the East German dream.

## Baghdad to Berlin

Two West German nationals were injured – one subsequently died – when angry masses took to the streets of Baghdad to oust the Iraqi monarchy and the al-Nuri government. This seemed ominous for future relations between the FRG and revolutionary Iraq, and the country's new Foreign Minister, Abdul Jabbar Jomard, met with the West German ambassador in Baghdad shortly after the revolution, reassuring him that the new government of Iraq had no intention of harming West Germany's interests – or its nationals – and that all the agreements and policies in place between Iraq and the FRG would remain in effect and unchanged.[28] Despite Jomard's reassurances, however, the Bonn authorities felt they had little reason to stay calm. On 10 October 1958, East German efforts to reach out to the Arab world solidified into the foundation of the German–Arab Society (Deutsch–Arabische Gesellschaft, DAG) an organisation aiming 'to provide a true image of the GDR's fight for freedom [and] to present an uncorrupted image of the Arab peoples' fight for freedom'.[29] The DAG planned to provide photographs, documentaries and speakers to universities, societies and cultural centres and set up information booths at international trade fairs or exhibitions – 'be they in Damascus, Cairo, Casablanca or Tunis' – in order to spread the image of 'pacific political, economic, and cultural aspects of life in the GDR to the Arab masses'.[30]

A GDR delegation arrived in Iraq less than two weeks after the revolution, led by Ambassador Paul Wandel, formerly Central Committee Secretary of Culture and Pedagogy.[31] Wandel had a long history of militancy in the German Communist Party, and during his exile years in the Soviet Union he had, among other roles, served as Wilhelm Pieck's personal secretary. Petty rivalries within the SED's Central Committee brought him a reprimand in 1957, due to an alleged lack of commitment to the East German *kulturpolitisch* mission.[32] And once in Iraq, Wandel could not, and did not, disappoint. His appointment as delegation head testified to the importance that East Berlin attached to cultural and propaganda matters in expanding its web of foreign influence. While GDR and Arab comrades had come together to establish the DAG in East Berlin, Wandel held high-level visits with new Iraqi Prime Minister Qasim and several of his ministers in Baghdad.[33] A visit from East German Deputy Minister for Foreign and Intra-German Trade Gerhard Weiss soon followed, culminating in a further trade agreement.[34] The Iraqi authorities granted the GDR permission to open their trade mission in Baghdad shortly thereafter. Joining the GDR representation in Cairo, this would be the second East German outpost in the heart of the revolutionary Arab world. Again, Bonn's ties with Israel proved to be a focal point for GDR propaganda. Weiss placed key emphasis on the two German states' differing attitudes towards Israel during his Baghdad press conference, condemning the Federal Republic's 'so-called reparation payments ... essential contribution to Israel's material and moral strength'.[35]

The possibility of harm to West Germany's ties with the Arab world in the wake of 1958 deeply worried Adenauer. As a preventative measure, he approved a credit transfer of over DM350 million to Nasser – to the great displeasure of the Americans, who, rather than appeasing Cairo, deemed it much more important to support the more conservative, and seemingly more reliable, Western allies in the region, such as Jordan and Lebanon. The Chancellor, however, was adamant that the Western countries should deploy their economic weapons in the Middle East. It was crucial, Adenauer insisted to explain to an exasperated Dulles, to tie the countries of the Middle East to the European economic sphere, as this would be the only effective way to keep the Soviets out of the region.[36]

The West Germans assured the Israelis that Bonn's openness towards Nasser should not alarm them. Three days after the Iraqi revolution, the Chancellor met with Israel's Ambassador to France, Maurice Fischer, to discuss the West German–Israeli relationship in the wake of the 1958 upheavals. Adenauer asked Fischer 'not to attribute the reserved tone in the German public announcements to any negative attitude towards Israel but only to their wish to act as a mediator in view of their good standing with the Arabs'. The Chancellor inquired whether Israel would support such mediation, and also about Israel's rumoured desired acquisition of a nuclear bomb.[37]

Fischer denied the latter, but confirmed the former on condition that Israel's existence and boundaries would be protected.[38] On both points, however, Fischer's replies were not quite the truth. Excavations had recently begun in the Negev area that would lay the grounds for Israel's first nuclear reactor.[39] And in private, Fischer scorned the self-deluded West German belief in themselves as mediators between the Arabs and the West – held 'no doubt in perfect sincerity' – which had come out of the 1958 crisis.[40]

Adenauer's worries, and those of his foreign policy establishment, further increased in November 1958, when Khrushchev demanded that the Western allies withdraw their occupation forces from Berlin within six months. Should they not comply, the Soviets would unilaterally transfer their sovereign rights in Berlin to the East German authorities, and the Western powers would be forced to somehow recognise and deal directly with them on all Berlin-related matters. The Soviet leader's diplomatic offensive forced Bonn's Western allies to reassess their own policy of non-recognition of the GDR, and a flurry of diplomatic activity ensued in the Western capitals – including in Bonn, although the Soviets had circumvented the FRG government by communicating exclusively with Paris, London and Washington.

While the Bonn establishment panicked, from Cologne Shinnar observed the evolution of the Berlin crisis with a pinch of optimism. 'It cannot be ruled out', he noted in January 1959, that 'during the next few months the Bonn government will itself propose appointing a permanent representative in Israel ... present and future developments definitely require that they be in possession of continuous reports from Israel, which is not necessarily the case for the neighbouring countries'.[41] While recognising the risks inherent in an escalation of the situation in Berlin, in a conversation with State Secretary von Eckardt, Shinnar commented that with the upcoming Four Powers talks on the German question it was possible that 'the problem of recognition of East Germany will disappear and will no longer be an obstacle to the establishment of relations with Israel' – to which Eckardt agreed.[42] From Jerusalem, Prime Minister Ben-Gurion concurred with Shinnar's assessment. Upon learning of secret talks going on between West German and Polish representatives about establishing some form of mutual recognition, the Israeli Prime Minister noted in his diary that 'if they succeed they will abolish the line of no diplomatic relations with countries that recognise East Germany and the fear of Arab states will diminish [and] then they will propose diplomatic relations with us'.[43]

Adenauer himself, in a forty-five-minute talk with Shinnar, had stressed that the two countries should formalise their relations soon – and certainly no later than 1960. The question of the timing of the exchange of ambassadors between Israel and the Federal Republic resurfaced periodically in conversations between Israeli and West German representatives. 'He added that the matter is very close to his heart and that he would be happy to close the circle [of his chancellorship] by giving expression to his feelings for Israel', reported Shinnar to the Foreign Ministry.[44] Such conversations went in parallel with concrete West German support for Israel – not only through the reparations programme and the covert security arrangements, but also politically, at the United Nations and at NATO meetings, where the FRG supported Israel's position at a time in which the country, post-Suez, found itself in a minority position; or at the Vatican, where West

German diplomats lobbied with the local authorities for the establishment of diplomatic relations between Israel and the Vatican state; and, finally, by supporting public engineering works, such as a pipeline project that would have rendered Israel's energy procurement efforts much more efficient.[45] The year 1959 even witnessed the filming of the first West German–Israeli movie co-production, *Burning Sand*.[46]

All of this overt and covert West German support for Israel notwithstanding, the official line of the Federal Foreign Ministry on the question of diplomatic relations remained unchanged: there was no point in exchanging ambassadors or consuls between the two countries – not just yet. Israeli attempts to reach out to the United States in the hope that Washington would exert enough power on the West German position proved fruitless. Despite Dulles' explicit endorsement of a diplomatic agreement between the Federal Republic and the Jewish state, the Bonn authorities remained adamant that this would be a mistake that would push the GDR in the arms of the Arabs, that may also negatively affect West German–Soviet relations. And – just to be sure to drive the point home with the Israelis – who could guarantee that such a move would not have endangered the smooth carrying out of the reparations agreement, negatively affecting the transfer of West German goods to Israel?[47]

## Pondering Palestine

Questions of *Israelpolitik* became even more complicated in the late 1950s, given the mounting competition in the region as to who would champion Palestinian national aspirations. Up to the Suez Crisis, Nasser had insisted on the need to find a solution to the living conditions and the eventual right of return of the refugees. But after 1956, he dramatically raised the stakes. His stated aim became 'the liberation of the Palestinian people, to which we shall restore its political and social rights' – a goal to be fought for by a Pan-Arab movement.[48] Nasser's dynamism notwithstanding, young members of the Palestinian diaspora would play an increasingly important role in shaping the politics of the region, shifting the narrative on the Palestinian struggle towards ever more militant tones, often accompanied by guerrilla incursions into Israeli territory.[49] The self-styled Movement for the Liberation of Palestine (*harakat al-tahrir al-filastini*, Fatah) began to gather ever more followers. At the head of the movement was a former engineering student, Yasser Arafat, who had founded the Palestinian society at Cairo University before relocating to work in the Gulf. Arafat was one of a number of disillusioned young Palestinians who had experienced first-hand expulsion and dispersal, feeling estranged within the Arab countries where they had resettled.[50]

The Fatah movement gathered around a simple but revolutionary message: waiting for the Arab states to act to protect Palestinian interests was a losing game. The liberation of Palestine was not an issue that should be delegated to the Arab leaders, whose record in defending the Palestinian cause had been disastrous over the previous decade – instead, the time had come for Palestinians to take matters into their own hands.[51] Membership spread quickly throughout the region, attracting many recruits, especially from Syria, which hosted a consistent part of the Palestinian diaspora and where the political union with Egypt began to reveal, to many, the brutal face of the Nasserist experiment.

Tensions and fractures between conservative monarchies and revolutionary Arab republics, adding to the intensified struggle for the representation of Palestinian nationalism, dominated the Arab world when the East German authorities began framing their own position regarding Palestine and Palestinian rights. The first East German body to openly advertise its stance on the matter was the East German Trades Union Confederation (Freier Deutscher Gewerkschaftsbund, FDGB). One of the key mass organisations through which the SED arranged the East German population's participation in the political process, the FDGB also served an important international role, keeping and expanding ties with equivalent organisations in third countries.[52] Just as the West German trade union movement had been expanding its links with the Israeli Histradut throughout the 1950s, the East Germans were attempting to do the same with their partner organisations in the Arab world. In a communiqué released in conjunction with the International Confederation of Arab Trade Unions, the East German union had promised support for the 'restoration of the legitimate rights of the Palestinian Arabs'.[53] But such a clear stance in favour of the recognition of the rights of Palestinian citizens, as expressed in the declaration of the Trade Union Confederation, did not generally feature in, or form part of, the East German narrative on the Middle East conflict at that time – and East Berlin's Foreign Ministry was eager to have its voice heard on the matter.

The Ministry circulated its very first memo to address and contextualise the questions of the East German attitude vis-à-vis Palestinian Arabs and of their political representation in July 1958, which stressed 'that we consider the Palestinian question as an internal affair of the Arab states'. A 'large part of Palestine', the memo added, 'was declared to be an Arab state by the UN [and] is indeed administered by Arab states'. The memo concluded with an odd note that recommended not to recognise, for the time being, the All Palestine Government – a body founded back in 1948, and that the Egyptian authorities would shut, for good, just a year after the circulation of the East German memo.[54] At the height of the first war between Israel and its Arab neighbours, it was supposed to serve as the embryonic governmental administration of a Palestinian state, although in subsequent years it served more as an Egyptian tool to undermine Jordanian claims to representation of the Palestinian cause rather than as anything resembling a functioning Palestinian government.[55] The message of the Foreign Ministry, in short, emphasised the importance of sticking to the side which held power, such as the UAR, and who might translate into important economic and political partners for the GDR.

Not until the 1970s did the East German state organs couple their anti-Israeli rhetoric with a pro-Palestinian message. They studiously avoided the question for most of the 1950s and 1960s, in order not to alienate Arab states whose recognition was much more strategically important for the GDR than that of any Palestinian grouping. The civil and political rights of the Palestinian Arabs, the living conditions of Palestinian refugees, the question of return – none of these issues mattered much to the East German authorities. From East Berlin's perspective, the Palestinians were simply not valuable, their cause worth paying neither attention nor lip service to. And although the East German government had, in principle, agreed to host a number of Palestinian students in the GDR, in fact no student with a Palestinian background was selected to study at East German universities until the mid 1970s.[56] The priority, for the East German authorities, was to not get ensnared in the complications of Palestinian and intra-Arab politics by avoiding statements focusing on the controversial subject – while at the same time bashing Israel, its ties with Bonn, and the latter's imperialist ambitions at any given opportunity.[57]

In contrast, the West Germans had been quietly making their voice heard on Palestinian matters in the way that they knew best – through economic support. Albeit at irregular intervals and with varying amounts, the Federal Republic had begun funding the UN Relief and Works Agency (UNRWA) in 1952, shortly after the signing of the agreement with Israel.[58] West German donations to UNRWA, the UN agency founded in 1949 to improve the living conditions of the Palestinian refugees across the Middle East, grew exponentially in just two years, jumping from DM105,000 in 1956 to a total of DM800,000 in 1958. Such increase in the West German contribution to the UNRWA budget had something to do with the renewed economic strength and political ambition of the Federal Republic but, partly, also with the insistence of Arab representatives themselves. In their talks with West German diplomats, envoys in Bonn, especially the Lebanese, Jordanian and Iraqi ones, often raised the question of the desperate living conditions of Palestinian refugees in their respective countries, asking for the Federal Republic's financial help to support their efforts at hosting them. In the attempt to convince West German representatives of the need to devote more funding to the question of Palestinian refugees, 'they [Arab representatives] constantly mention the comparison with our high transfers to Israel [and] any attempt [on our part] to convince them that the two cases are completely different and absolutely not comparable inevitably do not cut it'.[59] And, as Bonn's State Secretary Karl Carstens put it, a higher contribution to the UNRWA would 'undermine' the credibility of such arguments.[60]

In the end, the sum agreed for in the year 1958 – DM800,000 – was the result of a compromise between the UN and Middle East Departments within Bonn's Foreign Ministry. UNRWA's Director, Henry Richardson Labouisse, had broached the subject of higher West German spending during his visit to the Federal Republic in the summer of 1957, asking for a more active Federal involvement in funding the young UN agency, and in December UN Secretary General Dag Hammarskjöld had written a personal letter to West Germany's Permanent Observer at the United Nations echoing the message. As the Director of the Middle East Desk Voigt stressed, increasing the amount of West German donations to the UN agency for Palestinian refugees would not radically affect Bonn's finances. And it would be a beneficial move in terms of *Ansehen* – boosting West Germany's international prestige by displaying Bonn's compassionate understanding for 'a problem of substantial international significance'.[61]

In addition to increasing funding for the Palestinian cause via the United Nations, the West German authorities also foresaw avoiding overt statements in Israel's favour, especially as the tenth anniversary of the country's foundation drew nearer – an event referred to as the *Nakba*, the catastrophe, in the Arab world. Accordingly, in March 1958 the Chancellor declined an invitation to visit Israel to take part in the celebrations for the tenth anniversary of its founding, which were to take place in May; West German President Theodor Heuss and the mayor of West Berlin Willy Brandt received advice to do likewise.[62] It was important, the West German Foreign Office advised, to show a certain reserve regarding Israel, especially in light of the '*DDR-Problem*' in the wake of the 1958 revolutions.[63] From Cairo, Ambassador Becker recommended avoiding any type of visit, even personal ones, as they might give credibility to GDR propaganda aimed at the Arab states about dangerous West German–Israeli sympathies developing behind their backs.[64]

One of those who did not follow the guidelines coming from the Foreign Ministry was SPD politician and Bundestag Vice President Carlo Schmid. His party had historically been involved in promoting reconciliation between Germans and Israelis – as testified, for example, by the fact that the 1952 reparations agreement would not have been ratified by the Bundestag had it not been for the SPD votes, while at that time the ruling coalition was vocally against it.[65] Schmid himself had a significant experience in foreign policy matters having taken part in, among others, the delegation that accompanied Adenauer in his groundbreaking 1955 visit to Moscow. In 1950, Schmid's first encounter with Israeli politicians had taken place in Istanbul, where he attended the Inter Parliamentary Union meeting as a member of the FRG delegation. At that time, Israeli Knesset delegates had vehemently attacked the West Germans, asking for their exclusion from the Union's meetings. While, in public, the Israeli attacks mounted, Schmid had sat down with some of the Israeli delegation members, trying to help the two delegations to find some common ground. Almost a decade on, in utter defiance of the policy line recommended by the Foreign Ministry, he accepted an invitation to visit Israel on the occasion of its tenth anniversary.[66]

Schmid travelled in the company of his daughter.[67] They stayed in Israel for a week, visiting the main archaeological sites in the country and attending Israel's military parade, which Schmid admired from his seat – right between Prime Minister Ben-Gurion and Foreign Minister Moshe Sharett. 'Ben-Gurion asked me how I liked the march', noted Schmid in his memoirs. ' "Very good", I replied, "one may even get the impression that a Prussian army corps was parading" – the Prime Minister laughed.'[68] Schmid returned for a second visit to Israel shortly thereafter to deliver a lecture at the Hebrew University on European intellectual history while also finding the time for informal talks with both Ben-Gurion and the new Israeli Foreign Minister, Golda Meir. Again, the conversation returned to the topic of diplomatic relations between the two countries. SPD Chairman Ollenhauer had visited the country earlier in 1957 and had already made clear to the Israeli authorities that he, and his party, would try and influence Adenauer to change perspective on the question of diplomatic relations with Israel, in the attempt to speed up the process.[69]

Adenauer, exasperated, eventually lashed out at Carlo Schmid, trying to get across that the question of German–Israeli relations would carry with them global geopolitical implications: 'Because of how things are today, the establishment of official diplomatic relations between Israel and the Federal Republic would certainly arouse very big agitation and a witch-hunt of the strongest kind against the Federal Republic, and this agitation would also spread to non-Arab, Islamic countries such as Pakistan.'[70]

Such a scenario, Adenauer stressed, would compel the FRG to interrupt relations with a number of states, and the main beneficiaries of this would be 'Pankow [i.e. East Berlin] and Moscow'.[71] Unbeknown to Schmid, however, other avenues of cooperation remained wide open.

## The Finnish connection

As revolutionary zeal swept across the Arab Middle East and political uncertainty spread throughout most Western capitals, on the quiet banks of the Rhine five men had gathered in the elegant halls of the Hotel Königshof, in Bonn, to talk business.[72] The five had different backgrounds and goals, but they all shared a keen interest in the weapons procurement industry. The question on the table was whether the Finnish firm Tampella would be willing to negotiate a deal to provide the West German armed forces with grenade launchers and ammunition. With the signing of the Paris Treaties in 1954, the three Western powers had invited the Federal Republic to join NATO and allowed it to start the process of rearmament. Chancellor Adenauer promised that West Germany would reach a 500,000-man strong army within three years – a very ambitious goal, which was further complicated by a lack of equipment. The Defence Ministry soon turned to other countries in its search for tanks, aircraft, and warships.[73] By 1957, established French ammunition supplies had become expensive, while equivalent Finnish products promised to be cheaper and just as good. But there was a problem. A 1948 peace agreement signed between Finland and the Soviet Union committed the Helsinki government to hindering any future German rearmament plans. A Finnish–West German arms deal risked seriously irking the Soviets, with potentially disastrous consequences. How could the five avoid upsetting the Soviets and at the same time seal the deal between the Finnish firm and the West German Defence Ministry? Shlomo Zabludowicz suggested a creative answer to this thorny question.

Polish-born businessman Zabludowicz had survived five years in Auschwitz, losing most members of his family in the Holocaust. After the camp's liberation he relocated to Finland, from where he supported the Jewish Agency's arms procurement efforts as the first Arab–Israeli war was in the offing.[74] Now based in Tampere, Zabludowicz had made his name as a resourceful arms dealer. Among other activities, he had founded Soltam Ltd, a company jointly owned by the Luxembourg-based company Salgat, which in turn belonged to Tempella, and by the Israeli-based firm Soleh Boneh. The solution sketched by Zabludowicz foresaw that Tempella would order the grenade launchers and ammunition via Salgat, and that these would be produced in Israel by Soleh Boneh based on the original Finnish design.

Involving the Luxembourg- and Israel-based firms in the project was a brilliant solution – one that shielded the Finnish company and government from any possible Soviet accusation of working for the rearmament of the West German state in breach of the 1948 peace agreement. The fact that the Finnish representation in the Federal Republic at that time was also based in Cologne, just like the Israeli Mission, may have also smoothed the transaction logistics.[75] And so, in October 1958, the deal was finalised, following Zabludowicz's design. Having concluded this DM12 million trans-action, the Bundeswehr authorities concluded that they would not need to embark on any more grenade launcher purchases for at least a decade. But if the arrangement devised by Zabludowicz provided cover for the Finns while covertly dealing with Bonn, the problem would soon fall on David Ben-Gurion's shoulders.

At first, the Israeli Prime Minister consented to the finalising of the deal without notifying his Cabinet of the matter. He had consulted Peres and other representatives of the Defense Ministry, who supported his decision. But later, realising that bypassing his Cabinet members was, in fact, unconstitutional, he tabled a motion to support the Israeli firms working on national defence with retroactive effect.[76] When Health Minister Yisrael Barzilai expressed his concern, Ben-Gurion dismissed it. Barzilai insisted on a Cabinet discussion at the next meeting, but the topic quickly fell off the agenda.[77] The matter was not discussed at Cabinet level again until, in the summer of 1959, an article published in *Der Spiegel* laid out all the details of the Israeli involvement in the West German arms procurement efforts, causing commotion in Europe, the Arab Middle East, and beyond, and unleashing a severe governmental crisis in Israel itself. The Israeli public at large, and many members of parliament from within and without Ben-Gurion's Mapai party, were shocked to learn from the German press about their country's contribution to the West German rearmament programme. In the evening hours of 28 June 1959, Mapai cadres gathered to discuss the issue. Ben-Gurion stressed that the deal was crucial to strengthen the flow of foreign currency into the country. From a security perspective, it would lay the ground for building upon these exchanges, possibly also facilitating future Israeli armament – a prospect that seemed all the more important at a time in which it had become increasingly hard to obtain arms from Israel's traditional American and French partners. 'If anyone concludes that the Holocaust forbids us to negotiate with Germany', he warned, 'I say that that person lives in the past and not the present, [and] cares more about his feelings than about the existence of the Jewish people'. And to those who stressed that by providing the post-war German state with weapons he was dishon-ouring the millions who had died at the hand of Nazi Germany, Ben-Gurion replied that rather than focusing on the dead, Israelis should now focus on 'keeping the Jews living in this country from being slaughtered', among other ways by reinforcing ties with the Federal Republic, 'Adenauer is not Hitler', he insisted.[78]

The following day, Ben-Gurion reiterated the message in the Knesset. But while his words to the Mapai the night before had managed to convince all of his fellow party members to support him in this crisis, the same did not hold true for the members of other parties in the government coalition. Since July 1955, Ben-Gurion had presided over a heterogeneous and fragile coalition, including, on the right, the Progressive Party and the religious bloc, and Mapam and the Workers' Party on the left. Ben-Gurion counterbalanced the wide assortment of political factions in the Knesset with the prerogative to shape much of Israel's defence and foreign policy essentially on his own, as the case of the deal with West Germany demonstrated so clearly. The words of the opposition leader Menachem Begin further charged the already tense Knesset discussion: 'All those who washed their hands with Jewish soap', asked Begin, were they 'to carry Jewish weapons, too?'[79]

The news of Israel's decision to transfer grenade launchers and ammunition to Bonn's growing security apparatus appeared to shock audiences well beyond Israel. West German diplomats stationed throughout the region soon faced a renewed wave of Arab protests of varying degrees and intensity. Ben-Gurion's words did not help – addressing the Knesset, the Israeli Prime Minister had stressed that the trade with Germany would ultimately boost Israel's export sectors, benefiting Israel's workers, and that the money received from Bonn could be used to buy other weapons that Israel needed but did not produce. Especially the latter statement caused an uproar in the Arab world. In Jordan, thanks to the local West German envoy's close relations with the editors of the main newspapers and general good PR work, the reaction in Amman was comparatively mild.[80] But in countries such as Iraq and Libya things were much more complicated. Baghdad's Foreign Minister was furious. As he saw it, the problem went beyond the question of this transfer of ammunition and essentially revolved around the fact that the Federal Republic had allowed Israel to build up its weapons and ammunition industries in the first place, having agreed to paying reparations to the country with the Luxembourg Agreement in the early 1950s.[81] The real purpose of the entente between West Germany and Israel was 'to provide work for Zionists and help them to displace the Arabs of Palestine', explained Lybia's *Tripoli Mirror*: 'It seems that the West German government is either gambling with its excellent reputation in the Arab world or is undervaluing the changes that took place therein.'[82]

## The 'Swastika Epidemic'

In Jerusalem, Ben-Gurion asked the members of the Mapam and the Workers' Party to resign from the coalition. Faced with their refusal, Ben-Gurion himself resigned from his post as Prime Minister. New elections took place shortly thereafter, and in November 1959 the Israeli electorate granted Ben-Gurion his biggest electoral victory yet. Although the question of his policy vis-à-vis Germany was just one of the matters discussed in the electoral campaign, it really seemed that the Israeli electorate was ever more willing to endorse Ben-Gurion's policies – including his line on how to deal with the 'new' Germany. But just as things seemed to have calmed down in Israel, an unprecedented series of anti-Semitic incidents took place in the Federal Republic, casting serious doubt about the stable and renewed character of the West German state.

On the night of Christmas Eve 1959, the external walls of the synagogue in Cologne were smeared in red painted swastikas and anti-Semitic invective. In the weeks that followed, a multitude of anti-Semitic episodes – over 800 in seven weeks – occurred across the Federal Republic. The reaction to such numerous incidents, as described by the journalist Walter Hirsch, highlighted what at the time seemed to be the most disturbing elements of the wave of anti-Semitic events:

> We were told – and by no less than Ben-Gurion himself – that [in Germany] there were still a few irredeemable old Nazis, but that the new generation was objective, and [German] democracy open-minded and free. And yet the offenders are

mostly young people. We were told – and by no less than Germany's most radical enemies in Israel – that as long as the economic conjuncture was good nothing would happen – and yet these things have happened at a time of unprecedented economic prosperity in West Germany.[83]

After what many regarded as a far too premature end to the Allied denazification efforts due to Cold War imperatives, how much could one trust the German population to have changed, and to have left the Nazi past behind? The words uttered by Yosef Shofman of the Herut party during a Knesset debate held in January 1960 captured the uneasiness of many in Israel: 'You thought you would gain friendship by putting weapons into the hands of murderers, without knowing how they would use them. Is it not the same hand which daubs swastikas and anti-Semitic slogans which will grasp the "Uzi" which your Government, Mr. Prime Minister, will supply to Germany?'[84] In Moscow, Khrushchev declared that he was 'saddened' by the 'recent Fascist and anti-Semitic outrages in West Germany' and accused Chancellor Adenauer of having drawn 'no conclusions from the lessons of the past'.[85] Communist China, too, noted that 'militarism and Nazism [had] return[ed] to West Germany'.[86] Indeed, the 'swastika epidemic' in the Federal Republic, as it was known at that time, confirmed many of the allegations that East German propaganda had now been making for over a decade about the not-so-latent anti-Semitic and Nazi character of the Bonn Republic.

The acts of vandalism that took place between the end of 1959 and the beginning of 1960 served East German propaganda so well that many in West Germany suspected an East German involvement in the anti-Semitic outbursts.[87] Adenauer himself considered these incidents the result of an operation aimed at ruining Bonn's international image – especially in view of the upcoming conference in Paris, where the superpowers were to discuss the German question and seek a solution to the Berlin Crisis – and he was largely correct in his assessment.[88] According to him there was 'no doubt … that the [anti-Semitic] incidents have regrettably damaged the reputation of the Federal Republic. The best way of counteracting continuing criticism will be through action by the Government evidencing its serious intention to prevent any recrudescence of anti-Semitism'.[89]

For the first time in his life, the Chancellor visited a concentration camp, Bergen-Belsen. In his speech at the camp, he 'ask[ed] the public, not only in my country but the public of the word, to accept the assurance that we stand with all of our power so that … what most unfortunately occurred during the National Socialist time never happens again in the world'.[90] Adenauer again oscillated between asking the world to recognise that his Germany was different from the Germany of the past, but at the same time skirted away from assuming any responsibility for what, 'most unfortunately', had occurred in the Third Reich. On 18 February 1960, the West German Minister of the Interior, Gerhard Schröder, presented to the Bundestag the results of ministerial inquiries into the recent neo-Nazi incidents.[91] He stressed that the incidents had been the work of a tiny minority, and that the reaction of the population of the Federal Republic had immediately been one of 'revulsion and indignation'. And, while the attacks had taken place all over the territory of the Federal Republic, the number of incidents that had taken place in Berlin suggested 'a special role played by puppeteers based in the Soviet zone', confirmed, he claimed, by the fact that the 'sensation caused by the incidents in the world public opinion' had been 'exploited by the communist propaganda'.[92] In a private meeting with the political director of the World Jewish Congress, Foreign Minister Brentano reminded his counterpart that one of the vandals who attacked the synagogue in Cologne was not only a member of the banned rightist German Reich Party (Deutsche Reichspartei) but was also found in possession of SED party badges. 'It is widely known that today the East would do anything to shake the credibility of the Federal Republic', the Minister commented: 'One knows very well these National-Bolshevists from the East'.[93]

Despite Bonn's protests, not everyone believed that the GDR was behind the anti-Semitic incidents. In West Germany, the Social Democrats, for example, thought it 'improbable that [the incidents] were organised' lamenting instead that the 'East-West conflict, finding expression in a negative and cheap anti-communism, superseded the need for dealing politically and spiritually with the national-socialist past in Germany'.[94] In Israel, on the basis of an assessment made by the Mossad and further discussions internal to the Foreign Ministry, Israeli diplomatic personnel stationed abroad were instructed to 'reject the communist plot theory as the main cause of the anti-Semitic wave'.[95] As Gideon Rafael, Israel's ambassador to Belgium and Luxembourg, noted at that time, the 'wave of anti-Semitism and neo-Nazism', had 'considerably weakened [West] Germany's standing' and Israel should now 'exploit this situation'.[96] Ambassador to Paris Maurice Fischer, in agreement, encouraged Israeli Foreign Ministry personnel to 'continue focusing international attention on the neo-Nazi revival' in order to push Bonn to finally concede diplomatic relations.[97] And many, even in the West German Foreign Ministry, expected the establishment of diplomatic relations with Israel to be the outcome of Adenauer's upcoming trip to the United States.[98] While Shinnar chastised the West German turnaround on the question of diplomatic relations as a 'completely illogical' policy,[99] and his subordinate at the Israeli Mission in Cologne, Yohanan Meroz, suggested to 'force Germany to establish diplomatic relations, even against its will',[100] in fact David Ben-Gurion tacitly acquiesced to letting the matter rest for the time being. Instead, he insisted on the much more pressing objectives of obtaining increasing amounts of economic aid from Germany and developing security ties with it – possibly away from the public eye. For a country that, in 1960, had just got rid of the food rationing and price-control measures introduced by the British in 1939 and later confirmed by the Israeli government in 1949, reinforcing the economy and defence sectors was, after all, paramount.[101]

## Waldorf Astoria, March 1960

The subject of diplomatic relations did not even come up when Ben-Gurion and Adenauer met in person for the first time in March 1960, at the Waldorf Astoria Hotel in New York. For Ben-Gurion, the meeting was a breath of fresh air after the disappointing encounter he had had with the American President just a few days

Figure 5.1  Konrad Adenauer and David Ben-Gurion in New York, 1960.

earlier. Ben-Gurion was particularly worried about a recent Soviet decision to supply MiG-19 fighter planes to Egypt and pleaded with the President to supply Israel with ground-to-air missiles and electronic early warning equipment from the United States. Eisenhower, however, did not budge. He had long stressed the importance of bringing peace to the region while maintaining a position of neutrality – thus dampening potential arms racing.[102] The President expressed his sympathy for Ben-Gurion's worries, but he also stressed that 'the nations of Western Europe – France, Great Britain and even West Germany – could better supply arms to Israel than could the United States'.[103] The Israeli Cabinet had concluded as much during discussions prior to Ben-Gurion's journey. While efforts should be made to obtain more arms from, or with the support of, the United States, Israel should turn to France, Britain and Germany to get armaments that would boost Israel's deterrent power. And so, Ben-Gurion touched exactly upon this point in his first ever direct conversation with Konrad Adenauer.

Hannelore Siegel, the personal secretary who accompanied the West German Chancellor on his informal trip to the United States, was struck by how the two 'got along well immediately'.[104] The meeting took place in the immediate aftermath of the anti-Semitic outbursts in West Germany, which so blatantly contradicted the new image which Adenauer had portrayed, and on which Ben-Gurion also insisted. The East German Stasi would often refer to the 'secret deal' between the two leaders on that occasion, yet the two statesmen did not sign any protocol.[105] At that time, 'I could not give an exact answer' to the Israeli requests, Adenauer recalled in his memoirs.[106] He did, however, agree in principle to participate in the development of the Israeli state by providing it with funds to invest in 'industry, shipping and agriculture'.[107] And when Ben-Gurion highlighted the Israeli need for mini submarines and anti-aircraft missiles, the Chancellor readily gave his word regarding West Germany's willingness to support the Israeli arms procurement efforts, too. Alluding to Peres' covert visit to Rott am Inn, Adenauer added that he supported what had been discussed earlier on the matter with Defence Minister Strauss.[108]

After his meeting with Ben-Gurion, Adenauer travelled to the White House. The Chancellor seemed content about how the meeting with the Israeli Prime Minister had gone, and 'repeated a humorous remark about how highly a New York press photographer valued a picture of Mr. Adenauer and Mr. Ben-Gurion together'.[109] Indeed, the Chancellor was very aware of the importance of his country's public image and the recent swathe of anti-Semitic acts of vandalism, 'heightened by German maladroitness', had highlighted that fifteen years after the end of the Second World War much anti-German sentiment still existed in the world. Adenauer was determined to set things right. In the delicate months that preceded the Paris summit meeting where the Four Powers would discuss the prospect of German reunification and the status of Berlin this was more important than ever.[110]

News of Adenauer's assent to support Israel in matters of economic and military development leaked soon after the Waldorf Astoria meeting had taken place. As the West German Ambassador in Lebanon worriedly reported to Bonn, many in the Arab world now insisted on a boycott of the Federal Republic; a reassessment of relations with East Germany; and a break in diplomatic relations with Bonn.[111] West German representatives again pointed to the GDR to defend Bonn's own plausible deniability – the news of any prospective cooperation with Israel was portrayed as the latest in a long line of East German attempts to ruin West German credibility in the Arab Middle East: 'It is noted that these press reports are spread by ADN, the governmental news agency of the Soviet zone, with the goal of spoiling German-Arab relations', was the sentence that Voigt suggested West German diplomats in the region should use vis-à-vis their Arab colleagues to undermine their arguments.[112] Yet the months following the Ben-Gurion–Adenauer meeting witnessed a flurry of activity around the question of how to translate the prospect of West German economic support to Israel into practice – a project which in West German financial circles would soon receive the coded nickname 'Operation Business Friend' (*Aktion Geschäftsfreund*).[113]

## An unexpected announcement

By 1960, the two German states faced new geopolitical circumstances in the Middle East. GDR foreign policy, propaganda and economic organs became more concerted in their efforts to advance East Berlin's cause both at home and abroad – and, especially, to boost the GDR's appeal within the Middle East. The main objective of East Berlin's Cold War struggle was to demonstrate that, regardless of what Bonn maintained, the GDR, too, was a legitimate German state, capable of being recognised internationally. The Middle East was the arena in which the GDR had had its first successes in this regard and, as the East German efforts to reach out to the region intensified in the late 1950s, so did its propaganda against Bonn, against Israel, and against the ties between the two countries. East German representatives adopted the anti-colonial and anti-imperialist language of the nonaligned countries, adding elements of the German–German setup to it.[114] Bonn became a 'neo-colonialist' power, its links to Israel dictated by 'imperialist' aims, including that of subjugating the Arab populations of the Levant while providing Israel with weapons and other valuable goods.[115] An intricate web of public diplomacy efforts aimed specifically at audiences in the Maghreb and Mashreq was coupled with an increased East German economic presence in the region – which, however, remained considerably behind the West German one.

In an attempt to defend vital interests against perceived Soviet and East German threats, the West German government had become further enmeshed in the Middle East conflict, engaging in a double game that saw it drawing ever closer relations with both the conservative and revolutionary Arab states and also, less visibly but ever more importantly so, with Israel and its security establishment. Interpreting the out-break of the 1958 Arab revolutions as playing into the hands of the East Germans, the Chancellor devoted special efforts to protecting the FRG's own position vis-à-vis the East German and Soviet threats, especially given the huge loss of popularity and diminishing influence of Bonn's main European allies in the region, Great Britain and France. The West German political establishment increased both the FRG's economic and commercial support of the major Arab economies as well as the spending in favour of the UN agency dedicated to improving the living conditions of the millions of Palestinian refugees. And, while refraining from establishing official diplomatic relations with Israel, Bonn also began exchanging weapons with Israel and agreeing, at least in principle, to make a very generous financial contribution to the country's future economic development.

Following the swastika epidemic in Germany and the governmental reshuffle in Israel, the relations between the two countries appeared to be shaky. But underneath the surface of crises and tensions that characterised the bilateral relationship lay a series of adjustments, which testified to the increasing solidity of the West German–Israeli ties. These would soon be tested again, following David Ben-Gurion's unex-pected announcement, on 23 May 1960, that 'one of the greatest Nazi criminals, Adolf Eichmann' was 'now under arrest in Israel and [would] soon stand trial here, in accord-ance with the Nazi and Nazi Collaborators (Punishment) Law, 5710–1950'.[116]

# Notes

1 Shinnar, *Bericht eines Beauftragten*, p. 70.
2 DFPI, 1958–1959, Vol. 13, Doc. 252: Fischer (Jerusalem) to the Minister of Foreign Affairs, 31 July 1958.
3 This remained the case until 1983. For an overview on German and its uses in mandatory Palestine and Israel see H. Zabel (ed.), *Stimmen aus Jerusalem. Zur deutschen Sprache und Liteartur in Palästina/Israel* (Berlin: LIT, 2006).
4 R. Streppelhoff, 'On Pitches and Bridges: Sport in the Development of German-Israeli Relations' in *Opportunities and Challenges in Sport: Bilateral German-Israeli Symposium* (Berlin: International Council of Sports Science and Physical Education, 2016); R. Streppelhoff, *Gelungener Brückenschlag: Sport in den deutsch-israelischen Beziehungen* (Sankt Augustin: Akademia, 2012).
5 M. Lämmer, *Deutsch-israelische Fußballfreundschaft* (Göttingen: Die Werkstatt, 2018), pp. 65ff.
6 L. G. Feldman, 'The Role of Non-State Actors in Germany's Foreign Policy of Reconciliation' in A. M. Le Gloannec (ed.), *Non-State Actors in International* (Manchester: Manchester University Press, 2007); H. Von Hindenburg, *Demonstrating Reconciliation: State and Society in West German Foreign Policy toward Israel, 1952–1965* (New York: Berghahn Books, 2007).
7 PA AA B12 1018 Telex Washington to Bonn, 6 January 1958.
8 Yaqub, *Containing Arab Nationalism*.
9 W. R. Louis and R. Owen (eds), *A Revolutionary Year: The Middle East in 1958* (London: Tauris, 2002).
10 M. Kerr, *The Arab Cold War: Gamal 'Abd Al-Nasir and His Rivals, 1958–1970* (London: Oxford University Press, 1971).
11 F. Gerges, *Making the Arab World: Nasser, Qutb and the Clash that Shaped the Middle East* (Princeton, NJ: Princeton University Press, 2018), pp. 16–17.
12 PA AA: MfAA C 1575/153 Key facts on GDR-UAR Relations, signature illegible, 7 June 1958.
13 DDEL Eisenhower Library, White House Office of the Special Assistant for National Security Affairs, NSC Series, Policy Papers Subseries, Box 23, NSC 5801/1 Long-range US Policy towards the Near East.
14 For example, West Germany's exports to Syria and Lebanon doubled between 1953 and 1959, going from DM48.1 million to DM99.9 million and from DM62.5 million to DM119.7 million, respectively. Those to Egypt tripled, going from DM124.7 million in 1951 to DM326.4 million in 1959. Berggötz, *Nahostpolitik in der Ära Adenauer*, pp. 466ff.
15 DDEL Eisenhower Library, White House Office of the Special Assistant for National Security Affairs, NSC Series, Policy Papers Subseries, Box 23, NSC 5801/1 Long-range US Policy towards the Near East.
16 Deutsches Orient Institut, *Die Angriffe der SBZ gegen die Nahostpolitik der Bundesregierung* (1964), p. 107.
17 'Deutsch-arabisches Freundschaft: Delegierte aus der DDR und den arabischen Staaten bekräftigen Kampfbündnis gegen die Aggressoren', *ND*, 24 July 1958, p. 5.
18 Berggötz, *Nahostpolitik in der Ära Adenauer*, pp. 408ff.
19 'Sprungbrett Bundesrepublik', *Der Spiegel*, 23 July 1958, p. 13.

20 Vilenska was a member of the triumvirate at the head of the Communist Party when it was re-founded in 1944. See, e.g., S. Miller Rubenstein, *The Communist Movement in Palestine and Israel, 1919–1984* (Boulder: Westview Press, 1985), p. 342.
21 'In der DDR stehen wir auf die richtige Seite', *ND*, 15 July 1958, p. 1.
22 'Die Zukunft im Nahen Osten gehört den Völkern', *ND*, 16 July 1958, p. 6.
23 A. Greilsammer, *Le Communistes Israéliens* (Paris: Presses de la Fondation Nationale de Sciences Politique, 1978), p. 125.
24 On the political difficulties of the MAKI see Rubenstein, *The Communist Movement*, p. 345.
25 M. Thomas, *Communing with the Enemy: Covert Operations, Christianity and Cold War Politics in Britain and the GDR* (Oxford: Peter Lang, 2005), p. 75ff.
26 *Ibid.*, pp. 86ff.
27 FRUS, 1958–1960/IX, Doc. 278: Report Prepared in the Bureau of Intelligence and Research, 11 August 1958.
28 Ambasuisse an Politisches Bern [Telegramm Nr 43], 17 July 1958, Dok 145.
29 'Feste Form für feste Beziehungen: TLZ-Gespräch mit Frau Charlotte Ibrahim, Jena, über die Deutsch-Arabsche Gesellschaft', *Thüringer Landeszeitung*, 21 October 1958.
30 H. von Hauschild, 'Im Dienste der Völkerfreundschaft: Fünf Jahre Deutsch-Arabische Gesellschaft in der DDR', *Neue Zeit*, 1 October 1963, p. 6.
31 BAL-SAPMO, DY 30/IV 2/20/2, Wandel: Report to the Politbüro, 13 August 1958.
32 'Wandel, Paul' in H. Müller-Enbergs and O. W. Reimann, *Wer war wer in der DDR: Ein Lexikon ostdeutscher Biographien* fifth edn (Berlin: Links, 2010).
33 'Botschafter Wandel über Besuch in Irak', *ND*, 15 August 1958, p. 1.
34 'Handelsabkommen DDR-Irak', *ND*, 28 October 1958, p. 5.
35 'Erklärung des Leiters der Handelsdelegation der Regierung der Deutschen Demokratischen Republik, Gerhard Weiß, vor der Presse in Bagdad am 27. Oktober 1958', *Dokumente zur Außenpolitik der Regierung der Deutschen Demokratischen Republik*, Band VI, Vom 1. Januar bis zum 31. Dezember 1958 (Berlin: Rütten & Loening, 1959), p. 317.
36 StBKAH BIII/049, Notes, 26 July 1958.
37 DFPI, 1958–1959, Vol. 13, Doc. 248: Fischer to the Minister of Foreign Affairs, 18 July 1958.
38 *Ibid.*
39 A. Cohen, *The Worst-Kept Secret: Israel's Bargain with the Bomb* (New York: Columbia University Press, 2010); S. Hersh, *The Samson Option: Israel's Nuclear Arsenal and American Foreign Policy* (New York: Vintage Books, 1993).
40 DFPI, 1958–1959, Vol. 13, Doc. 252: Fischer (Jerusalem) to the Minister of Foreign Affairs, 31 July 1958.
41 DFPI, 1958–1959, Vol. 13, Doc. 257: Shinnar (Cologne) to the West European Division, 16 January 1959.
42 DFPI, 1958–1959, Vol. 13, Doc. 259: Shinnar (Cologne) to Eytan and Fischer, 4 March 1959.
43 DBGA, Ben Gurion Diary Entry, 20 April 1958, obtained and translated by Yiftach Shavit.
44 DFPI, 1958–1959, Vol. 13, Doc. 261: Shinnar (Cologne) to Fischer (Jerusalem), 21 May 1959.

45 On the FRG's support for Israel at the UN and NATO see DFPI, Vol. 11, 1956–1957, Doc. 259: Tsur (Paris) to the Director-General of the Ministry of Foreign Affairs and the West European Division, 31 December 1956.
46 Akademie der Künste Archiv [AdKA], Filmprogrammsammlung: 1,876. See also T. Ebbrecht-Hartmann, *Übergänge: Passagen durch eine deutsch-israelische Filmgeschichte* (Berlin: neofelis, 2014) and T. Ebbrecht-Hartmann, 'Projected Encounters: Rolf Vogel and the Beginnings of Cinematic Relations between Germany and Israel', *Leo Baeck Institute Year Book* 63:1 (2018), pp. 11–33, here esp. p. 12.
47 DFPI, Vol. 11, 1956–1957, Doc. 523: Shinnar to Eytan, 7 March 1957.
48 See, for example, Nasser's speech, 27 January 1958 quoted in Y. Hakarbi, *Arab Attitudes to Israel* (Jerusalem: Keter, 1972), p. 6; see also the dated, but still relevant, C. Bailey, *Jordan's Palestinian Challenge, 1948–1983: A Political History* (Boulder: Westview Press, 1984).
49 R. Khalidi, *The Iron Cage: The Story of the Palestinian Struggle for Statehood* (Boston, MA: Beacon Press, 2006), pp. 140ff.
50 S. K. Aburish, *Arafat: From Defender to Dictator* (London: Bloomsbury, 1998) and B. Abu Sharif, *Arafat and the Dream of Palestine* (New York: Palgrave Macmillan, 2009).
51 Y. Sayigh, *Armed Struggle and the Search for a State: The Palestinian National Movement, 1949–1993* (Oxford: Oxford University Press, 1997).
52 U. Gill, *Der Freie Deutsche Gewerkschaftsbund (FDGB): Theorie – Geschichte – Organisation – Funktionen – Kritik* (Opladen: Leske + Budrich, 1989).
53 PA AA: MfAA A12740/12 Report, 3 July 1958. L. Maeke, *DDR und PLO: Die Palästinapolitik des SED-Staates* (Berlin: De Gruyter Oldenbourg, 2017), pp. 30ff.
54 *Ibid.*
55 A. Shlaim, 'The Rise and Fall of the All-Palestine Government in Gaza', *Journal of Palestine Studies* 20:1 (1990), pp. 37–53; J. Caldwell, 'Inter-Arab Rivalry and the All-Palestine Government of 1948', *Jerusalem Quarterly* 62 (2015), pp. 50–64.
56 Timm, *Hammer, Zirkel, Davidstern*, p. 270.
57 MfS, HVA, Report, Nr. 683/59, *Bonner Störversuche gegen den wachsenden Einfluss der DDR in der Vereinigten Arabischen Republik.*
58 See chapter 1; J. F. Defrates, 'UNRWA, the Federal Republic of Germany and the Palestine Refugees', *Orient* 13:3 (1972), pp. 124–6.
59 PA AA B12 1018: Voigt to Department 300, 3 October 1958.
60 PA AA B12 1018: Carstens to Brentano, 23 December 1957.
61 PA AA B12 1018: Voigt to Department 300, 3 October 1958.
62 PA AA B12 1018: The Chancellor on the 10th anniversary of the State of Israel. Marchtaler, 31 March 1958.
63 PA AA B12 1018: Federal Foreign Office, Berlin Office. Telegram, Duckwitz, 16 April 1958.
64 PA AA B12 1018: Embassy BRD Cairo. Participation of a delegation of the Bundesregierung in the celebration of the 10th anniversary of the existence of Israel. Becker, 25 April 1958.
65 K. Meyer, *Die SPD und die NS-Vergangenheit 1945–1990* (Göttingen: Wallstein, 2015).
66 C. Schmid, *Erinnerungen* (Bern: Scherz, 1980), p. 503.
67 *Ibid.*, p. 637.
68 *Ibid.*, p. 639.

69  DBGA, Ben Gurion's Diary Entry, 1 January 1960, obtained and translated by Yiftach Shavit.

70  PA AA B12 1022: Adenauer to Schmid (draft), 23 December 1959.

71  *Ibid.*

72  'Granaten aus Haifa', *Der Spiegel*, 1959, pp. 18–20.

73  D. H. Kollmer, *Rüstungsgüterbeschaffung in der Aufbauphase der Bundeswehr: der Schützenpanzer HS 30 als Fallbeispiel (1953–1961)* (Stuttgart: Steiner, 2002).

74  A. Miettinen, 'Isänsä Poika', *Helsingin Sanomaat Kuukausiliite* (2011), pp. 25–33.

75  T. Forsberg, 'Finnland und Deutschland' in B. Auffermann and P. Visurri (eds), *Die Nordischen Staaten und die deutsche Herausforderung* (Nomos: Baden-Baden, 1995).

76  T. Segev, *The Seventh Million: The Israelis and the Holocaust* (New York: Hill & Wang, 1993), p. 311ff.

77  Segev, *The Seventh Million*, p. 313.

78  *Ibid.*, p. 314.

79  *Ibid.*

80  PA AA B12 1050: Jordanian reaction to the news about Israeli arms deliveries to the Bundesrepublik. Voigt, 2 July 1959.

81  PA AA B12 1050: Telegram, Dittmann (Bagdad), 18 July 1959.

82  PA AA B12 1050: Libyan press reaction to the German-Israeli arms trade, Beye, 8 July 1958.

83  PA AA B12 1019: Report: This month in Israel. Hirsch, 11 January 1960.

84  E.g. during the parliamentary debate that took place in the Knesset on 20 January 1960.

85  'Naziumtriebe in dreizehn Orten', *ND*, 1 January 1960, p. 6; and JTA, *Daily News Bulletin* 'Khrushchev Charges Germans Seek to "Whitewash" Nazi Regime', 15 January 1960, p. 1.

86  *Ibid.*

87  See Wolffsohn, *Die Deutschland Akte*. For sources documenting the Stasi role in the anti-Semitic outbursts that took place in the Federal Republic, and in particular on the operations codenamed *Aktion J* (Operation J) and *Aktion Vergißmeinnicht* (Operation Forget-Me-Not) see the files in: MfS, HA XX/4, Nr. 513.

88  Wolffsohn, *Die Deutschland Akte*.

89  DDEL, Dwight D. Eisenhower's Papers as President, Ann Whitman File, International Series, Box 15, Chancellor Adenauer's Visit, 14–17 March 1960, Background Memorandum (Herter).

90  Quoted in J. K. Olick, *The Sins of the Fathers: Germany, Memory, Method* (Chicago: Chicago University Press, 2016), p. 183.

91  Deutscher Bundestag, 103. Sitzung, 18 February 1960, p. 5575.

92  Wolffsohn, *Die Deutschland Akte*, p. 19.

93  PA AA B 12 1019: Weber, 7 January 1960.

94  FES 1/WKAD000298: Waldemar von Knoeringen Nachlaß. Diplomatische Beziehungen mit Israel (1960) SPD Auslandsreferat, Statement by the Social Democratic Party of Germany.

95  Protocol of a meeting of the Knesset Foreign Affairs and Defence Committee, 26 January 1960, quoted in: R. Stauber, 'Realpolitik and the Burden of the Past: Israeli Diplomacy and the "Other Germany"', *Israel Studies* 8:3 (2003), p. 108.

96  DFPI 1960, Comp. Vol. 14, Doc. 204: Rafael (Brussels) to the Minister of Foreign Affairs, 26 January 1960.

97  *Ibid.*

98  PA AA B12 1022: Telex. Federer, 12 February 1960.

99  'Aufzeichnung über den Besuch des israelischen Gesandten F.E. Shinnar im Auswärtigen Amt vom 27.1.1956', n.d. in Jelinek, *Zwischen Moral und Realpolitik*, p. 359.

100  DFPI, 1958–1959, Doc. 266: Meroz (Cologne) to Fischer (Jerusalem), 26 November 1959.

101  O. Rozin, 'The Austerity Policy and the Rule of Law: Relations between Government and Public in Fledging Israel', *Journal of Modern Jewish Studies* 4:3 (2005), pp. 273–90.

102  D. D. Eisenhower, *The White House Years: Waging Peace, 1956–1961* (Garden City: Doubleday, 1965).

103  Emphasis added. FRUS, 1958–1960/XIII, Doc. 131: Memorandum of Conversation, White House, Washington, 10 March 1960, 11 a.m.

104  Author's interview with Hannelore Siegel, Cologne, 21 July 2015.

105  See, for example, BStU, MfS, SdM, 12, Bericht des Ministers für Nationale Verteidigung an den Nationalen Verteidigungsrat der Deutschen Demokratischen Republik: *Schlussfolgerungen für die Landesverteidigung der Deutschen Demokratischen Republik aus der israelischen Aggression gegen die arabischen Staaten*, n.d. For the Stasi's assessment see BStU, MfS-ZAIG, 12970/216, Report on the military and economic cooperation between West Germany and Israel.

106  K. Adenauer, *Erinnerungen. Fragmente* Vol. 4 1959–1963 (Stuttgart: Deutsche Verlags-Anstalt, 1968), p. 36.

107  DFPI, Vol. 14, 1960, Doc. 214: Harman (New York) to the Ministry of Foreign Affairs, 14 March 1960.

108  *Ibid*. See also Z. Shalom, 'Document: David Ben-Gurion and Chancellor Adenauer at the Waldorf Astoria on 14 March 1960', *Israel Studies* 2:1 (1997), pp. 50–71 and Y. A. Jelinek and R. A. Blasius, 'Ben Gurion und Adenauer im Waldorf Astoria: Gesprächsaufzeichnungen von Israel-deutschen Gipfeltreffen in New York am 14. März 1960', *Vierteljahrshefte für Zeitgeschichte* 45:2 (1997), pp. 309–44.

109  DDEL, Dwight D. Eisenhower's Papers as President, Ann Whitman File, International Series, Box 15, Memorandum of Conversation between Adenauer and Eisenhower, 15 March 1960.

110  DDEL, Dwight D. Eisenhower's Papers as President, Ann Whitman File, International Series, Box 15, Chancellor Adenauer's Visit, 14–17 March 1960, Background Memorandum (Herter).

111  PA AA B12 1022: Hellenthal (Beirut), 21 March 1960.

112  PA AA B12 1022: Voigt (Bonn) to FRG Embassy Cairo, 23 March 1960.

113  R. A. Blasius, 'Geschäftsfreunschaft statt diplomatische Beziehungen. Zur Israel-Politik 1962/1963' in R. A. Blasius *Von Adenauer zu Erhard: Studien zur Auswärtigen Politik der Bundesrepublik Deutschland* (Munich: Oldenbourg, 1994), pp. 154–210.

114  In a remarkable example of how 'phrases' transferred 'from one social setting to another' during the Cold War, as in J. Suri, 'The Cold War, Decolonization, and Global Social Awakenings: Historical Intersections', *Cold War History* 6:3 (2006), p. 360.

115  'Ägypten weist Brentano zurecht, unverschämte Rundfunkrede des Bonner Aussenministers', *ND*, 1 September 1956.

116  'Prime Minister's Statement on the Arrest of Eichmann. Sitting 98 of the Fourth Knesset, 23 May 1960', in *Major Knesset Debates*, Vol. 4 (Lanham: University Press of America, 1991), p. 1141.

# 6

# Trials

On 28 May 1960, Walter Ulbricht received a memo from one of his trusted collab-orators: Albert Norden.[1] Son of a Rabbi murdered at Theresienstadt, Norden had managed to make a respectable name for himself among the highest echelons of the East German state machinery, not only becoming a Politbüro member but also rising to the role of director of the Committee for German Reunification within the SED Central Committee, an office focusing on anti-West German propaganda. Norden's position within the SED represented an astonishing achievement, given his background. Norden had spent his exile years mostly in the United States – and in Ulbricht's Germany he had had to work very hard in order to shed all of the prejudices that the other members of the East German Politbüro might hold against him because of his Jewish origins, the time he spent in the United States, or both. Within the newly founded GDR, he quickly rose up the ranks of the SED party-state, becoming the mas-termind behind East German propaganda aimed at both domestic audiences and the outside world. As head of the Agitation Commission of the Politbüro, shortly after Ben-Gurion's announcement of the capture and forthcoming trial of Adolf Eichmann in Jerusalem, Norden began playing with the idea of an East German hijacking of the trial – one that could serve as a spectacular indictment of the West German state from the media platform offered by the trial that was about to take place in Jerusalem.[2] 'One should consider', Norden wrote to Ulbricht in May 1960, 'whether the GDR could step in directly into the preparations for the trial. It would certainly strengthen the inter-national authority of the GDR – and be useful for the Israeli Communist Party – if we openly came forward about Eichmann's own crimes and his accomplices in the Bonn government'.[3] This was a markedly determined tone in East German messaging about the continuities between the West German government and the Nazi past and how to denounce them on the global stage. It was the start of a public relations offensive that would recur with great frequency as the Eichmann trial unfolded.

Norden's ideas about how to seize upon the Eichmann trial as a propaganda oppor-tunity came against the backdrop of intense German–German competition, which also involved rival narratives about the Nazi past and its legacy in each German state. The GDR's public discourse on the past focused on the Nazi persecution of Communists and on the Soviet Union's role as liberators. Internationally, this narrative legitimised the relationship between East Berlin and Moscow. At home, this reading of the past also served to emphasise that the new East German state – a Democratic Republic, at least in name – represented a clear break from the dictatorial past. Given the stark authoritarian characters of the East German state, the faults in this interpretation of the past are rather blatant. Yet this discourse served important political ends, both domestically and internationally. And while the West German narrative differed markedly from the East German one, in the Federal Republic, too, the public discussion about the past supported Bonn's political goals. The Adenauer government presented itself as representing a markedly different Germany from Hitler's Germany – yet the West German discourse on the Nazi past recognised that special responsibilities had been bestowed upon it, stemming from the horrors of the past. Apologising and assuming responsibility, or at least declaring to have done so, in the international arena also served to smooth the anti-German feelings harboured by the Western allies in the wake of the Second World War and contributed to crafting post-war West German legitimacy internationally.

No event would bring each Germany's interpretation of the Nazi past to clash like the Eichmann trial. Both German states sent officials to Jerusalem tasked with ensuring that the trial would not have negative repercussions on their image and prestige – or, in the East German case, to actively try and mould the trial into a political tool to wage against their German Cold War opponent. As the trial unfolded in Jerusalem, the efforts of West German foreign intelligence services, diplomats, and journalists became embroiled with those of East German propagandists and lawyers into a Cold War struggle that drew in Israeli prosecutors and security personnel, as well as members of the broader public in and beyond Israel. The means of German–German competition were swiftly moving to focus on the legacy of the past and were now headed for Jerusalem. As such, officials in both Germanys wondered how to best exploit, or contain, the global echo of the Eichmann trial.

## Contacts in Prague

By the turn of the 1950s, establishing relations with Israel was clearly not an option for East Berlin. The refusal to pay restitutions, and the GDR's increasing – avidly desired – closeness to the Arab countries, meant that the differences between the two countries were fundamentally irreconcilable. However, this did not mean that diplomats of the two countries did not engage at all with one another. Over the course of the decade, Israeli diplomats had quietly been making inroads with East German diplomats stationed in various parts of the world. While in the mid 1950s meetings between representatives of the two countries had taken place mainly in Moscow, at the turn of the decade the fulcrum of East German–Israeli exchanges became Czechoslovakia.[4] It was from Prague that the few East German citizens who received a permit to travel to Israel got their visa.[5] And it was from Prague that the East German Foreign Ministry received the most detailed and reliable information about the political developments that were taking place in and around Jerusalem.[6]

The East German–Israeli exchanges in Czechoslovakia were favoured by the fact that Bonn had no diplomatic presence in the country and that much of the East German personnel stationed there during the years of the Nazi regime had fostered personal connections to mandate Palestine, the future State of Israel, and had spent some of the most crucial moments of their lives in Prague. The second secretary of the East German embassy in Prague, Wolfgang Münzer, was born in a Jewish family in Magdeburg. He had fled Nazi persecution by relocating to Prague in 1933, from where he moved on to Palestine upon the request of the German Communist Party cadres. There, Münzer joined the local Communist Party as well as the Marxist-Zionist movement Poale Zion Left.[7] Münzer had also joined the ranks of Poale Zion Left's paramilitary guerrilla organisation, which fought against the British mandate forces until, in 1936, British guards arrested him and deported him back to Germany, handing him over to the Nazi authorities. He narrowly managed to escape, relocating first to Prague, again, then to England.[8] In 1960, sitting just a few desks away from him in the East German embassy in Prague, was the East German consul Horst Seydewitz, whose brother lived in Israel. Because his father's second wife was Jewish, many assumed that he was too. Seydewitz was only eighteen years old when he had to leave Germany and move to Czechoslovakia to escape Nazi persecution given that his father, Max Seydewitz, was a prominent leftist politician. The Liebsteins, family friends, had helped Horst and his two brothers to cross the border.[9] Now with the surname of Livneh, the family was stationed in Prague, where the father, Eliyahu, served as Israeli ambassador.[10] Prior to his Prague post, Livneh had long been stationed in Germany, first as the representative of the Jewish Agency in Berlin, then as Israeli Consul, and he had been involved in the conversations that led to negotiating the Luxembourg Agreement.

It was perhaps also because of his connection to Israel, as well as to the Liebsteins/Livneh family, that Seydewitz would end up talking for over two hours with Jehuda Raveh, his counterpart at the Israeli embassy, when they met on 15 January 1960.[11] Seydewitz had arranged the meeting following the death of an Israeli journalist and *Frankfurter Allgemeine Zeitung* contributor, who had passed away following a car crash near Magdeburg in November 1959.[12] He wanted to return the journalist's passport and other personal belongings to the Israeli authorities, but the meeting lasted much longer than initially planned, as the two turned to discussing the delicate topic of East German–Israeli relations.

## The mistake of Dr Seydewitz

In his conversation with Raveh, Seydewitz let go of his usually cautious approach to international diplomacy. The East German consul optimistically predicted that the time would come when his country and Israel would have 'normal relations'; his Israeli colleague commented that in fact, from a variety of points of view, the GDR was much more appealing (*sympatischer*) than West Germany. Seydewitz then replied that it was difficult for him to understand 'why Israel would have official relations with the Federal Republic'.[13] Three days later, Seydewitz forwarded his report of the meeting to the East German ambassador in Prague, and the embassy then passed on the document to the Foreign Ministry. Yet when sending the documents to East Berlin, the Second Secretary of the Embassy, Bernhard Neugebauer, characterised some of Seydewitz's statements as 'not thought through enough, politically speaking',[14] and his colleagues in the Foreign Ministry agreed. He had made a crucial 'mistake', the GDR Foreign Ministry personnel in Berlin stressed, when:

> He let the different developments of the two German states [on the issue of the relations to Israel] end on a note that hints that Israel has official relations with West Germany. The matter should be construed from the outset either as if we were against the relations of any state with West Germany, or as if we were interested in maintaining the same kind of relations with the state in question.[15]

Foreign Ministry personnel used the occasion to launch a review of the main guidelines dictating how West Germany should (or not) be talked about when meeting international colleagues. The 'mistake' that Simons, Head of the Department for Affairs of the Near and Middle East, condemned, did not focus on the specifics of East German–Israeli relations. Rather, the key problem was related to the way in which the relations between Israel and the Federal Republic, and indirectly therefore also between the German Democratic Republic and the Federal Republic, had been portrayed by the East German consul in Prague while dealing with Raveh. In other words, it was the German–German dimension rather than only the German–Israeli one that mattered. Simons pointed out that while it was true – in principle – that the GDR was interested in having peaceful relations with other states, it still was essential to weigh 'in front of whom' one would make 'such a statement'. Communications of this sort, Simons emphasised, might lead some to think that the GDR was ready to strengthen ties with the Jewish state – and 'I do not need to explain', the head of the Near and Middle East Division in East Berlin concluded, 'that this is not the case'.[16] Just a few months after the meeting with the Israeli consul, the course of Horst Seydewitz's career altered. He was recalled from his post in Prague to the GDR, where he was put to work in the archives of the Foreign Ministry, and he would remain there until his retirement. In condemning Seydewitz's openness to his Israeli counterpart as a 'mistake', East Berlin's Foreign Ministry re-emphasised that there could be no closeness between GDR and Israeli diplomats. But while the Ministry insisted on chastising those who seemed to display too warm an attitude towards Israel, in the aftermath of Eichmann's capture members of other East German organs were brainstorming about possible public relations strategies that would help them to connect with the Israeli public in their anti-West German struggle.

## Linking campaigns

For the GDR, news of the Eichmann trial was very well-timed. East German propaganda had long been carrying out attacks against Bonn's lack of confrontation with the Nazi past. Such campaigns were rather effective, especially given that the East Germans had a point. While GDR propagandists overlooked the key fact that several East German officials, too, had less than honourable connections to the Nazi era, it was true that the denazification process in the FRG had been, at best, superficial.[17] The East German propaganda strategy focused mainly upon locating people who occupied posts of responsibility in various sectors of society, in spite of their 'brown', i.e. Nazi, past. In 1957, for example, during an international press conference taking place in East Berlin, GDR propaganda officials disclosed information regarding the past of over a hundred West German judges, accusing them of having pursued Hitlerian justice in their judicial roles in Nazi Germany. As Norden recalled in his memoirs, soon after the disclosure of information about these judges, for whom the East German press coined the expression 'blood-judges' (*Blutrichter*), several papers in West Germany and abroad had started questioning the problematic past of several magistrates, incorporating the term *Blutrichter* in their writings.[18] Members of the judicial branch were not the only ones to be attacked by the SED propaganda machinery, which soon started targeting West German politicians and bureaucrats too. SED cadres soon got ready to strike against others whose importance in Adenauer's eyes were much more relevant, such as, most prominently, State Secretary Hans Globke.

Globke had started his career in the civil service in 1929 as an official in the Interior Ministry.[19] Although he had not joined the Nazi Party, among other activities related to his post in 1935 he helped to draft the first two Nuremberg race laws, which stripped Jews in Germany of their political rights and forbade marriages and sexual relations between Germans and Jews, and co-authored a legal commentary on the laws together with then Interior Minister Wilhelm Stuckart.[20] Later, Globke contributed to drafting the laws that forced all German Jews to take on the names of Israel or Sarah and that transferred the property of concentration camp victims to the German authorities. After the war, he came to play a crucial role within the West German Chancellery. Adenauer was convinced that Globke, who had never joined the Nazi Party, had worked to hinder, not promote, Jewish persecution in Germany.[21] While his skills and his long-standing experience in the Interior Ministry rendered him a valuable asset for the West German Chancellor, his past made him an ideal target for East Berlin propaganda. For the GDR, the Jerusalem trial thus appeared a perfect opportunity to emphasise how many Eichmanns were still actively involved in West German politics and society – a chance to upgrade the propaganda campaign against the FRG, transforming it into a systematic, sustained effort to demonstrate on the international stage the continuities between Bonn and the Nazi past, undermining once and for all any West German claim to international respectability.

## Public relations

In the autumn of 1960 an agent or informant of the Central Intelligence Agency (CIA) close to Bonn officials had spoken of the fears of 'his Nazi friends in the West German government ... afraid of the things that will come out of the EICHMANN trial next spring'.[22] To be sure, the upcoming trial generated a certain level of interest about the past of many West German officials, including, most prominently, Globke. 'It would appear', another Central Intelligence Agency report noted, 'that the Soviet bloc has mounted a major effort to exploit the EICHMANN case to implicate GLOBKE in Nazi activities, and thus injure the Adenauer government'.[23] Globke's presence so high up within Bonn's government was in fact disquieting for many, and not just in the East. For, in the words of West German Attorney General Fritz Bauer, 'it was in effect a dirty shame that Globke continued to hold on to his key job as principal adviser to the Chancellor'. Bauer, who headed the Central Office for the Investigation of National Socialist Crimes set up in Ludwigsburg in 1958, was deeply worried by the personnel continuities between the Nazi Reich and the Federal Republic. So much so, that upon receiving information about Eichmann's whereabouts he had decided to pass it on to the Israeli, rather than West German, authorities.[24] He was scathing in his judgement of Globke's role in the Chancellery. For him, 'A man who had, by his own admission, written the commentaries on the Nuremberg racial decrees, who had been responsible for the infamy of the "Jewish first names" and who had, from the beginning of the Third Reich to the very bitter end, remained in the very office which – of all things – had had charge of Jewish Affairs in the Reich Ministry of the Interior, should not, as a simple matter of principle and justice, occupy a position such as Globke had held in Bonn since 1949'.[25]

Protecting the image of the 'new' Germany by demonstrating a clear break from the Nazi past in front of both domestic and international audiences – in spite of so much of the evidence that suggested the contrary – became a key priority in Bonn. The discussion about how to do so effectively quickly spread among various West German offices. In their conversations with Israeli representatives working in Cologne, Federal Foreign Ministry officials emphasised their fears about the East German exploitation of the trial for political ends, expressing their hope that the Israeli authorities would not fall for such a line and would instead focus on supporting their true friend, the Federal Republic.[26] Yet the West German plan did not just rely on asking the Israelis for help. By the end of 1960, the Foreign Ministry's Foreign Information and Press Departments started planning an impressive public diplomacy offensive to be unleashed throughout the run-up to, and duration of, the Eichmann trial, promoting a positive image of the West German state and, contrarily to the East German nemesis, its readiness to confront its difficult past.

West German diplomats stationed all over the globe received precise instructions about how they should portray their government's stance on the upcoming trial in Jerusalem. The Foreign Ministry's Director and Head of the Ministry's Legal Department, member of the Nazi Party Friedrich Janz, circulated a missive directed to Bonn's embassies abroad emphasising the Bonn government's keenness to see 'Eichmann's crimes against the Jews' being 'dealt with'. But he also stressed that, 'for reasons that do not require any explanation', the Federal Republic had thus far reacted with a fair amount of 'reserve' on the question and would continue to do so in the near future.[27] Janz instructed Bonn's diplomats to follow, and report back to Bonn about, the 'treatment of the Eichmann case' abroad. Yet despite Janz's specific instructions, given the anti-Semitic outbursts that had spread over West German territory and beyond just the previous year, protecting the Republic's reputation (*Ansehen*) would not be an easy task.

From the bureau tasked with assisting German war criminals being tried abroad, the Central Office for Legal Protection (Zentrale Rechtsschutzstelle), Hans Gawlik argued that it was 'necessary' to rely on materials that demonstrated that the crimes of which Eichmann was accused had been 'committed by a small circle of people' and were 'surrounded by such secrecy' that 'those who were not directly involved could not have known about them'.[28] While fundamentally historically inaccurate, these words expressed something that many in West Germany wanted to believe, and wanted the world to believe, to be true. From New York, West German Consul Georg Federer highlighted that, while it was difficult to anticipate the possible effects of the trial, he deemed that lists and other materials regarding the number of concluded, ongoing and outstanding West German trials against crimes committed during the Nazi era might come in handy.[29] And, Gawlik's resistance notwithstanding, by February 1961 Justice Ministry personnel began compiling a list of the trials, so much so that the *New York Times* correspondent in West Germany, Sidney Gruson, shortly thereafter reported that 'suddenly' the Central Office for the Investigation of Nazi crimes, 'normally fiercely tightlipped about its work', of late had issued 'heaps of statistics' suggesting 'that the Germans themselves are about to speed the wheels of justice about Nazi criminals'.[30]

The release of such lists and information materials was very well-timed and formed a key component of the public relations counteroffensive mounted by the FRG in preparation for the trial. Nevertheless, the informed public would have easily been able to see through such numbers. As late as March 1960, many in the FRG worked to stop, rather than speed up, the judicial confrontation with the past, as illustrated by the Bundestag debate over extension of the statute of limitations on crimes of murder.[31] The debate, which came to overlap with the news of the upcoming Eichmann trial, stemmed from an SPD initiative proposing that the statutory limit for the prosecution of crimes punishable with life in prison be extended until 1969. At the time such crimes were prosecutable until only twenty years after they had been committed, and the SPD proposal aimed to change the symbolic starting date for the prosecution of such crimes from May 1945, the year of the end of the Second World War, to September 1949, the year of the founding of the West German state. On 24 May 1960, just one day after Prime Minister Ben-Gurion announced the capture and upcoming trial of Adolf Eichmann, the West German Bundestag rejected prolonging the opportunity to investigate crimes committed during the Nazi era, and thus de facto refused to support the West German judicial effort to prosecute Nazi criminals.[32] SPD member Walter Menzel later voiced his hope that the Eichmann trial would have important consequences for the pursuit of justice in the Federal Republic. He welcomed the prospect of what he saw as a positive development, because confronting the atrocities of the past, 'at least attempting to right past wrongs', was a duty of the Federal Republic – and not because East German propaganda insisted on this point, Menzel emphasised.[33] At the following Bundestag session, on 10 June 1960, another SPD representative, Karl Mommer, asked Justice Minister Schäffer about whether the government was 'aware that it very much damages the reputation of the Federal Republic if other states, especially a state as small as Israel' succeeded in tracking down the current location of former Nazi criminals, while the FRG did not.[34] Minister Schäffer's reply that the West German government was doing 'everything possible' to bring Nazi criminals to justice caused general laughter among those sitting on the SPD benches.[35] After all, it was no coincidence that West German Attorney General Fritz Bauer had not turned to the West German authorities with information on Eichmann's location. When asked about it in the Bundestag, Justice Minister Schäffer defended the Bonn government's unawareness of Eichmann's whereabouts, declaring that in the FRG it was believed that the architect of the Final Solution had relocated somewhere in the Middle East. In fact, West German intelligence had established that Eichmann was in Argentina as early as 1952.[36] The failure of the West German embassy in Buenos Aires, and of the Federal Republic's governmental and security institutions, to locate Eichmann seemed to undermine many of the claims about the strength of West German democracy, and rendered all the more urgent Bonn's public relations counteroffensive.

## Warsaw Pact preparations for the trial

The upcoming trial of Eichmann in Jerusalem caused a great deal of upheaval not, just in the Western, but also in the Eastern, bloc. Given that the crimes Eichmann had committed had taken place mostly in countries that now were under the Soviet sphere of influence, some of Moscow's junior allies pressed to get clear instructions about what their line on the trial should be, especially after Israeli diplomats stationed in Eastern Europe approached the Polish authorities to request Eichmann's extradition. While the Israeli authorities were adamant about trying Eichmann in Jerusalem, such a request on the part of a Warsaw Pact country would play into the hands of the Israelis by complicating the position of the Argentinian government, which, all but furious about Israel's violation of its sovereignty in the process that led to Eichmann's capture, instead insisted on trying Eichmann on its own territory. Confronted with increasing Israeli queries about possible extradition requests, Eastern European representatives, and especially the Polish, struggled to deal with such demands, while the Hungarians emphasised the importance of addressing certain crucial divergences among Socialist countries as to how to deal with the upcoming trial in time. Intra-Bloc consultations on the matter took place in August 1960.[37]

East German Foreign Minister Otto Winzer attended the meeting with a very specific goal in mind – that of persuading fellow Warsaw Pact representatives to sustain the East German propaganda efforts during the upcoming trial. As Winzer emphasised to his Eastern European colleagues, a deluge of East German documents and accusations against him could be used to sustain the propaganda offensive to be unleashed on the occasion of the Eichmann trial, drawing upon the connection between Eichmann and selected members of Bonn's establishment accused of having been active during the Nazi era. As Winzer related to the East German Politbüro upon his return, eventually Soviet, Czechoslovak, Polish, Romanian and Hungarian Foreign Ministry officials all agreed to publish and divulge the content of documents from their own archives that would undermine Bonn's 'neofascism' and 'Zionism', thanks to the East German insistence on the topic.[38]

But while Winzer had managed to induce his Soviet-bloc comrades to join the GDR in the offensive against West Germany, within GDR circles it quickly became clear that the propaganda battle over the Eichmann trial would be a risky one. First, because, as Norden himself put it in a private conversation with then Security Secretary within the SED Central Committee and future East German leader Erich Honecker, the propaganda could backfire and instigate the West German or foreign press to unmask the continuities with the past of the GDR's own personnel.[39] The gap between the East German rhetoric that attacked the West German continuities with the past and the GDR's own failure to address the question was acutely apparent to the highest echelons of the East German propaganda machine themselves. This inherent contradiction, claiming to represent a 'new' Germany that had no connections to the Nazi era and yet being aware of the many continuities between the Nazi past and the East German present, reflected a core element of the GDR's approach to the politics of memory: incongruous and obsessed with the Cold War fight against the other German opponent. A second peril highlighted by East German officials related to the broader question of the possible consequences of an active East German involvement with the trial, for example via the participation of GDR witnesses and plaintiffs. This, Norden worried, might lead some to conclude that the GDR entertained relations with Israel – a prospect that was very important to avoid. From the Division for Western Affairs (Westabteilung) of the SED Central Committee, the body in charge of contacts with organisations in the West, Arne Rehahn warned that 'Within the Eichmann trial … our interest is to unmask Bonn's regime and to reveal Globke's role [in the criminal actions of Nazi Germany]. We do not have the intention of giving the impression of the existence of some kind of official relations between the GDR and Israel'.[40] This was a preoccupation which was shared among colleagues sitting in various East German institutions, too.[41] Thus, for example, in preparation for Ulbricht's meeting with Secretary General of the Arab League Abdul Khalek Hassouna in May 1961, the Foreign Ministry suggested not mentioning the Eichmann trial at all. And, if Hassouna brought up the topic, Ulbricht was advised to respond exclusively by condemning the continuities with the past that characterised the Federal Republic.[42] Such preoccupations about possible geopolitical or strategic setbacks would only intensify as an improbable East German figure made his way to Jerusalem, attorney Friedrich Karl Kaul.

## Kaul's idea

Kaul was an extremely well-known personality, in both East and West Germany. At that time, he was one of the most influential German lawyers because, in fact, he was so much more than an ordinary attorney. As a member of the Berlin lawyers' chamber, throughout the late 1940s and until 1961, Kaul was allowed to appear before courts in both East and West Germany. This was a unique opportunity, which he used extensively, often managing to turn judicial situations into platforms from which to denounce what he and the GDR establishment saw, and portrayed, as the many fallacies of the West German state.[43] Author of more than thirty books and sixty screenplays, free to move between East and West Germany, and one of the very few East Germans to be able to indulge in a passion for expensive cars, Kaul demonstrated a creative approach to agit-prop that was possibly without equal in the workers' and builders' state. Just four days after Ben-Gurion's announcement of the trial of Adolf Eichmann in Jerusalem, Kaul had written to Heinz Stadler, one of Albert Norden's closest collaborators, pitching his ideas about how to approach the upcoming event.[44]

'I have had the impression that Eichmann's arrest is not very appealing to Bonn', Kaul noted.[45] He planned to set off to Jerusalem, where he could work as 'observer' or 'reporter'.[46] His intention was to appear before the Israeli court with East German Jewish victims of Nazi persecution who allegedly wanted – although they still had to be found – to take part in the trial as joint plaintiffs. He would contact the Israeli Justice Minister directly in his attempt to be granted the chance of representing his East German Jewish alleged clients. He stressed the need to act quickly, so as to make sure that the West Germans would not 'get in ahead of us' and declared himself willing to pay out of his own pocket for the trip.[47]

Kaul's notion of instrumentally using Jewish citizens for East German propaganda initiatives was not a new idea. Some of the most vicious propagandistic initiatives in the GDR had seen East German Jewish citizens being repeatedly asked to come forward in support of the governmental stance, supporting the East Berlin regime and especially its anti-Zionist and anti-Israeli positions.[48] Nonetheless, Kaul's initiative was groundbreaking, for several reasons. First, Kaul's move was innovative because of his readiness to travel to Israel – a country with which the GDR had no official relations; to which the East German regime had, since its inception, refused to pay any sort of compensation for the Nazi persecution of the Jews; and a country that, according to East German propaganda, was 'the spearhead of US imperialism', aiming to subjugate the 'national independence' of its Arab neighbours.[49] Second, because his proposal envisaged giving a new, global dimension to East Berlin's (Cold) War propaganda against Bonn. Indeed, while Kaul had long been using German courtrooms as platforms from whence to strike against the FRG, doing so from an Israeli courtroom meant placing, loudly, the Cold War between the two German states on an international stage, using the legacy of the Nazi past as a crucial weapon against the FRG's alleged respectability. Third, his idea also promoted an innovative, different implementation of the East German propaganda effort at a time in which the country's pamphlets on Bonn's continuities with the Nazi past aimed to reach an ever more global audience.[50] Indeed, the East German message crafted for the occasion of the Eichmann trial was aimed at a global public – 'from England to India', as Norden put it – in the attempt to come between these countries and Bonn and undermine West Germany's standing in the world.[51] Behind many of the measures that the Politbüro and the Division for Western Affairs of the SED would put forth as the Eichmann trial unfolded stood the initiative and creativity of this peculiar individual.[52]

Having to strike a delicate balance between attacking the FRG, by highlighting the question of the continuity with the past, while defending the GDR from the same accusations; and while attempting to persuade the Israeli authorities to let him take part in their trial albeit without giving the impression that the GDR might have formal relations with the Jewish state, Kaul set off to Jerusalem, for the first time, on 15 February 1961. He did so without the support of his Foreign Ministry – East Berlin's Foreign Minister Winzer claimed that from his point of view it would be far too complicated to send Kaul to Jerusalem and that the East Germans should instead send someone 'from West Germany' to Israel to do the job for them.[53] Yet Kaul's idea was too good not to give it a try, and Norden's office gave him the green light to proceed. A few weeks before his eventual departure, in January 1961, Kaul still lamented that everything that the GDR had done thus far about the Eichmann trial had been 'absolutely amateurish'.[54] Yet his initiative had contributed to unleashing a series of East German measures: Stasi officials brainstormed about possible individuals, preferably Jewish, to send to the trial from within or outside East Germany to sustain Kaul's efforts, while other SED officials organised a series of meetings in order to better pinpoint the East German strategy to tackle the forthcoming trial.[55]

In the meantime, however, contacts between the West German secret services and their American and Israeli counterparts had indeed expanded in the run up to the trial. As the news spread in the FRG that Adolf Eichmann had written a memoir, and that the family had then sold it to the American magazine *Life*, the Bonn government became increasingly 'worried re[garding] possible derog[atory] contents affecting members [of the Federal] government' and soon arranged for possible countermeasures. These involved asking the CIA for help. An agency cable dated 20 September 1960 indeed noted that *Life* magazine had agreed to omit a 'mention of Globke' under pressure from the CIA, possibly acting upon a West German request.[56]

Israeli officials denied having given Bonn assurances that the trial 'would be conducted in a way which would not hurt West German-Israeli relations'.[57] Yet, by the beginning of 1961 it became increasingly clear that albeit Eichmann might have revelations which would prove damaging for Globke or others within the West German political elite, the Israeli government 'would go particularly slowly with damaging allegations against prominent West Germans during the trial, for political and diplomatic reasons'.[58] Asked about how the security establishment handled the difficult months of the Eichmann trial in their expanding cooperation with the FRG, then Director of the Israeli Minister of Defense Asher Ben-Natan later recalled that he and his colleagues somehow knew that avoiding any stress on the link between Bonn and the Nazi past would ultimately pay off.[59] As he saw it, the message that the Bonn establishment was giving the Israelis was to not let the Nazi past darken the image that the West German state had been striving to construct for itself.

Thus, if East German propaganda was attempting to heighten the level of attention paid to the connection between Eichmann and Globke, and the Nazis and Bonn more generally, West German circles were striking back. In May 1961 a CIA cable from Munich reported that Robert Servatius, Eichmann's attorney, was 'considering bringing out fact Eichmann has turned communist, in order to make [the] story more sensational and profitable'.[60] At first the news had been considered credible, even at the top of the CIA. 'We have learned from a highly-placed source ... that Eichmann is now a Communist', reported CIA head Allen W. Dulles in April 1961.[61] In Dulles' words this was a 'highly sensitive' revelation, which would strike 'a severe blow to the Soviet propaganda effort'.[62] However, the claim soon appeared to be untenable. Only a few days later Dulles himself noted that, lacking the necessary evidence, he was inclined 'to let the matter rest for the time being'.[63] Only a West German tabloid published, in December 1961, news of Eichmann's conversion from Nazism to Communism. Otherwise, the bizarre news item remained largely unnoticed.[64]

Further to the public relations offensive, the West German Foreign Ministry had dispatched a team of observers to Jerusalem to observe the trial and other events related to it. The team comprised of nine individuals, including a university researcher, a journalist, a member of the Press and Information Office of the Federal Government, as well as Foreign Ministry personnel. At the head of the team was lawyer Gerhard Freiherr von Preuschen, whom Foreign Minister Brentano had warmly recommended for the job. His task in Jerusalem, as framed by the West German Cabinet, would be twofold – 'expressing' the 'moral interest' of the Bonn government at every possible opportunity and 'observing the political course of the process' and reporting back about it to Bonn.[65]

Five weeks before the beginning of the trial, Foreign Minister Brentano circulated to all FRG diplomatic and consular representations abroad the final specific guidelines related to the PR work (*Öffentlichkeitsarbeit*) that he expected them to carry out in conjunction with the trial.[66] It was important, Brentano stressed, to hinder the 'all too negative consequences' that the trial might have. He recommended, in particular, to be wary of Soviet and East German propaganda, and to rebuff any possible accusations against the FRG's continuities with the Nazi past by highlighting the anti-Israeli stance of the countries of the Soviet bloc. This, Brentano stressed, would be 'one of the most important tasks of the political PR work'. Brentano recommended emphasising that the FRG was keen to see Eichmann being prosecuted for his crimes; that the Bonn Republic had been very active in the pursuit of justice for crimes committed during the Nazi era; and attacking the GDR along three main lines. First, East Berlin had never agreed to pay reparations to Israel, while West Germany did. Second, the East German rulers were 'carrying on Hitler's dictatorship through the means of totalitarianism', while the FRG was a thriving democracy. Third, that while the GDR's propaganda was generally very anti-Israeli, Bonn instead had managed to 'win the trust of the Israeli government'.

In his first press conference in over two years, held shortly before the beginning of the trial in Jerusalem, Adenauer voiced his concerns over the negative impact that the trial might have on the international image of the Federal Republic.[67] Insisting upon a stance towards the Nazi past that had been typical of his chancellorship, Adenauer reminded his audience that only a 'relatively small percentage' of Germans had been convinced Nazis, while the 'great majority' had helped 'their Jewish fellow-citizens when they could'.[68] 'While the truth is, of course, the exact opposite of Dr Adenauer's assertion that only "a relatively small percentage" of Germans had been Nazis', typed Hannah Arendt in her *New Yorker* pieces, later to be published as *Eichmann in Jerusalem*.[69] Her work attracted a good deal of criticism from across the United States, Israel and Europe focusing on her treatment of the trial but, as Norman Podhoretz put it, what she had written also constituted 'perhaps the most severe indictment of Adenauer's Germany that has yet been seen this side of the Iron Curtain'.[70] And Arendt had a point. Increasingly, many of the allegations put forward by the GDR propaganda machine about the West German continuities with the Nazi past seemed to be disturbingly plausible.

## The German Cold War in Jerusalem

The commission for all-German matters of the East German Politbüro anticipated that the effect of Kaul's participation would be massive.[71] Prior to his visit, Kaul had appealed in writing to the Israeli Minister of Justice, Pinchas Rosen, with the request that he be permitted to represent some East German Jewish citizens who wanted to take part in the trial as joint plaintiffs.[72] He emphasised that, given that the West German lawyer Robert Servatius had, exceptionally, been granted permission to defend Eichmann in the Israeli court, a corresponding measure should be undertaken in order to allow East German citizens to participate in the prosecution of Adolf Eichmann in Jerusalem.[73] Israeli law had had to be changed to enable Servatius to defend Eichmann, as until that time foreign lawyers had no right of audience in Israeli courts. *Neues Deutschland* highlighted how different the roles of the two Germanys in the trial would be: West Germany was sending Robert Servatius to defend Eichmann; East Germany was

Figure 6.1   Gideon Hausner and Robert Servatius at the Eichmann trial. Jerusalem, 1961.

sending Kaul to represent Eichmann's victims.[74] Israeli Communist representatives joined in the attacks against Bonn, both in the Knesset and in the press.[75]

But the East German preparations for the trial suffered a huge blow when the Israeli Knesset ruled out the possibility that there could be any accessory prosecution in the trial.[76] Kaul claimed that by that point the West German and Israeli authorities had already reached an agreement as to how the trial should be conducted; and that the only way in which the GDR, and he himself, could proceed would be with the help of 'the Israeli comrades'.[77] The East German attempt to dominate the trial and use it as a weapon in the Cold War battlefield against West Germany had encountered a serious setback. Moshe Sneh (previously Kleinbaum), one of the founders of Maki, publicly attacked Israeli Justice Minister Pinhas Rosen during a Knesset debate for acquiescing to the West German wish to avoid mentioning Globke during the trial.[78]

When Rosen and Kaul met in person, on 20 February 1961, according to Kaul's account of the discussion, the message that he tried to convey to his Israeli interlocutors was that the trial was not just about history and the past. From the East German perspective, as he insisted, the trial had very much to do with the present. According to an excerpt of their conversation, as reported by Kaul in the account that he published in 1963 and where he wrote, in the third person, of his time in Jerusalem:

> Prof. Dr. Kaul asked: 'Mr Chief Prosecutor, do you really think that Eichmann could have hurt a hair of even a single Jew had others not created the conditions for this to happen?'
>
> 'Of course, during the trial we will have to speak also of Hitler and Himmler, Kaltenbrunner and Heydrich,'[79] the Israeli Chief Prosecutor conceded.
>
> 'You are only naming dead people! Why don't you name the names of those who are still alive today and are again in office in West Germany?'[80]

Kaul emphasised how difficult it would be for him to explain to the East German Jewish citizens that the Israeli state refused to allow them to take part in Eichmann's indictment, and left some documentary evidence, which purported to help prove Eichmann's culpability, with the Israeli Minister and the attorney. Despite his efforts, however, Kaul was only granted permission to attend the trial as an official observer.

Following his disappointing meeting with the Israeli Minister, Kaul organised an international press conference. There, he repeated that the importance of the trial was not just 'historical': for the GDR the 'extermination [*Ausrottung*] of Nazism' was a 'burning national interest' without which German reunification would never be possible.[81] Members of the West German observers delegation stationed in Israel for the trial repeatedly interrupted his speech, countering his allegations against the FRG – yet he nevertheless went on for two hours. It was clear that in Jerusalem representatives of East and West Germany were battling over the meaning and significance of the trial for their Cold War present. So much so, that an Israeli journalist reported in the *Jerusalem Post* that the discussion at Kaul's press conference resembled 'a private dispute between East and West Germans'.[82] At one point an Italian journalist had stood up and asked Kaul to please move on from the discussion with the West Germans and get to the heart of the new revelations.[83] A journalist working for the *New York Times* begged Kaul and the West Germans to have respect for his readers, and to please stop quarrelling, for their discussion had very little to do with the Eichmann trial.

Following months of disputes about where the trial should be conducted, and how, on the morning of 11 April 1961, in a small courtroom in the Beit HaAm auditorium in Jerusalem, two guards conducted Adolf Eichmann towards a glass booth from where he would be tried by the Israeli authorities for the crimes he committed when heading the Gestapo office charged with implementing the Nazi policy of Jewish extermination. Three thousand kilometres away, the East German People's Chamber (the Volkskammer) reunited to discuss the significance of the trial, emphasising in an official communication that 'The trial against Eichmann in Jerusalem is more than just a trial about the Hitlerian fascist past (*hitlerfaschisische Vergangenheit*). It is also a denunciation of the militaristic system which continues to exist on West German soil still today.'[84] In the final comments on the draft speech of chief prosecutor Gideon Hausner, who would play a key role in the trial, David Ben-Gurion reminded the attorney general of the importance of always employing the adjective 'Nazi' when mentioning 'Germany', so as to be very clear in the distinction between the Germany of the past and that, or rather those, of the present.[85]

The day after Kaul left Jerusalem to go back to East Berlin, on 5 May 1961, the Israeli authorities concluded that his mission in Jerusalem had 'failed'.[86] He had not been allowed to take part in the trial, and his outreach activities had had only limited effect. Yet the Israeli assessment was not entirely correct. Indeed, in the same communication, the Director General of the Israeli Ministry of Foreign Affairs himself, Chaim Yaḥil, had to concede that, although Kaul had not been allowed to speak at the trial, nonetheless it was 'impossible' to prevent the Israeli and international press from condemning Globke's presence in the West German Chancellery.[87] And that, too, was part of the GDR's means to a victorious end of the Cold War confrontation. For the aim of Kaul's presence and activities in Jerusalem was not – or not only – that of representing East German Jewish citizens and their accusations against Eichmann. He had managed to go to Jerusalem in spite of those who, both in the Eastern and Western bloc, warned of the pitfalls that might be cognate to his involvement in the trial. His activities in Jerusalem were planned with the explicit aim of attacking Bonn by highlighting the continuities between Hitler's Reich and Adenauer's Bundesrepublik, in a country where the majority of the electorate was still sceptical of Ben-Gurion's overtures to West Germany, and at a moment in which the Israeli and international public were particularly vulnerable to anti-German feelings.[88] His endeavours in Jerusalem had represented a continuation of the East Cold War struggle against the West by new, and innovative, means.

## Berlin and Belgrade

The unfolding of the Eichmann trial in Jerusalem coincided with a crucial turning point in the history of the Cold War. On the night of 12–13 August, East German soldiers set up coils of barbed wire, separating the Soviet sector of Berlin from the

Western one. These barriers, guarded by units of East German police, transport police, and GDR workers' militias, would later become the Berlin Wall.[89] In West Berlin, Mayor Willy Brandt encouraged his citizens to stand together 'for unity and the right to freedom', but panic ran high among governmental officials in Bonn. Once the immediate fears about a Soviet–American confrontation that might lead to a global nuclear war receded, Bonn's Foreign Ministry officials began sketching out what the longer-term consequences of the Wall could be for the German–German Cold War confrontation. Their main worry was that the construction of the Wall might give the decisive push to the East German quest for international legitimacy, signalling that the GDR state was there to stay, for quite a long time to come, and with full Soviet backing too.

The construction of the Berlin Wall was intended to halt the drain of citizens who fled from the GDR, a problem that was demographic and economic in nature, but which also reflected the astounding legitimacy deficit of the Ulbricht regime. Yet the Wall also bestowed upon GDR diplomats the confidence that from now on East Germany would be able to launch a revitalised foreign policy, finally leading to the achievement of East Berlin's crucial goal – that of international recognition.[90] The first challenge that West German diplomats had to face in this regard was the impending conference of non-aligned countries in a Belgrade where, due to the diligent application of the Hallstein Doctrine, Bonn had no diplomatic presence. The meeting was a crucial one, officially sanctioning the existence of a consistent bloc of non-aligned countries that had all intentions of playing an independent role within the global Cold War. Taking place in the wake of the construction of the Wall, the event was particularly delicate for the FRG. Just four years earlier, in 1957, Tito's Yugoslavia had attempted to challenge the rigidity of the West German claim to sole representation of the German nation by establishing relations with the GDR. At that time, Bonn's reaction was extremely severe, cutting off diplomatic relations to the country, as well as the generous economic aid that the FRG had granted it.[91] In 1957 the move had proved to be an effective warning against other countries tempted to provide the GDR with official recognition. However, in 1961 the lack of a West German presence in the country posed some limitations on Bonn's intention to influence and lobby the countries about to take part in the Belgrade conference.

The West German Foreign Ministry had anticipated that most of the participants would be loyal to Bonn's stance on the German question – but they could not be entirely sure. After all, the Wall in Berlin might, in fact, persuade the majority of the states represented in Belgrade that the time was ripe to recognise the East German state.[92] Several non-aligned leaders clearly expressed that, in their view, there were two German states, and that the non-aligned countries should recognise this new political reality. Indonesia's Sukarno demanded 'the recognition of the … de facto sovereignty of two Germanys'.[93] Prince Norodom Sihanouk of Cambodia claimed that the existence of two German states was 'a fact that we have to recognize', while the host, Marshal Tito, stressed that after the construction of the Berlin Wall the 'existence of two Germanys' was now, simply, a 'fact'.[94] As the CIA reported while the conference was ongoing, 'most of the views thus far expressed … on the German question, are closer to those of the Soviet Bloc than those to the West'.[95]

Yet the Conference's concluding communiqué only mentioned the German problem in passing, in the form of a broad call to 'all parties concerned not to resort to or threaten the use of force to solve the German question or the problem of Berlin',[96] and what nipped the blossoming non-aligned recognition of the GDR in the bud was, mainly, Nasser's vehement disagreement with the idea. He had experienced first-hand a series of West German recriminations after his overtures to the GDR in the 1950s and, at the turn of the decade, he seemed to want to reconcile his relationship with Bonn. While his attitude on the matter would change again shortly thereafter, at the Belgrade conference Nasser reminded his fellow non-aligned leaders that the construction of the Wall did not mean the 'end' of the German problem.[97] East Berlin had never been so close to official, massive recognition on the part of such a substantial portion of countries outside of the Soviet bloc – but, clearly, more remained to be done, especially about persuading Nasser (and Nehru) of the GDR's power and prestige. How could East German representatives avoid another Belgrade, and persuade him to distance himself from the West German line, bringing him to see the many positive sides of the GDR?[98] One way to impress him, the East Germans reflected, could be their fierce anti-Zionism – and the propaganda establishment swiftly drew up a plan to insist on anti-Israeli themes in preparation for the next meeting of the non-aligned countries, scheduled to take place in Cairo three years later.[99] As the GDR Commissioner in the United Arab Republic would soon emphasise, 'anti-Israeli rhetoric' was the 'catch-phrase' of every official communication in the country, whether aimed at a domestic or an international audience.[100] Thus defaming Israel, while stressing the similarities between the GDR and the Arab countries, should become a core feature of the East German efforts to reach international recognition.

Former SS-Obersturmbannführer Adolf Eichmann was hanged on 1 June 1962. Meeting with the Israeli Defense Minister Peres the following week, Adenauer expressed his gratitude for the 'correct and honourable way' in which the 'Eichmann problem' had been dealt with in Israel.[101] After having been halted as the trial was ongoing, the economic cooperation that had been agreed upon by Adenauer and Ben-Gurion in New York in 1960 could now finally start being implemented.

## Notes

1  BAL-SAPMO DY 30/IV 2/2.028/2: Norden to Ulbricht, 28 May 1960.
2  For background on the trial, including its global media coverage, see D. Lipstadt, *The Eichmann Trial* (New York: Schocken, 2011); for its media coverage in the GDR see J. Keilbach, 'The Eichmann Trial on East German Television', *VIEW: Journal of European Television History and Culture* 3:5 (2014), pp. 17–22.
3  Emphasis added. BAL-SAPMO DY 30/IV 2/2.028/2: Norden to Ulbricht, 28 May 1960.
4  Author's interview with Otto Pfeiffer, Berlin, 26 November 2013.
5  Timm, *Hammer, Zirkel, Davidstern*, p. 174.
6  PA AA: MfAA A 12609/1: Neugebauer (Prague), 9 December 1959.
7  D. Vital, *Zionism: The Formative Years* (New York: Oxford University Press, 1982).

8   K. Hartewig, *Zurückgekehrt: die Geschichte der jüdischen Kommunisten in der DDR* (Cologne: Böhlau, 2000), p. 82.
9   Author's interview with Manja Finnberg, 17 November 2013.
10  Y. Ben-Yaacov, *A Lasting Reward: Memoirs of an Israeli Diplomat* (Jerusalem: Hoffmann and Campe Verlag, 2007), p. 67.
11  PA AA: MfAA/A 13777/5: GDR Consular department, Prague. Memorandum of conversation with the Israelite [*sic*] Consul in Prague, Mister Raveh. Seydewitz, 18 January 1960.
12  'In Memoriam', *Der Spiegel*, 23 December 1959, p. 95. Timm, *Hammer, Zirkel, Davidstern*, pp. 171ff.
13  PA AA: MfAA/A 13777/5: GDR Consular department, Prague. Memorandum of conversation with the Israelite [*sic*] Consul in Prague, Mister Raveh. Seydewitz, 18 January 1960.
14  PA AA: MfAA/A 13777/3: Embassy GDR Prague. Conversation of comrade Dr. Seydewitz with the Israeli consul in Prague. Neugebauer, 21 January 1960.
15  PA AA: MfAA/A 13777/1: 3.AEA, Conversation Dr. Seydewitz with the Israeli representative. Simons, 2 February 1960.
16  *Ibid.*
17  See, i.e., H. Best and A. Salheiser, 'Shadows of the Past: National Socialist Backgrounds of the GDR's Functional Elites', *German Studies Review* 29:3 (2006), pp. 589–602; H. Waibel, *Diener vieler Herren. Ehemalige NS-Funktionäre in der SBZ/DDR* (Frankfurt am Main: Lang, 2011).
18  A. Norden, *Ereignisse und Erlebtes* (Berlin: Dietz, 1981), p. 229. The campaign against West German judges and their Nazi past continued, and in 1959 the GDR disclosed information about over 800 of them. On the problems linked to the contintuity of personnel in Bonn's judiciary system, see D. Rigoll, *Staatsschutz in Westdeutschland: von der Entnazifizierung zur Extremistenabwehr* (Göttingen: Wallstein, 2013).
19  On Globke's life see K. Gotto (ed.), *Der Staatssekretärs Adenauers. Persönlichkeit und politisches Wirkens Hans Globkes* (Stuttgart: Klett-Cotta, 1980) and E. Lommatzsch, *Hans Globke (1898–1973): Beamter in Dritten Reich und Staatssekretär Adenauers* (Frankfurt am Main: Campus, 2009). On how he transitioned to his role as State Secretary in the aftermath of the Holocaust see D. E. Rogers, 'Restoring a German Career, 1945-1950: The Ambiguity of Being Hans Globke', *German Studies Review* 31:2 (2008), pp. 303–24.
20  C. Essner, *Die Nürnberger Gesetzte oder Die VErwaltung des Rassenwahns, 1933–1945* (Paderborn: Schöningh, 2002). On Stuckart's role and actions see H. C. Jasch, *Staatssekretär Wilhelm Stuckart und die Bundesrepublik – Die Mythos von der sauberen Verwaltung* (Munich: Oldenbourg, 2012).
21  J. Bevers, *Der Mann hinter Adenauer: Hans Globkes Aufstieg vom NS-Juristen zur Grauen Eminenz der Bonner Republik* (Berlin: Christoph Links, 2009).
22  NARA II, RG 263: *CIA Name File: Adolf Eichmann. Directorate of Operations File, Vol. 3. '[excised] involvement with West Germany of Eichmann Case'*, CIA Dispatch, 2 December 1960; T. Naftali, 'New Information on Cold War CIA Stay-Behind Operations in Germany and on the Adolf Eichmann Case', https://fas.org/sgp/eprint/naftali.pdf [Accessed November 2019].
23  NARA II, RG 263: *CIA Name File: Adolf Eichmann. Directorate of Operations File, Vol. 3. 'Possible Communist Exploitation of Trial of Adolf Eichmann'. Munich, Air Pouch,*

26 March 1961. NARA II, RG 263: *CIA Name File: Adolf Eichmann. Directorate of Operations File, Vol. 2. 'Life to Publish Eichmann Memoirs'. CIA Cable,* 18 October 1960.

24   I. Wojak, *Fritz Bauer: 1903–1968: Eine Biographie* (Munich: Beck, 2009), pp. 284–316; Z. Aharoni and W. Dietl, *Operation Eichmann: Pursuit and Capture* (London: Cassel, 1999), p. 79. Conze et al., *Das Amt*, p. 257.

25   In NARA II, RG 263: CIA Name File: Adolf Eichmann. Directorate of Operations File, Vol. 3. 'The Eichmann Trial and Allegations Against Sec. State Dr. Globke'. US Consulate Frankfurt Dispatch, 7 February 1961. The document that Bauer is referring to here is: W. Stuckart and H. Globke, *Kommentare zur deutschen Rassengesetzgebung* (Munich: Beck, 1936). On the policy of name changes in Nazi Germany see S. Friedländer, *Nazi Germany and the Jews*, Vol. 1, *The Years of Prosecution 1933–1939* (New York: Harper Perennial, 1998), pp. 34–5ff.

26   ISA/RG 93.43/MFA/584/5 Hess (Cologne) to Savir (Cologne), 20 February 1960.

27   PA AA B7/10: Janz to the Embassies of the Federal Republic, n.d.

28   PA AA B7/10: Note: Obtaining documents that might be able to hinder certain effects of the Eichmann trial. Gawlik, 19 January 1961.

29   *Ibid.*

30   The quotes are from PA AA B7/10: Dallinger, 24 February 1961 and S. Gruson, 'Germans Striving to Counter Reaction Expected from Nazi's Trial in Israel', *New York Times*, 5 April 1961, p. 15, respectively.

31   This debate became known as the *Verjährungsdebatte* (i.e. the debate on the statute of limitations for Nazi crimes). Between May 1960 and January 1963, the upcoming trial of Adolf Eichmann was mentioned on just five occasions during Bundestag debates, mostly in connection to discussions on West German domestic issues. Deutscher Bundestag, *Zur Verjährung nationalsozialistischer Verbrechen: Dokumentation der parlamentarischen Bewältigung des Problems, 1960–1979, Teil 1* (Bonn: Deutscher Bundestag, Presse-und Informationszentrum, 1980).

32   This series of *Verjährungsdebatten* took place in 1960, 1965, 1969 and 1979. On 3 July 1979 a majority of Bundestag members (253 against 228) finally voted to abolish the statute of limitations on crimes of murder and genocide.

33   Deutscher Bundestag, 117. Sitzung, 24 May 1960, 6,684.

34   Deutscher Bundestag, 118. Sitzung, 22 June 1960, 6,796.

35   *Ibid.*

36   NARA II, RG 263: Adolf Eichmann, CIA Name File. Directorate of Operations File, Vol. 1, Doc. 42, 'Near Eastern Connections', 19 March 1958; T. Naftali, 'The CIA and Eichmann's Associates', in R. Breitman, N. W. J. Goda, T. Naftali and R. Wolfe (eds), *US Intelligence and the Nazis* (Cambridge: Cambridge University Press, 2005), pp. 337–74; Conze et al., *Das Amt*, pp. 604ff.

37   ISA/RG 130.09/MFA 2307/8: Avir (Warsaw) to Yaḥil (Jerusalem), 9 June 1960 and PA AA: MfAA A/16242: Vesper to Florin, 4 August 1960.

38   BA-SAPMO, DY30 J IV 2/2A/767: Working Protocol of the Politbüro, No. 35 of 16.8.1960, Annex 4, Consultation Questions of the Ministry of Foreign Affairs of the Hungarian People's Republic to the Ministry of Foreign Affairs of the Soviet Union, Poland, CSSR, the GDR, and Romania in connection with the Eichmann affair, 16 August 1960.

39   BA-SAPMO, DY 30 IV 2/2028/1: Norden to Honecker, 27 October 1960.

40   BA-SAPMO, DY 30 IV 2/2.028/21: Rehahn to Norden, 14 February 1961.

41 DY 30 IV 2/2.028/21: Rehahn to Norden, 11 January 1961; DY 30 IV 2/2.028/52: Winzer to Norden, 12 January 1961.

42 PA AA: MfAA A/11202, Discussion topics for the Ulbricht-Hassouna meeting in East Berlin, 13 May 1961.

43 In 1961 the West German Supreme Court banned him from serving as a defence lawyer in the West. Friedman, 'The Cold War Politics of Exile', pp. 308 and 315.

44 BAL-SAPMO DY 30/IV 2/2028/57: Kaul to Stadler, 27 May 1960.

45 *Ibid.*

46 BAL-SAPMO DY 30/IV 2/2.028/57: Kaul to Stadler, 30 May 1960.

47 *Ibid.*

48 Wolffsohn, *Die Deutschland Akte*, p. 87.

49 See, e.g., G. Krauss, 'Die zionistische Agentur des USA-Imperialismus', *ND*, 6 December 1952, p. 7; M. Amino, 'General Robertson mußte die Dienstbotentreppe benutzen', *ND*, 8 March 1951, p. 4.

50 PA AA B6/60 Propaganda of the Soviet zone distributed in Ceylon against the Bundesrepublik. Auer, 26 April 1962.

51 See BAL-SAPMO, DY 30/IV 2/2.028/39: Norden to Florin, 12 August 1960.

52 The most comprehensive work on Kaul to date is: A. Rosskopf, *Friedrich Karl Kaul: Anwalt im geteilten Deutschland (1906–1981)* (Berlin: Berlin-Verlag Spitz, 2002). See also the excellent M. P. Friedman, 'The Cold War Politics of Exile, Return, and the Search for a Usable Past in Friedrich Karl Kaul's *Es wird Zeit, dass du nach Hause kommst*', *German Life and Letters* 58:3 (2005), pp. 306–25; A. Weinke, '"Verteidigen tue ich schon recht gern …" Friedrich Karl Kaul und die westdeutschen NS-Prozesse der 1960er Jahre', in *Schuldig. NS-Verbrechen vor deutschen Gerichten*, Beiträge zur Geschichte der nationalsozialistischen Verfolgung in Norddeutschland (Bremen: Temmen, 2005), pp. 44–57.

53 BAL-SAPMO, DY 30 IV 2/2.028/52: Winzer to Norden, 12 January 1961.

54 BAL-SAPMO, DY 30 IV 2/2.028/57: Kaul to Norden, 15 January 1961.

55 MfS, HA IX, Nr. 22631, Foreign experts on the case of Globke, n.d.

56 NARA II, RG 263, CIA Name File: Adolf Eichmann. Directorate of Operations File, Vol. 2. 'Life to Publish Eichmann Memoirs'. CIA Cable, 18 October 1960.

57 JTA, 'Israel denies giving assurances to German Govt on Eichmann Trial', 22 March 1961, p. 1.

58 NARA II, RG 263, CIA Name File: Adolf Eichmann. Directorate of Operations File, Vol. 3. 'The Eichmann Trial and Allegations Against Sec. State Dr. Globke'. US Consulate Frankfurt Despatch, 7 February 1961.

59 Author's interview with Asher Ben-Natan, first Israeli Ambassador to the Federal Republic of Germany and former official of the Israeli Ministry of Defence (Ramat HaSharon, Israel: 20 January 2014).

60 Classified CIA Message, 9 May 1961, www2.gwu.edu/~nsarchiv/NSAEBB/NSAEBB150/box15_do_file_vol3/doc42.pdf [Accessed November 2019].

61 Memorandum. Allen W. Dulles to Brig. Gen. Chester V. Clifton, 'Adolph [*sic*] Eichmann', FOIA. www.foia.cia.gov/sites/default/files/document_conversions/5829/CIA-RDP80B01676R000800050072–2.pdf [Accessed November 2019].

62 *Ibid.*

63 Memorandum, 'Allegations that Eichmann is now a Communist', April 1961. www2.gwu.edu/~nsarchiv/NSAEBB/NSAEBB150/box15_do_file_vol3/doc36.pdf [Accessed November 2019].

64  Dispatch, 28 December 1961. www.foia.cia.gov/sites/default/files/document_
    conversions/1705143/EICHMANN,%20ADOLF%20%20%20VOL.%203_0077.pdf
    [Accessed November 2019].
65  143. Cabinet Meeting, 22 March 1961, *Die Kabinettsprotokolle der Bundesregierung.*
66  PA AA B7/10: Brentano to all Diplomatic and Professional Consular Representatives
    of the Federal Republic of Germany, 3 March 1961.
67  'Nazi Trial Issues Worry Adenauer', *New York Times*, 11 March 1961.
68  *Ibid.*
69  H. Arendt, *Eichmann in Jerusalem: A Report on the Banality of Evil*
    (New York: Penguin Books, 1994), p. 18. However, Gideon Hausner fiercely rebuffed
    Arendt's claims, see G. Hausner, *Justice in Jerusalem* (New York: Herzi Press, 1977),
    p. 455.
70  N. Podhorez, 'Hannah Arendt on Eichmann: A Study in the Perversity of Brilliance',
    *Commentary*, 3 September 1963, p. 6.
71  BA-SAPMO DY 30 IV 2/2021/31: Commission for all-German work at the Politbüro.
    Report for Comrade Norden about the work of the last weeks. Rehahn, 30 May 1961.
72  Kaul, *Der Fall Eichmann*, p. 119.
73  ISA/RG 74/A/3145/1 Kaul to Rosen, 19 February 1961; *ibid.* Rosen to Kaul, 21
    February 1961.
74  'DDR-Bürger klagen gegen Eichmann', *ND*, 30 October 1960, p. 2.
75  NARA II, RG 263: *CIA Name File: Adolf Eichmann. Directorate of Operations File,
    Vol. 3. 'Possible Communist Exploitation of Trial of Adolf Eichmann'. Munich, Air
    Pouch*, 26 March 1961, http://nsarchive.gwu.edu/NSAEBB/NSAEBB150/box15_do_
    file_vol3/doc26.pdf [Accessed November 2019].
76  'Als Nebenkläger abgelehnt', *Der Tag*, 13 March 1961.
77  BAL-SAPMO, DY 30 IV 2/2.028/57: Kaul to Norden, 15 January 1961.
78  NARA II, RG 263, CIA Name File: Adolf Eichmann. Directorate of Operations File,
    Vol. 3. 'Possible Communist Exploitation of Trial of Adolf Eichmann'. Munich, Air
    Pouch, 26 March 1961, http://nsarchive.gwu.edu/NSAEBB/NSAEBB150/box15_do_
    file_vol3/doc26.pdf [Accessed November 2019].
79  Both Ernst Kaltenbrunner and Reinhard Heydrich were high-ranking Nazi officials
    during the Second World War. See, respectively, P. B. Black, *Ernst Kaltenbrunner:
    Ideological Soldier of the Third Reich* (Princeton: Princeton University Press, 1984) and
    R. Gewarth, *Hitler's Hangman: The Life of Heydrich* (New Haven:
    Yale University Press, 2011).
80  Kaul, *Der Fall Eichmann*, pp. 133–4. The chief prosecutor against Adolf Eichmann,
    Gideon Hausner, also took part in the meeting. G. Hausner, *Justice in Jerusalem*
    (New York: Holocaust Library, 1958).
81  Kaul, *Der Fall Eichmann*, p. 138.
82  This and the following quotes are from PA AA B7/11: Telex from Jerusalem,
    Preuschen, 3 May 1961.
83  See 'Il tribunale denuncia il nazista Hans Globke', *L'Unità*, 13 May 1961, p. 9.
84  Erklärung des Präsidiums der Volkskammer der Deutschen Demokratischen Republik
    zum Eichmann-Prozeß, abgegeben durch den Präsidenten der Volkskammer, Dr.h.c.
    Johannes Dieckmann, auf der 17. Tagung der Obersten Volksvertretung am 12. April
    1961, Dokumente zur Außenpolitik der DDR (DADDR) 1961, p. 22.
85  ISA/RG 43.4/G/6384/1 Ben-Gurion to Hausner, 28 March 1961.
86  ISA/RG 93.43/MFA.584/5: Yaḥil to Savir, 5 May 1961.

87 *Ibid.* PA AA B7/11: Telex, Preuschen, 28 June 1961 and Telex, Stercken, 30 June 1961.

88 Stauber, 'Realpolitik and the Burden of the Past'.

89 On the Berlin Crisis and the construction of the Berlin Wall see, Hope, *Driving the Soviets Up the Wall*. A different interpretation of the events that led to 13 August is offered by M. Lemke, *Die Berlinkrise 1958 bis 1963. Interessen und Handlungsspielräume der SED im Ost-West-Konflikt* (Berlin: Akademie Verlag, 1995). For an overview of the historiography debating the East German and Soviet role in building the Wall see N. D. Cary, 'Wagging the Dog in Cold War Germany', *German History* 24:2 (2006): 268–93.

90 S. Bock and K. Seidel, 'Die Außenbeziehungen der DDR in der Peiode der Konsolidierung (1955 bis 1972/73)', in S. Bock, I. Muth and H. Schwiesau (eds), *DDR-Außenpolitik im Rückspiegel. Diplomaten im Gespräch* (Münster: LIT, 2004), p. 66.

91 See, for example, M. Anic de Osona, *Die erste Anerkennung der DDR. Der Bruch der deutsch-jugoslawischen Beziehungen 1957* (Baden-Baden: Nomos, 1990) and M. C. Theurer, *Bonn – Belgrad- Ost-Berlin: die Beziehungen der beiden deutschen Staaten zu Jugoslawien im Vergleich: 1957–1968* (Berlin: Logos, 2008), p. 112. The original announcement was published in *Bullettin der Presse- und Informationsamt der Bundesregierung*, 22 October 1957, Nr. 197, 'Der Abbruch der deutsch-jugoslawischen Beziehungen', 1807–8.

92 A. Das Gupta, 'The Non-Aligned and the German Question' in N. Mišković, H. Fischer-Tiné and N. Boškovska Leimgruber (eds), *The Non-Aligned Movement and the Cold War* (London: Routledge, 2014), p. 151.

93 Representatives from Ghana, Ceylon, Cuba and Iraq agreed. See *Conference of Heads of State or Government of Non-Aligned Countries* (Belgrade: Yugoslavia, 1961), pp. 36, 101, 112, 126, 149. The representatives of Afghanistan, Ethiopia, Nepal and Burma more generically called for the need to 'safeguard world peace' by guaranteeing 'free access to West Berlin' or starting 'peaceful negotiations'.

94 *Ibid.*, p. 157.

95 JFKPOF-104-004 Papers of John F. Kennedy. Presidential Papers. President's Office Files. Subjects. Non-Aligned Nations summit meeting, Belgrade, 1 September 1961. Central Intelligence Bulletin, 5 September 1961.

96 'Aus dem Kommuniqué der 12. Sitzung des Staatsrates der Deutschen Demokratischen Republik am 7. September 1961: Bericht der Sonderbotschafter und Einschätzung der Belgrader-Konferenz der nichtpaktgebundenen Länder' (1.-5. 9. 1961), DADDR 1961, p. 261.

97 *Ibid.*, p. 81.

98 On Nasser's tepid reaction to the news of the Berlin Wall see BAL-SAPMO, ZP SED 2/20/373: *Bericht über des Besuch des Sonderbotschafters des Vorsitzenden der Deutschen Demokratischen Republik, Minister Ernst Scholz, beim Präsidenten der vereinigten Arabischen Republik, Gamal Abdel Nasser*, 15 December 1961.

99 On the political uses of anti-Zionism, and their overlap with anti-Semitism see Jeffrey Herf (ed.), *Anti-Semitism and Anti-Zionism in Historical Perspective: Convergence and Divergence.* (London, New York: Routledge, 2007), and on the East German case in particular see Angelika Timm's contribution, pp. 186–205.

100 PA AA: MfAA A 13355: Office of the GDR Representative in the UAR, Schüßler, 31 March 1964.

101 StBKAH BIII/61: Note, 8 June 1962.

Part III

# Consolidation and cleavages, 1962–69

# 7

# New leaders, old questions

On 4 March 1962, Israeli Finance Minister Levi Eshkol arrived in Brussels to push forward a key point of his government's agenda – fostering closer economic ties between Israel and the European Economic Community. The Israeli Ambassador to Belgium, Emile Najar, accompanied him, as did Felix Shinnar from the Israeli Mission in Cologne. Their agenda was packed with meetings – including with the Foreign Ministers of Belgium, France and Luxembourg, and with the Federal Republic's Economic Minister, Ludwig Erhard. Yet the content of the meeting with Erhard was rather different from the others, as it also touched upon a topic that was particularly dear to the Israeli delegation and had to do specifically with the future of the West German–Israeli relationship. One of the main questions that the Israelis intended to ask Erhard was a clarification about the flow of payments that Bonn would direct towards the Jewish state in the years to come to support the country's development, as Adenauer and Ben-Gurion had briefly discussed during their meeting in New York and as the Chancellor had seemed to endorse in the previous months. From an Israeli perspective, these payments were crucial. Defence- and security-related expenses had increased substantially at the turn of the decade as the country expanded its armaments arsenal just as reparations from Germany and other foreign investments and capital transfers were declining.[1] But strengthening economic ties was not just important for the Israelis. In fact, such economic cooperation also acted as a multiplier of commercial opportunities to promote both West German and Israeli goods in third countries. Each side could, thanks to the other, access markets and partners that would have otherwise remained much harder to get to. The FRG could play a crucial role in promoting Israel as a key partner of the European market area, while the Israelis provided Bonn with key contacts and opportunities building upon their partnership with Third World countries, ranging from Bolivia to Togo.[2]

Just like ten years earlier, when Adenauer had announced the West German readiness to pay reparations to Israel without even consulting the Economics Minister on the subject, in the early 1960s Erhard again had been left out of the Chancellor's decision to transfer funds to Israel. This became painfully clear during the Brussels meeting, when Erhard learned from the Israelis themselves of the West German intention to transfer funds to Israel.[3] And while he was then let into the secret arrangements and made an important contribution to carry them out successfully, Erhard's initial unawareness about them was indicative of the kind of relationship that Adenauer had crafted both with his Israeli counterparts and with his Economics Minister. By the end of 1963, Eshkol and Erhard would become the respective heads of government in Israel and the FRG. They inherited a complex situation from their predecessors, who had advanced the bilateral relationship to a level that would have been unthinkable just a decade earlier, but who at the same time had left out or alienated many of their closest advisers in the process, thus making it possible for the East German and Arab representatives to attempt to strain the bilateral relationship at such a delicate moment of leadership transition.

## Operation Business Friend

The first tranche of the West German financial transfers arrived in Israel in December 1961.[4] The funds came from a state-owned development bank created in 1948 as part of the Marshall Plan, the Credit Institute for Reconstruction (Kreditanstalt für Wiederaufbau).[5] This new and substantial form of cooperation stemmed from a decision of the Chancellor himself – implemented only after Ben-Gurion, Peres and Shinnar had insisted over months, with polite reminders, in order to get the Chancellor to commit, in practice, to such payments. 'Operation Business Friend', as the series of transactions was codenamed, was kept highly secret among West German circles. Official records marked the transfers as disburses arising from bilateral agreements with unspecified developing countries, and although such secrecy would later be declared unconstitutional, at that time it was deemed crucial to limit the circle of people who would be aware of them in order to ensure the smooth carrying out of such exchanges.[6] The total sum of the funds transferred under the umbrella of 'Operation Business Friend' would amount to over DM629 million in four years.[7] Following up the informal agreement reached in Bavaria in the winter of 1957, substantial exchanges between the West German and Israeli Ministries of Defence evolved in parallel to Operation Business Friend. Codenamed Operation 'Frank.[reich]./Kol.[onien]' (for France/Colonies), the cooperation between the two countries' defence establishments increased substantially in the early 1960s. And from Washington there would be no objection 'should Embassy Bonn feel it could inquire … re rumors that Israel and GFR [West Germany] have concluded secret pact for mutual cooperation with respect to nuclear weapons development', noted Dean Rusk from the US State Department in the summer of 1961.[8] While never confirmed, such rumours had gained traction 'in Mideast grapevines' just as the secret donations from the West German credit institute to Israel were increasing.[9]

    Just three months after the meeting between the West German and Israeli Economics and Finance Ministers in Brussels, Peres and Strauss met in Germany in order to discuss the transfer from the Federal Republic to Israel of a wide series of armaments – including French planes, German tanks, American helicopters and possibly also submarines. The cooperation would also entail military personnel training – the Germans were to instruct Israeli 'artillerymen with good German language skills' about how to operate many of these devices, and upon their return to Israel they would act as instructors themselves.[10] While earlier in the day Strauss had been fiercely opposed to the prospect of the Federal Republic's transfer of reparation payments to Israel, by the early 1960s the Defence Minister had become one of the most pivotal figures in the development of West German–Israeli cooperation in the realm of security. He greatly valued Peres as a strategic interlocutor – it was thanks to him that the West German Defence Minister had managed to expand his network to, and even close important deals with, the defence establishment of key countries such as Kenya and Portugal.[11] Furthermore, given that many of the West German weapons manufacturers' industries were based in his own Bavaria, by promoting the sale of German-made weapons to third countries in Africa, the Middle East and beyond, Strauss was also promoting the interests of his constituents.[12] But the summer of 1962 would not just bring more business to the West German security industry or increase the flow of West German funds streaming into Israel. A new headache was just coming Bonn's way, passing from Cairo, and further ensnaring the German–German Cold War into the rivalry between Israel and its Arab neighbours.

## Nasser's missiles

The summer of 1962 was to be a celebratory season in Egypt. At the parade organised for the tenth anniversary of the Free Officers revolution, on 23 July 1962, Nasser wooed his Egyptian and international audience by revealing new types of missiles, made in Egypt. The two models – *Al Qahir* (the Conqueror) and *Al Zafir* (the Victor) – had been successfully tested two days prior to the parade.[13] They were able, as Nasser put it, to strike 'south of Beirut'.[14] In other words, for the first time in the history of the Arab–Israeli conflict, all of Israel's territory was within the range of Egyptian firepower. Nasser's announcement followed less than one year after Ben-Gurion had announced the successful launch of an Israeli rocket built allegedly for 'meteorological purposes', the *Shavit II* (the Comet II – although a Comet I had never been launched and the addition of the Roman number two to the name served more decorative, rather than informative, purposes).[15] The missile race in the Middle East was already well underway by the time Nasser displayed the missiles to the crowd. From 1962 onwards, however, the arms race would take a much more sinister turn.

The potency of the new Egyptian missiles had taken the Israeli intelligence by surprise, causing deep shock especially to Mossad director Isser Harel, whose attention focused on a group of German scientists stationed in Egypt who seemed to have played a crucial role in the development of the new rockets. In particular, *The Conqueror* 'appeared generally similar to the improved World War II German V-2' missile, as the US Defense Intelligence Agency also noted.[16] As the then head of Shin Bet, Amos

Manor, put it, this was the beginning, for Harel, of something 'much more profound than an obsession' – the fear that German scientists were working in Egypt arming Israel's archenemy to complete the extermination of the Jews that Hitler's Germany had begun and only partially accomplished.[17] As Harel himself later recalled, for him 'the scientists' crisis was not only a matter of politics and security but it also embodied and exposed Israel's extreme sensitivity to any activity which could risk its security and existence in the generation after the Holocaust', and 'the fact that the Nasser regime used especially Germans, many of whom active Nazis in the past, sharpened the security anxiety and gave it also a heavy emotional dimension'.[18]

Israeli Prime Minister Ben-Gurion had long been aware of the presence of the German scientists in Egypt. Indeed, German scientists had been at work in Egyptian weapons manufacturing laboratories since the days of King Farouk, and most of them remained in place after the 1952 revolution.[19] Furthermore, following the coup the newly instated Egyptian officers had turned to German experts in order to strengthen the country's military, navy and secret services engaging with direct discussions with the top echelons of the then budding West German security services.[20] Head of West German intelligence Reinhard Gehlen put forth for this crucial task Otto Skorzeny – a former SS-Standartenführer who remained in Egypt for about one year heading a staff that included several former Wehrmacht and SS officers. By the early 1960s, a relatively consistent group of German expats was active in Cairo working in various functions for the Egyptian government.[21] The lack of job prospects for missile experts in postwar West Germany rendered the work offers that the scientists received from Cairo in the late 1940s and early 1950s particularly appealing. But the fact that most of these scientists had acquired their know-how in Hitler's Germany and that the German community in Cairo largely revolved around former Nazi officials, did them no favours in Israeli eyes.

The Israeli secret service had been successfully infiltrating the group of German expats in Cairo since the early 1950s and at an increasing pace over the course of the 1960s. A crucial asset in this endeavour was the arrival of Wolfgang Lotz in Cairo. Originally from Germany, Lotz had arrived as a teenager in mandate Palestine in 1933, changing his name to Ze'ev Gur-Arie. Once in Palestine, he gathered military experience that would prove crucial to his later espionage activities. Gur-Arie served in Egypt both during the Second World War, when he was stationed there by the British, and during the Suez War of 1956 as an IDF soldier. By then, he had already joined Aman, Israel's military intelligence directorate headed by Meir Amit, where he worked as a member of Unit 188, which was in charge of human intelligence (HUMINT) collection in the Arab world.[22] His superiors approached him with a new mission in 1959 – given his German origins, his task would be infiltrating the consistent group of former Nazi officials living, working and thriving in Egypt, in the attempt to extract as much information as possible about the extent of the scientists' contributions to the Egyptian armament process and, more broadly, about Cairo's military plans and capabilities. This was something that Gur-Arie – now back to his surname of Lotz – very easily managed to do, arriving in Egypt and posing as an ex-Wehrmacht officer and Nazi official with a passion for horse breeding. Hosting lavish parties in his villa in the Heliopolis suburb near Cairo, where he impressed his guests with invented stories about his service in Rommel's Afrika Korps during the Second World War, he quickly began forming precious contacts among even the highest echelons of the Egyptian security and defence establishments, dutifully reporting all of the intelligence he collected back to Jerusalem.[23]

Lotz's mission in Egypt exemplified exactly the kind of approach that Ben-Gurion deemed best to solve the nuisance of the German scientists working for the Egyptian authorities – investing in covert operations and gathering information about the Egyptian armament goals and know-how without giving too much prominence to the issue at high level bilateral meetings with the West German counterparts. But on this – as well as on many other aspects of his German-policy – Ben-Gurion faced severe and mounting criticism even from his closest advisers. This would sharply intensify after Nasser's 1962 display of the newly crafted missiles. Ben-Gurion and Defence Minister Peres, on the one hand, and Foreign Minister Golda Meir and Mossad director Isser Harel, on the other, heavily disagreed on the type of visibility that should be given to the presence and role of the German scientists in Egypt, and on the type of pressure that should be put on the Federal Republic to deal with the matter.[24] The tension was further heightened by the intense rivalry between two main Israeli intelligence agencies – the Mossad, which Harel headed, and the intelligence branch of the Israeli military, Aman, which was under the control of Meir Amit.[25] Defence Minister Peres contacted the head of the Israel Mission in Cologne, Shinnar, shortly after the Egyptian missiles' parade, with the request to pass on his concerns about the scientists' presence and activities to the German Defence Minister. In the coming months, Shinnar discussed the matter with a wide number of West German politicians and commentators, in an attempt to influence public opinion and persuade Bonn's political elite to take action against the scientists, albeit with limited results.[26]

Meanwhile, other Israeli politicians tried to reach out to the American superpower for support. In her conversation with President Kennedy at Palm Beach in December 1962, Golda Meir stressed that Israel had been aware of the Egyptian progress on the missile programme 'with German help' since 1960, but that the situation was all the more worrying in the wake of the beginning of the Egyptian involvement in the Yemen civil war. Betraying much of his narrative about Arab unity and pan-Arab sentiments, from 1962 onwards Nasser began sending troops and weapons from Egypt to Yemen, engaging in a disastrous and protracted proxy war with Saudi Arabia.[27] 'Israel has seen that Soviet supplied TU 16s have been able to fly from Egypt to Yemen, drop bombs and fly back to Egypt. If they can do that', Meir asked, 'what can they do to Israel?'[28] Just a few weeks before Meir's visit to President Kennedy in Florida, when the former head of the German delegation that had finalised the reparations agreement, Franz Böhm, visited Israel, Meir had seized the opportunity to drum in to him that it was unacceptable that 'so soon after the catastrophe of the Nazi persecution of the Jews again Germans [are] taking part in planning the death of Jews, the destruction of Jewish cities and of Jewish land'.[29] Through him, Meir requested that the German government issue a declaration condemning the work of the scientists, possibly withdrawing their passports, as well and making sure they would not lift a finger in support of the Egyptian armaments efforts.

But the measures Meir suggested would have violated the German Basic Law, which did not foresee the possibility that the Federal government might constrain freedom of movement of its citizens.[30] The discussion about what the Federal Republic could do to address the question of the German scientists' presence and work in Cairo became the fulcrum of heated debates in Jerusalem, Bonn and the United States.

Despite the remonstrations of those who, like the Director of the Anti-Defamation League (*B'nai B'rith*), deemed a 'merely legalistic approach to this extremely serious problem' to be 'totally insufficient to meet the psychological and political requirements of this situation',[31] an inter-party committee was set up in the Bundestag, and headed by Böhm himself, with the task of exploring legal mechanisms to force the reluctant scientists to leave their Egyptian posts. This, paradoxically, had the potential to serve the East Germans well – they had long been trying to convince the Egyptians of their technical expertise, although East German engineers never really gained the status of their West German colleagues in Egypt. But just as the West Germans were slowly attempting to find a way to remove the scientists from Egypt without breaching their constitutional rights nor playing too much into the hands of the East Germans, the Mossad had sprung into action.

## Targeted killings

Wolfgang Pilz, one of the scientists based in Egypt, began receiving a series of parcel bombs through the post in November 1962. Between 1943 and 1945 Pilz had worked on the Nazi missile programme at the Peenemünde Army Research Centre – the secret lab facility where, at its peak in 1943, about 12,000 people worked, most of them hard labour convicts, captives of the concentration labour camp on site. The lab's main successes had taken place in 1942, when the Germans superseded the American and Soviet missiles by creating the world's first long-range, liquid-fuelled ballistic missile, the A4. After the end of the Second World War, and after a stint at the Stuttgart Research Institute for Jet Propulsion Physics, together with his colleague Eugen Sänger, Pilz had founded INTRA, a company that would provide expertise to Nasser's missiles project.[32] Pilz, Sänger and two other veteran Wehrmacht specialists, Paul Goercke and Hans Krug, began collaborating with the Egyptian authorities in 1959. With the exception of Krug, who remained in the Federal Republic to coordinate the work with the project's various suppliers, Sänger, Pilz and Goercke all relocated to Egypt in 1961, hiring some thirty-five other German scientists to join them in the programme of developing the Egyptian missiles. Their key contact in Egypt was General 'Isam al-Din Mahmoud Khalil, who headed the Egyptian army's research and development unit and who had had no difficulty in attracting them to Egypt given the frustration that reigned among missiles engineers in post-war Germany.[33]

After opening one such parcel sent to her boss, Pilz's secretary remained permanently blinded in one eye, with her hearing impaired.[34] Pilz, however, was unharmed. Between the end of 1962 and the early months of 1963, further explosives sent to Pilz's workplace ended up killing six members of the personnel working at the Egyptian

333 rocket plant and injuring five more, but always missing the intended target. Another scientist, Hans Kleinwachter, was shot at while leaving his German office in Lörrach in February of the same year. He, like Pilz, narrowly survived the assassination attempt. But just a few months before the targeting of Pilz another scientist, Heinz Krug, had mysteriously disappeared. An anonymous phone call to the West German police confirmed that he was dead – his body would never be found. The authorities of the Federal Republic, whose territory had suddenly become the stage of a proxy war between Israel and Egypt over the fate of the German scientists, let the Mossad carry out its work, handling these incidents with 'extreme discretion' despite the fact that BND reports had already concluded that the German scientists were not helping Egypt develop weapons of mass destruction (WMDs).[35]

Building upon Cicero's maxim 'that there can be nothing happy for the person over whom some fear always looms' Mossad's chief Isser Harel codenamed this campaign of targeted killings of the scientists – the first in Israel's history – Operation Damocles, to evoke the mythical looming sword that would now be dangling over the scientists' heads.[36] He had come to the conclusion that physically removing them from the Egyptian missile project was a crucial step to hamper its progress and safeguard Israel's peaceful existence alongside, or rather despite, its neighbour. But the missile programme had been plagued by various technical and financial difficulties since its inception.[37] One of the key issues that transpired from the information collected by the CIA was that, while the missile technology itself had made substantial progress, the technology crucial to the missiles' guidance systems was lagging far behind. Until the guidance systems were fixed – which was the German scientists' key task – there was no way that the missiles could go into mass production. While the CIA highlighted that 'in the unlikely event that the Germans do leave, the Arab engineers and technicians would find it difficult to continue the program alone and probably would seek other outside assistance',[38] the elimination of the German scientists involved in the project, concluded Harel, was essential to preserve Israel's security – at least for the time being.

It was a young German woman who eventually managed to expose the hand of the Mossad behind this string of assassinations attempts. Heidi Goercke, daughter of one of the German scientists, became suspicious after having an awkward conversation with a man who had walked up to her introducing himself as Otto Joklik, an acquaintance of her father from Cairo. He had urged her to meet him and another friend in Switzerland in a few days' time to discuss the matter further and to do all she could to convince her father to quit his Egyptian job. Goercke alerted the Swiss police about the strange conversation and reported to the local authorities the unusual behaviour of the two men, who were later arrested. The attempts of the Mossad's head to have the two men freed met with firm resistance from the Swiss police.[39] While Prime Minister Ben-Gurion was on holiday in Tiberias and Defence Minister Shimon Peres away for work in Paris, Harel strived to find a backchannel deal with the Swiss to avoid the capture of the two Mossad agents from becoming public knowledge. Struggling to do so, he then opted for a very different approach.

On 16 March, Harel organised an impromptu press gathering on the top floor of the Mossad's headquarters in Tel Aviv, where he briefed a group of leading Israeli journalists about the 'chemical, biological and radiological weapons' that German scientists were helping Nasser to build.[40] Harel's involvement of the press in the matter of the German scientists had begun even earlier – for some time he had been leaking news to the press about the German scientists' involvement in the Egyptian missile programme. But on 16 March Harel went further than that and, after the conference in the Mossad headquarters, he went on to make an announcement on the national radio about the activities of the German scientists in Cairo. The reaction of the Israeli public was shock and outrage. The press soon began talking about the scientists' key contribution to Egypt's nuclear weapons programme, too, with which Egypt could hit Israel once the rockets were completed.[41] The news came as a big surprise to Ben-Gurion, who had never approved of the organisation of such a media stunt and reacted furiously to Harel's initiative. Never before had Harel operated outside of the realm of Ben-Gurion's wishes – so much so that, in his earlier days as head of the domestic intelligence services he had often used the agency's power to spy against Ben-Gurion's detractors and worked to reinforce the Old Man's political strength. Now he had dramatically departed from his mentor's instructions because he was sure, he insisted, that 'Adenauer was playing a double game with Israel, and [was] presumably helping Nasser to develop atomic weapons'.[42]

In an address to the Knesset delivered shortly thereafter, with Ben-Gurion still vacationing in Tiberias, Golda Meir denounced what she saw as Bonn's unacceptable stillness on the matter. She, too, had grown increasingly uncomfortable with Ben-Gurion's policy of rapprochement with West Germany and with his insistence on the alleged existence of an 'other Germany' – one very different from that of the past.[43] 'The German Government cannot remain indifferent to the fact that eighteen years after the fall of Hitler's regime, which caused the deaths of millions of Jews, the sons of that nation are working to destroy Israel, where the remnant of the Holocaust has found shelter', argued Meir in front of her fellow Knesset members.[44] And if this was the rhetoric coming from Ben-Gurion's own party ranks, other Knesset members were even more critical concerning the matter. The parliamentary debate on the question of the German scientists in Egypt showcased the deep animosity amongst the various political parties in Israel at the time and it quickly turned into a golden opportunity for Ben-Gurion's opponents to bash his policy of conciliation with the Federal Republic, and his leadership more broadly. Maki representative and prominent Communist leader Shmuel Mikunis condemned the government's 'fatuous cooperation with the neo-Nazi leaders in Bonn'[45] while members of the Haredi-Hassidic party Agudat Yisrael condemned the fact that 'Hitler's pupils ... are prepared to hire themselves and their knowledge out to the Egyptian tyrant'.[46] Consistently with his decade-long fierce speeches against any semblance of rapprochement with Germany, Herut leader Menachem Begin did not miss the occasion to attack the Bonn government, and, indirectly, also Ben-Gurion's:

Only a few years have passed since the smoke ceased to ascend from the German-manufactured furnaces ... The Bonn government claims with despicable hypocrisy that it can do nothing against its citizens, who go to and from

Egypt, bringing our enemies knowhow, equipment and training ... We accuse Germany of playing a double game. It has given the Jewish state a fraction of a percentage, in money, of what it stole from the homes, businesses and bodies of our murdered brethren. In return for that money it has obtained moral rehabilitation [and] because of its own selfish, impure motives, it is playing that game with our enemies, telling them: we gave the Jews money; we will give you other things. And it gives those things that most endanger our security and existence.[47]

Golda Meir hastily rebuked Begin, but she did not counter his arguments. Ben-Gurion's policy of rapprochement with the Federal Republic had been attacked from all sides, and the Foreign Minister had not rebuffed the points made by the Prime Minister's critics – possibly because she agreed with much of the gist of what had been said. The debate ended with the passing of a parliamentary motion that highlighted three main points. First, 'that the involvement of German scientists and experts in Egypt in the production of weapons of destruction ... constitutes a grave threat to the security of Israel and its population'. Second, that 'it is incumbent upon the German Government to stop this dangerous activity by its citizens forthwith, and to take all the necessary steps to prevent this cooperation with the Egyptian government' and, third, to appeal 'to enlightened world opinion to exert its influence to put a stop to this activity by German experts'.[48] Ben-Gurion, indignant about the increasing attacks against his government and policy coming from both within and outside his government after the media stunt, summoned Harel to Tiberias. The two had a very harsh exchange, which ended with Harel's submission of his resignation. Ben-Gurion readily accepted it and charged Amit with heading the Mossad. It was the end of an era in the history of Israeli intelligence. Ben-Gurion's break with Harel, in addition to the increasing distance between the Prime Minister and Foreign Minister Golda Meir, signalled the beginning of the end of the Ben-Gurion era, too.

Despite international pressure mounting against the Federal Republic to ensure that the scientists would move back to Germany, or at least cease being involved in the Middle Eastern arms race, in Bonn's Foreign Ministry the Head of the Countries' Division, Josef Jansen, reiterated that regardless of any urge coming from abroad, it was important to deal with the issue of German scientists in a way that would 'not negatively influence' the stance 'of the Arab states on the German question'.[49] This was especially important as the upcoming non-aligned conference in Cairo, scheduled for September 1964, neared. Mindful of how crucial Egyptian backing within the German–German competition had been in 1961 in Belgrade, it was key not to give in to the Israeli hysteria on the matter.[50] In Bonn, Golda Meir's Knesset speech was cast as 'objectively incorrect' and even 'defamatory'.[51] The US State Department released a communiqué stressing that Washington had 'no evidence that weapons of mass destruction are being produced or that the UAR has a capability to produce them', concluding that 'our evidence supports the German Government'.[52]

The intelligence assessments that President Kennedy had been receiving on the question of the participation of the German scientists in the Egyptian rocket programme hinted that the Israeli 'campaign' on the matter was not related to 'genuine Israeli concern but also that they (1) are trying to justify their agent operations in Europe; and (2) may also be attempting to create justification for going ahead on their own nuclear program.[53] In addition to questioning Israeli motives behind the huge publicity given to the question of the German scientists, head of the NSC Robert Komer also emphasised that after reviewing the Israeli intelligence the conclusion was that 'this effort looks far less menacing than the Israelis suggest' and that it would also be 'beyond UAR capabilities' to arm the rockets with radiological warheads.[54] Hundreds of letters from concerned private citizens began pouring into the Kennedy White House. A group of US Senators started lobbying the President, urging him to discourage the participation of German scientists in the Egyptian programme by applying pressure on the West German government.

But, as both American and West German officials recognised, there could be some value in having West German citizens involved in Egypt's programme. As the Department of State Executive Secretary noted, their participation reduced the Egyptian reliance on the Soviets in this matter and, at least in this way the 'West can control sources of materials and parts if need be'.[55] As the Under Secretary for Political Affairs, Averell Harriman, put it in the reply to one of the many protest letters flocking through Washington, 'German citizens working on the UAR rocket program are few in number' and 'it is by no means certain they would all obey the summons from their Government to return home'.[56] Removing the West German scientists may even backfire, given how crucial a forum for Cold War rivalry the Middle East had become. Aware of the long-standing East German attempts to convince the Egyptians to hire more personnel from the GDR and enhance the East German–Egyptian cooperation on several levels, it could not at all be guaranteed, Harriman stressed, 'that [the scientists] would not be replaced by Soviet bloc personnel equally qualified in such work, again forcing the UAR into greater reliance on the USSR'.[57] As Harriman pointed out, it was a crucially important matter – for the United States as much as for the West Germans – to impede further Soviet bloc advances into the Middle Eastern region and leaving West German scientists in place in Egypt may, after all, aid the West in the Cold War struggle.

## East German stakes

While the Adenauer government planned its next steps vis-à-vis Israel and the West German Foreign Office attempted to push back on the question of the scientists, East German authorities continued to walk the fine line between bashing the Federal Republic in third countries, including Israel, and trying to appeal to the Arab states, and Nasser in primis, to possibly convince some of them to politically recognise the GDR. Events related to the complex non-relations between East Germany and Israel again brushed against Horst Seydewitz's career in February 1962. While working in his new post at the archives of the East German Foreign Ministry, Seydewitz was instructed to avoid any kind of official communication with Israeli officials. This order came in response to a request for historical materials dating back to the seventeenth century that a research institute linked to the Israel Museum in Jerusalem had made to the GDR.[58] 'Given the current stance of the relations between Israel and the GDR', Seydewitz read, 'this type of contact is in general to be prohibited'.[59] This line of conduct was also to be applied in case of possible future requests originating from any other governmental, cultural and scientific institutes. 'Direct correspondence with Israeli offices', the ministerial response concluded, 'is not allowed'.[60] The Foreign Ministry also condemned the contacts between societal organisations and interested Israeli partners. 'Given the current state of East German-Israeli relations', the East German Foreign Ministry stressed, it was advisable to avoid any kind of contact with the Israelis.[61] A ministerial report dated January 1963 dismissed any prospect of relaxation in official East German–Israeli relations. The document pointed out that Israel had, in fact, several reasons to oppose an establishment of relations with the GDR; including, for example, that East Berlin had not agreed to pay reparations to the Jewish state, and Israel's own links to the FRG, which would have blocked any attempt to breach the Hallstein Doctrine by recognising the GDR. It emphasised that not having official relations with Israel was the GDR's most convenient choice. 'The relatively good relations with certain Arab states, at the present stage of the battle for international recognition of the GDR, cannot be complicated or disturbed by establishing relations with Israel.'[62] Furthermore, from the economic perspective, the consequences of a possible retaliatory Arab boycott would simply be devastating for the GDR economy.[63]

The distance that the East German Foreign Ministry intended to keep from Israel, however, was contradicted by two kinds of exchanges. First, and paradoxically, at a moment in time in which the GDR professed its absolute loyalty to the Arab states, the GDR had commercial exchanges with Israel. A special effort was needed to keep these economic ties alive, and covert, and specific, guidelines were issued, by both the East German Foreign Ministry and the Ministry for Foreign and Inter-German Trade, on the matter. Their aim was not to halt them, but merely to ensure that the commercial ties with Israel remained secret, so as to protect the slow but tangible progress that the GDR was making in accessing the Arab markets. In order to ensure that the exchanges remained secret, East German–Israeli trade was to be administered by firms based in third countries, East German Minister for Foreign Trade Julius Balkow stressed.[64] Thus, firms were established and registered in third countries – for example Cistella and Egonia, in Austria – and economic exchanges were carried out. Such secrecy and caution, however, were not always successful. In 1963 and 1964, the Arab and West German press repeatedly denounced the existence of East German–Israeli commercial exchanges,[65] which then led the director of the UAR trade mission in the GDR to confront the GDR Deputy Minister for Foreign Trade, Gerhard Weiss, about the existence of such economic exchanges with Israel. The UAR representative had even brought a basket of oranges to the meeting with Weiss, and as the label clearly showed, these were from Jaffa, in Israel – and he had bought them at the East German food market nearby.[66]

Second, East German propaganda efforts in Israel against Bonn continued, and these were carried out via direct contacts with Israeli organisations. In terms of soft power, the GDR seemed to have made some progress. One of the Israeli participants in the Women's Day events in East Berlin in 1962 had been so impressed with the positive developments she had witnessed in the GDR that on returning to Israel she had given a series of pro-GDR talks in various Israeli cities.[67] In April 1963 the Israeli association of the Anti-Nazi Resistance Fighters organised a commemorative event to mark the twentieth anniversary of the Warsaw Ghetto uprising, and forwarded an invitation to the GDR. Norden welcomed the idea of East German participation in the event.[68] Taking part in the ceremony and the ensuing press conference would ensure that the East German standpoint could be represented, and the 'documentation regarding Globke' could once more be publicised in an international arena, continuing on the path set forth by Kaul at the Eichmann trial.[69] Günter Stillmann, a Communist German Jew who had played a crucial role in the resistance against the Nazis in Berlin, was selected to go and represent the GDR. Stillmann had spent his exile years (1939–48) in mandate Palestine and had decided to move back to his native Berlin to take part in the foundation of a new, democratic, socialist German state.[70] In the GDR he worked as a journalist and eagerly made his way back to the country that had now become Israel to take part in the ceremony, which would be attended by many of the people he had met during his participation in the underground communist activities in mandate Palestine.[71] Against the prediction of the Israeli conference organisers, Stillmann managed to receive his visa without any problems, thanks to the contacts established between East Germans and Israelis in Prague. To welcome him at Lod airport were former Knesset member and head of the Israeli chapter of the International Federation of Resistance Fighters Abraham Berman, who had been a founding member of the 1942 Anti-Fascist Bloc in the Warsaw Ghetto that had led the 1943 anti-Nazi uprising, as well as Maki General Secretary and Knesset member Shmuel Mikunis.

Stillmann had an important role to play at the commemoration – he was to be one of only two international representatives called to speak at the ceremony, attended by some 800 people, with several more waiting outside the Mughrabi Theatre in Tel Aviv. While upon landing in Lod he had spoken with the press in Hebrew, at the conference Stillmann decided to address the audience in German and promote the image of the East German state that he represented. Speaking on behalf of the GDR's National Front (Nationale Front der Deutschen Demokratischen Republik) Stillmann stressed all of the key points of the East German propaganda on questions of *Israelpolitik*.[72] For example, Stillmann answered a question on the lack of East German material compensation to Israel by specifying that the GDR should not be seen as the successor state of Nazi Germany, given that victims of Nazism made up the majority of the East German population. The best way to atone for Nazi crimes, Stillmann explained, was to prevent such atrocities ever being repeated in the future – which was exactly what the Democratic Republic was doing by ensuring that former Nazis would not have any say in politics or state bureaucracy and pursuing the socialist cause at the international level.[73] During the press conference he insisted on what a scandal Globke's presence in Bonn was, especially since he was so high up within the West German government hierarchy, sitting in the Chancellor's very office. His words were reprinted in a dozen Israeli publications, which went on to criticise Globke's presence in the Federal Republic.[74] Stillmann also took advantage of his stay in Israel to reach out to Yad Vashem, distributing further materials about Globke and promising to deliver even

more about other former Nazis now active in the West German bureaucratic apparatus. While Stillmann underlined several times that he was 'not a representative of the
East German government' and had therefore nothing concrete to say about the current or future state of East German–Israeli relations, he stayed very close to the official
line in his answers to the Israeli journalists. As the East German Foreign Ministry had
summarised just a few months earlier: 'With the help of the [reparations] agreement
the West German monopoly succeeded in penetrating the Israeli market and to gain
predominance in strategic domains, earning massive profits. The world public opinion
shall be deceived about the character of the West German state, as the agreement is
viewed as an expression of the West German willingness to repay debt.'[75]

In the report drafted upon his return to East Germany, Stillmann highlighted the
complexity of the Israeli public's perception of West Germany, and how this could play
out in favour of the GDR. On the one hand, he noted, issues such as the reparations
payments had had overall a very positive impact on the Israeli attitude vis-à-vis the
FRG – one that could be tough for East German speakers to undermine given that the
GDR had never even agreed to discuss the question with Israel. On the other hand, he
also emphasised how easily the Israeli public opinion could be turned against Bonn, as
demonstrated during the recent scandal over Nasser's German scientists. He had gone
to study the country's political turmoil in person following Harel's explosive interview
on the national radio. From the benches of the Knesset visitors' gallery in Jerusalem,
Stillmann had taken a close look at the multi-party attacks waged against Ben-Gurion's
policy of reconciliation with the Federal Republic, and at Golda Meir's essential lack
of a rebuttal, and included these observations in the notes he circulated back to Albert
Norden and the East German Politbüro office 'For All-German Affairs'. As he put it,
the climate of widespread anxiety about the activities of the German scientists in Egypt
had very much helped him promote his message about the inherent danger of a revival
of Nazi forces in West Germany and abroad.[76]

## Managing the attacks

The continuous attacks against the Federal Republic, which had increased in conjunction with the crisis of the German scientists in Egypt, and the fact that so much of the
Israeli public had virulent opinions on the matter, did, in fact, bother the West German
Chancellor. Why keep bringing up the question of the Nazi past, after Bonn had spent
so much time and effort in trying to rebuild its image as a responsible and reliable
player in international affairs? During a meeting with the head of the Israel Mission in
Cologne, Shinnar, Adenauer lamented the 'circa 2,000 trials' for Nazi-era crimes that
were 'still' being prepared in Germany as of May 1963.[77] 'This', the Chancellor commented, 'is intolerable'. 'Maybe', he suggested, 'this matter could be terminated in conjunction with the diplomatic recognition of Israel?' Shinnar reassured the Chancellor
and reminded him that during the Eichmann trial in Jerusalem Ben-Gurion had
clearly stressed that 'the most important thing about the trial was that it provided documentation about that time, a sort of demonstration for the youth' and that this was

'now over'. 'Well it should be over', the Chancellor countered, 'because it damages the German image immensely'.[78]

By then, Adenauer had been in power for fourteen years, and his chancellorship was drawing to a close. Aiming to cement a lasting political legacy as a testimony to his efforts for international reconciliation, Adenauer began reconsidering the idea of solving the question of Israel's recognition before the end of his mandate. Why, after all, had ambassadors not yet been exchanged between the two countries? As he put it to Foreign Minister Schröder in 1963, Adenauer now firmly believed that 'the time has arrived to establish diplomatic relations with Israel. I know that many Arab states object that in such case they would immediately recognise the government in the Soviet occupation zone [but] I do not think this will happen. In my opinion, our investments in development aid are a strong enough incentive to withhold the Arab countries from undertaking such a measure'.[79] Among the ranks of the SPD, impatience with the Hallstein Doctrine was on the rise, too. During a Bundestag debate in May 1963, the leader of the SPD, Carlo Schmid, admitted that he did not 'think that it would harm us much if indeed – which I don't even expect – some Arab states were to recognize Pankow [East Germany]',[80] testifying to the increasing willingness of the Bundestag members to discuss and question the assumptions underlying Bonn's *Israelpolitik*.

But the Chancellor's seeming readiness to move on to diplomatic relations with the Jewish state deeply alarmed Foreign Ministry officials. As State Secretary Karl Carstens put it, such a move would be 'fraught with risks'.[81] Foreign Minister Schröder contacted the Chancellor to inform him that he was 'confident in a consistent continuation of our long-standing, fixed policy' on Israel. In any case, he added, the 'Foreign Ministry has reassured the embassies of the Arab states … that regarding its attitude about the problem of the recognition of Israel nothing has changed'.[82] Schröder reminded Adenauer about the uniqueness of the Federal Republic's 'Israel-problem' stressing that Bonn 'must reckon with the high likelihood that the Arab states, which about the question of Israel react predominantly in an emotional manner, would respond to the establishment of diplomatic relations between us and Israel with the establishment of diplomatic relations with the so-called GDR'.[83] When the President of the West German Bundestag, Eugen Gerstenmaier, had visited Israel, in December 1962, he declared that the establishment of diplomatic relations between West Germany and Israel would 'certainly occur' – 'one day'.[84] President Gerstenmaier was the most prominent German politician to have accepted an invitation from the Israeli government until that moment, and his words provoked dismay not only among Arab, but also among West German, representatives. 'Is the formal establishment of German-Israeli relations important enough to Israel to take into consideration that in this way the Federal Republic would quietly let the Soviet occupation zone overtake the West German position, constructed over the years, allowing it to further expand the Eastern sphere of influence in the Arab countries?'[85] wondered Bonn's ambassador to Egypt, Walter Weber. Giving in to the pressures coming from his Foreign Office, Adenauer's final answer would be no.

The establishment of diplomatic relations did not crown the end of Adenauer's chancellorship and of Ben-Gurion's premiership – the situation was simply too tense, overlapping with the questions of the scientists, the global Cold War rivalry, and the overarching fear that the East Germans would benefit from any West German diplomatic misstep.[86] Adenauer and Ben-Gurion retired, one shortly after the other, respectively in June and October 1963. By that point, the question of diplomatic relations remained unsolved, as did the issue of the German scientists involved in the Egyptian rocket programme, as well as the 'political time-bomb'[87] of West German–Israeli covert security cooperation, which threatened to explode at any time. To the delight of the East Germans it did, soon after Adenauer's and Ben-Gurion's retirements, in the hands of their successors: Ludwig Erhard and Levi Eshkol.

## 'That pudgy and popular fellow': Chancellor Erhard

Adenauer left his post as Chancellor under severe pressure coming from the ranks of his own party.[88] And while he never liked his successor, many other people did.[89] Indeed, Erhard had been suggested for the post of Chancellor exactly because of his popularity, largely derived from 'his' *Wirtschaftswunder* – the 'miracle' at the base of the spectacular recovery of the West German economy in the post-war era as Erhard served as Federal Economics Minister.[90] But 'that pudgy and popular fellow', as *Time* magazine described him in 1963,[91] while certainly extremely popular among the West German electorate, did not enjoy the same degree of popularity within the ranks of the CDU. In fact, Erhard had really not been very involved within the life of the Christian Democratic Party at all during his political career.

Despite having served as Adenauer's Minister of Economics for over fourteen years, Erhard joined the CDU only in 1963 – after it became absolutely clear that his name would be put forward as Adenauer's successor. While the records were backdated to indicate that he had been a party member since March 1949,[92] in fact this meant that Erhard became Chancellor without having a real power base he could rely upon within his own party. This was to bear crucial relevance on the course of Erhard's chancellorship, and on his management of complex and delicate political issues such as that of the Federal Republic's relations with Israel. Erhard was an economist, with an academic background consisting of a doctorate and honorary professorship in Munich. The thorough consideration that he had given to the issues at hand during the course of his earlier career characterised his approach to statecraft, too. The new Chancellor developed his overall policy orientation after consulting with his ministers and relying on expert advice – two details which were not to be taken for granted in the Chancellery of the Federal Republic where Adenauer had been in office for so long. In the foreign political domain this difference would have important, tangible effects. As Peres put it, early West German–Israeli relations 'rested to a large extent on the mutual trust and friendship between individuals'.[93] This very feature made them particularly vulnerable to governmental changes. As 'individuals went', Peres considered, 'their policy was likely to go with them'.[94] The new Chancellor was thus in a unique position to shape the future of Bonn's *Israelpolitik*.

With the swearing-in of Chancellor Erhard, the international campaign to isolate East Germany assumed unprecedented political significance.[95] While the superpowers'

Cold War morphed into a phase of détente following the Cuban missile crisis, this coincided with an intensification of the German–German Cold War.[96] Adenauer had been able to adapt the Hallstein Doctrine to the type of relations that he was interested in forging with Israel, and he did so by allowing the West German *Israelpolitik* to bifurcate into two main branches, one overt, one covert. At the beginning of his chancellorship, Erhard seemed inclined to do the opposite: adapting West German–Israeli relations to meet the requirements of Bonn's international isolation campaign against the GDR, which was his most prominent foreign policy goal.

In May 1963, in a statement to the Bundestag, Foreign Minister Schröder emphasised that within Bonn's struggle to be the 'only really legitimate German voice internationally' the West German moves in the Middle East had to be planned and executed with extreme care.[97] Erhard's Foreign Minister was determined to keep working for the isolation of the GDR, and the reasoning behind his thinking on West German–Israeli relations was essentially focused on Germany and its division. As he later put it: 'From a German point of view, special attention had to be given to the fact that the further planning of the relations with Israel could not be developed in isolation from the reality of German division and from the USSR-backed East German strive for international endowment.'[98] His vision aimed to make the most of the overall atmosphere of détente by turning it against East Germany – for example by reaching out to the countries of Eastern Europe, in an attempt to isolate the GDR in its own backyard.[99]

Erhard shared Schröder's foreign political vision. During a press conference in December 1963, the new Chancellor showed his determination regarding the prospect of establishing diplomatic relations with Israel: 'Today we are in a situation in which we do not want to let the question of relations with Israel translate into a resuscitation of the topic of recognition of the GDR, especially in the Arab world ... If you ask me directly whether I have the intention to start this type of procedure in the cabinet then I must tell you: not for the time being.'[100] During the press conference the Chancellor also shelved the question of the German scientists in Egypt, stating that he did not believe that the matter had enough weight to justify taking any 'big political action'.[101] The Chancellor reiterated his take on the matter during a conversation with Felix Shinnar a few days later. The Israeli statements on the issue of the German rocket scientists in Egypt were, according to Erhard, 'evidently excessive'.[102] Shinnar reminded the Chancellor of the 'emotional significance' that the matter had for the Israeli public, but his point did not seem to register, while the parliamentary proceedings to find a legal solution to the matter were also slowly coming to a halt.[103]

However, as the Foreign Office was focusing on the effort to buy the favour of the non-aligned states, and especially the Arab countries, among West German Bundestag members interest in the development of German–Israeli relations was growing. Some of the members of the Bundestag who had been informed about the ongoing West German–Israeli covert security cooperation grew impatient of keeping the matter secret.[104] Hans Merten of the SPD was one of them. During the summer of 1963, his declarations whipped up a storm as he declared that, yes, the Federal Republic was training Israeli soldiers. An inter-party working group to study the issue of relations with Israel was formed in November 1963.[105] The issues of relations with Israel, and of the scientists, were frequently debated within the Bundestag, within its Foreign Affairs Committee, and within the Cabinet. The interest of West German public opinion in the matter also seemed to have increased. This reflected a broader societal concern with what increasingly appeared to be the deficiencies of the confrontation of the recent German past that had taken place in the Federal Republic spurred, partially, by East German propaganda on the failure of West Germany in coming to terms with the past (*Vergangenheitsbewältigung*), but also by other events that were taking place in the Federal Republic itself.[106] Of these, the most important was the onset of the second Auschwitz trials in Frankfurt in 1963, led by Attorney General Fritz Bauer, in order to try former personnel of the Auschwitz-Birkenau concentration camp. The trial contributed to a gradual amplification of the voices of those who, within the West German public, were critical of the lack of confrontation with the Nazi past and, indirectly, also translated into greater popular interest in the question of the relations that should exist between the Federal Republic and the Jewish state.[107]

Meanwhile, in the Bundestag, the initiative to draft a Federal law that would force the scientists to come back to Germany gathered significant consensus. Spearheaded by Böhm after his visit to Israel in October 1962 – and after Gold Meir's insistence with him on the gravity of the situation – in May 1963 the Bundestag interparty committee submitted a bill, with retroactive effect, that would have impeded West German citizens from working on the development of atomic, biological and chemical weapons – anywhere in the world. Those engaged in such activities would be required to seek permission from the West German Foreign Ministry. But the proposal came under heavy criticism – mostly from the ranks of CDU representatives, who lamented that such a measure would anyhow be ineffective, unconstitutional, or both. Instead, the Bundestag discussion only resulted in passing a resolution requiring the government to submit alternative legislation.[108] A later proposal made by an inter-ministerial committee formed by the Foreign, Interior, Economic and Justice Ministers to introduce a law which would have led to the withdrawal of passports from scientists who continued their work without a government permit did not lead anywhere either. While Article 26 of the Federal Basic Law made any contribution to preparations for an aggressive war a punishable offence, various proposed amendments to the constitution in order to allow for the withdrawal of the scientists' passports were brushed aside.[109]

The Bundestag debates about possible measures to take in order to render the work of the scientists illegal took place in the aftermath of a decision that had been very hard for Nasser to accept: the US President's eventual assent to providing Israel with Hawk missiles.[110] Kennedy did so in the hope that increasing the traditional weaponry stocks would deter the Israelis from getting the nuclear bomb. But it was too late for that already – the Israelis had successfully tested their first nuclear warhead in France in 1960 and the first test on Israeli soil would take place shortly thereafter, in 1963, in the Negev region.[111] Nasser viewed the US decision to provide Israel with Hawk missiles, and the West German preparations to remove the scientists from his rocket programme, as yet another sign of the West's siding with Israel and against Egypt. In a conversation with McCloy in Cairo, 'he referred to the announcement … of the conclusion of the US loan to Israel for the Hawks and of the "Action of the Bundestag" in making illegal the assistance of German citizen-scientists to any foreign countries in the manufacture of weapons. Clearly', as Nasser saw it, 'this was aimed directly at Egypt'.[112]

Eventually, in 1964 Chancellor Erhard himself wrote to President Nasser confirming that he would not support the drafting of a law forcing the scientists to leave Egypt, regardless of the debates ongoing in the Bundestag.[113] He had no interest in doing so. In 1964, much of the energies of West German economic diplomacy, which Erhard given his past as Economics Minister believed in the most, were spent in an attempt to ensure that the upcoming conference of the non-aligned countries would not register any strategic improvement in the GDR's quest for international recognition. The trade agreement signed with Yugoslavia in July 1964, the agreement of October 1964 to transfer DM70 million of capital aid to Algeria, in addition to the DM130 million loan agreement signed with Egypt in April 1963, all testified to proactive engagement of the Chancellor and the Foreign Ministry in the global isolation campaign against the GDR.[114]

But Erhard was ready to go even further to please Nasser. In April 1964, the Chancellor communicated to the American Ambassador, George C. McGhee, his intention to invite Egyptian President Nasser to Bonn for an official visit. In contrast, he stressed, alas it would not be possible to accommodate Israeli President Levi Eshkol's request to visit the FRG given that Bonn did not officially recognise the State of Israel.[115] 'Obviously', commented the Ambassador, 'the Chancellor conceives of it [the invitation of Nasser to Bonn while resisting Israeli Prime Minister Eshkol's idea that he might also visit] largely as a continuation of the Hallstein Doctrine'.[116] But if Erhard's public moves seemed to be only aimed at not upsetting – or rather, actively pleasing –the Arab partners, between 1962 and 1964 the Federal Republic's covert commitment to the economic and military security of the Jewish state had broadened significantly, with the new Chancellor's reluctant support.

## Delegating tanks

In the summer of 1963, US military intelligence spotted something unusual in Israel – the IDF seemed to possess US-made helicopter gunships, of a kind that the United States had never supplied Israel with. President Lyndon B. Johnson, upon Kennedy's assassination in November 1963, continued on the track set by his predecessor. He significantly widened the scope and scale of US assistance to Israel, however, aiming to strengthen its role as a bulwark against Soviet inroads in the region, and came to see the West Germans as a useful tool the United States could employ to this end.[117] The helicopter gunships that US military intelligence had located in Israel in 1963 were part of the weapons transferred as part of the Frank./Kol. informal agreement between Peres and Strauss. By the following summer, the West German support of the Israeli weapons procurement effort would broaden to include the covert transfer of 150 US-made tanks to Israel, via Italy.

The idea had taken shape through a series of consultations among US, Israeli and West German representatives and crystallised after Erhard's visit to Washington in

June 1964, which took place less than ten days after Eshkol's. Erhard explained to Johnson that Bonn needed to 'proceed very carefully because of possible adverse Arab reaction'.[118] The Chancellor hinted at the fears that a number of non-aligned countries would push for the recognition of the GDR at the upcoming Cairo conference and that this 'could complicate the prospects for a German solution'.[119] And the German question, the Chancellor had stressed at the very beginning of his talk with the US President, was 'the most important question that lay at the heart of everything'.[120] Erhard was reluctant to send the tanks directly from West German territory to Israel and proposed shipping the tanks to Italy instead, where they would be equipped with weapons and ammunition and then shipped on to Israel.[121] Despite his closest aides' warnings that 'Italian security is *not rpt not* so good as German and risk of leak could be increased',[122] President Johnson welcomed Erhard's suggestion. He thanked the West German Chancellor for Bonn's help and said that he 'felt sure that it would be a long time before the true nature of the deal was recognized'.[123] The President, as it turned out, was sorely mistaken.

News of the arms transfers soon leaked to the press, unleashing, as Abba Eban put it, '[a] volcanic emotion which spread from Cairo across the Arab world' that severely challenged Bonn's credibility within the region.[124] At first, West German representatives attempted to reassure their Arab counterparts with their usual arguments, pointing to the rumours spread by East German propaganda in the attempt to drive a wedge between Bonn and its Arab partners. The 'press campaign' concerning the arms shipments, so went Bonn's explanation, was being orchestrated on the part of 'interested parties' with the purpose of putting further strain on the German–Arab relationship. Especially given that, as they emphasised, this was already damaged after the episode of the German scientists in Egypt and was continuously stressed due to the recurring debate on the establishment of diplomatic relations with Israel.[125] The Lebanese press denounced, 'in particularly aggressive tone', West German–Israeli cooperation in the production of WMDs.[126] From Damascus, Ambassador Hans Joachim Mangold 'urgently' requested clarification as to what the 'official version' of events was, and so did Müller from Cairo.[127] The Egyptian regime's mouthpiece, *Al Gumhuriya*, commented that the Arab countries would now be very carefully in assessing 'who is deserving of their friendship and who of their animosity', hinting at the different behaviour of the two German states vis-à-vis Israel and the Arab world.[128] Indeed, as an East German representative in Cairo had boasted in relation to a West German journalist, the polemic on Bonn's military assistance to Israel in the Arab world was worth 'many millions' for the GDR.[129] The West German denial of the arms shipments was simply no longer tenable.[130] In the West German Bundestag, disillusionment was tangible, as its members were astounded to learn of the government's dealings behind their backs. Even within the Chancellor's party, the CDU/CSU, bitterness soared – its membership stressed that they would oppose any motion regarding establishing diplomatic relations with Israel after all that had happened in relations with that country without them being informed.[131]

News of the arms transfer to Israel that leaked in autumn 1964 was followed, in January 1965, by a renewed series of articles on the topic, which not only exposed many of the details of the latest agreements between Bonn and Washington about the transportation of US tanks to Israel – they also portrayed the deal as having been pushed by the West Germans. Four days after the news leaked, in a spectacular vendetta against the West German establishment, Egyptian President Nasser officially announced that he had personally invited East German leader Walter Ulbricht to visit Egypt. Bonn's long-winded and carefully orchestrated double game to simultaneously strengthen ties to Israel and Egypt while keeping the East Germans in isolation on the global stage seemed to have spectacularly backfired.

## Notes

1  Rivlin, *Israeli Economy*, p. 42.
2  PA AA, B12 1043, La Paz, Telegram, 27 April 1961, Köster; PA AA B36 43, Berlin, Cooperation between the Federal Republic and Israel in Togo, 17 January 1963.
3  G. Heimann, 'The Need to be Part of Europe: Israel's Struggle for an Association Agreement with the EEC, 1957–1961', *Israel Studies* 20:1 (2015), pp. 86–109.
4  AAPD 1965, Doc. 2, Weapons Transfers to Israel, Notes of State Secretary Carstens, 4 January 1965.
5  On the early history of the credit institute see A. Grünbacher, *Reconstruction and Cold War in Germany: Kreditanstalt für Wiederaufbau (1948–1961)* (Aldershot: Ashgate, 2004).
6  Four people in several key offices – besides the Chancellor, Ben Gurion and Shinnar, the only ones to be informed were State Secretary for Foreign Affairs Lahr, the Finance Minister, the Economics Minister and the Minister for Economic Cooperation.
7  Referenced in Jelinek and Blasius, 'Ben Gurion und Adenauer im Waldorf Astoria', p. 314.
8  NARA, RG 59, Central Foreign Policy Files, 1960–1963, Box 1,372, Outgoing Airgram, Dean Rusk (Department of State) to Embassy Bonn, 5 July 1961.
9  *Ibid.* H. Rühle, '"Aktion Geschäftsfreund": Wie Deutschland das israelische Nuklearwaffenprogramm finanzert hat', *Internationale Politik – Die Zeitschrift*, 4 June 2015; on an alleged West German re-export to Israel of unsafeguarded uranium from Argentina, see BNA: PRO FO 371/1745844 R. J. T. McLaren, Eastern Department, Foreign Office, to British Embassy Bonn, 22 June 1964, https://digitalarchive.wilsoncenter.org/document/117193 [Accessed March 2020]; rumours have developed to this day but the evidence of a West German involvement in the Israeli nuclear project is scant.
10 BAF/BW/1/2473 Training of Israeli army officers in the field of conventional air defense, Strümpel, 27 November 1962. In June 1962, acting upon the Chancellor's instructions, two members of each of the main political parties in the Federal Republic were let in on the existence and shape of these covert agreements – the group would be codenamed in the Defence Ministry paperwork as the 'Subgroup Technical Assistance' and it comprised Wehler and Ender of the FDP, Mommer and Schäfer of the SPD, and Kierling and Leicht of the CDU. BAF/BW/1/2473, Note: Israel, creation of the 'Untergruppe Ausrüstungshilfe' Acker, 3 November 1964.
11 On Peres' role in the making of West German–Kenyan ties see, for example, Archiv für Christlich-Soziale Politik (ACSP), Hanns-Seidel-Stiftung (HSS), NL Strauss, BMVg 725, Strauss personal note, 30 January 1962.

12 BAF/BW/1/185994, Economic defence relations with Israel, Herzog, 1 August 1967. The matter was also discussed in the Israeli Parliament on 8 June 1961. Czech representatives asked clarifications on the matter shortly thereafter: National Archive of the Czech Republic [NACR] Box 109/23, Record of Conversation Kozusnik-Livneh, 10 January 1962, obtained and translated by Mikuláš Pešta for CWIHP. W. G. Gray, 'Waffen aus Deutschland? Bundestag, Rüstungshilfe und Waffenexport 1961 bis 1975', *Vierteljahreshefte für Zeitgeschichte* 64 (2016), pp. 327–64. See also M. Milosch, *Modernizing Bavaria: The Politics of Franz Josef Strauss and the CSU, 1949–1969* (New York: Berghahn, 2006).

13 Directorate of Science and Technology, Office of Scientific Intelligence, 'The United Arab Republic Ballistic Missile and Space Programs', OSI-SR/65–29, 2 August 1965. CIA (CREST/FOIA), www.cia.gov/library/readingroom/docs/CIA-RDP78T05439A000500320027–6.pdf [Accessed November 2019].

14 R. Howard, *Operation Damocles: Israel's Secret War against Hitler's Scientists, 1951–1967* (New York: Pegasus Books, 2013), p. 148.

15 S. Aronson, *David Ben Gurion and the Jewish Renaissance* (Cambridge: Cambridge University Press, 2011), p. 295.

16 FRUS, 1961–1963/XVIII, Doc. 140, Assessment prepared by the Defense Intelligence Agency: Missile Potential of the United Arab Republic, 24 January 1963.

17 Quoted in R. Bergman, *Rise and Kill First: The Secret History of Israel's Targeted Killings* (New York: Random House, 2018), p. 73.

18 I. Harel, *Mashber ha-madaanim ha-Germanim, 1962–1963* (Tel Aviv: Maariv Library, 1982), p. 12.

19 O. L. Sirrs, *Nasser and the Missile Age in the Middle East* (London: Routledge, 2006).

20 O. L. Sirrs, *A History of the Egyptian Intelligence Service: A History of the Mukhabarat, 1910–2009* (Abingdon: Routledge, 2010), p. 33.

21 M. Abediseid, *Die deutsch-arabischen Beziehungen – Problemen und Krisen* (Stuttgart: Seewald, 1976); T. W. Kramer, *Deutsch-ägyptische Beziehungen in Vergangenheit und Gegenwart* (Tübingen: Erdmann, 1974).

22 U. Bar-Joseph, 'Israel' in D. Robert, M. S. Goodman and C. Hillebrand (eds), *Routledge Companion to Intelligence Studies* (London: Routledge, 2015).

23 W. Lotz, *The Champagne Spy: Israel's Master Spy Tells His Story* (New York: Manor Books, 1973).

24 Several members of the Israeli intelligence community, however, disagreed with Harel. See, for example: P. Z. Malkin and H. Stein, *Eichmann in My Hands* (London: Muller, 1990), p. 80.

25 Bergman, *Rise and Kill First*, p. 67.

26 Shinnar, *Bericht eines Beauftragten*, p. 134. AAPD, 1963, Vol.1, Doc. 142, Memorandum of Conversation Schröder-Shinnar, 5 April 1963.

27 J. Ferris, *Nasser's Gamble: How Intervention in Yemen caused the Six-Day War and the Decline of Egyptian Power* (Princeton: Princeton University Press, 2013). A. Orkaby, *Beyond the Arab Cold War: The International History of the Yemen Civil War, 1962–68* (New York: Oxford University Press, 2017).

28 FRUS, 1961–1963/XVIII, Doc. 121, Memorandum of Conversation with Israel Foreign Minister Meir, Palm Beach, 27 December 1962.

29 Böhm passed on the message to Adenauer. ACPD I-200 006/5, NL Böhm. Adenauer to Böhm, 16 October 1962.

30 ACPD I-200 006/5, NL Böhm. Adenauer to Böhm, 16 October 1962.

31 BAK/N1239/60, NL von Brentano, Epstein to Brentano, 27 March 1963. As Lotz writes in his memoirs, 'in 1964 the exodus of the German experts had already begun in earnest', *Champagne Spy*, p. 239.

32 M. J. Neufeld, *The Rocket and the Reich: Peenemünde and the Coming of the Ballistic Missile Era* (New York: The Free Press, 1994); J. Erichsen and B. M. Hoppe (eds), *Peenemünde: Mythos und Geschichte der Rakete 1923–1989* (Berlin: Nicolai, 2004).

33 Bergman, *Rise and Kill First*, pp. 61ff.

34 As to why the secretary was in a hurry to open this particular envelope see Bergman, *Rise and Kill First*, p. 69.

35 AAPD 1963, Vol. II, Doc. 133, Departmental Reunion in the Federal Chancellery, 26 March 1963.

36 'Nihil esse ei beatum, cui semper aliqui terror impendeat', Cicero 5.62. Cicero, *Tusculan Disputations*, translated by J. E. King. Loeb Classical Library (Cambridge, MA: Harvard University Press, 1927).

37 CIA Directorate of Science and Technology, Office of Scientific Intelligence, 'The United Arab Republic Ballistic Missile and Space Programs', OSI-SR/65–29, 2 August 1965. CIA (CREST/FOIA), www.cia.gov/library/readingroom/docs/CIA-RDP78T05439A000500320027–6.pdf [Accessed November 2019].

38 *Ibid.*; Bergman, *Rise and Kill First*, pp. 61ff.

39 For a detailed overview on the issue of the German scientists in Egypt, including an account of their past activities in Nazi Germany see '36, 135 und 333', *Der Spiegel*, 8 May 1963, pp. 56–71. For an example of West German frustration at being accused of the deeds of the scientists see, for example, 'Die Deutschen sind an an allen Schuld', *Der Stern*, 23 April 1963.

40 Sirrs, *Nasser and the Missile Age*, p. 66; Howard, *Operation Damocles*, p. 190.

41 M. Bar Zohar, *Spies in the Promised Land* (London: Davis Poynter, 1972), p. 258.

42 Recollection of Amos Manor, Harel's successor as Shin Bet director between 1952 and 1963, quoted in D. Raviv and Y. Melman, *Spies Against Armageddon: Inside Israel's Secret Wars* (Sea Cliff, NY: Levant Books, 2012), p. 76.

43 F. Klagsbrun, *Lioness: Golda Meir and the Nation of Israel* (New York: Schocken Books, 2019), p. 468.

44 *Knesset Debates*, Vol. 4, Sitting 234 of the Fifth Knesset, 20 March 1963, p. 1347.

45 *Ibid.*, p. 1354.

46 *Ibid.*, p. 1355.

47 *Ibid.*, pp. 1347–8.

48 *Ibid.*, p. 1358.

49 AAPD, 1963, Vol. II, Doc. 133, Departmental Meeting in the Federal Chancellery, 26 March 1963.

50 AAPD, 1963/I, Doc. 146, Memorandum of Conversation between Schirmer and Nasser, Cairo, 16 April 1963.

51 AAPD, 1963/II, Doc. 133, Departmental Meeting in the Federal Chancellery, 26 March 1963.

52 ISA/RG 130.23/MFA/3399/9 Israel Embassy in Washington, DC to the United States Department Jerusalem: 'Statement by the US State Department on the work of German scientists in Egypt', 26 March 1963. www.archives.gov.il/archives/#/Archive/0b0717068001c167/File/0b07170684e04e87/Item/0907170684fd3e1f [Accessed March 2020].

53 FRUS, 1961–1963/ XVIII, Doc. 197, Memorandum from Robert W. Komer of the National Security Council Staff to President Kennedy, 22 March 1963.

54 *Ibid.*
55 FRUS, 1961–1963/XVIII, Doc. 240, Memorandum from the Department of State Executive Secretary (Brubeck) to the President's Special Assistant for National Security Affairs (Bundy), 8 May 1963.
56 Library of Congress (LOC), W. Averell Harriman Papers 474/1, Letter to Senator Thomas J. Dodd, Harriman, 12 April 1963.
57 *Ibid.*
58 PA AA, MfAA A13357/1, Schwab to Simons, 2 February 1962.
59 PA AA, MfAA A13357/2, Weitz an Seydewitz, 6 February 1962.
60 *Ibid.*
61 PA AA, MfAA 13341/6, Meske to Rothe, 8 November 1963.
62 PA AA, MfAA A12608/1, Assessment of relations between the GDR and Israel, 22 January 1963.
63 *Ibid.*
64 BA-SAPMO, DY 30/IV A 2/20/826, Background talks with former employees of Israeli companies.
65 Timm, *Hammer, Zirkel, Davidstern*, pp. 373ff.
66 *Ibid.*, p. 363.
67 PA AA, MfAA 13341/16, Transcript of a letter from Mrs. Zilly Iram, Haifa, Israel, who was in Berlin during the convention in December 1962.
68 PA AA, MfAA A 13358/1, Office of the Presidium, National Council of the National Front of Democratic Germany, Dengler to Bierbach, 3.AEA, 1 April 1963.
69 *Ibid.*
70 G. Stillmann, *Berlin-Palästina und Zurück: Erinnerungen* (Berlin: Dietz, 1989).
71 Hartewig, 'Die Loyalitätsfälle', pp. 48–62.
72 The NF was an East German political party, represented in the *Volkskammer* but controlled by the SED. See K. Schneider and D. Nakath, 'Demokratischer Block, Nationale Front und die Rolle und Funktion der Blockparteien' in G. D. Stephan, A. Herbst, C. Krauss, D. Küchenmeister and D. Nakath, *Die Parteien und Organisationen der DDR: Ein Handbuch* (Berlin: Dietz, 2002), pp. 78–102.
73 PA AA, MfAA A13358/7, Report on the visit to Israel, Stillmann, 22 April 1963. Although, as put by a 1955 Israeli note, these measures could 'hardly be said to touch the core of the problem, seeing that the bulk of these victims have long ago left Germany', PA AA, MfAA A 682/29 Embassy of Moscow, file note on the meeting of Israeli Ambassador Joseph Awida with Ambassador König, 20 April 1956.
74 PA AA, MfAA A13358/7, Report on the visit to Israel, Stillmann, 22 April 1963.
75 PA AA, MfAA A12608/25 3. AEA, The attitude of West Germany towards Israel, 25 January 1962.
76 PA AA, MfAA A13358/4, Report on the visit to Israel, Stillmann, 22 April 1963.
77 AAPD, 1963, Vol. II, Doc.182, Memorandum of Conversation Adenauer-Shinnar, 28 May 1963.
78 *Ibid.*
79 Quoted in: AAPD, 1963, Vol. I, Doc. 121, Schröder to Adenauer, fn. 2.
80 74. Sitzung, Deutscher Bundestag, 8 May 1963.
81 AAPD, 1963, Vol. II, Doc. 310, Annotation of State Secretary Carstens, 17 August 1963.
82 AAPD, 1963, Vol. II, Doc. 318, Schröder to Adenauer, 27 August 1963.
83 Emphasis added. *Ibid.*
84 'Geheimaktion Gerstenmaier', *Der Spiegel*, 12 December 1962, pp. 74–5.

85  AAPD, 1962, Vol. III, Doc. 479, Weber (Cairo) to the Foreign Office, 11 December 1962.

86  AAPD, 1963, Vol. II, Doc. 341, Adenauer to the Foreign Office, 16 September 1963. On the topic see also H. J. Küsters (ed.), *Adenauer, Israel und das Judentum* (Bonn: Bouvier, 2004).

87  Schwarz, *Konrad Adenauer*, p. 443.

88  See, e.g., B. Ruhm von Oppen, 'The End of the Adenauer Era', *The World Today* 19:8 (1963), p. 350.

89  G. Schröder, 'Außenpolitik im Übergang Adenauer-Erhard' in D. Blumenwitz (ed.), *Konrad Adenauer und seine Zeit. Beiträge von Weg- und Zeitgenossen* (Stuttgart: Deutsche Verlangs-Anstalt, 1976), Vol. I, p. 720; L. Erhard, 'Was uns trennte, was uns einte. Zu Konrad Adenauers 100. Geburtstag' in K. Hohmann (ed.), *Ludwig Erhard: Gedanken aus fünf Jahrzehnte. Reden und Schriften* (Düsseldorf: Econ, 1988), p. 1053.

90  A. J. Nicholls, *Freedom with Responsibility: The Social Market Economy in Germany 1918–1963* (Oxford: Clarendon Press, 2004), pp. 151ff.

91  'West Germany: Waiting for the Call', *Time*, 15 February 1963.

92  A. C. Mierzejewski, *Ludwig Erhard: A Biography* (Chapel Hill: The University of North Carolina Press, 2004), p. 184.

93  Peres, *David's Sling*, p. 78.

94  *Ibid.*

95  See F. Eibl, *Politik der Bewegung: Gerhard Schröder als Außenminister, 1961–1966* (Munich: Oldenbourg, 2009).

96  J. L. Gaddis, *We Now Know: Rethinking Cold War History* (Oxford: Clarendon Press, 1997); A. Stephanson, 'Rethinking Cold War History', *Review of International Studies* 24:1 (1998), pp. 119–24.

97  PA AA, B36/110 Schirmer, 5 June 1964.

98  Schröder, 'Außenpolitik im Übergang Adenauer-Erhard', p. 741.

99  F. Eibl, *Politik der Bewegung: Gerhard Schröder als Außenminister 1961–1966* (Berlin/ Boston: Oldenbourg Wissenschaftsverlag, 2001), p. 258; Kilian, *Die Hallstein-Doktrin*, pp. 163–86.

100  PA AA, B36/42: Diplogerma Cairo. Following wording of the statement by Federal Chancellor Prof. Erhards in front of the press on 3.12. Böker, 4 December 1963; R. Blasius, 'Geschäftsfreundschaft statt diplomatischer Beziehungen. Zur Israel-Politik 1962/63' in R. A. Blasius (ed.), *Von Adenauer zu Erhard: Studien zur auswärtigen Politik der Bundesrepublik Deutschland 1963* (Munich: Oldenbourg, 1994), p. 205.

101  *Ibid.*

102  *Ibid.*

103  Shinnar, *Bericht eines Beauftragten*, p. 134.

104  Merten had only partially said the truth, however, stressing that there was no weapons transfer taking place between the two countries. Files on Merten's declarations and subsequent reactions can be found in: PA AA, B36/44.

105  PA AA, B36/42: Notation. Relations to Israel. Balken, 11 November 1963.

106  E. Gassert and A. E. Steinweis (eds), *Coping with the Nazi Past: West German Debates on Nazism and Generational Conflict, 1955–1975* (New York: Berghahn Books, 2006).

107  See R. Gross and W. Renz (eds), *Der Frankfurter Auschwitz-Prozess: 1963–1965, kommentierte Quellenedition* (Frankfurt am Main: Campus, 2013); H. von Hindenburg, *Demonstrating Reconciliation: State and Society in West German Foreign Policy toward Israel, 1952–1965* (New York: Berghahn Books, 2007).

108  AAPD, 1963, Vol. I, Doc. 133, Departmental Reunion in the Federal Chancellery, 26 March 1963.

109  Gray, *Germany's Cold War*, p. 301, fn. 151.

110  W. Bass, *Support Any Friend: Kennedy's Middle East and the Making of the US-Israeli Alliance* (Oxford: Oxford University Press, 2003), A. Ben-Zvi, *John F. Kennedy and the Politics of Arms Sales to Israel* (London: Frank Cass, 2003).

111  Hersh, *The Samson Option*; S. Aronson, *The Politics and Strategy of Nuclear Weapons in the Middle East: Opacity, Theory, and Reality, 1960–1991* (Albany: State University of New York Press, 1992); Cohen, *The Worst-Kept Secret*.

112  FRUS, 1961–1963/XVIII, Doc. 285, Telegram from the Embassy in the United Arab Republic to the Department of State, 30 June 1963 (McCloy).

113  AAPD, 1964/II, Doc. 340, Erhard to Gerstenmeier, 16 November 1964.

114  Gray, *Germany's Cold War*.

115  FRUS, 1964–1968/XV, Germany and Berlin, Doc. 25: Telegram from the Embassy in Germany to the Department of State (McGhee), 11 April 1965.

116  *Ibid.*

117  See A. Ben-Zvi, *Lyndon B. Johnson and the Politics of Arms Sales to Israel: In the Shadow of the Hawk* (London: Frank Cass, 2004).

118  FRUS, 1964–1968/XV, Doc. 49: Memorandum of Conversation Between President Johnson and Chancellor Erhard, 12 June 1964.

119  *Ibid.*

120  *Ibid.* On the relationship between Erhard and Johnson see T. A. Schwartz, *Lyndon Johnson and Europe: In the Shadow of Vietnam* (Cambridge, MA: Harvard University Press, 2003), p. 22 and G. McGhee, *At the Creation of a New Germany. From Adenauer to Brandt: An Ambassador's Account* (New Haven: Yale University Press, 1989), pp. 104–40.

121  FRUS, 1964–1968/XV, Doc. 49: Memorandum of Conversation Between President Johnson and Chancellor Erhard, 12 June 1964.

122  Emphasis added. Lyndon Baines Johnson Presidential Library (LBJL), National Security File (NSF) Country File Israel, 145, Harrimann to McGhee, Eyes Only, n.d.

123  FRUS, 1964–1968/XV, Doc. 49: Memorandum of Conversation Between President Johnson and Chancellor Erhard, 12 June 1964.

124  A. Eban, 'Reality and Vision in the Middle East: An Israeli View', *Foreign Affairs* 43:4 (1965), p. 626.

125  PA AA, B36/114, Vermerk, Deutsche Waffenlieferungen an Israel, 29 October 1964.

126  PA AA, B6/78, Telegramm: Munzel an AA, 31 October 1964.

127  PA AA, B6/78, Telegramm: Mangold an AA, 30 October 1964; PA AA, B36/114, Fernschreiben aus Kairo. Mueller, 3 November 1964.

128  PA AA, B36/114, Fernschreiben aus Kairo. Mueller, 3 November 1964.

129  *Ibid.*

130  PA AA, B6/78, Vermerk, Deutsche Israel-Politik und Öffentlichkeitsarbeit in arabischen Staaten. Matz, 13 November 1964.

131  PA AA, B36/114, Vermerk. Sitzung des Außenpolitischen Arbeitskreises der CDU am 5. November 1964–19.00 Uhr, 6 November 1964.

# Wrangling diplomacy

With the exposure of the West German–Israeli arms deal began the 'most critical phase' for Bonn's Middle East policy.[1] Were Ulbricht really to reach Cairo, noted the West German Foreign Office, this would pose the 'most difficult challenge to date' to Bonn's claim of being the sole representative for the whole of Germany – the principle of sole representation (*Alleinvertretungsanspruch*) upon which the West Germans had based a decade of foreign relations with third countries was seriously at risk.[2] For the FRG, it was necessary 'to take a tough line' with Egypt in order to 'frighten other states who were toying with the idea of acting similarly', commented the First Secretary of the British Embassy in Bonn.[3] The problem, however, was understanding which tactics to pursue to achieve this end. The discussion went beyond the question of Bonn's *Israelpolitik* to encompass the core of the West German Cold War dilemma. It addressed a peculiar tension, stemming from two issues: first, the unique obligations to Israel that the FRG had, since 1952, openly and repeatedly stressed derived from Germany's Nazi past; and second, the present circumstances in which the German–German Cold War competition was intersecting with the Arab–Israeli conflict, within the context of a hazardous arms race that had been taking place in the Middle East since the 1950s and which was now gaining momentum. Successive attempts to persuade Nasser to withdraw his invitation to the SED leader failed, and consensus emerged in Bonn about the need to extricate the FRG from the delicate position it currently found itself in.[4] Nobody, however, agreed as to how this should be done.

## Weeks of indecision

Foreign Minister Schröder, as well as the majority of West German diplomats stationed in the region, was appalled at the news of Ulbricht's imminent arrival in the Middle East, and more broadly at the opportunity given to the head of the GDR, for the first time in history, to visit a country outside of the Soviet bloc. The West German Foreign Office, which had been kept largely in the dark concerning the issue of arms transfers to Israel, swiftly began exhorting the Bonn government to immediately stop the weapons delivery. From Cairo, West German ambassador Federer highlighted the importance of halting the 'vicious circle' that the secret arms transfers to Israel had initiated and which in turn fostered, and possibly also justified, Arab mistrust towards Bonn. Foreign Office officials recommended proposing a significant increase in the amount of aid destined for Cairo as a way of protecting the FRG from the prospect of an Arab recognition of the GDR in reaction to the news of Bonn's support of Israel.[5] Given the stakes that West German firms had in the commercial partnership with Egypt and the Arab world, it was now more crucial than ever to outspend the GDR and avoid any financial blackmail by Egypt, claimed Bonn's diplomats.[6] The Foreign Office also recommended extreme care when discussing the option of breaking off diplomatic relations with Egypt. Veteran diplomat Herbert Müller-Roschach, who in 1957 had handled Bonn's break in relations with Yugoslavia,[7] stressed that only in the event that Nasser established diplomatic relations with East Berlin could Bonn claim to have a reason to break off relations with Egypt.[8]

Having been close to recognition on the part of non-aligned countries for a while now, with limited results, with the revelation of the West German–Israeli arms deal the GDR potentially had a lot to gain. The 1964 Non-Aligned Movement conference in Cairo had ended without any tangible gains for the East German regime – only a generic paragraph featured in the final communiqué proclaiming non-aligned support for the reunification of all divided nations. This was mostly thanks to the West German pre-emptive profusion of 'development aid' to the participants, and especially the UAR, in the months running up to the conference.[9] But the scandal involving the Federal Republic towards the end of 1964 also came against the backdrop of a leadership change in the Kremlin that promised to broaden the East German margins for manoeuvre in the international domain. In the wake of Khrushchev's ousting in mid-October 1964, former KGB chief and Soviet deputy premier Alexander Shelepin visited the UAR, offering substantial financial aid to the country, as well as support for Nasser's disastrous military adventure in Yemen. And, crucially from East Berlin's perspective, he had also negotiated a date for an official invitation for Ulbricht to visit the UAR.[10] Things had changed remarkably from just a decade earlier, when the Soviets curbed their East German partners' insistence on the question of recognition from Arab countries. Slowly, the GDR's struggle for international recognition seemed to be bearing fruit. As the East German press vehemently attacked Bonn's dealings with Israel, on 5 February 1965 East German Foreign Minister Lothar Bolz wrote an open letter to West German Foreign Minister Schröder urging his counterpart to terminate the transfer of any arms and military equipment to Israel. To refuse, Bolz stressed, meant automatically involving the West German people in 'military aggressions against the freedom and independence of the Arab peoples'.[11]

Ideally, Chancellor Erhard explained to the CDU's executive committee, Bonn should aim for a solution that would not unleash 'a chain of recognition of the GDR', but without giving the impression that Bonn had ceded to Nasser's blackmail either.[12] The closer Erhard came to making a decision on the issue of Ulbricht's invitation, however, the more worried the Western allies became. The prospect that the Federal Republic might stop delivering weapons to Israel gave rise to widespread criticism of the West German state on the part of Jewish organisations based in the FRG, North America, and beyond, which called for a boycott of West German goods.[13] When the American ambassador in Bonn, George McGhee, stated that it would be 'embarrassing' for the United States if the FRG halted the transfers to Israel, Schröder replied that Bonn could not jeopardise Germany's 'vital interests'.[14] Hinting at the possibility of capitalising upon the West German willingness to confront the Nazi past, Bonn's ambassador to the United States, Knappstein, noted that the ongoing Bundestag discussion about prolonging the statute of limitations for Nazi crimes might perhaps be useful in smoothing the Israeli and international resentment against the FRG, showcasing how readily the West German regime was dealing with the legacy of the Nazi past.[15] But displaying a (rather ambiguous) remorseful attitude vis-à-vis the Nazi past could now do little to extricate the Federal Republic from the geopolitical crisis that unfolded in the weeks leading up to, and following, Ulbricht's Egyptian trip. Bracing for the upheaval to come, Bonn requested assistance from London, Paris and Washington.[16]

On 12 February, Erhard finally announced that the FRG would not in the future transfer weapons to areas of international tension. The West German Chancellor summarised the three main pillars of his decision. First, Bonn would no longer sell weapons to countries that were located in sensitive areas. Second, therefore, Bonn was to stop the arms transfers to Israel. Third, unless Nasser agreed to not invite Ulbricht to Egypt after all, the Federal Republic would halt its economic assistance to Cairo. Israeli Prime Minister Levi Eshkol disapproved of Erhard's decision, despising what he saw as a 'German capitulation to Nasser'.[17] Indeed, Erhard seemed to have both lost the stakes West Germany had invested in the long-standing partnership with Egypt and to infuriate the Israelis, without coming to any concrete, forthcoming resolution of the issues of the scientists, of diplomatic relations, or of what to do about the outstanding weapons deliveries. A sustained press campaign against the Federal Republic followed, but during a Bundestag debate on 17 February, Erhard, undaunted, stressed the need to not let go of the cardinal principles behind Bonn's *Deutschlandpolitik*. He would soon be made to change his mind.

## Ulbricht in Cairo

After sailing through the Mediterranean from Dubrovnik and onto the delta of the River Nile aboard the ship *Friendship among Peoples* (*Völkerfreundschaft*), on 24 February 1965 the East German delegation ended its Egypt-bound journey with a train ride from Alexandria to Cairo.[18] There, they were welcomed by Nasser himself. A group of uniformed Egyptian students lined up to welcome the East German leader, chanting something that to German ears sounded like: 'Achlen, Herr Olbraccht!' (Welcome, Mr Ulbricht!).[19] The twenty-one-gun presidential salute was fired; twenty-three foreign ambassadors, mostly from Soviet and non-aligned countries, were present to witness Ulbricht's arrival; and carpets adorned the station's interior. Just outside, a long line of East German flags adorned the pavement next to the railway station.

All seemed well – except for one detail. The East German emblem had been printed only on one side of each flag, so that, when moved by the wind, from one side they looked exactly like West German flags would.[20] While probably overlooked by the majority of those present, and especially non-German observers, the issue of the two-sided flags poignantly symbolised the German–German dilemmas regarding Ulbricht's trip to Cairo. Did this visit signify that the GDR was on the right track in its efforts to break through the West German campaign to exclude it from the international society? Or would the FRG manage to contain even this East German attempt at recognition?

The Bonn Foreign Office circulated to all of its consular and diplomatic agencies abroad a brochure on Ulbricht, which claimed he had 'joined forces with Hitler' in the early 1930s, recalled the 17 June uprising 'against his dictatorship', and attacked his 'complete subjection to Moscow's party line'.[21] It was up to 'any nation which feels some patriotism' to judge whether 'an invitation to Ulbricht can be a honor to his host'.[22] The East German party mouthpiece, *Neues Deutschland*, victoriously – albeit prematurely – announced the death of the Hallstein Doctrine, which for the East Germans had long amounted to 'the diplomatic expression of an economic and political extortion'.[23] Just a few days before their departure from East Berlin, the second wife of the East German leader, Lotte Ulbricht, jotted down in her travel diary: 'I feel so excited ... I have in front of me an extensive copy of the travel programme. From what I can gather, all the ceremonies generally in store for the visit of a head of state of a foreign country will be displayed for Walter Ulbricht's arrival. Our workers' and peasants' state then does count for something in the world!'[24] For years, the SED leaders had endured, and challenged, the constraints imposed not just by the Federal Republic, but also by Moscow, on the East German room for manoeuvre in the Arab Middle East. In 1965, Ulbricht could finally sit face to face with Nasser.

During his very first meeting with the 'tiger' and 'fox' of Egypt, Colonel Gamal Abdel Nasser – thus nicknamed for his toughness and cunningness[25] – Ulbricht condemned the West German double-dealing (*Doppelspiel*) in the Middle East, and denounced Bonn's secret arms transfers to Israel. He put in Nasser's mouth words that went very close to underlining an implicit Egyptian recognition of the GDR, and of the existence of two German states. 'You are in a difficult position', the East German leader sympathised with Nasser, 'You have relations with two German states, both of which claim to be speaking for the whole of Germany'.[26] It was Ulbricht though, not Nasser, who repeatedly hinted at the existence of *two* German states. It was he who described the Egyptian leader's move of inviting him to the UAR as 'resistance against Bonn's oppression', and expressed the hope that this would 'encourage other Arab and African states to unmask' the colonialist politics of the West German state.[27] Ulbricht commented that the GDR and Egypt were each the respective specialist in the fight against 'imperialism'; in Europe, the GDR against the FRG, and in the Middle East, Egypt against the former colonial powers.

The UAR leader easily saw through Ulbricht's words. In contrast to what the East German delegation expected, and to what the Egyptian delegation to the Arab League had done just a few weeks before, during his meeting with Ulbricht Nasser did not condemn Bonn's foreign policy conduct – not even its ties with Israel. It was Washington,

Figure 8.1  Walter Ulbricht and Gamal Abdel Nasser in Cairo, 1965.

Nasser lectured the East German leader, which had pressured the FRG to sell weapons to Israel. 'We want to cause misunderstandings between West Germany and Israel; we want to bring West Germany to a point where it stops delivering weapons to Israel', he explained.[28] On the question of Germany's future, Nasser reiterated the 1964 non-aligned stance, and expressed the hope that reunification would happen through pacific means, without mentioning a word that even came close to official recognition of the East German state by the UAR. He then briefly outlined the costly economic problems that the UAR was suffering due to its war in Yemen and welcomed the prospect of increased economic cooperation with the East Germans.[29] Following new measures introduced as part of the economic seven-year plan outlined in 1963, the GDR was now in the position to offer support to expand the economic, scientific and technical cooperation between the two countries.[30] In return, the East German leader asked for Nasser's cooperation in attempting to procure the GDR the much-needed oil resources that countries 'very close' to the UAR possessed, as well as for support of the East German attempts to be admitted to the United Nations.[31]

Further details were dealt with during a meeting between the East German Deputy Minister for International and Inter-German Trade, Gerhard Weiss, and his Egyptian counterpart, Mahmoud Fawzi. Weiss noted that it was not only in the UAR's interest, but also in that of the GDR, that the ties between the FRG and Israel did not strengthen any further – although, as East Berlin's *Israelpolitik* and the SED's propagandistic insistence on West German–Israeli ties highlighted, this was evidently not the case. In an interview published in one of the most influential Egyptian newspapers, the daily *Al Ahram*, Ulbricht explained that the GDR's stance was one of opposition to the 'attempts made by the international monopoly capital to build up Israel as an imperial outpost in the Arab region', and that for this reason the GDR watched the ever strengthening military ties between Bonn and Jerusalem with concern.[32] Especially given that, Ulbricht claimed, this also included a joint 'cooperation in the preparations for the production of nuclear weapons'.[33] The East German news agency Allgemeiner Deutscher Nachrichtendienst (ADN) published an interview with Winzer 'on the crisis of Bonn's Middle East policy',[34] in which the East German Minister did not just speak of Bonn's endeavours in the Levant. He also condemned the 'fake pathos' with which Erhard spoke of the Nazi past, stressing that such a stance was simply not credible in a West German state that was still packed with unpunished former Nazis. Transferring arms and ammunition to Israel, Winzer claimed, had nothing to do with a process of coming to terms with the Nazi past; rather, it served the 'preparation for a new genocide', which, this time, would be taking place in the Middle East against the Arab peoples.[35]

Before Ulbricht's departure, Nasser agreed to write a joint communiqué with his guest; to open a UAR consulate in East Germany; and to accept Ulbricht's invitation to visit '[East] Germany'.[36] The two leaders signed a series of agreements relating to economic and technical cooperation, as well as scientific and cultural relations. The GDR granted Egypt a long-term credit of US$70 million and a short-term credit of approximately US$11 million.[37] Members of the East German delegation alternated high-level political meetings and interviews with local and international journalists with visits to some of the most impressive archaeological sites on earth.[38] 'Photographers of the West German press are constantly between our feet, as they hope to catch an image of an exhausted Ulbricht – but in vain!',[39] noted Lotte.

Upon his return to East Berlin, Ulbricht declared that he was 'very satisfied' with how the visit had gone.[40] He dismissed earlier West German attempts to prevent it from taking place as 'unwise' (*töricht*): 'given that Bonn's government sits in the proverbial glass house it should not be throwing stones', the SED leader commented.[41] The fact that the trip had taken place in spite of West German attempts to the contrary; that the UAR and the GDR had signed a series of important agreements in various crucial fields; and that the Egyptian leader had agreed both to establish a consulate in the GDR as well as to visit the East German state – all of this signalled the success of Ulbricht's visit to the UAR. Instead of proposing overly ambitious goals that he was likely not to achieve, such as an exchange of ambassadors with Nasser, Ulbricht had been quick to adapt to aim at modest, and therefore more easily achievable, goals. In addition, his generous offers spanned from commercial agreements that would help the UAR to achieve the goals delineated in its five-year plan, to matters of cultural and technical cooperation. The GDR was now in the position to capitalise on the visit, turning a tactical victory into a major strategic success. The East German visit had secured a huge, prestigious victory – or so it seemed at the time.

## To Lod and Bonn and back again

On 7 March 1965 West German special envoy Kurt Birrenbach landed in Lod, Israel, tasked with a secret mission. His aim was to pacify the Israelis after Bonn's recent decision to halt arms and ammunition shipments and negotiate a possible compensation for them.[42] This was to include the establishment of an embryonic West German diplomatic presence in Israel, possibly a consulate, and the conversion of the arms deliveries into a financial arrangement. And yet, soon after his flight had landed, Birrenbach got the impression that somehow many in Israel were aware of his 'secret' mission. What was even more puzzling to him was that upon his arrival several people congratulated him on the commencement of diplomatic relations between the two countries.[43] In fact, as special envoy Birrenbach was on his way to Lod airport to begin the delicate round of negotiations, Chancellor Erhard had formally proposed that Bonn and Israel establish diplomatic relations – which was not what the Chancellor had planned to do when he had parted company with his envoy just the previous day. Furious about not having been informed in time about the Chancellor's intentions, Birrenbach flew back to Bonn shortly after his arrival in Israel. After being briefed about the new developments he returned to Jerusalem. There, he finalised the terms of the financial compensation to the Israelis for the arms equipment that Bonn had failed to deliver, and the establishment of diplomatic – not consular – relations.

Birrenbach's back-and-forth between Bonn and Lod epitomised the extent to which Erhard's *Israelpolitik* was being pulled in multiple directions. Just two days before Birrenbach's arrival in Jerusalem, the Chancellor had met with the American, British and French ambassadors. The meeting was to be a memorable one. The French ambassador commented to Erhard's foreign policy adviser that 'no Russian could command Ulbricht more than [US Ambassador] McGhee had just done' with Erhard. A close friend of President Johnson, 'robust and rosy-cheeked' McGhee was described in US media outlets as a 'hybrid strain of a Texan – a cross between a Rhodes Scholar and a wildcat oil boomer'.[44] An energetic and skilled diplomat who relished the opportunity to dress up in orientalist sheikh costumes when partaking in masquerade balls,[45] McGhee had started his career as an oil tycoon before the war. He then entered the State Department in 1951, travelling the Middle East widely while negotiating and disbursing US aid to the region, prior to being posted to Turkey. He had a clear understanding of the geostrategic importance of Middle Eastern countries, and of their oil reserves, and vigorously stressed with the Chancellor the importance for Bonn of not alienating Nasser. The FRG could not break relations with Egypt, the American ambassador declared 'energetically', as this would automatically send the Egyptians into 'the hands of the Communists'.[46] While the US ambassador had essentially dominated the meeting, his opinion was in line with those of the British and the French allies. But the pressure on the Chancellor was not just coming from the United States, France, Britain or Israel. Criticism of Erhard's perceived tentative and clumsy management of the crisis was increasingly mounting within the ranks of the Christian Democrats themselves. Rainer Barzel, former Minister of All-German Affairs and now CDU/CSU parliamentary group leader, recently back from the United States, fiercely argued with Erhard that it was essential for the Chancellor to adopt a more openly pro-Israeli stance. Will Rasner, the party's chief whip, noted that the Chancellor's reputation had fallen so sharply in the opinion polls, because of his indecisiveness in handling the crisis, that CDU/CSU members intended voting him out of office on the forthcoming Monday 8 March 1965.[47]

Faced with harsh criticism on the part of the Western allies and with the prospect of being ousted from government and from his own party, on Sunday 7 March 1965 Erhard announced one of the most striking policy reversals since the beginning of his chancellorship. The West German stance on the 'Middle East crisis' was now fixed, announced West German press spokesman von Hase. First, he stressed, Bonn would freeze the economic aid agreed with Egypt. Second, Bonn intended to regard any 'enhancement' of the East German position as an unfriendly act. The key word used in 1955, recognition (*Anerkennung*) had now been substituted by a much more encompassing enhancement (*Aufwertung*) of East Germany's international position.[48] Third, the Chancellor proposed the establishment of diplomatic relations with Israel. The fourth and fifth points were more generic; the FRG would no longer export weapons to areas of tension, and it declared itself in favour of a de-escalation of tension in the Middle East.

The King of Morocco indefinitely postponed his planned trip to West Germany on the same day as the announcement, and Iraq and Yemen announced that they were planning countermeasures to put in place against Bonn. A conference of Foreign Ministers of Arab League countries stressed that in the event of the actual establishment of diplomatic relations between West Germany and Israel, several of their members would break relations with West Germany. The SED, naturally, cherished the news: 'Only the German state that stands for the national freedom and independence of the Arab peoples, and that opposes the neo-colonialism of the imperialist powers can speak in the name of Germany. Only the German Democratic Republic!'[49] The East German government further stressed that the exchange of ambassadors between West Germany and Israel could not be interpreted in any way other than as a 'provocation to the Arab states and all anti-imperialist and anti-colonialist powers'.[50] The agreements signed between the GDR and Egypt when Ulbricht visited the country were followed by new ones signed with Syria, and the opening of an East German *Generalkonsulat* in the Republic of Yemen (South Yemen). 1965 also marked the year in which the GDR began militarily assisting Egypt with a programme of arms shipments to Cairo.[51] Reviewing the recent GDR foreign policy successes, Politbüro member Hermann Axen stressed that in 1965 Bonn witnessed its 'biggest political defeat', which culminated in the establishment of relations with Israel.[52]

In Bonn, Schröder was furious. Disappointed and embittered, he lamented Erhard's move, which, he claimed, represented a fundamental departure from 'our' *Deutschlandpolitik*.[53] As McGhee himself noted, 'the fact that CDU party leaders could seriously talk of forcing Erhard's resignation is evidence of the degree to which the Chancellor's display of indecisiveness during recent weeks has weakened his position and his prestige'.[54] Since rumours about a possible West German recognition of Israel had begun spreading throughout the Middle East and North Africa, Bonn had become 'the blackest beast in the Arab chamber of imperialist horrors' in much of the regional press coverage, although behind the scenes some Arab representatives, such as the Jordanian and Lebanese Foreign Ministers, attempted to reign in the harsh line advocated by Nasser, who called for a boycott of the Federal Republic and immediate all-Arab recognition of the GDR.[55] Erhard's handling of the crisis was not just bashed by vocal leaders such as Nasser or the Baathist Amin al-Hafiz in Syria. The regional powers interested in keeping relations with the Federal Republic – such as Jordan, Saudi Arabia and Sudan – condemned the 'stupidity' displayed by the Federal government and its 'very silly' management of the Middle East crisis, which let the issue 'become one between FRG and Arabs generally rather than handling matter to focus dispute solely between FRG and UAR'.[56]

For all the criticism of him, however, Chancellor Erhard had had to face a complex situation, arising from decisions that had mostly pre-dated his entry in office, and had attempted to face it in a way that would not betray any of the core principles of the Federal Republic's foreign policy. Throughout the crisis he had often repeated that it was necessary to preserve Bonn's claim to sole representation. He had reaffirmed, on different occasions, his frustration at the Western allies' inability to take Bonn's foreign political stance on the German question seriously. What the Chancellor had attempted to do, in light of McGhee's loud exhortation not to dare break off relations with Egypt, as well as on the basis of public opinion polls which saw his popularity falling worryingly in West Germany and the United States, was to preserve at least the facade of a West German position of autonomy, independence and power in the international domain. In the process, it had become clear that the majority of leaders in the Arab Middle East were not at all interested in damaging their relations with the Federal Republic, and the Israeli government, albeit vocally protesting against the suspension of the arms transfers from West Germany, treasured the opportunity to solidify its diplomatic ties to one of the strongest countries in Europe. Transcending the specificity of German–Israeli or German–Arab relations, in Bonn the debate on the Middle Eastern crisis had become, effectively, a West German debate on how to wage the inter-German global Cold War. In spite of the divergences, there was one point on which most observers agreed: the events of 1965, which culminated in the exchange of ambassadors between the Federal Republic of Germany and Israel, epitomised a crucial, and crucially German, Cold War crisis. 'In the final analysis', reflected a US diplomat in Bonn, 'one can regard the FRG's Government's actions in this instance as demonstrating (however haphazardly) something like diplomatic genius'.[57]

## An impossible normalisation

The establishment of diplomatic relations with another country was not usually a matter of discussion in the Israeli parliament – but the German case constituted an exception. 'It is not like establishing diplomatic relations with any other country [and] the moral and historical account arising from the Holocaust goes beyond any framework of political action', explained Prime Minister Levi Eshkol to the Knesset.[58]

'Both emotion and intellect, both heart and mind', stressed Herut party leader Menachem Begin, 'tell us not to accept full normalisation, before the whole world, in the generation of the destruction, between the nation which was destroyed and the people which destroyed it'.[59] Mapam party member Yisrael Barzilai deplored the 'renazification' taking place in the Federal Republic and warned about the real character of the allegedly 'new' Germany, while Shmuel Mikunis of the Maki denounced Erhard's proposal to exchange ambassadors as simply the latest move within 'West Germany's policy of foolhardy expansionism in our region'.[60] Eventually, with sixty-six votes for, twenty-nine against, and ten abstentions, on 16 March 1965 the Knesset approved the establishment of diplomatic relations with Bonn despite fierce opposition arising from the ranks of the opposition. The vote took place just before Birrenbach's final work trip to Jerusalem to take care of the final practicalities before the establishment of the respective embassies. While Israeli politicians debated about how to respond to Erhard's offer and Birrenbach shuttled between Bonn and Jerusalem, another West German emissary, Alex Böker, was touring the Arab capitals, assuring his interlocutors of the fact that the Federal Republic would no longer export weapons to Israel and that Bonn would wait for the actual exchange of ambassadors to give the Arab countries the time to adjust to the situation. His strategy worked. As the US State Department's Head of Near Eastern Affairs would later put it, 'each day that recognition of Israel was deferred had been a gain from a German viewpoint'.[61]

It took some five months after the Knesset vote before West German ambassador Rudolf Pauls presented his credentials to the Israeli authorities. The West German Embassy would be located in Tel Aviv – not Jerusalem – and for the moment would be housed at the Sheraton Hotel, right on the seafront. To some of the embassy staff members, the temporariness of this housing measure seemed to mean that there were such low expectations about the future of the newly established diplomatic mission that the initial location where the West German delegation set up its office was a hotel – so as to be ready to pack up and leave at any moment.[62] If he were an insurance broker, would he sell a life insurance policy to the incoming German ambassador to Israel, was Böker's favourite joke in US diplomatic circles.[63]

Erhard had hoped that the establishment of diplomatic relations between the Federal Republic and Israel would represent a new beginning in German–Israeli relations. Instead, these would continue to be embroiled with the political anxieties of actors on both sides of both conflicts – German–German and Arab–Israeli – for decades to come. Heavy protests, denounced by members of the Bonn Cabinet as 'irresponsible' and 'deeply regrettable', took place to condemn Pauls' arrival.[64] 'I was sure that he would have to be recalled', later recalled then Foreign Minister Golda Meir, who had been 'outraged' by his nomination.[65] While US observers praised the ambassador's 'pleasing, courteous personality' and cast him as a 'good conversationalist as well as a good listener', the ambassador faced severe criticism in Israel.[66] While Pauls had not been a member of the Nazi Party, he had served in the Wehrmacht in the Eastern Front and, in December 1944, had received one of the most prestigious military decorations in Nazi Germany – the Knight's Cross – for having broken through the Russian lines. After losing an arm in battle, he was relocated to Nazi Germany's embassy in Turkey, where he

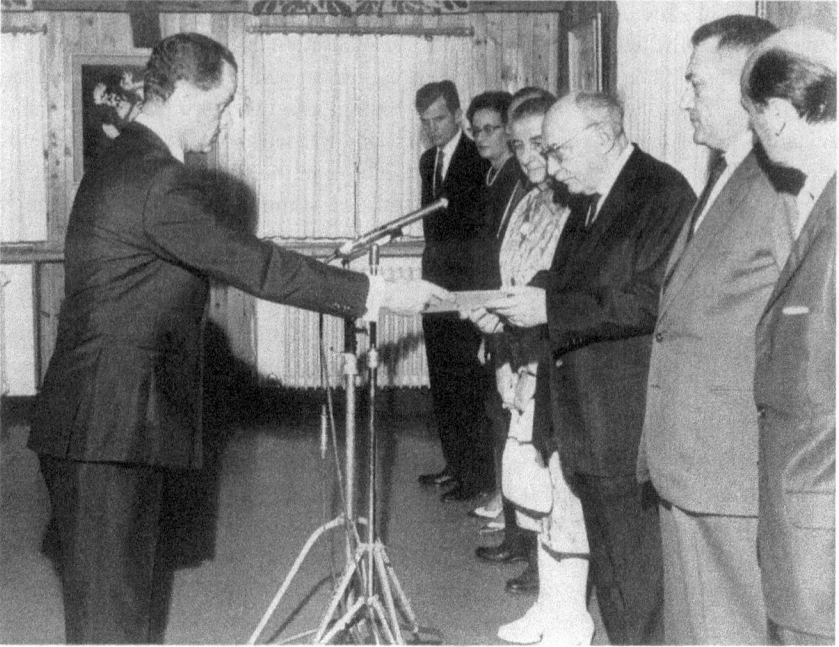

Figure 8.2　Ambassador Pauls presenting his credentials in Jerusalem, 1965.

served as a deputy military attaché under Franz von Papen, the former Chancellor who had played a crucial role in paving Hitler's rise to power. But his nomination was not the only one to spark outrage. Pauls' hand-picked second-in-command at the embassy, Alexander Török, who would serve as Embassy Councillor and Charge d'Affaires, had an even more disturbing past. Török was born in Hungary and had served in the Hungarian Foreign Service under dictator Miklós Horthy. In 1944, when the Germans marched into Hungary, Török was sent to Berlin as Legation Secretary – just when the Hungarian mission in Berlin became a crucial crossroads for receiving and forwarding Nazi orders, including those related to the planned annihilation of Hungarian Jewry. In the wake of the Holocaust he had 'admitted knowledge of the deportations but said he was powerless to do anything about it'.[67] Török had then remained in Berlin following the end of the war, where he applied and received German citizenship and, in 1950, joined the Federal Foreign Service. His appointment to Tel Aviv followed earlier postings in Tunisia, Togo and Bonn. The reaction of the Israeli public to his appointment was of shock and disgust – but after an internal investigation the Foreign Ministry confirmed Török's fitness for the post, where he remained until 1968.

But the West Germans, in turn, were uneasy with the person who had been chosen to represent the State of Israel in Bonn, Asher Ben-Natan. Originally from Austria, Ben-Natan had illegally migrated to Palestine in 1938. He soon became involved with the Haganah and the Bricha, assisting Jewish refugees fleeing from Europe and playing a crucial role in the identification and eventual capture of several Nazi criminals right

Figure 8.3 Ambassador Ben-Natan presenting his credentials in Bonn, 1965.

after the Second World War. In the early 1950s he took up a job seemingly as a pioneer of the Israeli food industry – as the governmental representative at Inkoda, a company that supplied Israel with meat from Northern African countries. But Ben-Natan's tasks in Ethiopia and Sudan went beyond suppling Israel with meat, as an important part of his job also revolved around 'the creation of important political and security contacts' in loco that would complement Israel's strategy of the periphery, in an attempt to circumvent the geostrategic isolation that the Arab neighbours aimed to impose on it.[68] Ben-Natan then went on to the Israeli Ministry of Defence, becoming its Director General, a position which he held from 1959 to 1965. It was in that post that he had worked with Shimon Peres, among others, to forge the West German–Israeli security ties, and it was from there he took up his ambassadorial post in Bonn.

While many in the FRG were eager to forget about the secret arms deals forged with the Israeli security establishment, Ben-Natan did not miss a chance to take part to public debates and to appear in the media and pursued his representative duties in one of the most difficult countries. Unlike his counterpart, Ben-Natan was fluent in the language of the host country, his native German. He was outgoing, smart and a very charming communicator. The same could not be said for Pauls. His first public speech, made on 30 June 1966 on the occasion of the German Day at the Tel Aviv Trade Fair, attracted widespread criticism, as the ambassador pointed out that West Germany was no longer in need of any special dispensation for past deeds, adding that some Israelis seemed to be unfortunately prone to stirring up the past 'for political reasons'.[69] Pauls further elaborated on his points a few days later, when he met a journalist of the Israeli daily *Yedioth Aharonot* aboard a ship in Haifa harbour just prior to his departure on home leave, to whom he emphasised that he considered his speech 'moderate and balanced'. What he had done, he said, was express some criticism. After all, 'full diplomatic relations mean full mutual rights, including that of criticism. Criticism is not Israel's exclusive right, and you will have to get used to it'.[70]

Pauls' utterances had come after a series of tense interactions between West Germans and Israelis in the wake of the exchange of ambassadors. In particular, Adenauer's visit to Israel and, a few days later, Abba Eban's trip to Warsaw stirred unease in the unfolding special relationship – just at a time when many West German commentators were insisting on the importance of a 'normalisation' of relations between the two countries. In May of that year, during the first and only visit of former Chancellor Adenauer to Israel, ninety-year-old Adenauer, too, was greeted by protesters at the airport. But by then the campaigns of the Herut party, of the Ghetto Fighters' Association, and others, did not spark much discussion among the German or Israeli publics anymore. What irked the former Chancellor was the reception he received from the Israeli authorities. At a dinner party in Adenauer's honour, Prime Minister Levi Eshkol did not spend a single word praising Adenauer's Germany support for Israel, economically and otherwise.[71] Notwithstanding a letter to Goldmann written upon his return in which Adenauer characterised his visit as 'a moving experience and, I believe, a successful one too',[72] the incident had seriously disappointed the Old Man.

Abba Eban's work trip to Poland in the spring of 1966 presented another source of tension between the West German and Israeli authorities. Prime Minister Eshkol had long attempted to push for a rapprochement between Israel and the Eastern bloc, and the Israeli Foreign Ministry organised a gathering of Israeli ambassadors to Eastern European countries in Warsaw on 12 May 1966 to discuss the matter.[73] Despite Ambassador Pauls' recommendations not to release any statement on the issue, on the occasion of the diplomatic gathering in Warsaw the Israeli government cabled a communication to the Polish authorities expressing Israel's 'energetic support' for the maintenance of the Oder-Neiße line – the contested border between Poland and the GDR which the Federal Republic did not recognise – and declaring its opposition 'to any change in the border which might cause political tension',[74] to Bonn's huge disappointment. The timing of the declaration was particularly unfortunate, because it came right after the one significant achievement in the bilateral relationship, an economic agreement, which foresaw West German payments to Israel that would extend over a period of twenty-five years, thus overshadowing the one element that could have been celebrated as a successful continuation of the West German–Israeli partnership through economic means.[75] Prior to leaving for his annual holiday Pauls further declared that he 'felt that the results of his first year in Israel could be described as positive'.[76] Not many would have agreed with him at the time.

## Operation Marabu

While the Federal Republic and Israel struggled to find a new footing for their bilateral, now fully institutionalised, ties, the East German regime attempted to seize the benefits arising from the Arab discontent with Bonn's diplomatic overture to Jerusalem. The prospect of gaining diplomatic recognition from the Arab Middle East, however, remained elusive. Somehow, the GDR's assurances were not managing to overcome the Arab fear of the losses that their countries would incur should they break with the FRG and opt instead for an exclusive relationship with the GDR, and the effects of the East German diplomatic fiasco were increasingly visible. In June 1965, for example, the Allgemeiner Deutscher Nachrichtendienst (ADN) reported on a worrying 'Israeli offensive' against the GDR that was taking place in Havana.[77] There, the Israeli ambassador was doing everything possible to counter the East German narrative that ridiculed Bonn's spectacular diplomatic fiasco in the Middle East. He repeatedly pointed out that, as a matter of fact, it was the GDR that had lost the 1965 diplomatic contest in the Levant, for although several Arab countries had broken relations with Bonn, none of those countries had diplomatically recognised the GDR.

The Israeli ambassador in Cuba had a point. While the GDR had made crucial gains in the wake of Bonn's foreign policy 'mess' in 1965, it had not attained diplomatic recognition from any of the countries that had threatened, and then went on, to break relations with the FRG.[78] At the time, this could have been interpreted either as a sign of the futility of East Germany's efforts to overcome the diplomatic isolation Bonn imposed on it – as the Israeli representative in Cuba was arguing; or as a sign that slowly, but surely, the GDR would also gain recognition on the part of countries that did not belong to the Soviet bloc – as the East German leadership chose to see it. In hindsight, the crisis indicates that already by the mid 1960s the FRG was on the right track to win the German–German Cold War confrontation. No country could afford to make such an affront to the Federal Republic as to recognise the GDR and the West Germans were extremely skilled at making under-the-table deals with the Arab partners – so as to allow them, openly, to break off diplomatic relations with the FRG while keeping their economic ties relatively unaltered. Yet the SED leadership was not ready to give in. On the contrary, from East Berlin's perspective the progress made thus far, albeit limited, showed that the GDR *was* gaining international recognition.[79] Thus, the East German fight against Bonn for international recognition continued, and with it, the GDR's own *Israelpolitik*.[80]

As a 1966 East German Foreign Ministry memo made clear, vehemently attacking Israel, and emphasising the close relations between West Germany and Israel, was – still – considered essential to capture the interest of Arab audiences, steering them towards the GDR.[81] But the Foreign Ministry was not the only East German body working to spread anti-Israeli propaganda. During a meeting of East German foreign intelligence branch (Stasi- Hauptverwaltung Aufklärung, HVA) officers and KGB officials which took place in Moscow in mid-April 1966, the two parties agreed to boost their cooperation in the field of foreign intelligence activities, especially in the Middle East, and initiate wide-ranging consultations on the matter. During the talks, Stasi and KGB officers agreed to continue and strengthen some of their existing joint foreign influence and counterintelligence operations, such as Operation Marabu – a disinformation offensive aimed at driving a wedge between the FRG and the Arab countries by emphasising the military, political and economic cooperation in place between Israel and the Federal Republic. The East Germans would provide the KGB with relevant information and materials – and the Soviets would do their best to spread the information as widely as possible.[82]

East German and Soviet activities aiming at pushing aside the curtain of non-recognition intensified after the end of Erhard's chancellorship, in December 1966. The ensuing Grand Coalition government under Kurt Georg Kiesinger (CDU/Christian Social Union (CSU)) and Foreign Minister (SPD) Willy Brandt insisted on a 'new Eastern policy' which aimed at reaching out to countries of the Eastern bloc while keeping the GDR in isolation. Ulbricht's regime responded to the new and dynamic duo at the helm of Bonn's foreign policy by multiplying its efforts at international recognition, including by the countries of the Levant, with the help of the Soviets. One key pillar of such efforts was inviting Arab representatives to visit the GDR. UAR Vice-President Hassan Ibrahim, who had 'the time, a new wife, and no hard currency for a honeymoon', and who resigned from his post less than a month after his return from East Berlin, had not made for a particularly prestigious guest – and in general the East German policy did not seem to be effective in bringing about the boost that East Berlin's cadres would have hoped.[83] Undeterred, by 1966 the GDR welcomed an average of three official Arab visitors per week, and East German Foreign Minister Otto Winzer embarked upon frequent tours of the Arab Middle East, rehashing the usual messages about the historical support given by the Communist half of Germany to the Arab countries, in contrast to the 'nefarious' West German support of Israel. In March 1967, Moscow telegrammed several Arab capitals guaranteeing that in the event of their diplomatic recognition of East Germany, the Soviets would step in and counterbalance any resultant economic harm inflicted by West Germany.[84] The West German government reacted to the East German offensive by moderating its public expressions of support for Israel, for example with Ambassador Pauls declining the invitation to attend the military parade for Israel's Independence Day, which in May 1967 would be held, controversially, in Jerusalem; and by inviting Secretary General of the Arab League Abdul Khalek Hassouna to Bonn for official talks.[85] But if East German courtships and Soviet reassurances seemed to be falling on deaf ears, rising tensions in the Middle East were to bring about deep changes in the political geography of the Arab–Israeli conflict, offering new openings to East Berlin.

## Six days of war

Blaming the 'abundance of Machiavellian minds' in the State Department, and conceding that 'we could be letting our thinking get too Byzantine', in December 1966 the US Ambassador to Jordan, Findley Burns, Jr., sent a cable to the State Department in which he hypothesised that 'a short Arab-Israeli war' may soon take place, and tried to map out its possible consequences.[86] In a few months, anxiety was on the rise throughout the whole region. Rumours had been spreading about a new round of hostilities, and on 13 May 1967 Moscow provided Cairo with faulty intelligence claiming that Israel had amassed eleven brigades at the border with Syria and was ready to begin hostilities against Damascus with the ultimate aim of toppling the Baath regime.[87] The intensification of border skirmishes between the two countries prior to Moscow's distribution of the faulty intelligence report rendered the information contained in it plausible. Nasser reacted by asking for the withdrawal of the peacekeepers stationed in the Sinai, and on 18 May UN Secretary General U Thant instructed the withdrawal of UNEF forces, which he praised as having 'contributed greatly to the maintenance of quiet and peace in the area'.[88] Five days later, the Egyptian president announced that the Straits of Tiran were closed to Israeli shipping – an act that, a decade earlier, then Israeli Foreign Minister Golda Meir, speaking at the UN, had stated would be considered a *casus belli* in Jerusalem. In Bonn, Ambassador Ben-Natan reached out to Foreign Minister Brandt. Many in Israel were feeling encircled by Nasser's manoeuvres. There were also increasing worries that, after the Egyptian campaign conducted in Yemen where Israeli intelligence and International Red Cross reports confirmed the use of poisonous gas against the civilian population, the UAR would use poison gas against Israeli civilians. Ben-Natan asked for a shipment of 20,000–30,000 gas masks and urged Brandt to please provide him with a positive response – or a negative one, but at least quickly so that he could start looking elsewhere in the shortest possible time.[89] A reply in the affirmative came from the West German Foreign Office that afternoon.[90] The next day, Jordan announced the sealing of a military alliance with Egypt, which foresaw that each of the two countries would come to the defence of the other in case of an Israeli attack, along the lines of a similar deal signed six months earlier between Egypt and Syria.

Then, in the early hours of 5 June 1967, a pre-emptive Israeli air assault destroyed most of the Egyptian air forces.[91] Over the next five days, Israeli forces captured the Gaza Strip and the Sinai Peninsula from Egypt, drove the Jordanians out of East

Jerusalem, and conquered the West Bank and the Golan Heights. After the hostilities in the Middle East broke out, West German Chancellor Kiesinger reiterated his government's policy of 'non-interference' with the parties in the conflict – a policy which, however, did not mean 'moral indifference' nor 'neutrality of the heart', as Foreign Minister Brandt put it before the Bundestag.[92] Throughout East Germany, the Stasi steered its domestic surveillance to gauge what the population thought about the unfolding events in the Middle East, focusing in particular on churches and industrial factories – especially those that were trading internationally. Worryingly, it seemed that 'not all' East German citizens were convinced of the need to condemn Israel's culpability in waging the war. Some East German factory workers expressed views that differed from regime propaganda – an attitude which the domestic intelligence organs were examining as a matter of very serious concern. Officials at the receiving end of this information looked at the question as having broader significance – using what the East German people thought of Israel in June 1967 as a thermometer to gauge the actual warmth of their loyalty to the regime. A Stasi informant in East Berlin, for example, passed on that four workers at a chemical factory had refused to sign a resolution that called Israel the aggressor;[93] another pointed out that at least two of the workers at DIA Elektrotechnik – the chief accountant and the director of the contract handling office no less – had consulted Western media to gather a fuller picture of the onset and course of the war unfolding in the Near East. The two pointed to the fact that Israel was armed by the Federal Republic and the United States, while the Arabs by the Soviets, as the reason behind Israel's military success.[94]

East German military experts, too, looked at the Six Day War to extract lessons that had little to do with Middle Eastern conflict dynamics and more with the ongoing Cold War confrontation in Europe. East German Minister of National Defence Heinz Hoffmann was, for example, extremely grave in his assessment of the war. According to him, the conflict should not be interpreted simply as 'a local military confrontation' but rather it reflected global geopolitical tensions and, disturbingly, constituted a perfect illustration of the West German desire to infiltrate the Middle East.[95] Hoffmann evoked the West German–Israeli reparations agreement of 1952 and claimed that Bonn's support for Israel in 1967 did not differ substantially from Kaiser Wilhelm II's imperialist enterprises in the region prior to the First World War.[96] But his points were not just historical. He thought that the GDR should learn from the events of the June War, in particular as it exemplified the clear ability of imperialist countries to mobilise their populations for combat. Given how close the Israeli and West German establishments were at that time, it was extremely likely, he underscored, that in the event of an attack against East Germany the FRG would use similar military tactics and plans to those Israel had used against Egypt.

Albeit overstating the number of divisions available to the Israelis, and not quite grasping how the IDF had entered into Syrian territory, East German military experts gathered an overall precise understanding of what had happened on the battlefield during the June War (see maps 8.1 and 8.2). Shortly after the end of the hostilities Stasi officials gathered to analyse and study the shockingly rapid course of the war. An internal Stasi working paper pointed to the IDF's use of electronic warfare as a specific point of concern, given how quickly and easily Israel had rendered the Egyptian Soviet-made SA-2 missiles inoperative.[97] The National Defence Council of the GDR, chaired by

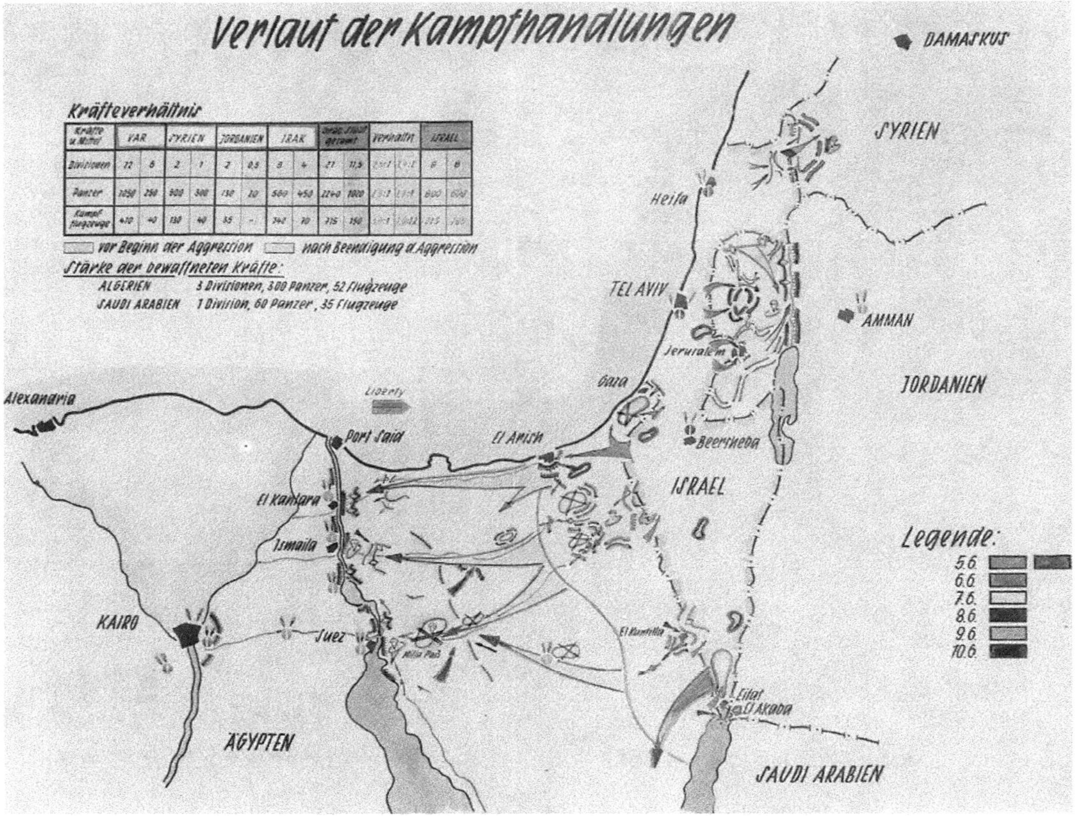

Map 8.1 Stasi map of the Six Day War, 'The Course of the Fighting', 1967.

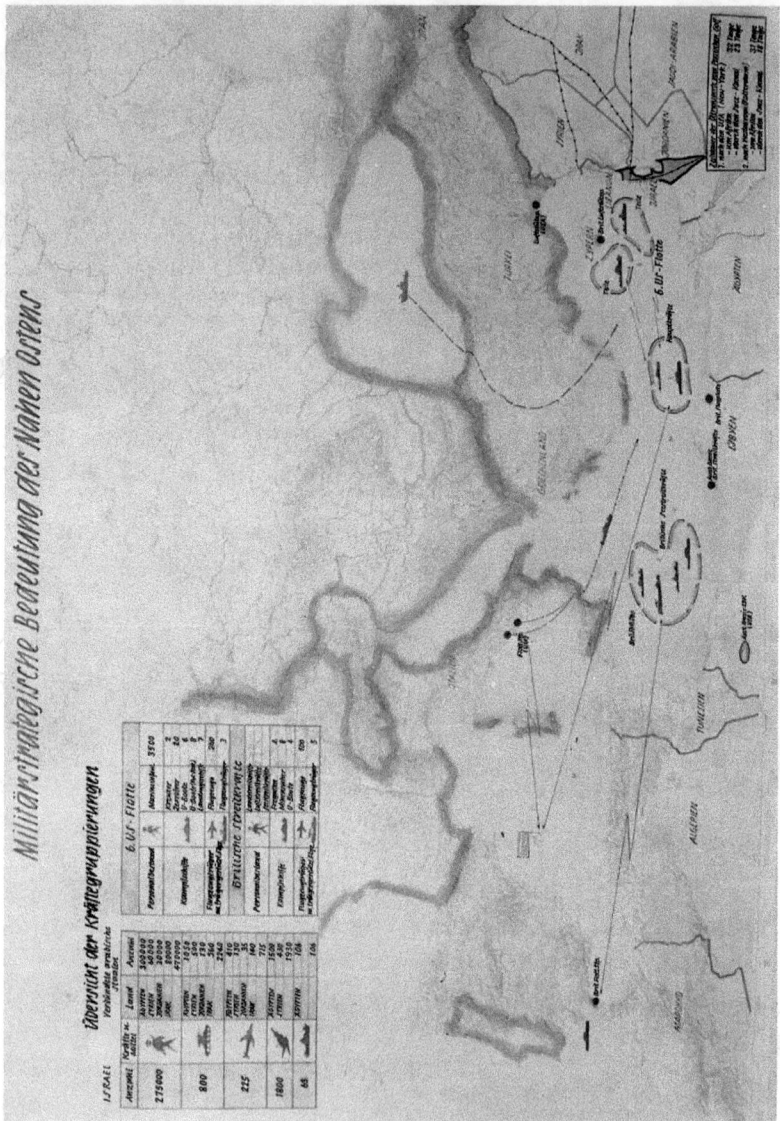

Map 8.2 Stasi map, 'Military-Strategic Significance of the Middle East', 1967.

Ulbricht, reconvened shortly thereafter to discuss the events – identifying the use of military intelligence and espionage, in addition to air power, as key explanatory factors behind Israel's rapid and overwhelming victory.[98] Further studies on the lessons that the East German People's Navy should gather from the Six Day War followed.[99]

Within the Eastern bloc, the GDR used the Six Day War to reiterate East Berlin's loyal commitment to the Soviet superpower, at a time when this was challenged by other junior allies, such as Romania, which had not only gone it alone in January 1967 by establishing diplomatic relations with West Germany (something that was not taken lightly in East Berlin), but also refused to follow the Soviet directive to break off relations with Israel.[100] As a letter that Ulbricht wrote to Brezhnev shows, the East German leader was keen to demonstrate to the Soviets how proactive and eager the GDR was in support of the Arab cause. Once the fighting halted, Ulbricht called for 'effective, [Soviet bloc-]coordinated, fast, political and material support for overcoming the consequences of the [Israeli] aggression', which would include 'solidarity measures towards the Arab countries', as well as initiatives to fully exploit the visibility provided by the UN and the other international platforms from whence to denounce the Israeli aggressor.[101]

The East German propaganda machine quickly mounted a sustained attack against Israel. The main thrust of the campaign revolved around the usual leitmotifs. First, Israel was 'following the tracks of the Hitlerist-fascist aggressors'.[102] Second, the root cause of Israel's aggression was to be found in Western imperialism, with special blame being attached to West Germany. The message circulated widely among the highest echelons of the East German security establishment: 'The connection between … years of extensive supply of tanks and other munitions from West Germany to Israel, and Israel's aggression, is clear'[103] denounced the East German Council of Ministers on 8 June 1967 – though most of the weapons used by Israel in the war did not come from West Germany nor did the later cooperation between the Federal Republic and the Jewish state have to do with the post-Holocaust restitutions agreement. Indeed, East Germany was being 'more anti-Israeli than other Eastern European countries and sometimes more than the USSR itself', noted Israeli officials, who also closely followed the 'intensified activity' of East Germany's alleged reporters at the UN who were in fact lobbying vis-à-vis Third World representatives.[104] In the region, the conflict provided the GDR with a new opportunity to support the Arab states – and to up the ante of this support to an extent that been impossible for East Berlin until then. The GDR intensified its deliveries of tanks, jet fighters and other weapons, as well as sending over pilots, military advisers and medical equipment.[105] The arms deliveries continued well after the end of the war, marking a turning point in the GDR's level of engagement with the region. In fact, however, East German provisions to the Arab Middle East would remain torn between the 'willingness and readiness of the GDR to provide assistance' to the Arab countries on the one hand, and the 'limits of its actual capacities' on the other, as Stasi officials would elegantly put it.[106]

At the June Plenum of the Soviet Communist Party, West Germany was cast as having 'thoroughly prepared' Israel for imperialist aggression and as a key contributor to Israel's arms procurement efforts.[107] The Soviets praised the East Germans for having no relations with Israel and adamantly condemned the Federal Republic: 'Speaking of the role of the powers of the West in the events in the Middle East, one cannot ignore [that] the Kiesinger-Brandt government manoeuvred in every possible way while outwardly observing neutrality. In fact, its sympathies were entirely on the side of Israel.'[108] This was especially noteworthy given that 'in previous years the Federal Republic of Germany delivered a considerable amount of armaments to Israel, strengthened relations with it on all lines and tried to strengthen its influence in the Middle East … From this we can draw only one conclusion: it is necessary to continue our pressure on the FRG and to expose German militarism and revanchism'.[109]

Ulbricht tried to drill the same message into UAR, Syrian and Yemeni representatives, contrasting West Germany's support to Israel with the 'total solidarity' that East Germany instead devoted to the Arab cause. Coupled with a far-reaching propaganda campaign, which claimed that West Germany had sent some ten submarines and thirty tanks to Israel and that 500 West German volunteers had travelled in secret from Luxembourg to join the IDF, the East German insistence on Bonn's involvement in the war did have some effect – alongside the United States and the United Kingdom, the Federal Republic was subjected to a selective oil embargo, which remained in place until 2 September 1967.[110] After having been deceived about the arms shipments from the Federal Republic to Israel in the Adenauer and Erhard years, Arab representatives were extremely susceptible to believing such rumours, which Bonn's diplomats tried hard to deny, with mixed results. The new round of fighting in the Middle East had, in fact, witnessed an outpouring of solidarity gestures on the part of West German citizens, and many of them had proclaimed their willingness to fight alongside Israeli soldiers, with letters inundating the desk of Asher Ben-Natan at the Israeli embassy.[111] Private organisations and individuals arranged collections for, and donations to, Israel, and student societies, political parties, trade unions and churches held several demonstrations in all major West German cities.[112] While the personnel of most other embassies in Israel, including that of the United States, received evacuation orders, at the German Embassy the personnel received no such instructions. 'Perhaps they forgot to evacuate us', as Hannelore Siegel put it with a smile. The war therefore also marked a turning point in the integration of the West German embassy personnel with Israeli civil society – one that would eventually ease the embassy's work on the ground after the hostilities had ended.[113]

## Walking the tightrope between Khartoum, Bonn and East Berlin

The Arab leaders reacted to Israel's rapid and overwhelming victory by scheduling a series of conferences to discuss their (ideally) coordinated response. In an attempt to counter East German insinuations about the alleged West German role in the conflict, the Bonn government submitted a memorandum to the UN General Assembly on 3 July 1967 in which it denied the rumours that its arms transfers to Israel had resumed. The months of July and August were filled with a flurry of diplomatic activity among Arab capitals, and the organisation of several conferences, including a round of preliminary talks between Arab Foreign Ministers in Khartoum at the beginning of August and, two weeks later, consultations among Arab Ministers of Finance, Economics and Oil in Baghdad and another conference in Khartoum at the end of the month.

East German Deputy Prime Minister Gerhard Weiss arrived in Egypt on 6 July, and from there he moved on to Damascus, to discuss with the both political leaderships how East Germany could best support the Arab states in their rearmament efforts.[114] Observers from the Bonn Foreign Ministry viewed these developments with preoccupation. The East German manoeuvres in the region at the time of the inter-Arab consultations in the wake of the Six Day War, coupled with the East German efforts 'to slander the Federal Republic with every possible means as a one-sided supporter of Israel' might well end up with a recognition of the GDR during the course of the summer, when a final conference of Arab leaders was planned.[115] But the Khartoum conference, which took place at the end of August, would be remembered for a very different outcome – the declaration of three 'no's that were to lay the 'framework of the main principles to which the Arab states adhere [in the formulation of their policy vis-à-vis Israel], namely: no peace with Israel, no recognition of Israel, no negotiations with it.[116] The conference closed with an implicit and tacit decision to lift the oil embargo against those countries that had been perceived to be siding with Israel during the war, including the Federal Republic, and West German policy over the following months walked a delicate thread in the attempt to regain Arab favour and counter the East German diplomatic offensive. For example, Bonn declined the request of the Israeli ambassador Ben-Natan to allow an Israeli brigadier general to visit the country to gather information on new developments in the West German tank design and industry for fear that doing so would lead credence to the East German, Soviet and Arab rumours about the renewal of the security ties between the two countries.[117]

But West German diplomats were not just busy rebutting East German propaganda claims. Less than a week after the cessation of the hostilities the Federal government approved the transfer of DM5 million to be destined to the German Red Cross in the Middle East,[118] and the West German commitment was reinforced, on 20 September 1967, by a Cabinet decision to designate DM50 million over a period of five years to projects improving the living conditions of Palestinian refugees. They should be 'clearly recognisable as German', as this would have helped the process of West German–Arab rapprochement.[119] The West German campaign to regain the favour of the Arab countries also included extensive bilateral consultations with Arab representatives and with Arab League functionaries.[120] These went in parallel with a steady improvement in the relations between the Federal Republic and Israel at the bilateral level, supported by a strengthening of the economic ties between the two countries and by Bonn's commitment to help Jerusalem to broker favourable deals with the countries of the European Economic Community.[121]

The East German attempt to capitalise on the Six Day War and the West German campaign to regain prestige in the Middle East came against the backdrop of mounting protests in Eastern Europe. While in Poland ruling Władysław Gomułka responded to these developments by adopting increasingly repressive measures, the leadership in Czechosloviakia attempted to qualm the population's demands by promoting reform. In 1968, newly appointed leader Alexander Dubček lifted press censorship and replaced key ministries officials, while assuring the Soviet superpower and its Warsaw Pact allies that nothing would change in terms of Prague's political alignment with the Eastern bloc. The Soviets responded by planning a military intervention. To bolster the legitimacy of their operation, having learned from what had happened in Hungary in 1956, in August 1968 Soviet forces marched on to Prague with the support of some 80,000 more troops from Poland, Bulgaria, Hungary and the GDR.[122] At the United Nations, the Israeli delegation expressed 'shock at the invasion and military control of the Czechoslovak Republic', adding that 'the participation of German troops in the invasion and occupation this time as part of the forces of the Warsaw Pact arouses in us particularly terrible memories'.[123] While Egyptian officials avoided outright declarations on the matter, Iraqi, Syrian and Southern Yemeni officials endorsed the Warsaw Pact invasion of Czechoslovakia, in the hope that doing so would strengthen their relationship with Moscow.[124]

But if the region seemed to be reacting to the invasion of Czechoslovakia along Cold War lines – with the majority of the Arab countries siding with the Soviets, and Israel vocally against the intervention – the reality on the ground was much more complex. The West German establishment had been able to understand and navigate this complexity, pushing for reconciliation and establishing diplomatic relations with Israel while promoting its interests in the Arab world and stepping up as one of main donors contributing, for example via the UNRWA and the German Red Cross, to improving life conditions for Palestinian refugees. The GDR, in contrast, had not. In focusing so centrally on anti-Israeli and anti-West German propaganda for the Arab world, the SED regime lost sight of the multiple channels that Bonn's (often economic) diplomacy was pursuing in the region, managing to reach out simultaneously to Israel, the Arab states and the Arab League. When six Arab countries recognised the GDR, in 1969, East German cadres celebrated what seemed to be a major breakthrough. Taking place twenty years after the establishment of both German states, however, the wave of recognition coming from key Arab countries did not really damage the FRG. The incoming Social Democratic government in Bonn – the first in the history of the Federal Republic – quickly dismantled any remains of the Hallstein Doctrine and moved on, signalling a broader ideological shift away from the stark global Cold War confrontation of the previous decades towards a period of détente.

## Notes

1   AAPD 1965, Doc. 1, Cabinet Proposal of the Federal Foreign Office, 4 January 1965.
2   AAPD 1965, Doc. 41, Record of the Ministerial Director Krapf, 27 January 1965.
3   FRO 371/183081 [RG 113116/1], Hwyel I. Duck, Bonn to Peter H. Laurence, North and East African Dept, 6 February 1965.
4   On the attempted Spanish mediation between the FRG and the UAR, see I. González García, *Relaciones España-Israel y el Conflicto del Oriente Medio* (Madrid: Biblioteca Nueva, 2001).
5   AAPD 1965, Doc. 32, Cabinet Proposal of the Federal Foreign Office, 25 January 1965.
6   *Ibid.*
7   And whom in 1942 had taken part in an internal meeting of the Foreign Ministry to discuss the implementation of the policies agreed upon at the Wannsee Conference in the occupied territories, Conze et al., *Das Amt*, p. 528.
8   AAPD 1965, Doc. 56, Notes of the Ministerial Director Müller-Roschach, 5 February 1965.

9  Das Gupta, 'The Non-Aligned and the German Question', p. 153. See also PA AA, B7/46, *Fernschreiben, Federer,* 1 October 1964.

10  'Moskau setzte Nasser unter Druck', *Der Spiegel,* 10 February 1965, p. 22.

11  DARDDR 1965, Telegram Bolz (East Berlin) to Schröder (Bonn), 5 February 1965, p. 118.

12  CDU Bundesparteivorstand, Nr. 18, 9 February 1965, p. 822.

13  AAPD 1965, Doc. 58, Ambassador Knappstein (Washington) to the Foreign Office, 6 February 1965.

14  AAPD 1965, Doc. 74, Ambassador Knappstein (Washington) to State Secretary Carstens, 12 February 1965.

15  For an example of the intention to use the *Verjährungsdebatte* at the service of Bonn's *Alleinvertertungsanspruch* see, for example: AAPD 1965, Doc. 77, Notes of the Ministry Director Meyer-Lindenberg, 15 February 1965.

16  AAPD 1965, Doc. 84, Telegraphic Instructions State Secretary Carstens, 17 February 1965.

17  FRUS 1964–1968/XVIII, Arab-Israeli Dispute, Doc. 150, Telegram from the Embassy in Israel to the Department of State, 15 February 1965.

18  R. A. Blasius, '"Völkerfreundschaft" am Nil: Ägypten und die DDR im Februar 1965', *Vierteljahrshefte für Zeitgeschichte,* 46:4 (1998), pp. 747–805.

19  '"Du Lotte, der konnte nachts die Pyramiden sehn"', *Der Spiegel,* 1 December 1965, p. 72.

20  *Ibid.*

21  PA AA, B7/138, Soviet Agent in Germany – Walter Ulbricht, n.d. Annexed to: Krapf an alle diplomatischen und berufkonsularischen Vertretungen der Bundesrepublik Deutschland, 12 February 1965.

22  *Ibid.*

23  'Hallstein Doktrin in der Sackgasse', *ND,* 3 February 1965 and PA AA, MfAA C 912/20, Gedanken und Argumente zur Diplomatie des sozial. Deutschland, 9 August 1965.

24  '"Russisch half hier wenig": Lotte Ulbricht über den Staatsbesuch des SED-Regierungschefs am Nil', *Der Spiegel,* 1 December 1965, p. 68.

25  'Egypt's Tiger and Fox: Gamal Abdel Nasser', *New York Times,* 2 April 1956, p. 3.

26  Quoted in Blasius, 'Völkerfreundschaft', p. 777.

27  *Ibid.,* p. 778.

28  *Ibid.,* p. 784.

29  A. Orkaby, *Beyond the Arab Cold War: The International History of the Yemen Civil War* (New York: Oxford University Press, 2017).

30  H. Berghoff and U. A. Balbier, *The East German Economy, 1945–2010: Falling Behind or Catching Up?* (Cambridge: Cambridge University Press, 2013); A. Steiner, *The Plans That Failed: An Economic History of the GDR* (Oxford: Oxford University Press, 2010).

31  Blasius, 'Völkerfreundschaft', p. 781. In 1965 the overall GDR oil imports came from the UAR (2.1%) and from the USSR (97.9%). Wippel, *Die Außenwirtschaftsbeziehungen der DDR,* p. 48.

32  DADDR 1965, Interview der VAR-Zeitung 'Al Ahram' mit dem Vorsitzenden des Staatsrates der Deutschen Demokratischen Republik, Walter Ulbricht, über den Freundschaftsbesuch in der Vereinigten Arabischen Republik. Veröffentlicht am Februar 23, 1965, p. 847.

33  *Ibid.*

34  DADDR 1965, Interview des Allgemeinenen Deutschen Nachrichtendienstes (ADN) mit dem Ersten Stellvertreter des Ministers für Auswärtige Angelegenheiten der

Deutschen Demokratischen Republik, Staatssekretär Otto Winzer, über die Krise der westdeutschen Nahostpolitik. Veröffentlicht am Februar 23, 1965, p. 121.

35  *Ibid.*

36  *Ibid.*, p. 799.

37  M. G. Winrow, *Foreign Policy of the GDR in Africa* (Cambridge: Cambridge University Press, 1990), p. 69.

38  S.A. Scham, 'The Political Theatre of the Past: Visits by State Leaders to Archaeological and Historical Sites', *Journal of Eastern Mediterranean Archaeology and Heritage Studies* 1:1 (2013), pp. 66–87; S. Derix, 'Facing an "Emotional Crunch": State Visits as Political Performances During the Cold War', *German Politics and Society* 25:2 (2007), pp. 119 and 123.

39  ' "Russisch half hier wenig": Lotte Ulbricht über den Staatsbesuch des SED-Regierungschefs am Nil', *Der Spiegel*, 1 December 1965, p. 68.

40  DADDR 1965, Rundfunk- und Fernsehinterview, 7 March 1965, p. 866.

41  *Ibid.*, p. 872.

42  E.g. 'Deutsche Kernphysiker in Israel', *Frankfurter Rundschau*, 26 October 1964; 'Defence aid to Israel from Germany', *The Times*, 30 October 1964.

43  K. Birrenbach, *Meine Sondermissionen: Rückblick auf zwei Jahrzehnte bundesdeutsche Außenpolitik* (Düsseldorf: Econ, 1984), p. 101.

44  H. Scott, 'George McGhee: Oilman, Scholar, Diplomat – America's Ambassador to West Germany', *The Stars and Stripes*, 1 December 1963, p. 11.

45  Georgetown University Archive (GUA), George C. McGhee Papers, McGhee Scrapbooks, Box 5.

46  Quoted in H. Osterheld, *Aussenpolitik unter Bundeskanzler Ludwig Erhard, 1963–1966: Ein dokumentarischer Bericht aus der Kanzleramt* (Düsseldorf: Droste, 1992), pp. 171 and 166, respectively.

47  R. Zundel, 'Regisseur der CDU-Fraktion. Will Rasner halt "Stall wache" in Bonn', *Die Zeit*, 31 July 1959.

48  Gray, *Germany's Cold War*, p. 292, fn. 26.

49  DADDR 1965, Erklärung der Regierung der Deutschen Demokratischen Republik vom 14. Mai 1965 zur Aufnahme diplomatischer Beziehungen zwischen der Bundesrepublik Deutschland und Israel, p. 146.

50  *Ibid.*

51  K. Storkmann, *Geheime Solidarität: Militärbeziehungen und Militärhilfen der DDR in die 'Dritte Welt'* (Berlin: Links, 2012), p. 183.

52  DADDR 1965, Bericht des Politbüros an das 10. Plenum des ZK der SED, erstattet von Hermann Axen, Kandidat des Politbüros, am Juni 23, 1965, p. 166.

53  Osterheld, *Aussenpolitik*, p. 172.

54  NARA, RG 59, ANF 64–66, Box 2226, McGhee (Bonn) to the Secretary of State, 11 March 1965.

55  *Ibid.*, Akins (Baghdad) to the Secretary of State, 11 November 1964.

56  *Ibid.*, Rountree (Khartoum) to the Secretary of State, 13 March 1965; Hart (Jidda) to the Secretary of State, 19 March 1965; Barnes (Amman) to the Secretary of State, 24 March 1965.

57  NARA, RG 59, ANF 64–66, Box 2226 Palmer (Tel Aviv) to the Secretary of State, 13 April 1965.

58  N. Lorch (ed.), *Major Knesset Debates, 1948–1981*, Sitting 460 of the Fifth Knesset, 16 March 1965, p. 1,429.

59  *Ibid.*, p. 1439.

60  *Ibid.*, p. 1454.

61  NARA, RG 59, ANF 64–66, Box 2,205, Memorandum of Conversation, 'German Relations with Near Eastern and North African Countries', 7 April 1965.

62  Hannelore Siegel, interview with the author, Cologne, 20 July 2015.

63  NARA, RG 59, ANF 64–66, Box 2,205, Memorandum of Conversation, Boeker-Davies.

64  177. Cabinet meeting, 25 August 1965, *Die Kabinettsprotokolle der Bundesregierung.*

65  G. Meir, *My Life* (London: Futura, 1979), p. 144.

66  NARA, RG 59, ANF 64–66, Box 2,226, Mouser (Bonn) to State Department, 20 May 1965.

67  NARA, RG 59, ANF 64–66, Box 2,226, Hillenbrand (Bonn) to the Secretary of State, 3 August 1965.

68  A. Ben-Natan, *The Audacity to Live* (Jerusalem: Mazo Publishers, 2007), p. 92.

69  Vogel, *The German Path to Israel.*

70  *Ibid.*

71  J. Hestermann, *Inszenierte Versöhnung: Reisediplomatie und die deutsch-israelische Beziehungen von 1957 bis 1984* (Frankfurt: Campus Verlag, 2006), esp. pp. 119–41.

72  StBKAH, B2 52, Adenauer to Goldmann, 12 May 1966.

73  G. Laron, *The Six-Day War: The Breaking of the Middle East* (New Haven: Yale University Press, 2017), pp. 89ff.

74  'Israel Reiterates Its Support for Poland's Present Boundaries', JTA *Daily News Bulletin*, 13 May 1966, p. 1.

75  For details on the agreement see Fink, *West Germany and Israel*, pp. 40ff.; Feldman, *The Special Relationship between West Germany and Israel*, pp. 104ff.

76  *Ibid.*

77  PA AA: MfAA A 13355, Report of the ADN Correspondent in Havana: Diplomatic offensive of the Israeli Embassy in Havana, 15 June 1965. On earlier anti-Bonn East German propaganda in Cuba see PA AA B6 71, New campaign of the Soviet zone against members of the Federal Foreign Service. Raab, 12 January 1962.

78  'Bonn's Mideast Muddle', *New York Times*, 16 February 1965. For a brief overview of Israel–Cuba relations see M. Bejarano, 'Israel and Cuba: A New Beginning?', *Israel Journal of Foreign Affairs* 9:1 (2015), pp. 75–85.

79  J. McKay, *The Official Concept of the Nation in the former GDR: Theory, Pragmatism and the Search for Legitimacy* (Aldershot: Ashgate, 1998), p. 19.

80  Herf, *Undeclared Wars.*

81  SAPMO-BA, DY 30/IV A2/20.832, Ministry of Foreign Affairs Information Department, 'Some Aspects of Israel's Foreign Policy and the GDR's Position Toward Israel', 10 February 1966.

82  BStU, MfS, SdM, 1465, Protocol of the negotiations between representatives of the MfS of the GDR and the KfS at the Council of Ministers of the USSR on common proactive measures for the year 1967, n.d.

83  NARA, RG 59, ANF 64–66, Box 2205, Battle (Cairo) to the Secretary of State, 7 June 1966.

84  Gray, *Germany's Cold War*, p. 201.

85  AAPD 1967, Doc. 136, Memorandum of Conversation, Brandt- Hassouna, 21 April 1967.

86  LOC, Averell Harriman Papers 432/10, Burns (Amman) to the Secretary of State, 12 December 1966.

87  Laron, *The Six-Day War*, p. 49ff.

88  Cable, UN Secretary General to the Commander of UNEF, 18 May 1967, reprinted in Directorate of History, Canadian Forces Headquarters, Report N. 16, *The Withdrawal of UNEF from Egypt*, 1 April 1968. www.canada.ca/content/dam/themes/defence/caf/militaryhistory/dhh/reports/cfhq-reports/book-egypt-unef-1967-en.pdf [Accessed November 2019].

89  AAPD 1967, Doc. 188, Memorandum of Conversation Brandt-Ben-Natan, 29 May 1967.

90  AAPD 1967, Doc. 190, Notes of Director Meyer-Lindenberg re: Conversation Brandt-Ben-Natan, 29 May 1967.

91  M. Oren, *Six Days of War: 1967 and the Making of the Modern Middle East* (Oxford: Oxford University Press, 2002); T. Segev, *1967: Israel, the War and the Year that Transformed the Middle East* (New York: Metropolitan Books, 2007); I. Ginor and G. Ramez, *Foxbats over Dimona: The Soviets' Nuclear Gamble in the Six-Day War* (New Haven: Yale University Press, 2007); Laron, *The Six-Day War*.

92  Sitzung, Deutscher Bundestag, 7 June 1967. For a detailed analysis of the political debate in the FRG, and of the reaction of the public, see Fink, *West Germany and Israel*, p. 55ff. as well as the dated, but still relevant, Lavy, *Germany and Israel*, p. 150ff.

93  BStU, MfS, HA XVIII, Nr. 7,622, Department XVIII/7, Information – Nr. 2, Kulka, 9 June 1967.

94  *Ibid.*

95  BStU, MfS, SdM, 12, Report of the Minister of National Defense to the National Defense Council of the German Democratic Republic on the agenda item: 'Conclusions for the Defense of the German Democratic Republic resulting from the Israeli aggression against the Arab states'.

96  S. McMeeking, *The Berlin-Baghdad Express: The Ottoman Empire and Germany's Bid for World Power* (Cambridge, MA: The Belknap Press of Harvard University Press, 2010).

97  BStU, MfS, ZAIG 4624, The Aggression committed by Israel against the Arab countries and the American Global Strategy, 30 August 1967.

98  Bundesarchiv Online, DW 1/39486, 29. Sitzung des NVR am 01. September 1967. www.argus.bstu.bundesarchiv.de/DVW1_NVR/mets/DVW1_NVR_39486/index.htm?target=midosaFraContent&backlink=/argus-bstu/DVW1_NVR/index.htm-kid-48095897-ad24-457a-bc41-c78f4f7adac8&sign=DVW%201/39486 [Accessed November 2019].

99  J. Bielesch, *Zur Strategie und Taktik des Aggressors Israel im Krieg gegen die arabischen Staaten im Juni 1967 – die Schlußfolgerungen für die Erhöhung der Verteidigungsbereitschaft der Volksmarine*, Thesis Defended at the University of the Ministry for State Security (Stasi) on 3 January 1969.

100  For an overview, see Raphael Vago (ed.), *Romania-Israel: Diplomatic Documents, 1948–1969* (Bucharest: Romanian Ministry of Foreign Affairs, 2013).

101  SAPMO-BA, NY 4182/1206, Ulbricht to Brezhnev, 14 June 1967.

102  'Aufrichtige Freundschaft mit Araberstaaten', *ND*, 12 June 1967, p. 1.

103  While the FRG had supported the Israeli arms procurement efforts in the run-up to the war – and Israel's heavily armoured tanks played a key role in the war – the deliveries of Skyhawks, Mirages, Ouragan and Super Frelons agreed upon by the United States and France between 1964 and 1967 were much more substantial than the West German deliveries and played a key role in guaranteeing Israel's victory in the Six Day War. A. Gluska, *The Israeli Military and the Origins of the 1967 War: Government, Armed Forces and Defence Policy, 1963–1967* (London: Routledge, 2007).

104 ISA/RG 103.1/MFA/4081/20 Israeli Embassy (Bonn) to the Ministry of Foreign Affairs (Jerusalem), N. Hadas, 23 June 1967. www.archives.gov.il/archives/#/Archive/0b0717068031bdef/File/0b07170680b34828 [Accessed March 2020]. On Hadas's information-gathering efforts regarding the two Germanys' readings of the Six Day War, see I. Ginor and G. Remez, *Foxbats Over Dimona: The Soviets' Nuclear Gamble in the Six-Day War* (New Haven: Yale University Press, 2007), pp. 164–5.

105 Herf, *Undeclared Wars*.

106 BStU, MfS, SdM, 1465, Proposal for the reception of the Minister of the Interior of the Republic of Iraq by Comrade Mielke, 8 October 1969.

107 Lamont Library, Harvard University, Archives of the Soviet Communist Party and Soviet State: Russian State Archive of Contemporary History (RGANI) Collection, fond 2, opis 3, delo 64, reel 108, Central Committee Meeting of the CPSU, 6 June 1967, translated by Marcus Chavasse.

108 *Ibid.*

109 *Ibid.*

110 M. S. Daoudi and M. S. Dajani, 'The 1967 Oil Embargo Revisited', *Journal of Palestine Studies* 13:2 (1984), pp. 65–90; AAPD 1967, Doc. 257, Ministerialdirektor Meyer-Lindenberg an die Botschaft in Paris, 11 July 1967.

111 A. Ben-Natan, *Briefe an den Botschafter* (Frankfurt: Ullstein, 1972).

112 Deutschkron, *Israel und die Deutschen*, pp. 330ff.

113 Asher Ben-Natan, interview with the author, Ramat Ha Sharon (Tel Aviv), 20 January 2014.

114 'Sonderbotschafter Dr. Weiß in Kairo', *ND*, 7 July 1967, p. 1.

115 AAPD 1967, Doc. 283, Aufzeichnung des Ministerialdirektors Meyer-Lindenberg, 27 July 1967.

116 C. D. Smith, *Palestine and the Arab-Israeli Conflict: A History with Documents* (Boston: Bedford/St. Martin's, 2007), p. 307.

117 AAPD 1967, Doc. 320, Aufzeichnung des Ministerialdirektors Meyer-Lindenberg, 15 September 1967.

118 Deutscher Bundestag, Stenographische Berichten, Vol. 64, p. 5732.

119 AAPD 1968, Doc. 50, Gespräch zwischen Duckwitz und Cabani, 8 February 1968, fn. 6.

120 See AAPD 1968, Doc. 34, Legationsrat I. Klasse Harder, Kairo, an das Auswärtige Amt, 29 January 1968; AAPD 1968, Doc. 126, Botschafter Hille, Amman, an das Auswärtige Amt, 11 April 1968; AAPD 1968, Doc. 167: Botschafter Böker, z.Z. Bagdad, an Staatssekretär Duckwitz, 17 May 1968 for examples of the West German dialogue with Egypt, Jordan, and Iraq, and on Bonn's reaching out to the Arab League see in the same volume Doc. 50, Gespräch des Staatsekeretärs Duckwitz mit dem Leider des Bros der Arabischen Liga, Cabani, 8 February 1968.

121 See, e.g., AAPD 1968, Doc. 168: Notes of State Secretary Lahrs, 22 May 1968.

122 A. Kemp-Welch, 'Eastern Europe: Stalinism to Solidarity', in Kieran Williams, *The Prague Spring and its Aftermath: Czechoslovak Politics, 1968–1970* (Cambridge: Cambridge University Press, 1997).

123 Quoted in AAPD 1968, Doc: 267 Knoke (Tel Aviv) to the Foreign Office, 23 August 1968.

124 CIA Intelligence Memorandum, *Third World Reaction to Soviet Invasion of Czechoslovakia*, 17 September 1968. www.cia.gov/library/readingroom/docs/DOC_0000126875.pdf [Accessed November 2019].

# Conclusion: German–Israeli relations between past and future

'We can look back on what we have achieved and, without exaggerating, call it a miracle', declared Bundeskanzler Angela Merkel in an interview marking the fiftieth anniversary of diplomatic relations between Israel and the Federal Republic of Germany. But can we?[1] This book has analysed the genesis of such a 'miracle', focusing instead on the contradictions and dilemmas that characterised so much of German and Israeli foreign policy during the 1950s and 1960s. It has examined how and why the historic rapprochement was achieved between Bonn and the Jewish state, and not East Berlin and Israel; and how and why it was achieved against the backdrop of the German Cold War and the intensifying Arab–Israeli conflict. By doing so, this study has placed the origins of the entente between West Germany and Israel, and the estrangement between the GDR and the Jewish state, within the context of the global Cold War.

The Cold War or, rather, invocations of its importance for German *Israelpolitik*, influenced Bonn's and East Berlin's stance towards Israel in complex ways. In the wake of the enunciation of the Hallstein Doctrine in 1955, the federal Foreign Office's Middle East experts intensified their warnings against formalising Bonn's ties with Israel. For example, FRG ambassador to Egypt Walther Becker, in 1956, emphasised that the question of relations with Israel constituted a 'negative mark' for the West German reputation in the Egypt, and the Arab Middle East at large,[2] and the head of the Foreign Office's Middle East Department, Voigt, repeatedly stressed that the question of relations with Israel was closely interconnected to that of possible GDR advances in the region.[3] Hallstein himself was initially sceptical about the existence of a nexus between West German–Israeli relations and the global isolation campaign against East Berlin. So too was Wilhelm Grewe, the prime mover behind Bonn's foreign political doctrine. The insistence of diplomats stationed from Cairo to Islamabad, however, convinced them both that such a nexus existed. And the Chancellor, too, came to appreciate the risks that exchanging ambassadors with Israel might involve for Bonn's Cold War against the GDR. In 1958, Khrushchev's Berlin ultimatum gave rise to a sense of unease in Bonn's political circles, and the Eisenhower Doctrine undermined the West's appeal in the Middle East.[4] Within such a complex international scenario, Adenauer came to fear that the negative effects for the FRG of an exchange of ambassadors with Israel would extend well beyond the realm of Bonn's relations with the Arab world.[5]

The West German diplomats who, from the early 1950s onwards, had insistently advocated keeping the Jewish state at a distance had all served in the Foreign Office during the Nazi era. Most of them had been stationed in the Arab Middle East just at a time in which Hitler's Reich attempted to mobilise a global *jihad*.[6] The level of continuity of personnel between the pre- and post-war diplomatic service testifies to the relevance of what Norbert Frei has termed the 'politics of the past' (*Vergangenheitspolitik*) of the Adenauer government.[7] Nonetheless, the *Arabisten*'s stance on Israel implied something more than a continuation of pre-war anti-Semitism by other means. Their warnings on the Cold War relevance of Bonn's *Israelpolitik* were gradually accepted by the highest levels of Bonn's foreign policy echelons. After the 1956 Istanbul Conference, their arguments dictated Bonn's stance on the question of relations with Israel for a decade. It was they who drew the connection between German–German Cold War rivalry and Bonn's ties to the Jewish state. SED cadres adopted it, too, and emphasised West German–Israeli closeness to woo their Arab interlocutors. The *Arabisten*'s ability to persuade both West and East German foreign policy framers that a connection between the German–German Cold War and *Israelpolitik* existed, also testifies to just how malleable the concept of a rigid Cold War system was, in either Germany. It emphasises how issues that originally had little to do with the Cold War, such as postwar German–Israeli relations sparked by the Israeli request to receive compensation for Nazi crimes against the Jews, could be cast as crucially interwoven with it.[8]

In the GDR, Cold War constraints crucially shaped *Israelpolitik* concerns. In the early 1950s, the huge amount of reparations that the Soviet Union took from East Germany meant that the GDR would not have been in the position to make *Wiedergutmachung* payments to Israel. And, especially during Stalin's years, GDR leaders would hardly have been able to pursue a radically different policy than that adopted by the Soviet superpower. After 1948, Moscow soon abandoned its initial pro-Israeli stance, and this influenced the GDR's approach to the region, at a time in which the German–German competition intensified. The Arab Middle East seemed to offer concrete prospects for advancing the East German claim that the GDR, too, was a legitimate German state, which could conclude economic, and perhaps one day also political, deals with countries outside of its own bloc.

The GDR's *Israelpolitik* was clearly influenced by, and in turn aimed to influence, the German–German Cold War rivalry. East German representatives planned to woo their Arab counterparts by adopting a fierce anti-Zionist and anti-Israeli stance. This was especially visible during Ulbricht's visit to Cairo in 1965 – but it was a development that dated back to the early 1950s. The very first article published in the SED's mouthpiece to comment upon the *Wiedergutmachung* agreement denounced the very dangerous implications that the deal had for the peaceful coexistence of Arabs and Israelis in the Middle East. As SAPMO files illustrate, East German representatives received, and studied, documents forwarded to them from Moscow, that Arab League representatives sent to Bonn to illustrate their reasons for protesting the Luxemburg Agreement. Successive East German defamations of West German–Israeli ties pointed to the consistent material support that Bonn gave to Israel by means of its restitutions. Such themes were reiterated in the wake of the Suez Crisis, the 1958 Crises and the Six Day War. Although Bonn had played a limited role in either of these situations, East German propaganda portrayed the FRG as sternly supporting the enemies of the Arab states. GDR press organs constantly referred to Bonn's *Wiedergutmachung* to Israel, using it as evidence of the anti-Arab stance of the FRG, in contrast to the GDR. Yet East German *Israelpolitik* formulations gradually began referring to broader issues, too. These included, for example, East Berlin's support for anti-colonial struggles in and beyond the Middle East, and the GDR's commitment to protecting the common good of the German people as a whole. The significance of these points, expressed when expounding the GDR's *Israelpolitik*, extended beyond the mere rationalisation of East Berlin's approach towards a third country. Rather, these issues summoned the key pillars of the self-definition of the GDR in international politics during a Cold War which increasingly became entangled with other types of conflicts – such as the Arab–Israeli wars, or the anti-colonial struggles.

This book has demonstrated that questions of *Israelpolitik* raised issues that, for both Germanys, were uniquely related to conflicts that existed independently of, but shaped and were shaped by, the bipolar confrontation. The early interactions between German and Israeli diplomats took place in the wake of the Israeli request for restitution for the crimes committed by the Nazis against the Jews. Therefore, the way in which either Germany negotiated the legacy of Nazism featured prominently in the early encounters between German and Israeli representatives. The Arab protests against German restitutions to Israel later translated into broader wariness regarding the strengthening of West German–Israeli ties and, especially after 1955, the two Germanys began taking into account the reverberations that their actions towards Israel might have vis-à-vis the Arab countries.

## The German Cold War and the legacy of the Nazi past

*Israelpolitik* matters expose the contradictions that characterised the policies of the two Germanys towards a country that posed them with unique challenges, related both to the present and to the legacy of Nazism. West Germany paid financial restitution to Israel for Nazi crimes, while East Germany did not. Bonn transferred financial aid and weapons to Israel, while East Berlin engaged in rampant anti-Israeli propaganda. West Germany established full diplomatic relations with Israel, while East Germany never did. Nevertheless, one issue bound both Germanys' *Israelpolitik* together: namely, the necessity of representatives of both Germanys to explain, and justify, their relationship with the past and the legacy of Nazism when dealing with *Israelpolitik* matters. Notwithstanding significant differences both in East and West German discourses on the Nazi past and in the stances that East and West Germany adopted towards Israel, representatives from both Germanys explained their *Israelpolitik* by putting forth specific explanations of the legacy of Nazism. No other country presented German representatives with such complexity in seeking to reconcile past legacy with present interests.

Both Germanys attributed pivotal importance to spreading specific messages on their attitude to the Nazi past, and this aspect was central to both Germanys' *Israelpolitik* and to the self-definition of each Germany within the Cold War system.

While works dealing with the politics of memory and commemoration in divided Germany generally focus their analysis on examining monuments, memorials, commemoration ceremonies and similar, diplomatic cables, too, can reveal a great deal about the discourse that either Germany put forth about the Nazi past, and its relevance for the (then) present. Adenauer soon understood that portraying his Germany as ready to pay for the consequences of the criminal policies of the Nazis could ease the FRG's entrance into the family of nations. At the same time, as he emphasised in his 1951 Bundestag speech, *Wiedergutmachung* did not imply admittance of a German collective guilt.[9] And he did not refrain from stressing, in front of Israeli representative Shinnar, or his own Cabinet, the urgency of halting trials against Nazi criminals, because of the issues these created to the FRG's public image internationally.[10]

While BND files on the matter are still largely classified, CIA records declassified under the FOIA, and certain federal Foreign Office files, do illustrate the brainstorming, among West German representatives, regarding how to speak of the Nazi past in the early 1960s, as the Eichmann trial approached. Moreover, while East German propaganda continuously stressed the links between Bonn and the Nazi past, West German representatives talked of the 'National-Bolshevists' in the East, and of the GDR's 'spiritual continuation with Nazism' when dealing with Israeli interlocutors.[11] Despite important differences between the uses of the Nazi past in the two German states, the evidence presented in this book shows that West German officials, too, viewed the legacy of Nazism as something that could be used as leverage for political benefits – either to fend off East German attacks, or to resist Israeli pressure on troublesome issues. Indeed, the utilisation of the past was integral to the diplomatic efforts of both German states.

*Israelpolitik* and the East German institutional memory of the Nazi past were also closely interlinked. The SED alleged, for example, that the *Wiedergutmachung* agreement benefited the big monopolists in West Germany and Israel, the same ones who had produced Zyklon B for the gas chambers of the extermination camps.[12] Arguments such as this, in turn, aimed to justify East Berlin's not paying restitutions to the Jewish state. The official memory of the Nazi past, and the recurring denunciations of the continuities between Adenauer's Bundesrepublik and Hitler's Reich, were supposed to give the impression that the GDR had little reason for having to make good for the crimes committed by the Nazis. This translated onto the official East German justifications as to why East Berlin did not have to engage in *Wiedergutmachung* talks with Israeli representatives. Discourses on the past could, and did, serve very important functions in the international domain – and they could be, and were, used as a tool against international competitors.[13]

# Intra-bloc constraints

Studying the German *Israelpolitik* considerations also highlights the complexity of the relationship of each Germany with the respective superpower. For example, Mohamed Heikal, Nasser's friend and confidant, and editor-in-chief of one of the oldest and most important Egyptian newspapers, *Al Ahram*, recalled that 'Adenauer was … ordered by Kennedy to give arms to Israel'.[14] He also claimed that the West German ambassador to Egypt justified Bonn's decision to sign the *Wiedergutmachung* agreement by pointing out that 'this is not Germany's will', and that '[West] Germany behaved according to the dictates of the allies, especially America'.[15] Speaking to the executive of the CDU/CSU in 1965, Adenauer himself seemed to confirm, at least partially, Heikal's version of the events. 'About the question of the arms transfers I would like to say the following: it was at the Americans' request'.[16] Authors of the calibre of Klaus Hildebrand ('the foremost historian of German diplomacy')[17] have claimed that Washington was the initiator of the arms transfer arrangements between West Germany and Israel.[18] But the question of an Allied – especially US – intervention pushing Bonn to supply weapons or material compensation to the State of Israel is much more complex than Heikal's and Adenauer's claims might suggest. As chapters 1, 5 and 7 illustrated, it is not correct to argue that West Germany concluded the Luxemburg Agreement, or the weapons transfer deals, in spite of the will of its Western allies.[19] And, while at several points the Allies did urge Bonn to conclude the agreement, the initial phases of West German–Israeli interactions were not the result of unidirectional Allied or superpower pressure on Bonn's policy makers. Nor was Adenauer's initial statement on his Germany's determination to 'make good again' with the Jews the result of Allied demands, nor were the initial talks of arms transfers between the two countries.

In the East, as fellow Warsaw Pact countries recognised, the case of East Berlin's *Israelpolitik* was unique. Within the Soviet bloc, several countries were interested in using such uniqueness as a spearhead to help the socialist advance in the countries of the Arab Middle East. While Moscow seemed mostly willing to restrain the GDR's outreach to the Arab capitals – for example by restricting it to economic, rather than political, matters – fellow socialist countries instead intervened to restrain the GDR's gestures towards Israel that, in their view, Arab representatives might interpret as being too friendly. This was the case, for example, in the run-up to Kaul's attempts to be at the forefront of the East German involvement in the Eichmann trial, when Hungarian, Czechoslovak, Polish and Romanian representatives expressed their concern over East German activism on the matter, and their opinion mattered for at least two reasons. First, because the structure of the East German economy meant that the GDR needed to import raw materials from fellow COMECON countries, below world market prices, to foster the export of manufactured goods to the countries of the Arab Middle East.[20] Thus, the backing of fellow Socialist countries was vital to sustain East German foreign trade with the Levant. Second, given that the GDR's diplomatic and consular representations were not particularly numerous until the mid 1960s, the representative offices of fellow Soviet bloc countries, especially Czechoslovakia,[21] provided crucial support in spreading East German propaganda internationally. And, most importantly, in the run-up to 1965 Soviet intercession was crucial to obtaining Ulbricht's invitation to Cairo, finally rewarding East Berlin's intentions to persuade, slowly but surely, the Kremlin into supporting Ulbricht's political ambitions.[22]

## Global and regional power dynamics

This book has argued that the geostrategic acrobatics of either Germany were aimed at ensuring that their *Israelpolitik* would not negatively impact on their own Cold War and, vice versa, that their Cold War rivalry would not hamper their political and economic advancements in the Middle East.[23] The historical-political context in which the *Wiedergutmachung* agreement of 1952 was signed saw both parties, the Federal Republic and Israel, involved in their own existential conflicts, against their respective nemeses. In other words, Israel's and Bonn's enemies read the agreement in terms of the conflicts they were involved in, even though these had little to do with the West German–Israeli negotiations.

Arab perceptions, and the accompanying public attacks, meant that the Luxemburg Agreement came to symbolise a Western decision to take Israel's side, yet again.[24] Nasser often insisted on this point, perhaps most memorably during his speech on the nationalisation of the Suez Canal. Then, he explicitly mentioned the Luxemburg Agreement as a sign of Western support for Israel.[25] East German press organs went a step further and argued that the Luxemburg Agreement would harm both the German and the Middle Eastern peoples. The press organs of the GDR portrayed the agreement as a betrayal of the German population, subjected to yet another costly reparation treaty on behalf of the Bonn government – and emphasised that the agreement was tantamount to a 'preparation for mass murder in the Middle East'.[26] Despite all of its propaganda efforts, however, the GDR failed to exchange ambassadors with the Arab Middle East for the first twenty years of its existence, as Bonn successfully dictated its own political priorities to the Arab leaders and was able to influence the policies of several regional powers, in its attempt to ensure that they would not negatively impact upon Bonn's Cold War against East Berlin.

The interplay between Arab–Israeli hatreds and Cold War dynamics ran deeper and started earlier than is generally understood. Authors such as Fawaz Gerges and Odd Arne Westad have long claimed that Cold War dynamics heightened tension in the region and that the bipolar rivalry 'created international frameworks that made the internal conflicts in the region more difficult to solve'.[27] Yet the literature assessing the relative prominence of bipolar versus local dynamics generally focuses on the interactions of the two superpowers with regional players. Authors dealing with German–German interactions with the Middle East concentrate on the post-1955 period – i.e. the enunciation of the Hallstein Doctrine and its consequences. But the onset of the German–German rivalry in the Middle East, too, translated into a Cold War intrusion into regional politics, which exacerbated local dynamics even before 1955, further irritating the already strained relations between Israel and its Arab neighbours against West German and American wishes.[28] This was not the intention of the Bonn government – quite the contrary.[29] However, the attitude that one or the other Germany adopted towards Israel could be used to portray the German state in question as taking sides within the Arab–Israeli conflict, as Bonn's diplomats warned, and East German politicians understood. And understanding them is crucial if one intends, vis-à-vis the latest developments within Cold War historiography, to 're-assess and re-emphasise the place of Europe in the global Cold War' and 'to demarcate Germany's place and role in it'.[30]

## The End-*ing*[31]

Following Ulbricht's Middle Eastern travels, the Arab recognition of the GDR and the opening of the West German embassy in Israel, unresolved questions and unsatisfactory answers related to the evolving German–Israeli relationship, and to the overlap between German–German and Arab–Israeli rivalries, remained. During the late 1960s, the 1970s and for most of the 1980s, East Germany was one of the prime suppliers of weapons to Israel's bitterest enemies.[32] In 1973, the GDR was the first state to welcome a diplomatic representation of the Palestinian Liberation Organization on its territory – two years before the USSR.[33] Only after decades of covert and overt antagonism, in April 1990, did the East German government present an official apology to the Jewish state. It beseeched 'the Israeli people to forgive us for the hypocrisy and hostility in GDR policy towards the Israeli state [and] to forgive us for the persecution and degradation Jewish citizens were exposed to in our country, even after 1945'.[34] But it was too late. On 3 October 1990, Germany was reunified, and the GDR passed into history.

Today, the Federal Republic is the recipient of recognition and trust from both sides of the Middle East conflict. And the country's unique ability to engage countries as diverse as Iran, Turkey and Israel, both bilaterally and within the EU, characterises Germany's position in the region. In this context, the significance and uniqueness of the first two decades of *Israelpolitik*, and of German–German competition in the Middle East more broadly, should not be underestimated. Rather than neglecting the German Democratic Republic as a Soviet relic to be swept into the dustbin of history, the extensive archival evidence available since the fall of the Berlin Wall clearly shows that the Federal Republic's experience of diplomacy in the region (and beyond) was crucially shaped by the competition with its former nemesis, especially in the first two decades of its existence. The analysis of this seminal period in the evolution of German–Israeli relations in particular, and of German foreign policy more broadly, is therefore not only crucial to understanding the Cold War and Germany's role within it – both in the respective bloc and in the Middle East – but it also offers a new lens for understanding contemporary political developments.

Processes of (inter)national reconciliation – including, but not limited to, the German–Israeli case – are not defined by overall constant harmony. Rather, they are supported by the existence of cooperative frameworks that allow countries or groups to manage or resolve differences. As later events illustrate only too well, the formalisation of diplomatic relations between the Federal Republic and Israel in 1965 did not reduce the difficulties characterising much of the 'special relationship'. These included the mutual recriminations in the wake of the 1973 war;[35] sorrow and outrage following the massacre of the members of the Israeli Olympic team at the hand of Black September terrorists in Munich in 1972, later released by the Bonn government without even consulting the Israeli authorities;[36] and the accusations that Israeli Prime Minister Menachem Begin made against Chancellor Helmut Schmidt in February 1982, reminding him in particular of 'what his countrymen perpetrated under the National Socialist regime against my country at the time when Mr Schmidt remained faithful to the personal oath he had given to Adolf Hitler as a soldier and officer in his army'.[37] The efforts towards a 'normalisation' of such ties did not represent an end to the many problems that characterised German–Israeli relations, marking instead one episode within a continuing story of recriminations, cooperation and conflict complicated by the legacy of a difficult past. But while the GDR until the 1980s intensified its anti-Israeli message and policies, the long and complex process of West German–Israeli reconciliation that had taken place against the backdrop of global Cold War tensions, fierce German–German rivalry, and successive Middle Eastern wars, would never be reversed.[38]

# Notes

1 'Angela Merkel on 50 Years of German-Israeli Relations', https://archived.wixsite.com/de50il-eng/blank [Accessed November 2019].

2 PA AA, B2 94/150, Ambassador Becker: Political report on Egypt, n.d.

3 'Referat von Generalkonsul I, Voigt, AA, über die politische Lage im Nahen Osten', 23 January 1956. In Jelinek, *Zwischen Moral und Realpolitik: deutsch-israelische Beziehungen 1945–1965*, pp. 368–9.

4 Fursenko and Naftali, *Khrushchev's Cold War*; Yaqub, *Containing Arab Nationalism*.

5 See chapter 5.

6 Motadel, *Islam and Nazi Germany's War*; Becker, 'Post-War Antisemitism'.

7 Frei, *Adenauer's Germany and the Nazi Past*.

8 Stephanson, 'Fourteen Notes on the Very Concept of the Cold War'.

9 Deutscher Bundestag, 165. Sitzung, Bonn, 27 September 1951, p. 6,698. http://dipbt.bundestag.de/doc/btp/01/01165.pdf [Accessed November 2019]. K. Jaspers, *The Question of German Guilt* (New York: Dial Press, 1947).

10 See chapter 7.

11 PA AA, B 12 1019, Notation. Weber, 7 January 1960.

12 R. Herrnstadt, '"Wiedergutmachung" – für wen?', *ND*, 25 November 1952, p. 1.

13 T. Hopf, *Reconstructing the Cold War: The Early Years, 1945–1958* (Oxford: Oxford University Press, 2012), p. 26.

14 M. Heikal, *Nasser: The Cairo Documents* (London: New English Library, 1972), p. 294.

15 *Ibid.*, p. 292.

16 Quoted in Buchstab, *Adenauer: 'Stetigkeit in der Politik'*, 9 February 1965, p. 869.

17  Gray, *Germany's Cold War*, p. 7.

18  Hildebrand, *Von Erhard zur Großen Koalition* (Stuttgart: Deutsche Verlags-Anstalt, 1984), p. 112; M. Wolffsohn, *Ewige Schuld? 40 Jahre deutsch-jüdisch-israelische Beziehungen* (Munich: Piper, 1991), p. 32.

19  M. Wolffsohn, 'Das deutsch-israelische Wiedergutmachungsabkommen von 1952 im internationalen Zusammenhang', *Vierteljahrshefte für Zeitgeschichte* 36:4 (1988), pp. 691–731.

20  BAK B 206/619, Statements by the new deputy foreign minister of the 'GDR', Sepp Schwab, 7 July 1956; Lorenzini, 'Comecon and the South in the Years of Détente'; R. Ahrens, 'Debt, Cooperation and Collapse: East German Foreign Trade in the Honecker Years' in H. Berghoff and U. A. Balbier (eds), *The East German Economy, 1945–2010: Falling Behind or Catching Up?* (Cambridge: Cambridge University Press, 2004), p. 161.

21  See Bontschek, *Die Tschechoslowakei und die DDR*. See also Wentker, *Außenpolitik*, pp. 89–108. Contrast the Czechoslovak–East German relations with those between the GDR and Poland: S. R. Anderson, *A Cold War in the Soviet Bloc: Polish-East German Relations, 1945–1962* (Boulder: Westview Press, 2001).

22  Harrison, *Driving the Soviets Up the Wall*.

23  On the Cold War and the Middle East see, for example, N. J. Ashton, 'Introduction: The Cold War in the Middle East, 1967–1973' in N. J. Ashton (ed.), *The Cold War in the Middle East: Regional Conflict and the Superpowers, 1967–1973* (London: Routledge, 2007), p. 11. On why 'the Cold War "belongs" to the Middle East' see also Westad, 'Foreword' in M. Trentin (ed.), *The Middle East and the Cold War: Between Security and Development* (Newcastle: Cambridge Scholars, 2012), pp. vii–ix.

24  Even though in the early 1950s the attitude of Washington's policy makers was hardly pro-Israeli. See, for example, Bass, *Support Any Friend*, pp. 15–49 (on the situation 'inherited' by Kennedy); and D. Little, *American Orientalism: The United States and the Middle East since 1945* (Chapel Hill: University of North Carolina Press, 2002), pp. 77–116.

25  Documents on International Affairs 1956, 'Speech by President Nasser at Alexandria announcing the nationalization of the Suez Canal Company, 26 July 1956', p. 99.

26  For example in M. Amino, 'General Robertson mußte die Dienstbotentreppe benutzen', *ND*, 8 March 1951, p. 4; Interview des Allgemeinen Deutschen Nachrichtendienstes (ADN) mit dem Ersten Stellvertreter des Ministers für Auswärtige Angelegenheiten der Deutschen Demokratischen Republik, Staatssekretär Otto Winzer, über die Krise der westdeutschen Nahostpolitik. Veröffentlicht am 23. February 1965, DADDR, 1965, p. 121ff.

27  F. Gerges, *The Superpowers and the Middle East: Regional and International Politics, 1955–1967* (Boulder: Westview Press, 1994); see O. A. Westad's foreword to M. Trentin (ed.), *The Middle East and the Cold War: Between Security and Development* (Newcastle: Cambridge Scholars, 2012), p. viii.

28  Gerges, *The Superpowers and the Middle East*.

29  See, e.g. FRUS, 1952–1954/IX, Doc. 479, The Acting United States High Commissioner for Germany (Donnelly) to the Department of State, 6 September 1952.

30  F. Romero, 'Cold War Historiography at the Crossroads', *Cold War History* 14:4 (2014), p. 697.

31  C. Steedman, *Dust* (Manchester: Manchester University Press, 2001), pp. 142–56.
32  E.g. K. P. Storckmann, *Geheime Solidarität: Militärbeziehungen und Militärhilfen der DDR in die 'Dritte Welt'* (Berlin: Links, 2012); Herf, *Undeclared Wars against Israel.*
33  B. Stöver, *Der Kalte Krieg, 1947–1991: Geschichte eines radikalen Zeitalters* (Munich: Beck, 2011 [2007]), p. 244.
34  Translated and quoted in A. Timm, 'The Burdened Relationship between the GDR and the State of Israel', *Israel Studies* 2:1 (1997), p. 43. This declaration was aimed, however, not just at Israel but also the United States. See, for example, C. Ostermann, 'Die USA und die DDR (1949–1989)' in U. Pfeil (ed.), *Die DDR und der Westen: Transnationale Beziehungen 1949–1989* (Berlin: Links, 2001), pp. 165–84.
35  See, for example, G. Lavy, *Germany and Israel: Moral Debt and National Interest* (London: Frank Cass, 1996), pp. 146ff.
36  For an analysis of the massacre and its impact on German politics and society, see K. Schiller and C. Young, *The 1972 Munich Olympics and the Making of Modern Germany* (Berkeley: University of California Press, 2010), pp. 187–220.
37  Israel Ministry of Foreign Affairs, 108th Statement by Prime Minister Begin on Remarks made by Chancellor Schmidt, 25 February 1982, http://mfa.gov.il/MFA/ForeignPolicy/MFADocuments/Yearbook5/Pages/108%20Statement%20by%20Prime%20Minister%20Begin%20on%20Remarks%20m.aspx [Accessed November 2019]. For background see H. Leber, 'Der deutsch-israelische Raketenstreit von 1978. Zum Umgang der sozialliberalen Bundesregierung mit Rüstungsexporten aus Koproduktion', *Vierteljahreshefte für Zeitgeschichte* 67:4 (2019), pp. 621–60.
38  L. De Vita, 'German-Israeli Ties in 1965 and 2015: The Difficult Special Relationship', *International Affairs* 91:2 (2015), pp. 835–49.

# Note on the sources

This book is based on an archival strategy that places the origins of German–Israeli relations in the aftermath of the Holocaust within the global geostrategic context of the 1950s and 1960s, characterised by the intensifying Cold War in Europe and Arab–Israeli conflict in the Middle East. The most important sources for this book are documentary records from former East and West German archives. In order to analyse the Cold War politics of Bonn's *Israelpolitik*, I have consulted Federal Archive files stored in Koblenz (*Bundesarchiv Koblenz*, BAK) pertaining to the Chancellery, the relevant Ministries and the Office of the Federal President. The fact that during my visits to Germany, I was also allowed to peruse various reports of the West German intelligence services (BND), some of which are still largely classified, made the archival research *in loco* all the more worthwhile. I have also consulted Chancellery files at the Chancellor Adenauer Foundation in Rhöndorf (*Stiftung Bundeskanzler Adenauer Haus*, StBKAH), the place of Adenauer's private residence where, upon his retirement as Chancellor in 1963, he brought the documents he deemed most relevant for his memoirs. I have relied upon materials from the BAK, the Chancellors' parliamentary group (CDU/CSU) and the Foreign Ministry, among others, to analyse Erhard's and Kiesinger's *Israelpolitik* and to assess similarities and differences between their and Adenauer's approach to such a complex policy area.

Files of the West German Foreign Ministry (*Politisches Archiv des Auswärtigen Amtes*, PA AA) as well as the published collection of documents on Bonn's foreign policy (*Akten zur Auswärtigen Politik der Bundesrepublik Deutschland*, AAPD) have proved crucial, despite the fact that many years covered in this work are not yet included in the AAPD series.[1] Because legitimacy and recognition, which are among Bonn's key foreign policy goals, rely both on material power as well as public perception, I have specifically sought to include materials from the press and international information departments of the West German Foreign Ministry (*Auswärtiges Amt*, AA) that would shed light on West Germany's public diplomacy strategies and tactics (*Öffentlichkeitsarbeit*).[2] However, I have also gathered materials from other more obvious Foreign Office desks, such as the Minister's bureau and desks that cover the political and economic exchanges between Bonn and the Middle East. Party files located at the CDU party archive in Sankt Augustin (*Archiv für Christlich-Demokratische Politik*, ACDP), the CSU party archive in Munich (*Archiv für Christlich-Soziale Politik, ACSP, Hanns-Seidel-Stiftung*) and the SPD archive in Bonn (*Friedrich Ebert Stiftung*, FES) have supplemented evidence available in the respective parties' collections of their published documents.

My analysis of East Germany's *Israelpolitik* relies upon the files of Politbüro meetings, of Walter Ulbricht's and Otto Grotewohl's offices, and of various departments of the Central Committee of the East German ruling party (SED), especially the International Relations Department. While few in number for the period under scrutiny, files of the sword and shield of the SED, namely the East German Ministry for State Security (Stasi) and its foreign intelligence services (*Hauptverwaltung Aufklärung*), show just how captivating the West German–Israeli relationship was from an East German perspective. To understand the SED party line and its evolution on crucial issues pertaining to East Berlin's *Israelpolitik*, I have often relied upon the SED's official press organ, *Neues Deutschland*. The historiography has often emphasised that despite its status, *Neues Deutschland* did not reach – let alone manage to indoctrinate – the East German population.[3] Yet, as the main means of communication of the ruling party, *Neues Deutschland* has provided an invaluable source for understanding the version of reality that the party aimed to mediate to its audience. Indeed, as Robert Wistrich emphasised, '*Neues Deutschland* is official and [it] matters'.[4]

East German Foreign Ministry (*Ministerium für Auswärtige Angelegenheiten*, MfAA) documents as well as files of the Ministry for Inter-German and International Trade (*Ministerium für Außenhandel und Innerdeutschen Handel*, MAI) and the agit-prop organs linked to the Politbüro were all crucial to deepening my understanding of the tension existing among various East German offices and personalities regarding the most efficient way to wage the German–German Cold War, and how to adapt East Berlin's *Israelpolitik* to this end. Because the GDR had such difficulties in establishing diplomatic ties with third countries – though it found it possible to expand its economic ties with most countries of the Middle East – some of the MAI personnel stationed abroad assumed the political analysis and consultancy tasks otherwise delegated to diplomatic personnel.[5] Thus, files of MAI personnel in East Berlin as well as in Arab countries have enriched the analysis of East German formulation and implementation of *Israelpolitik* and of East Berlin's Cold War.

Hermann Wentker in particular has noted the crucial, and what he sees as excessive, importance that the East German establishment attributed to the uses of propaganda for foreign policy purposes.[6] It is perhaps because of a general consideration of the GDR propaganda campaigns as failures that the literature has thus far largely overlooked the peculiar, creative ways in which East German state and party organs attempted to convince peoples around the globe of the vileness of the FRG. East German declarations on Bonn's and East Berlin's *Israelpolitik* were considered a crucial way to advance the GDR's quest for international recognition, in the Middle East and beyond. Thus, I treat East German propaganda – and, while maintaining a crucial distinction between the two, also the West German *Öffentlichkeitsarbeit* – not merely as an 'adjunct to policy' but as an 'integral part of strategy'.[7] By engaging with the topic of GDR propaganda for global audiences while paying specific attention to the Middle East, this book also points to a severe imbalance in the existing literature. Indeed, while the domestic aspect of East German propaganda via radio, print media, television and film is very well researched, little is available on the adaptation of East Berlin's propaganda for global Cold War purposes.[8]

Some of the most vicious *Israelpolitik*-related initiatives in the GDR saw East German Jewish citizens being repeatedly asked to come forward in support of the governmental anti-Zionist, anti-Israeli stance.[9] Files of the chief propagandist of the SED, Albert Norden, his collaborators within the Agitation Commission of the *Politbüro*, as well as files from the *Centrum Judaicum Archiv* (CJA), have allowed me to get a first-hand account of the difficult dynamics at play between SED organs and East German Jewish citizens. West German sources, too, have provided useful insight into East German activities and the GDR's *Israelpolitik* – for example, the reports of the West German intelligence services (BND) or of the AA desk dealing with *Öffentlichkeitsarbeit* (PA AA).[10] Thus, I have decided to include them in my analysis of the GDR's moves in the international domain – while keeping in mind that West Germany's observation of East Germany might possibly tell us more about Bonn than East Berlin, and vice versa.

Accessing the personal papers of a number of personalities involved in the formulation and implementation of foreign policy in either German state has proven invaluable for differentiating between the various versions of *Israelpolitik* supported by different actors, or by the same actors over a period of time. Published and unpublished memoirs, letters and travel diaries provided insight into the perspectives of key personalities involved in the making, or evaluating, of the early West and East German *Israelpolitik*. My use of these sources took into account that recollection-driven narratives – especially, though not exclusively, those of policy-makers and members of the intelligence service – need to be treated with caution. Consciously or not, these authors often tend to present a certain version of the past in order to reinforce specific narratives.

As the analysis of sources from both sides of the Iron Curtain and of the Arab–Israeli conflict makes abundantly clear, neither East nor West Germany formulated their *Israelpolitik* in a void. Evidence from the United States and the former Soviet Union showed that both superpowers played an important – if ambivalent – role in the shaping of the foreign policies of their respective German junior ally, and each German state attempted to pursue their own interests in the region while navigating the complex relationship with the respective superpower. The combination of sources from the US National Archives and relevant presidential libraries, as well as private papers held at the Library of Congress and Georgetown University, and Soviet documents from the Russian State Archive of Recent History (RGANI) held at the Lamont Library of Harvard University make this abundantly clear. Archival documents from other partner countries – Britain in the Western, and Czechoslovakia in the Eastern Bloc – further illustrate each Germany's decision-making process and its contradictions. Sources from British and Czech archives show that a certain degree of competition vis-à-vis their partner countries, and not just against their German nemesis, characterised each Germany's Middle East policy.

The evidence showed that during the Cold War, competition existed not only between the blocs, but also within them – and that the Middle East conflict was a crucial stage on which this multi-faceted competition unfolded. Press clippings from Arab newspapers, Arab League documents, as well as speeches and memoirs, corroborated the findings from the former Eastern and Western bloc, showing the importance of the German–German competition from the perspective of the Arab states. In turn, these states also competed with each other for prestige in the region, while attempting – not always managing – to project an image of unity and cohesion, especially when dealing with the Palestinian question. While this book focuses on German *Israelpolitik* formulations, Israeli and Arab sources complemented my research in German, American, British and Czech archives. Sources from the Israeli National Archives, minutes from Knesset debates, and the memoirs and private papers of key personalities such as David Ben-Gurion and Menachem Begin, show just how fraught and difficult the question of what relations the state of Israel should have with either German state was, for both the Israeli political establishment and the Israeli public.

For the purpose of this work, oral history interviews served only as a complement to the wealth of published and unpublished written source material on the topic. Nevertheless, the interviews I conducted were all crucial in order to shed light on various aspects of the formulation and implementation of East and West German *Israelpolitik*, as well as on the foreign policy of the Israel, the FRG and GDR more generally. Conversations with former East German diplomats, such as Otto Pfeiffer, or their relatives, such as Manja Finnberg, have allowed me to gather a fuller sense of East German policy making and the reverberations of the personal experiences of East German representatives of East Berlin's struggle against Bonn's claim of sole representation of the German nation (*Alleinvertretungsanspruch*). Personal meetings with two of the three secretaries who worked in the Chancellery during Adenauer's era, Johanna Müller (née Seither) and Hannelore Siegel, have allowed me to gather a unique perspective on the work of 'Germany's Old Man' (*Der Alte Herr*). Their insights are particularly valuable because they also provided me with first-hand accounts of the workings of the first FRG embassies in two key locations, including Moscow, where Müller was stationed from the moment the embassy opened until 1961, when she landed her position at the Chancellery, and Tel Aviv, which Siegel joined from the day it opened. The conversation with Israel's first Ambassador to the Federal Republic, Asher Ben-Natan, has allowed me to gather further insight into the Ambassador's experiences in West Germany, as well as his earlier involvement in the Israeli arms procurement efforts and in forging links with Bonn's defence establishment during the late 1950s and early 1960s. This has allowed me to triangulate some of the claims made by the two then defence ministers in their memoirs, Shimon Peres and Franz Josef Strauss, on a theme that, to date, is still one of the most contentious issues in German-Israeli relations. Understanding, mapping and acknowledging the complexity of the German–Israeli reconciliation process and of the various actors involved in it, while avoiding the grand, often facile, narrative often employed to describe it in public discourse, has been the guiding principle in the conduct of the research for this book.

# Notes

1 I am referring to the gap between 1953 and 1963 in the AAPD volumes.
2 I. Clark, *Legitimacy in International Society* (Oxford: Oxford University Press, 2005).
3 See, for example, M. Allinson, *Politics and Popular Opinion in East Germany, 1945–1968* (Manchester: Manchester University Press, 2000), p. 71.
4 R.S. Wistrich, 'Neues Deutschland and Israel. A Diary of East German Reactions' in Robert S. Wistrich (ed.), *The Left Against Zion: Communism, Israel and the Middle East* (London: Vallentine-Mitchell, 1979), p. 114.
5 Wentker, *Außenpolitik*.
6 *Ibid.*, p. 195.
7 G. Rawnsley, 'Introduction' in G. Rawnsley (ed.), *Cold War Propaganda in the 1950s* (Basingstoke: Macmillan, 1999), p. 5.
8 On propaganda via radio see the essays collected in K. Arnold and C. Classen (eds), *Zwischen Pop und Propaganda: Radio in der DDR* (Berlin: Links, 2004); on propaganda via newspapers see, e.g., the contributions available in A. Fiedler and M. Meyen (eds), *Fiktionen für das Volk: DDR-Zeitungen als PR-Instrument. Fallstudien zu den Zentralorganen Neues Deutschland, Junge Welt, Neue Zeit und Der Morgen* (Berlin: LIT, 2011); on propaganda via television see for example the volume by H. Heinze (ed.), *Zwischen Service und Propaganda: Zur Geschichte und Ästhetik von Magazinsendung im Fernsehen der DDR, 1952–1991* (Berlin: VISTAS, 1998); on propaganda through the medium of cinema see, e.g., M. Lange, *Das politisierte Kino: ideologische Selbstinszenierung im "Dritten Reich" und der DDR* (Marburg: Tactum Verlag, 2013).
9 See Wolffsohn, *Die Deutschland Akte*, for example p. 87; P. Maser, 'Juden in der DDR' in Eppelmann, et al., *Bilanz*, p. 218.
10 Although on a later time period, see H. Wentker, 'Die DDR in den Augen des BND (1985–1990)', *Vierteljahrshefte für Zeitgeschichte* 56:2 (2008), pp. 323–58. See also P. Maddrell, 'Im Fadenkreuz der Stasi: Westliche Spionage in der DDR: Die Akten der Hauptabteilung IX', *Vierteljahrshefte für Zeitgeschichte* 61:2 (2015), pp. 141–71, and T. Wegener Friis, K. Mackrakis and H. Müller-Embergs (eds), *East German Foreign Intelligence: Myth, Reality and Controversy* (Abingdon: Routledge, 2010).

# Select bibliography

## Primary sources

### Unpublished

*Czech Republic*

National Archives of the Czech Republic (NACR)

*Germany*

Archiv für Christlich-Demokratische Politik (ACDP)
Archiv für Christlich-Soziale Politik (ACSP), Hanns-Seidel-Stiftung (HSS)
Bundesarchiv Berlin-Lichterfelde (BAL) and Stiftung Archiv der Parteien und
  Massenorganisationen der DDR im Bundesarchiv Berlin-Lichterfelde
  (BAL-SAPMO)
Bundesarchiv Freiburg (BAF)
Bundesarchiv Koblenz (BAK)
Bundesbeauftragte für die Unterlagen des Staatssicherheitsdienstes der ehemaligen
  Deutschen Demokratischen Republic (BStU)
Centrum Judaicum Archiv (CJA)
Friedrich Erbert Stiftung – Archiv der Sozialen Demokratie (FES AdsD)
Landesarchiv Nordrhein-Westfalen (LNW)
Politisches Archiv des Auswärtigen Amtes (PA AA) and Ministerium für Auswärtige
  Angelegenheiten der Deutschen Demoktaischen Republik (MfAA)
Rheinisch-Westfälisches Wirtschaftsarchiv zu Köln (RWWA)
Stiftung Archiv Akademie der Künste (AdK)
Stiftung Bundeskanzler Adenauer Haus (StBKAH)

*Israel*

Beit Lohamei HaGetaot Archives (BLGA)
David Ben-Gurion Archives (DBGA)
Israeli State Archives (ISA)
Menachem Begin Archives (MBA)
The Moshe Sharett Israel Labor Party Archive – Berl Katznelson Foundation

*United Kingdom*

British National Archives (BNA), Public Record Office (PRO)
Wiener Library Archive (WLA)

United States

Archives of the Soviet Communist Party and Soviet State: Russian State Archive of
    Contemporary History (RGANI), Harvard University
Dwight D. Eisenhower Presidential Library (DDEL)
Georgetown University Archives (GUA)
Harry S. Truman Presidential Library (HSTL)
Hoover Institution Archives (HIA)
John F. Kennedy Presidential Library (JFKL)
Library of Congress (LOC)
Lyndon B. Johnson Presidential Library (LBJL)
National Archives and Records Administration (NARA)


**Author's interviews**

Otto Pfeiffer, former East German diplomat, Berlin (Germany), 26 November 2013.
Manja Finnberg, niece of Horst Seydewitz and family history researcher, (via Skype) 17
    November 2013.
Asher Ben-Natan, former Israeli diplomat and first Israeli Ambassador to the Federal
    Republic of Germany, Ramat HaSharon (Israel), 20 January 2014.
Johanna Müller, former secretary of Chancellor Adenauer and employee of the first
    West German Embassy in Moscow, Berlin (Germany) 18 March 2015.
Hannelore Siegel, former secretary of Chancellor Adenauer and employee of the first
    West German Embassy in Tel Aviv, Cologne (Germany) 20 July 2015.


**Published**

*Akten zur Auswärtigen Politik der Bundesrepublik Deutschland*, Auftrag des Auswärtigen
    Amts vom Institut für Zeitgeschichte (Munich: Oldenbourg, 1994–).
Blasius, R. A. 'Völkerfreundschaft am Nil: Agypten und die DDR im Februar 1965,
    Stenographische Aufzeichnungen aus dem Ministerium für Auswärtige Angelegenheiten
    über den Ulbricht-Besuch bei Nasser', *Vierteljahreshefte für Zeitgeschichte* 46:4 (1998),
    pp. 747–806.
Bock, S., Muth, I. and Schwiesau, H. (eds) *DDR-Außenpolitik im Rückspiegel. Diplomaten
    im Gespräch* (Münster: LIT, 2004).
Buchstab, G. (ed.) *Adenauer: 'Wir haben wirklich etwas geschaffen'. Die Protokolle des CDU-
    Bundesvorstandes 1953–1957* (Düsseldorf: Droste, 1990).
——. *Adenauer: 'Stetigkeit in der Politik'. Die Protokolle des CDU-Bundesvorstandes
    1961–1965* (Düsseldorf: Droste, 1998).
Burdett, A. L. P. *The Arab League: British Documentary Sources, 1943–1963* (Slough: Archive
    Editions, 1995).
Deutsches Orient Institut. *Die Angriffe der SBZ gegen die Nahostpolitik der Bundesregierung*
    (Hamburg: Deutsches-Orient-Stiftung, 1964).
*Die Kabinettsprotokolle der Bundesregierung*, Vols 1–10 (Boppard am Rhein: Harald Boldt,
    1982–2000).
*Documents Diplomatique Français* (Paris: Ed. Ministère des Affaire Étrangères, Commission
    de Publication des Documents Diplomatique, 1988–97).
*Documents on the Foreign Policy of Israel* (Jerusalem: Hamakor Press, 1981–97).

*Documents on the Foreign Policy of Israel, 1961–1967: Israel-Federal Republic of Germany Relations 1961–1967* (Jerusalem: Israel State Archives, 2013).
*Documents on International Affairs* (London: Oxford University Press for the Royal Institute of International Affairs, 1956).
*Documents on Israeli-Soviet Relations, 1941–1953* (London: Frank Cass, 2000).
*Dokumente zur Außenpolitik der Deutschen Demokratischen Republik* (Berlin [East]: Staatsverlag der DDR).
*Foreign Relations of the United States (FRUS)*.
Jelinek, Y. A. (ed.) *Zwischen Moral und Realpolitik. Deutsch-israelische Beziehungen 1945–1965: eine Dokumentsammlung* (Gerlingen: Bleicher, 1997).
Lorch, N. (ed.) *Major Knesset Debates, 1948–1981*, Vols 2–4 (Lanham: University Press of America, 1993).
Sharett, Y. *The Reparations Controversy: The Jewish State and German Money in the Shadow of the Holocaust, 1951–1952* (Berlin: De Gruyter, 2011).
Vogel, R. (ed.) *The German Path to Israel: A Documentation* (Chester Springs: Dufour, 1969).
——. *Der deutsch-israelische Dialog: Dokumentation eines erregenden Kapitels deutscher Aussenpolitik*, Vols 1–8 (Munich: Saur, 1987–90).
Weissbuch und Erklärung der Bundesregierung. *Die antisemitische und nazistische Vorfälle* (Bonn, 1960).

*Newspapers, periodicals and news agencies*

Allgemeiner Deutscher Nachrichtendienst (ADN)
*Frankfurter Allgemeine Zeitung (FAZ)*
*Frankfurter Rundschau*
*The Jerusalem Post*
*Jewish Telegraphic Agency (JTA)*
*LaMerhav*
*Maariv*
*Neues Deutschland (ND)*
*New York Times*
*Der Spiegel*
*The Times*

*Memoirs, correspondence and speeches*

Adenauer, K. *Erinnerungen* (Frankfurt am Main: Fischer Bücherei, 1965–68).
Ben-Natan, A. *The Audacity to Live* (Jerusalem: Mazo Publishers, 2007).
——. *Brücke bauen – aber nicht vergessen. Als erster Botschafter Israels in der Bundesrepublik (1965–1969)* (Düsseldorf: Droste, 2005).
Ben-Natan, A. and Hansen, N. (eds) *Israel und Deutschland: Dorniger Weg zur Partnerschaft. Die Botschafter berichten über Vier Jahrzehnte diplomatische Beziehungen* (Cologne: Böhlau, 2005).
Birrenbach, K. *Meine Sondermissionen. Rückblick auf zwei Jahrzehnte bundesdeutscher Außenpolitik* (Düsseldorf: Econ, 1984).
Eban, A. *An Autobiography* (New York: Random House, 1977).

Goldmann, N. *Staatsmann ohne Staat* (Cologne: Kiepenheuer & Witsch, 1970).

Hausner, G. *Justice in Jerusalem* (New York: Holocaust Library, 1968).

Heikal, M. H. *Nasser: The Cairo Documents* (London: New English Library, 1972).

Kaul, F. K. *Der Fall Eichmann* (Berlin: Das Neue Berlin, 1963).

Lotz, W. *The Champagne Spy: Israel's Master Spy Tells His Story* (New York: Manor Books, 1973).

Meir, G. *My Life* (London: Futura, 1979 [1975]).

Norden, A. *Ereignisse und Erlebtes* (Berlin: Dietz, 1981).

Peres, S. *David's Sling* (London: Weidenfeld & Nicholson, 1970).

Schmid, C. *Erinnerungen* (Bern: Scherz Verlag, 1979).

Shinnar, F. *Bericht eines Beauftragten. Die deutsch-israelischen Beziehungen, 1951–1966* (Tübingen: Wunderlich, 1967).

Stillmann, G. *Berlin-Palästina und zurück. Erinnerungen* (Berlin: Dietz, 1989).

Strauß, F. J. *Die Erinnerungen* (Berlin: Siedler, 1989).

Ulbricht, L. *Eine unvergessliche Reise* (Leipzig: Verlag für die Frau, 1965).

Ulbricht, W. *Die nationale Frage in heutiger Sicht: Reden, Erklärung, Ansprache, Interview* (Berlin: Dietz, 1965).

## Secondary sources

Arendt, H. *Eichmann in Jerusalem: A Report on the Banality of Evil* (New York: Penguin Books, 1994).

Aronson, S. *David Ben-Gurion and the Jewish Renaissance* (Cambridge: Cambridge University Press, 2011).

Ashton, N. J. (ed.) *The Cold War in the Middle East: Regional Conflict and the Superpowers, 1967–1973* (London: Routledge, 2007).

Balabkins, N. *West German Reparations to Israel* (New Brunswick: Rutgers University Press, 1971).

Bartos, H. *West Germany's Relations to Israel in the Conservative Era 1949–1969: Reappraising the Reparations-, Arms-, and Diplomatic Relationship* (Doctoral Thesis, University College London, 2012).

Bass, W. *Support Any Friend: Kennedy's Middle East and the Making of the US-Israeli Alliance* (Oxford: Oxford University Press, 2003).

Bauerkämper, A. *Doppelte Zeitgeschichte: Deutsch-deutsche Beziehungen 1945–1990* (Bonn: Dietz, 1998).

Ben-Zvi, A. *Lyndon B. Johnson and the Politics of Arms Sales to Israel: In the Shadow of the Hawk* (London: Frank Cass, 2004).

Berggötz, S. O. *Nahostpolitik in der Ära Adenauer: Möglichkeiten und Grenzen* (Düsseldorf: Droste, 1998).

Bialer, U. *Between East and West: Israel's Foreign Policy Orientation, 1948–1956* (Cambridge: Cambridge University Press, 1990).

Booz, R. M. *'Hallsteinzeit'. Deutsche Außenpolitik 1955–1972* (Bonn: Bouvier, 1995).

Borchard, M. *Eine unmögliche Freundschaft: David Ben-Gurion und Konrad Adenauer* (Freiburg im Breisgau: Herder, 2019).

Brenner, M. *After the Holocaust: Rebuilding Jewish Lives in Postwar Germany* (Princeton, NJ: Princeton University Press, 1997).

Cesarani, D. *Eichmann: His Life and Crimes* (London: Heinemann, 2004).

Chubin, S. (ed.) *Germany and the Middle East* (London: Pinter, 1992).

Citino, N. J. 'The Middle East and the Cold War', *Cold War History* 19:3 (2019), pp. 441–56.

Conze, E., Frei, N., Hayes, P. and Zimmermann, M. (eds) *Das Amt und die Vergangenheit. Deutschen Diplomaten im Dritten Reich und in der Bundesrepublik* (Munich: Karl Blessing Verlag, 2010).

Craig, C. and Logevall, F. *America's Cold War: The Politics of Insecurity* (Cambridge, MA: Belknap Press of Harvard University Press, 2009).

Crump, L. *The Warsaw Pact Reconsidered: International Relations in Eastern Europe, 1955–1969* (London: Palgrave Macmillan, 2015).

Deutschkron, I. *Israel und die Deutschen. Das schwierige Verhältnis* (Cologne: Verlag Wissenschaft und Politik, 1983).

De Vita, L. 'German-Israeli Ties in 2015 and 1965: the Difficult Special Relationship', *International Affairs* 91:4 (2015), pp. 835–49.

——. 'Overlapping Rivalries: The Two Germanys, Israel and the Cold War', *Cold War History* 17:4 (2017), pp. 351–66.

Diner, D. *Rituelle Distanz: Israels Deutsche Frage* (Munich: Deutsche Verlags-Anstalt, 2015).

Edkins, J. *Trauma and the Memory of Politics* (Cambridge: Cambridge University Press, 2003).

Eibl, F. *Politik der Bewegung: Gerhard Schröder als Außenminister 1961–1966* (Munich: Oldenbourg, 2001).

End, H. *Zweimal deutsche Außenpolitik. Internationale Dimensionen des innerdeutshen Konflikts, 1949–1972* (Cologne: Verlag Wissenschaft und Politik, 1973).

Epstein, C. *The Last Revolutionaries: German Communists and Their Century* (Cambridge, MA: Harvard University Press, 2003).

Feldman, L. G. *The Special Relationship between West Germany and Israel* (Boston: Allen & Unwin, 1984).

——. *Germany's Foreign Policy of Reconciliation: From Enmity to Amity* (Lanham, MD: Rowman & Littlefield, 2012).

Fink, C. *West Germany and Israel: Foreign Relations, Domestic Politics, and the Cold War, 1965–1974* (Cambridge: Cambridge University Press, 2019).

Frei, N. *Vergangenheitspolitik. Die Anfänge der Bundesrepublik und die NS-Vergangenheit* (Munich: C. H. Beck, 2012 [1996]).

Frei, N. and Freimüller, T. *Karrieren im Zwielicht: Hitlers Eliten nach 1945* (Frankfurt a. Main, Campus Verlag, 2001).

Frei, N. and Steinbacher, S. *Beschweigen und Bekennen. Die deutsche Nachkriegsgesellschaft und der Holocaust* (Göttingen: Wallstein, 2001).

Fulbrook, M. *The Two Germanies, 1945–1990: Problems of Interpretation* (Houndmills: Macmillan, 1992).

——. *German National Identity After the Holocaust* (Cambridge: Polity Press, 1999).

Fursenko, A. and Naftali, T. *Khrushchev's Cold War: The Inside Story of an American Adversary* (New York: W. W. Norton & Company, 2006).

Gaddis, J. L. *We Now Know: Rethinking Cold War History* (Oxford: Clarendon Press, 1997).

Gerges, F. *The Superpowers and the Middle East: Regional and International Politics, 1955–1967* (Oxford, Boulder and Colorado: Westview Press, 1994).

Gerlach, F. *The Tragic Triangle. Israel, Divided Germany and the Arabs 1956–1965* (Doctoral Thesis, Columbia University, 1968).

Giordano, R. (ed.) *Deutschland und Israel: Solidarität in der Bewährung: Bilanz und Perspektive der deutsch-israelische Beziehungen* (Gerlingen: Bleicher, 1992).

Goodin, R. E. and Tilly, C. (eds) *The Oxford Handbook of Contextual Political Analysis* (Oxford: Oxford University Press, 2006).

Gorem, H. (ed.) *Germany and the Middle East: Past, Present, and Future* (Jerusalem: The Hebrew University Press, 2003).

Goschler, C. *Schuld und Schulden. Die Politik der Wiedergutmachung für NS-Verfolgte seit 1945* (Göttingen: Wallstein, 2005).

Gray, W. G. *Germany's Cold War: The Global Campaign to Isolate East Germany, 1949–1969* (Chapel Hill: University of North Carolina Press, 2003).

Grossmann, K. R. *Germany's Moral Debt: The German-Israeli Agreement* (Washington, DC: Public Affairs Press, 1954).

Hanrieder, W. (ed.) *West German Foreign Policy, 1949–1979* (Boulde: Westview Press, 1980).

Hansen, N. *Aus dem Schatten der Katastrophe. Die deutsch-israelischen Beziehungen in der Ära Adenauer und Ben-Gurion* (Düsseldorf: Droste, 2002).

Harrison, H. *Driving the Soviets up the Wall: Soviet-East German Relations, 1953–1961* (Princeton: Princeton University Press, 2003).

Herf, J. *Divided Memory: The Nazi Past in the Two Germanys* (Cambridge, MA: Harvard University Press, 1997).

—— (ed.) *Anti-Semitism and Anti-Zionism in Historical Perspective: Convergence and Divergence* (London and New York: Routledge, 2007).

——. *Nazi Propaganda for the Arab World* (New Haven: Yale University Press, 2010).

von Hindenburg, H. *Demonstrating Reconciliation: State and Society in West German Foreign Policy towards Israel, 1952–1965* (New York: Berghahn Books, 2007).

Hopf, T. *Reconstructing the Cold War: The Early Years, 1945–1958* (Oxford: Oxford University Press, 2012).

Hughes, R. G. *Britain, Germany and the Cold War: The Search for a European Détente, 1949–1967* (London: Routledge, 2007).

Illichmann, J. *Die DDR und die Juden: die deutschlandpolitische Instrumentalisierung von Juden und Judentum durch die Partei- und Staatsführung der SBZ/DDR von 1945 bis 1990* (Franfurt am Main: Lang, 1997).

Jaspers, K. *The Question of German Guilt* (New York: Dial Press, 1947).

Jelinek, Y. *Deutschland und Israel 1945–1965. Ein neurotisches Verhältnis* (Munich: Oldenbourg, 2004).

Kerr, M. *The Arab Cold War: Gamal 'Abd Al-Nasir and His Rivals, 1958–1970* (London: Oxford University Press, 1971).

Keßler, M. *Die SED und die Juden – zwischen Repression und Toleranz. Politische Entwicklungen bis 1967* (Berlin: Akademie Verlag, 1995).

Kilian, W. *Die Hallstein-Doktrin. Der diplomatische Krieg zwischen der BRD und der DDR, 1955–1973. Aus den Akten der beiden deutschen Außenministerien* (Berlin: Duncker & Humblot, 2001).

Kleßmann, C. *Die doppelte Staatsgründung: Deutsche Geschichte 1945–1955* (Göttingen: Vandenhoeck & Ruprecht, 1991).

Kupper, S. *Die Tätigkeit der DDR in den nichtkommunistischen Ländern. Arabische Staaten und Israel* (Bonn: Forschungsinstitut DGAP e.V., 1971).

Laron, G. *The Six-Day War: The Breaking of the Middle East* (New Haven, CT: Yale University Press, 2017).

Lavy, G. *Germany and Israel: Moral Debt and National Interest* (London: Frank Cass, 1996).

Lebow, R. N. and Gross Stein, J. *We All Lost the Cold War* (Princeton: Princeton University Press, 1993).

Lein, C. *Die Beziehungen beider deutscher Staaten zu Israel, 1949–1963* (Doctoral Thesis, Technische Universitat Dresden, 2006).

Lipstadt, D. E. *The Eichmann Trial* (New York: Nextbook/Schocken, 2011).

Litvak, M. and Webman, E. *From Empathy to Denial: Arab Responses to the Holocaust* (London: Hurst & Co., 2009).

Lorenzini, S. *Il Rifiuto di Un'Eredità Difficile: La Repubblica Democratica Tedesca, gli Ebrei e lo Stato di Israele* (Florence: La Giuntina, 1998).

Loth, W. *Stalins ungeliebtes Kind: warum Moskau die DDR nicht wollte* (Berlin: Rowohlt Berlin Verlag, 1994).

Ludi, R. *Reparations for Nazi Victims in Postwar Europe* (Cambridge: Cambridge University Press, 2012).

Mastny, V. *The Cold War and Soviet Insecurity: The Stalin Years* (Oxford: Oxford University Press, 1996).

Maulucci Jr., T. W. *Adenauer's Foreign Office: West German Diplomacy in the Shadow of the Third Reich* (DeKalb: Northern Illinois University Press, 2012).

Meining, S. *Kommunistische Judenpolitik: die DDR, die Juden und Israel* (Münster: LIT, 2002).

Mertens, L. *Davidstern unter Hammer und Zirkel. Die jüdischen Gemeinden in der SBZ/DDR und ihre Behandlung durch Partei und Staat 1945–1990* (Hildesheim: Olms, 1997).

Mierzejewski, A. C. *Ludwig Erhard: A Biography* (Chapel Hill: University of North Carolina Press, 2004).

Moeller, R. G. *War Stories: The Search for a Usable Past in the Federal Republic of Germany* (Berkeley: University of California Press, 2001).

Mohr, M. *Waffen für Israel: Westdeutsche Rüstungshilfe vor dem Sechstagekrieg* (Berlin: Köster, 2003).

Motadel, D. *Islam and Nazi Germany's War* (Cambridge, MA: The Belknap Press of Harvard University Press, 2014).

Nicholls, A. J. *The Bonn Republic: West German Democracy 1945–1990* (London: Longman, 1997).

Podhorez, N. 'Hannah Arendt on Eichmann: A Study in the Perversity of Brilliance', *Commentary*, 3 September 1963, pp. 201–8.

Rombeck-Jaschinski, U. *Das Londoner Schuldabkommen. Die Regelung der deutschen Auslandsschulden nach dem Zweiten Weltkrieg* (Munich: Oldenbourg, 2005).

Rubin, B. M. and Schwanitz, W. G. *Nazis, Islamists, and the Making of the Modern Middle East* (New Haven: Yale University Press, 2014).

Sachar, H. M. *Israel and Europe: An Appraisal in History* (New York: Knopf, 1998).

Sagi, N. *German Reparations: A History of the Negotiations* (Jerusalem: The Magnes Press, The Hebrew University, 1980).

Schwanitz, W. G (ed.) *Deutschland und der Mittlere Osten im Kalten Krieg* (Leipzig: Leipziger Universität Verlag, 2006).

Schwarz, H. P. *Die Ära Adenauer: Gründerjahre der Republik, 1949–1957* (Stuttgart: Deutsche Verlags-Anstalt, 1981).

——. *Die Wiederherstellung des deutschen Kredits: Das Londoner Schuldenabkommen* (Stuttgart: Belser, 1982).

Segev, T. *The Seventh Million: The Israelis and the Holocaust* (New York: Hill & Wang, 1993).

Shlaim, A. and Sayigh, Y. (eds) *The Cold War and the Middle East* (Oxford: Clarendon Press, 1997).

Sirrs, L. O. *Nasser and the Missile Age in the Middle East* (London: Routledge, 2006).

Stagneth, B. *Eichmann vor Jerusalem: das unbehelligte Leben eines Massenmörders* (Zurich: Arche, 2011).

Stauber, R. 'Israel's Quest for Diplomatic Relations: The German-Israeli Controversy 1955–1956', *Tel Aviver Jahrbuch für deutsche Geschichte* 41 (2013), pp. 215–28.

Select bibliography

——. 'Realpolitik and the Burden of the Past: Israeli Diplomacy and the "Other" Germany', *Israel Studies* 8:3 (2003), pp. 100–22.

Stein, S. *Israel, Deutschland und der Nahe Osten. Beziehungen zwischen Einzigartigkeit und Normalität* (Göttingen: Wallstein, 2011).

Storkmann, K. *Geheime Solidarität. Militärbeziehungen und Militärhilfen der DDR in die 'Dritte Welt'* (Berlin: Links, 2012).

Timm, A. *Hammer, Zirkel, Davidstern. Das gestörte Verhältnis der DDR zu Zionismus und Staat Israel* (Bonn: Bouvier Verlag, 1997).

——. *Jewish Claims against East Germany: Moral Obligations and Pragmatic Policy* (Budapest: Central European University Press, 1997).

Tooze, A. 'Reassessing the Moral Economy of Post-War Reconstruction: The Terms of the West German Settlement in 1952', *Past and Present* 6 (2012), pp. 47–70.

Tovy, J. 'All Quiet on the Eastern Front: Israel and the Issue of Reparations from East Germany, 1951–1956', *Israel Studies* 18:1 (2013), pp. 77–100.

Trentin, M. '"Tough Negotiations": The Two Germanys in Syria and Iraq, 1963–1974', *Cold War History* 8:3 (2008), pp. 353–80.

Trimbur, D. *De la Shoah à la Réconciliation? La Question des Relations RFA-Israël (1949–1956)* (Paris: CNRS Editions, 2000).

——. 'Eine deutsche Präsenz in Israel – Die bundesdeutsche Beobachtermission anlässlich des Eichmann-Prozesses in Jerusalem', *Tel Aviver Jahrbuch für deutsche Geschichte* 41 (2013), pp. 229–52.

Uhlmann, M. (ed.) *Die deutsch-israelischen Sicherheitsbeziehungen. Vergangenheit, Gegenwart, Zukunft* (Berlin: Berliner Wissenschafts-Verlag, 2008).

Weingardt, M. A. *Deutsche Israel- und Nahostpolitik: die Geschichte einer Gratwanderung seit 1949* (Frankfurt: Campus, 2002).

Weinke, A. *Die Verfolgung von NS-Tätern im geteilten Deutschland: Vergangenheitsbewältigungen 1949–1969 oder: eine deutsch-deutsche Beziehungsgeschichte im Kalten Krieg* (Paderborn: Schöningh, 2002).

Wentker, H. *Außenpolitik in engen Grenzen. Die DDR im internationalen System 1949–1989* (Munich: Oldenbourg, 2007).

Westad, O. A. (ed.) *Reviewing the Cold War: Approaches, Interpretations, Theory* (London: Frank Cass, 2000).

——. *The Global Cold War: Third World Interventions and the Making of Our Times* (Cambridge: Cambridge University Press, 2005).

Wistrich, R. (ed.) *The Left against Zion: Communism, Israel and the Middle East* (London: Vallentine Mitchell, 1978).

Witzthum, D. *Tehilatah shel yedidiut muflaʾah? Ha-piyus ben Yisraʾel le-Germanyah, 1948–1960* (Tel Aviv: Schocken, 2018).

Wolffsohn, M. *Deutsch-israelische Beziehungen. Umfragen und Interpretationen 1952–1986* (Munich: Landeszentrale für Politische Bildungsarbeit, 1986).

——. *Ewige Schuld? 40 Jahre deutsch-israelische Beziehungen* (Munich: Piper, 1991).

——. *Die Deutschland Akte. Tatsachen und Legenden* (Munich: Ferenczy bei Bruckmann, 1996 [1995]).

Yablonka, H. *The State of Israel vs. Adolf Eichmann* (New York: Schocken, 2004).

Yaqub, S. *Containing Arab Nationalism: The Eisenhower Doctrine and the Middle East* (Chapel Hill: University of North Carolina Press, 2004).

Zimmermann, M. 'Chameleon and Phoenix: Israel's German Image', *Tel Aviver Jahrbuch für deutsche Geschichte* 26 (1997), pp. 265–80.

Zubok, V. M. *A Failed Empire: The Soviet Union in the Cold War from Stalin to Gorbachev* (Chapel Hill: University of North Carolina Press, 2009).

Zweig, R. W. *German Reparations and the Jewish World: A History of the Claims Conference* (London: Frank Cass, 2002 [1987]).

# Index

EU authorised representative for GPSR:
Easy Access System Europe, Mustamäe tee 50,
10621 Tallinn, Estonia
gpsr.requests@easproject.com

www.ingramcontent.com/pod-product-compliance
Lightning Source LLC
Chambersburg PA
CBHW052000270326
41929CB00015B/2727